Ohio Real Estate

LAW

13th Edition

HONDROS LEARNING™

4140 Executive Parkway

Westerville, Ohio 43081

www.hondroslearning.com

22 21 20   1 2 3

ISBN: 978-1-59844-405-6

For more information on or to purchase our products, please visit www.hondroslearning.com.

SUGGESTED SYLLABUS

OHIO REAL ESTATE LAW—DAY CLASSES

COURSE DESCRIPTION: This course covers responsibilities and requirements for real estate sales and broker licensing. Topics include sources of real estate law, Ohio's judicial structure, the procedures in a typical legal action, and an introduction to process law.

COURSE OBJECTIVES: On completion of this course, students will be able to:
1. Demonstrate a basic knowledge of Ohio real estate law.
2. Demonstrate a basic knowledge of real estate legal terms.
3. Recognize instruments used in real estate practice.

COURSE TEXTBOOK: *Ohio Real Estate Law*, 13th edition, ©2020 Hondros Learning™

COURSE NUMBER: RE120

COURSE CREDIT HOURS: 40 clock hours or 4 credit hours awarded on successful course completion.

PREREQUISITES: None

INSTRUCTION METHOD: Lecture

COURSE OUTLINE:

DAY ONE:	MODULE 1	Introduction and Overview
		Chapter 1 - Introduction to Law
		Chapter 2 - Ohio Real Estate Licensing Law
	MODULE 2	Chapter 2 - Ohio Real Estate Licensing Law (continued)
DAY TWO:	MODULE 3	Chapter 3 - Agency Law
	MODULE 4	Chapter 4 - Fair Housing
DAY THREE:	MODULE 5	Chapter 5 - The Nature of Real Property
		Chapter 6 - Interests in Real Property
	MODULE 6	Chapter 6 - Interests in Real Property (continued)
		Chapter 7 - Deeds

DAY FOUR:	MODULE 7	Chapter 7 - Deeds (continued)
		Chapter 8 - Contracts
	MODULE 8	Chapter 9 - Decedents' Estates
		Chapter 10 - Land Use Controls
		Chapter 11 - Landlord/Tenant
		Review
		Final Examination
		Review of Final Examination

CLASSROOM HOURS ALL CAMPUSES: 8:00 a.m. - 5:35 p.m.
Module (a.m.): 8:00 a.m. - 12:35 p.m.
Lunch Break: 12:35 p.m. - 1:05 p.m.
Module (p.m.): 1:05 p.m. - 5:35 p.m.

ATTENDANCE: Attendance is mandatory to receive course credit.

GRADING: Final grade is based 25% on classroom participation and attendance, and 75% on Final Exam and Quiz grades.

NOTES: Tape recorders are not permitted during class lecture sessions.

OHIO REAL ESTATE LAW—NIGHT CLASSES

COURSE DESCRIPTION: This course covers responsibilities and requirements for real estate sales and broker licensing. Topics include sources of real estate law, Ohio's judicial structure, the procedures in a typical legal action, and an introduction to process law.

COURSE OBJECTIVES: On completion of this course, students will be able to:
1. Demonstrate a basic knowledge of Ohio real estate law.
2. Demonstrate a basic knowledge of real estate legal terms.
3. Recognize instruments used in real estate practice.

COURSE TEXTBOOK: *Ohio Real Estate Law*, 13th edition, ©2020 Hondros Learning™

COURSE NUMBER: RE120

COURSE CREDIT HOURS: 40 clock hours or 4 credit hours awarded on successful course completion.

PREREQUISITES: None

INSTRUCTION METHOD: Lecture

COURSE OUTLINE:

MODULE 1	Introduction and Overview
	Chapter 1 - Introduction to Law
	Chapter 2 - Ohio Real Estate Licensing Law
MODULE 2	Chapter 2 - Ohio Real Estate Licensing Law (continued)
MODULE 3	Chapter 3 - Agency Law
MODULE 4	Chapter 4 - Fair Housing
MODULE 5	Chapter 5 - The Nature of Real Property
	Chapter 6 - Interests in Real Property
MODULE 6	Chapter 6 - Interests in Real Property (continued)
	Chapter 7 - Deeds
MODULE 7	Chapter 7 - Deeds (continued)
	Chapter 8 - Contracts
MODULE 8	Chapter 9 - Decedents' Estates
	Chapter 10 - Land Use Controls
	Chapter 11 - Landlord/Tenant
	Review
	Final Examination
	Review of Final Examination

CLASSROOM HOURS: 6:00 p.m. - 10:30 p.m.

ATTENDANCE: Attendance is mandatory to receive course credit.

GRADING: Final grade is based 25% on classroom participation and attendance, and 75% on Final Exam and Quiz grades.

NOTES: Tape recorders are not permitted during class lecture sessions.

TABLE OF CONTENTS

PREFACE

Real estate education has changed dramatically over the past years. Ohio educational requirements encourage a higher caliber of real estate professional. This text was written with those higher standards in mind—and the goal of preparing you to successfully pass your licensing examination.

Ohio Real Estate Law, now in its 12th edition, has helped thousands of students gain a solid understanding of the legal aspects of real estate by looking at both theory and real-world application. Still offering all that and more. Key features include:

- Explores the basics of real estate law
- Provides students with real life case examples, which illustrate key laws
- Includes discussions of Ohio statutes, agency law, fair housing, deeds, contracts, landlord/tenant rights and duties, and other pertinent aspects of real estate law
- Key terms are highlighted and defined throughout the text, and reviewed in a comprehensive glossary, to assist you in understanding definitions required for state exams

The effectiveness and quality of Hondros Learning's educational materials are directly attributable to the quality of the instructors at Hondros College of Business. Their involvement and contributions to the development of this text are critical to its effectiveness in the classroom and in your career.

According to the Ohio Division of Real Estate, only 66% of Ohio's new licensees are in the real estate business after their first year. Survey results indicate that more than 91% of Hondros College of Business graduates are active in the industry after their first year. We directly attribute that success to the practical, comprehensive education provided through our program. Hondros Learning's course materials provide a full understanding of both the very basic and the very complex studies of real estate and its application to a real estate career.

Hondros Learning™

Hondros Learning is the leading provider of classroom materials for real estate prelicensing and continuing education. Together with Hondros College of Business, we have provided training and educational products to more than one million students.

Successful completion of this course is essential to your career. To help you with that— and passing your licensing exam the first time— these additional real estate products are available from Hondros Learning:

Ohio Real Estate Salesperson CompuCram® Online Exam-Prep

Real Estate Vocab Crammer™ Flashcards

Real Estate National Sales Review Crammer™

Ohio Real Estate State-Specific Sales Review Crammmer textbook

Real Estate Principles and Practices textbook

Ohio Real Estate Appraisal textbook

Ohio Real Estate Finance textbook

Real Estate Sales Review Crammer™ Course: National (text included)

Real Estate Sales Review Crammer™ Course: Ohio State Specific (text included)

Recognitions: Reviewer Acknowledgments

Hondros Learning™ would like to thank the following expert reviewers for their comments and suggestions:

Al Batteiger

Robert Kutschbach

Larry Press

Jerry Siebert

William A. Thompson

INTRODUCTION

"Do it once, do it right, and never do it again!" That is the philosophy I believe in for everything in life—and preparing for the Real Estate Licensing Exam is no different. If you have taken all your pre-licensing courses and built a strong foundation of real estate knowledge, the *Ohio Real Estate State-Specific Sales Review Crammer*™ book, combined with the Crammer Course and CompuCram® Online Exam-Prep, are all you need to pass the exam! In these, you'll focus on the concepts, subjects, and topics you need to know for the Ohio State-Specific Real Estate Licensing Exam—presented it in the format you'll see on the exam!

Our instruction methods can make a major difference in your exam success, but the choice is yours. While we have the knowledge and experience you need, you have a significant role in making the *Ohio Real Estate State-Specific Review Crammer*™ materials work for you. We'll give you the necessary skills and concepts to pass the Ohio State-Specific Real Estate Licensing Exam, but it's up to you to follow our directions and guidelines *for the best opportunity for exam success.*

The *Ohio Real Estate State-Specific Sales Review Crammer*™ really works! We have developed, and continually update, our program with the knowledge gained in our 40 years. Our results speak for themselves. Hondros College students, on average, score more than 12% higher on the Ohio Real Estate Licensing Exam than others. The students who take advantage of our CompuCram™ Exam Preparation Software consistently increase their opportunities of passing the exam the first time even more!

Simply put, if you follow the Hondros College plan from start to finish, you'll not only pass the exam but also be on your way to a rewarding career in the real estate industry! The statistic we are most proud of at Hondros College is the high percentage of our graduates still in the business at the end of one year, versus the statewide average for the same statistic—91% vs. 60%! That says a lot about our instructors, our classes, our materials, and our ability to prepare you for the real estate licensing exam. So, let's get to it and see how to do it once, do it right, and never do it again!

—John G. Hondros

Test-Taking Techniques

It has probably been years since you have taken an exam. So, let's review a few test-taking techniques that will easily add between 10 and 15 points to your score. First, you need to have a relaxed attitude toward taking the test. If you study and prepare, you'll do fine. Telling your family, friends, and colleagues you are taking the exam places pressure on you by creating expectations, and worrying about everyone's expectations for success may have the opposite effect on your ability to comfortably, and successfully, complete the exam. Go back and tell everyone you have decided to wait a while before taking the exam. Their expectations will disappear, and the sense of pressure will be gone. Try it; it works!

Here Are Some Other Tips:

1. Test moderators enforce the regulations closely. **NO eating, drinking, or smoking**, and **no breaks**. Calculators must be simple, basic calculators. You are limited to one piece of scrap paper. If you run out of scrap paper, hold it up for a replacement. Listen to the guidelines and follow them closely.

2. When you begin the exam, we suggest you immediately write down the concepts and formulas on your scrap paper. This way, you'll be ready to go when you need them (e.g., capitalization rate formulas).

3. Read the question. Read the question. Read the question. Read the question at least **three times** before you look at the answers. Then, read the answers at least two times before selecting the best one.

   People tend to read the questions quickly. Don't do this since you'll often read it so fast you will fall into the "sounds alike" trap and confuse words, (e.g., grantor versus grantee, gross income versus net income).

   When reading a question, do not jump to conclusions. Most questions will have "loss leaders"—statements that do not relate to anything or answers choices with unfamiliar words that sound like possible answers. Before you choose an answer, be sure you have read the entire question and all answer choices.

4. Do not spend a lot of time on one question. Go through the exam and answer only those questions that you *can answer* for certain. If you're in doubt about an answer, skip the question and go to the next one. It's best to move through the questions you can answer as quickly as possible and return to the others later, if you have time. If you are in doubt about a question, "mark" it, skip it, and move on. At the end of the test, after answering the questions you know, review all marked questions, if you have time. Sometimes other questions in the exam will help you answer a question you are unsure of.

5. Maintain your concentration. You may lose your train of thought because of am ambiguous question. This type of question is one that appears to be poorly written, make no sense, or has more than one correct answer. Getting stuck on one of these can throw you off for a series of questions. When this happens, relax—your mind and your muscles—and skip the question. There may be others of these questions on the exam. If, by chance, you miss these because you guess, it will not cause you to fail. What can cause you to fail the exam is becoming so frustrated that you miss the following questions. Keep your composure. Remember, even if you miss these and no others, you will still pass.

6. If a question on the exam appears to have more than one correct answer, look for the best answer based on the supplied information—not your assumptions.

7. Answer all questions, even if you have to guess. Two of the four answers are often not worth considering. Narrow your choices by process of elimination—weed out the obviously incorrect answers or answers you know are wrong. Pick one of the remaining answers when guessing.

8. Your first answer is usually the right one. Don't change it unless you're sure.

9. Answers with absolutes such as *must, always, greatest, never,* and *has to be* are generally not the correct ones.

10. Be careful of "except" questions. You tend to read these questions too fast and even though you know the correct answer, you will choose the opposite.

Example

1. ***All of the following are examples of a specific lien, EXCEPT:***
   a. property taxes.
   b. judgment.
   c. mechanic's lien.
   d. mortgage.

   *The best way to answer these questions is to cover the word **except** or **not** when reading the question.*

   Answer: b

11. Watch your time to ensure you budget it wisely, but remember time is ***not*** your enemy. You'll have plenty of time to complete the exam as long as you work consistently. Do not spend 15 minutes on one question to get one point, when you could have answered 10 questions for 10 points.

    If you try to answer every question the first time through, you may end up wasting valuable time on the questions you are unsure of. This will only increase your anxiety level. A good time to recognize this behavior is in the Sales Review Crammer™ course—our test has the same type of questions. If you see this happening, make a concerted effort to answer only the questions you know and can complete quickly. After you've regained your sense of balance, answer the difficult questions. If you have used your time well on our exam, you will be prepared for the real exam.

12. Finally, if you have time to review the questions you skipped, take the time to **read the question completely** again. Then, dissect the question into parts (like clauses and prepositional phrases). This will help you understand what the test is asking. This is true even for math questions. When you cannot determine the answer, and before you guess, ask yourself, "What concept is the test trying to make sure I know?" Ask yourself which answer best illustrates that.

    Keep in mind that the purpose of the exam is to make sure you have the minimum amount of knowledge needed to function in the real estate industry.

13. Above all—**don't panic!** During the exam, you may lose your train of thought. When this occurs, stop and take a moment to relax. Take a deep breath, let your shoulders drop; relax your muscles, and your mind, before proceeding. Remember what you've studied. You know more than you think—just relax enough to let it become clear.

14. Be positive and have confidence in yourself. Starting today, say to anyone who will listen, "I'm going to pass the exam," and *mean it*!

Remember there's only one sure-fire way to pass the exam—***study***!

How To Study

The Basics of Good Study Methods

To give yourself the best chance for success on the real estate sales exam, it's important to follow our instructions.

Time is of the essence. Taking longer to complete your classes (more than 6 weeks) decreases your odds of passing the state exam by 63%.

Once you've completed the pre-licensing course(s), immediately begin studying for the Real Estate Sales exam. Do the following:

a) Read *Test-Taking Techniques*, and put these ideas into practice as you take the sample exams at the end of the book. Learn the techniques so they become second nature. This can increase your exam score by at least 10 points.

b) Read the appropriate *Real Estate Sales Exam Outline and Subjects Covered*. The outline does not necessarily represent the order in which you'll see topics on the test, but it will tell you exactly which subjects are covered on the exam and the percentage of questions you can expect in each area.

c) Read ***all*** of the chapters, and the *Glossary*, and *read it no fewer than 3 times!* If a word is in the glossary, it is in the bank of test questions. More than 70% of the state test questions are simply definitions.

   Know the words in the glossary. When you read the glossary the first time, *mark the terms you don't know.* Read the glossary a second time, focusing on the marked terms. Highlight terms you don't know the second time and repeat this review process.

   There's an added benefit to knowing all the terms in our glossary: **If you do not know what a word means in a test answer, then it is probably NOT the right answer.**

d) As you read chapters the first time, *mark the concepts you don't know.* Read the textbook a second time, focusing only on the marked parts. Highlight concepts you don't know on the second reading and repeat this review process. Focus on state-specific law, agency rules, fiduciary duties, and disclosures. These are areas often missed on the exam. **Read, review, and focus on these areas!**

e) There are charts or graphics in this text designed to help you in certain areas, covering things that have a good chance of appearing on the exam.

f) The exams at the end of the book contain questions similar to those on the exam. Grade your exam and review the questions you missed by re-reading those areas in your book.

g.) Practice the math problems! Many students assume they can pass the stae exam without the math - this assumption is a formula for failure. For aditional help, take our *Real Estate Math Formulas and Applications* class.

g) CompuCram, Use It!

Golden Rules

If you have studied all the material in this textbook, and followed our advice for test taking and studying, you should do well on the Real Estate Sales exam.

To recap the most pertinent points:

1) **Time is of the essence.** Taking longer to complete your classes (more than 6 weeks) decreases your odds of passing the state exam by 63%.

2) Utilize your Compucram it is key to your success along with your classes.

1) Read the question. Read the question. Read the question! Read *all* of the answers, too, before you make a choice.

2) Answer all questions, even if you have to guess.

3) Your first answer is usually the right one. Don't change it unless you're sure.

4) Answers with absolutes such as *must, always, greatest, never*, and *has to be* are generally not the correct ones.

5) Know definitions! Study the glossary in this book—if you don't, you are doing yourself a disservice.

6) If you have thoroughly studied the glossary and see an answer on the exam containing a word you don't know, it probably is NOT the right answer.

7) Know the ways you can lose your license.

In conclusion, if you do it once, do it right, and do it as outlined in this book, you'll never have to do it again—and you'll be on the road to success in your real estate career!

Introduction to Law

The law has a tremendous impact on the work of a real estate agent. Hundreds of federal, state, and local laws control the use and transfer of real property affecting property values and shaping transactions. In addition, the real estate profession itself is strictly regulated. Laws prescribe the agent's qualifications and duties to clients, customers, and employees.

This chapter is a broad survey of the legal system in the United States, with a particular focus on Ohio's system. It begins with a discussion of the nature and purposes of the law and explains some fundamental legal categories and concepts. It goes on to discuss the sources of law: Constitutions, legislatures, courts, and administrative agencies. It also examines the judicial system in detail.

Key Terms

Case Law Rules of law developed in court decisions, as opposed to constitutional law, statutory law, or administrative regulations.

Civil Litigation A lawsuit in which one individual sues another for compensation.

Criminal Litigation A lawsuit in which the government sues an individual to punish the wrongdoer and protect society.

Damages An amount of money a defendant is ordered to pay to a plaintiff.

Due Process A fair hearing before an impartial judge. Under the U.S. Constitution, no one may be deprived of life, liberty, or property without due process of law.

Precedent A previously decided case concerning the same facts as a later case; a published judicial opinion that serves as authority for determining a similar issue in a later case.

Pretrial Discovery Using depositions and interrogatories to learn more about the disputed facts in a case from the opposing parties and reluctant witnesses.

Settlement An agreement between the parties to a civil lawsuit, in which the plaintiff agrees to drop the suit in exchange for a sum of money or the defendant's promise to do or refrain from doing something.

Stare Decisis The legal doctrine that requires a judge to follow precedent (decided in the same jurisdiction) to make the law consistent and predictable.

Tort A breach of the standards of reasonable conduct imposed by law (as opposed to a duty voluntarily taken on in a contract) that causes harm to another person, giving the injured person the right to sue the one who breached the duty.

The Nature and Functions of Law

The law is a system of rights and duties established and enforced by a government in the form of general rules that citizens and visitors in the government's domain must obey.

The law serves a number of related functions. Most basically, it establishes order. Without law, "might makes right:" The strong and ruthless use violence, and the threat of violence, to dominate the weak. But the law lays down rules of conduct based on considerations other than brute force, and a court or similar tribunal serves as a forum for resolving disputes without violence.

An important function of the law in any complex society is the enforcement of promises. Commerce depends on promises: A builder agreeing to construct a house must be able to rely on the owner's promise to pay for the house. Otherwise, the builder would have to demand payment in advance. Then, the owner would have to rely on the builder's promise to complete the work. By enforcing certain promises through contracts, the law makes it possible to plan ahead and deal with unfamiliar persons.

In the United States today, the law reflects widely accepted ideas of fairness and equality. We have laws intended to protect people, not merely from physical force but from other forms of exploitation as well. For instance, a real estate agent is not allowed to take unfair advantage of a buyer by misrepresenting facts about a property. We also have laws that promote equal treatment.

For Example

A real estate agent may not refuse to show people a house because of their race or religion.

Historical Background

When English settlers colonized the New World, they brought English law with them. After gaining independence, the United States retained many aspects of English law and legal institutions. These are still the foundation of the U.S. legal system. Many of our basic legal concepts and rules were inherited directly from England. This accounts for much of the strange legal terminology used in real property law: "Escheat," "emblements," and "estate pur autre vie" were all part of English law centuries ago.

Early English law was known as the common law of England. As a result, long-established rules based on English law can be referred to as "common law rules."

Legal Categories and Concepts

In a complicated society like ours, the law covers a vast territory. Mapping out fundamental categories and concepts makes it easier to explore.

Criminal Law and Civil Law

One of the most basic divisions in the law is the distinction between *criminal law* and *civil law*. **Criminal law** is the body of law concerned with wrongs that an individual commits against society. **Civil law** is the body of law concerned with the rights and liabilities of one individual in relation to another. A person who fails to live up to a legal duty or to respect another's legal right may cause harm to another person or property. The failure may be accidental or deliberate, and the injury may be slight or serious, physical, emotional, or financial.

Criminal Litigation

Criminal litigation is *a lawsuit brought by the government against an individual to punish wrongdoing and protect society*. A criminal suit has the broad goals of punishing the individual to prevent more crimes from being committed and to deter others from committing similar crimes.

Crimes are classified as certain harmful or potentially harmful acts defined by statute for which the government may prosecute in the name of the state. In general, crimes are those acts that are particularly dangerous to society.

For Example

Accidentally rear-ending another car causes harm, but it is not necessarily a crime. Drunk driving is a crime (even if the driver has not caused an accident) because it has the potential to cause a great deal of harm.

If a person is found guilty of a crime, punishment may be imposed in the form of a fine or imprisonment. Fines are generally not based on paying for damage done, although this is becoming a trend in some areas. Usually, a person convicted of a crime would have to pay a heavy fine to the government, even if the criminal act (such as drunk driving) did not result in any actual damage. This fine is often in addition to the possibility of serving a jail sentence.

Because of the presumption that all accused of crimes are innocent until proven guilty, there is a higher standard of proof required by the prosecution. Instead of having to prove one guilty by the greater preponderance (weight) of the evidence, as in civil matters, a prosecutor must prove his case beyond a reasonable doubt.

Civil Litigation

Civil litigation is *a lawsuit in which one individual sues another for compensation*. A person injured by another's act generally has the right to sue that person. The government offers the courts as a forum for resolving these disputes. The person who sues is the **plaintiff**; the person sued is the **defendant**. Either one is called a **litigant**. Any litigant may be either a "natural person" (a human being) or an "artificial person" (a legal entity, such as a corporation).

Civil suits and criminal prosecutions have different purposes; thus, bringing criminal charges against a defendant will not prevent a civil lawsuit against the same person. The goal of most civil suits is to compensate the injured person for the harm done. **Damages** are *the monies a defendant is ordered to pay the plaintiff*. This monetary award is usually the remedy granted to the injured party and paid by the person who caused the harm. Damage awards are usually limited to financial losses the injured person incurred. This might include lost profits or wages, money spent on repairs, or hospital bills. Another form of compensation the court may award is an **injunction** ordering the defendant to do something or refrain from doing something.

But while the basic purpose of most *civil suits is to compensate the injured person* and the basic purpose of *criminal suits is to punish the wrongdoer*, that distinction is sometimes blurred in civil suits. When a civil defendant's conduct was deliberate and outrageous, the court may order the defendant to pay the plaintiff **punitive damages** (also called **exemplary damages**). This is a sum of money over and above the **compensatory damages** award (also called **actual damages**), compensating the plaintiff for actual financial losses. As the name indicates, punitive damages punish. They are awarded quite frequently in a few specific types of lawsuits, like those based on violations of the Federal Fair Housing Act (see Chapter 4). But punitive damages are the exception.

Real estate lawsuits are nearly always civil, not criminal. The main exceptions to this are cases involving fraud or embezzlement. For example, a victim of fraud can bring a civil suit for compensation. Furthermore, in very serious cases, the government will also impose criminal penalties (see Chapter 3 regarding fraud).

Since most real estate disputes do not involve crimes, the focus in this chapter, and the book as a whole, will be on civil law.

 The general rule to remember is that civil suits compensate and criminal suits punish.

Basic Civil Law Concepts

Civil law has three fundamental categories: Contracts, torts, and property. Each represents a group of basic legal concepts and principles.

Contracts

A **contract** is a legally binding promise. When two people enter into a contractual relationship, they voluntarily take on legal duties toward one another.

There is a whole body of rules that govern legal relationships based on contracts. These rules apply to any kind of contract, whether it concerns employment, the sale of a condominium, or commercial shipping. These basic rules as applied to contracts concerning real property are discussed in Chapter 8.

Torts

A **tort** is *a breach of the standards of reasonable conduct imposed by law that causes harm to another person*. Unlike contract law, these legal duties are not voluntarily assumed. Rather, the law requires everyone to take reasonable care to avoid injuring others or damaging others' property.

For Example

While running through the train station to catch a train, A accidentally knocks B down. B's arm is broken in the fall. A has breached the legal duty to use reasonable care in passing through a public place. In other words, A has committed a tort against B.

Torts connected with real estate are discussed in Chapter 3 (fraud in the agency relationship) and Chapter 11 (injuries on leased property).

Property

Property is something that is owned, real or personal, tangible or intangible, and includes the rights of ownership in that thing. The rights of ownership allow the owner to use, possess, transfer, or encumber the property owned. Property law includes rules about acquiring ownership and losing ownership, and about the rights and duties that ownership carries with it. These rules, of course, are one of the main focuses of this book.

Contract, tort, and property issues can be tangled together in a single legal problem.

For Example

Suppose two neighbors have a dispute about their property boundary and each claims to own a particular strip of land. One neighbor's tenant slips and breaks her collarbone. It is not clear whose property she was on when she slipped, because of the boundary dispute. To determine whether either of the neighbors must compensate the tenant for her injury, the lawyers will have to sort out property issues (Who owned that strip of land?), contract issues (What rights and duties did the lease give the tenant?), and tort issues (Did the tenant slip because the owner failed to maintain the property in a safe condition, or because of her own carelessness?).

Sources of Law

Who makes laws? The simple answer is the government, but in the United States "the government" has several facets—and all play a role in lawmaking.

Governmental power is divided between the federal government and the 50 independent state governments; in each state, there are also regional and local governmental bodies. To complicate matters even further, there are different sources of law within the federal government and each state's government: Constitutions, legislatures, courts, and administrative agencies.

Constitutions: Constitutional Law

A **constitution** is a fundamental document that grants power to a government. It establishes the government's structure and defines the limits of the government's power. **Constitutional law** then, is the fundamental law with which all other laws must comply. A law is said to be **unconstitutional** and cannot legally be enforced if the government exceeds its constitutional power in the passage of the new law. Even a constitutional law can be applied by a government official in a way that oversteps the limits of the government's power. In that case, the law still stands, but the official's action is unconstitutional.

In the United States, there is a federal Constitution that applies to the whole country, and each of the states has its own constitution as well.

Federal Constitution

The United States Constitution was drawn up at the Constitutional Convention in 1787, approved by the states, and adopted in 1789. The Constitution declares itself to be the "supreme law of the land."

The U.S. Constitution defines the relationship between the federal government and the state governments. Only the federal government may make laws concerning such matters as wars and the military, immigration, copyrights and patents, and currency (Article I, section 8).

There are many other areas in which both the federal government and the state governments can, and do, make laws. Discrimination and environmental protection are examples. There are also many matters that are left up to the state governments, including the ownership and transfer of real property.

If a conflict arises between a federal law and a state law, the stricter rule prevails.

For Example

When a federal air pollution law is tougher than an Ohio law, a factory in Ohio must comply with the federal standard. On the other hand, if the federal law is looser than the Ohio law, the factory must comply with the Ohio standard.

Protection of Individual Rights

The first ten amendments to the U.S. Constitution are known as the Bill of Rights. They were adopted in 1791. The Thirteenth, Fourteenth, and Fifteenth Amendments were added soon after the Civil War. Together, these amendments protect the rights of individuals by limiting governmental power. Some of them have a particular impact on property.

Due Process. The Fifth and Fourteenth Amendments state that no one shall be "deprived of life, liberty, or property without due process of law." This is known as the due process requirement. **Due process** means *a fair hearing by an impartial judge.*

Equal Protection. The Fourteenth Amendment also provides that the government may not deny an individual "equal protection of the laws." The equal protection requirement prohibits the government from adopting laws that unfairly discriminate between different groups of people.

Just Compensation. The Fifth Amendment further prevents the government from taking private property for public use "without just compensation." The government has the power to turn a citizen's land into a public garden or parking lot, but the Constitution requires the government to pay for it (see Chapter 10).

State Action. The Bill of Rights and other Amendments to the Constitution are designed to protect individuals against abuse by the government. The Constitution generally does not protect a person in relation to private individuals. Rather, its protections apply when there is state action by the government or a government official.

For Example

The First Amendment protects freedom of speech. A city cannot pass a law or take action to prevent protesters from gathering in city parks for political rallies. That interference with their freedom of speech would violate the First Amendment.

On the other hand, as far as the Federal Constitution is concerned, the owner of a shopping center may prevent the same groups from gathering in the center's parking lot. The shopping center is private property, so the policy does not involve state action and therefore is not considered a violation of the First Amendment. *Hudgens v. NLRB,* 424 U.S. 507 (1976).

Ohio's State Constitution

Ohio's original constitution was adopted in 1802 but was replaced with a more comprehensive constitution in 1851. The state constitution opens with a Bill of Rights. Among many other guarantees, it provides that everyone has a right to acquire, possess, and protect property (Article I, Section 1). Many of the state constitutional rights overlap with those safeguarded by the U.S. Constitution. These overlapping rights include freedom of speech and protection from unreasonable searches and seizures of property.

After its Bill of Rights, the Ohio constitution outlines the structure of the state government. It also sets forth fundamental law concerning a variety of subjects including education, taxation, and elections.

Legislatures: Statutory Law

Legislatures are the branches of government that have primary responsibility for passing laws and, as such, are the dominant source of new laws in the United States.

- **Statutory law** refers to laws adopted by a legislative body.

- **Acts** or **statutes** refer to laws adopted by Congress and state legislatures.

- **Resolutions** or **ordinances** refer to laws adopted by counties and city councils.

Representatives elected to the U.S. Congress, state legislatures, and county and city councils across the country make thousands of new laws every year.

The Legislative Process

The members of a legislative body write and adopt laws through a process of argument and compromise. Each legislative body has its own procedures. As an example, here is a brief outline of the procedures used to write and pass a bill in the United States Congress:

- Congress is divided into two houses—the Senate and the House of Representatives. A proposed law (called a **bill**) is introduced in each house, often at the suggestion of a government agency (such as the Department of Housing and Urban Development) or a lobbying group (such as the National Association of REALTORS®).

- In each house, a legislative committee (such as the Ways and Means Committee) analyzes and revises the bill. A Senate committee and a House committee often make different changes in a bill; thus, two different versions are developed.

- Next, the Senate and House each consider and vote on their versions of the bill. If a majority in either house votes against the bill, it dies. If a majority in each house votes in favor of it, the two versions must be reconciled. A conference committee comprised of members from both houses works out a compromise version of the bill. If a majority in each house votes for this new compromise version, the bill is passed.

- The final stage of the legislative process involves the president. The president can expressly approve the bill by signing it, or can take no action on it. Either way, the bill becomes law. On the other hand, if the president **vetoes** (rejects) the bill, it will not become law unless Congress votes to override the veto. To override a presidential veto, a two-thirds majority in each house must vote in favor of the bill. If the veto is **overridden**, the bill becomes law in spite of the president's disapproval. If the bill can't muster strong support in Congress, it dies.

Ohio's legislature, the Ohio General Assembly, follows a similar procedure. It also is divided into two houses: The state Senate and the state House of Representatives. The state governor has the power to veto legislation. The collection of state statutes (laws adopted by the general assembly) is known as the Ohio Revised Code.

The Courts: Case Law

The courts fall under the judicial branch of government and are primarily responsible for enforcing laws. Although legislatures are the main source of new laws, the courts have become an important source of new laws as well. Judges, however, do not issue general rules in the same way legislatures do. A legislature can make laws on any subject it chooses (as long as it does not violate the federal or state constitution). A judge, on the other hand, can address a point of law only if it is at issue in a lawsuit. Thus, **case law** *refers to the rules of law developed by judges in court decisions.* These rules of law must be extracted and interpreted based on the opinions and reasoning used by the judge in deciding how to apply the law to the particular circumstances in those court cases.

Historically, the courts were the primary source of law in the English common law system (in contrast to other European countries, where statutory law was dominant). As a result, case law is sometimes called common law. Thus, the term "common law" can refer either to rules of law that we inherited from England or to case law (judge-made law) in general, as opposed to statutory law.

Dispute Resolution and Lawmaking

A judge's primary task is to resolve disputes. One such dispute may involve one person who accuses another of breaching a contract but the other denies it. The two individuals are unable to work out their disagreement, so there is a lawsuit. The judge acts as a referee and settles the argument by applying the law to the facts of the particular dispute.

In the course of resolving a dispute, a judge will often have to engage in a form of lawmaking. Applying the law to the facts is not a mechanical process. Nearly every case presents a new combination of circumstances, and many raise issues that have not been settled by existing law. A judge will often have to extend and reshape established rules of law, and sometimes will have to forge new ones.

For Example

It is an established rule that if someone selling a house is aware of any hidden defects in the property, the seller must tell a prospective buyer about them. A defect is considered hidden if the buyer would not discover it through a reasonable inspection of the house.

S sold B his house. S did not tell B that there were rotten beams in the attic. The attic can be reached only by climbing through a trap door. B inspected the house before closing, but did not bother to look at the attic. If B had gone to the attic, he would have seen the rotten beams.

After moving into the house, B discovered the rotten beams. B sued S. The judge must decide whether S had a duty to tell B about the beams. Were they a hidden defect, or did B fail to make a reasonable inspection? Was B required to climb into the attic? The established rules do not address these particular questions.

The way the judge answers these questions will, of course, directly affect the parties involved in the lawsuit. In the previous example, if the judge says the rotten beams were a hidden defect, then S had a duty to tell B about them. S will owe B compensation for failing to disclose that information.

The judge's conclusion, however, could also affect other people in a similar situation. Any seller who knows about a problem in an attic that can be reached only through a trap door will have to tell prospective buyers about it or risk potential liability. In other words, the judge's decision in this case will have become a rule of law to be followed in other similar cases.

Stare Decisis and Precedent

The **doctrine of stare decisis** means that *a judge's decision in a specific case can become a rule of law applied to all cases.* "**Stare decisis**" is a Latin phrase that means, roughly, "*to abide by the decision.*" The doctrine holds that once a judge has decided a particular point of law, other judges faced with the same issue must decide it the same way. The first judge's decision is called a precedent. A **precedent** is *a previously decided case concerning the same issues presented in a later case and, under certain circumstances, it is considered **binding** on other judges.* This makes the law consistent and predictable. Referring to the previous example again, if the judge ruled that S had to tell B about the problem in the attic, the doctrine would require another judge in a later case involving a similar attic to rule the same way.

Stare decisis is not a law, but a policy inherited from English common law that judges have followed for centuries. This policy tries to ensure that two people who do the same thing will be treated the same way by the law.

Not every court decision is a binding precedent for all other judges, however. A judge is bound by the decision of another court only if it is in the same **jurisdiction**—the area under the authority of a particular court.

For Example

The jurisdiction of the Ohio Supreme Court is the state of Ohio, so its decisions are not binding on another state's courts.

Within each jurisdiction, courts are arranged in a hierarchy, with numerous courts on the lowest level and a lesser number of courts on each higher level. There may be one judge or several judges on a given court, depending on its function and the population of the area it serves. A judge is required to follow the precedents decided by a higher court in the same jurisdiction.

For Example

Here is an imaginary, simplified court system case and diagram:

Intermediate Court A hears a case involving an attic that can be reached only through a trap door and rules that the buyer was not required to inspect it. All judges on Lower Courts A1, A2, and A3 are supposed to follow that precedent if they hear a similar case.

When a judge on Lower Court B2 decides a similar case, the judge is free to hold that the buyer was required to inspect the attic because Lower Court B2 is not in the same jurisdiction as Intermediate Court A.

Intermediate Court B is generally not bound by the precedents of Intermediate Court A, since Court A is not higher than Court B. However, after the case is ruled on by the Highest Court, then both intermediate courts and all lower courts are bound by the Highest Court's decision.

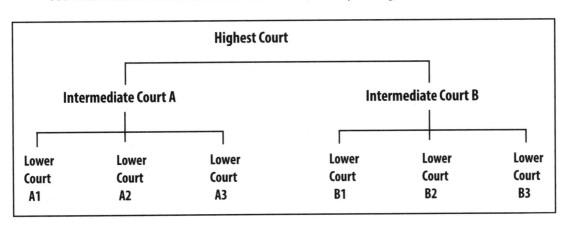

A judge also is expected to follow the earlier decisions of the judge's own court. The judge, however, does have the power to depart from those precedents. Conditions may have changed significantly since the earlier case was decided, or the earlier decision may simply seem wrong. If so, the judge may modify the rule, or **overrule** the precedent altogether, as long as that precedent was not decided by a higher court.

No decision can be a binding precedent unless a written **opinion** is published. In addition to stating the court's decision, an opinion describes the facts of the case and the court's reasoning. Some courts publish an opinion for every case decided; others publish opinions only for their most important cases.

By reading the higher court's opinion, a lower court judge can determine how similar the facts of that earlier case were to the case currently being decided and whether the same reasoning applies. When the facts are significantly different, the current case is **distinguished** from the earlier case. If the current case can be distinguished, the lower court judge can reach a different result than was reached in the earlier case.

Keep in mind that even though judges are not bound by lower court decisions or decisions from other jurisdictions, they often take them into consideration. When an Ohio judge is confronted with an issue that has not been decided by Ohio courts before, the judge is likely to read decisions from courts in other states. A well-reasoned opinion from another jurisdiction can have a persuasive influence.

Administrative Agencies: Regulations

Administrative agencies are part of the executive branch of government. Regulations issued by these various agencies have become another source of law at the federal, state, and local levels. Executives (the president, governors, mayors) and legislatures do not have the time or expertise to take care of all details of a complex area of law, so they create administrative agencies to oversee and guide specific areas. Federal agencies range from the Department of Housing and Urban Development to the Internal Revenue Service. State agencies include the Ohio Real Estate Commission and the Ohio Civil Rights Commission. Usually, each county and city also has its own zoning board, building department, and other local agencies.

An administrative agency has broad powers within its area of authority, including the power to issue regulations that have the force of law.

For Example

The Ohio Real Estate Commission has issued a regulation requiring real estate agents to give prospective buyers a **Consumer Guide to Agency Relationships** brochure or document. An agent who fails to comply with this regulation may have his license suspended or revoked.

Detailed regulations give rise to many disagreements: Permits and benefits are denied or revoked; rules are violated. These disputes would overwhelm the court system, so most of them are decided by the agencies themselves.

Many of these disputes are handled through an informal process of negotiation. But when a significant liberty or property interest (such as a real estate license) is at stake, the agency usually must hold a formal administrative hearing in order to comply with the constitution's due process requirement. These cases are decided by administrative law judges.

An administrative law judge is part of the agency, and is an expert in the agency's area of authority. The judge is supposed to consider disputes impartially, rather than simply taking the agency's side. If an individual is unhappy with an administrative law judge's decision, there may be a board of appeals within the agency that will reconsider his case. And if he is dissatisfied with that decision, he can appeal to the court system.

Case Law Citations

Judicial opinions are published in books called **case reporters**. Case citations—references to particular cases in the reporters—are given in a standardized form.

Example: *Deyling v. Flowers*, 10 Ohio App. 3d 19 (1983)

The citation includes the name of the case, followed by the volume (10) of the case reporter (Ohio App. 3d) where the opinion can be found. It then states the page number (19) the opinion begins on. The citation ends with the year that the case was decided, in parentheses (1983).

There are separate case reporters for most state appellate courts in the country, as well as federal case reporters. In addition, there are regional reporters that compile important cases from state courts in a given region (the Northeastern Reporter and the Pacific Reporter, for example). Each reporter's title has its own abbreviation for purposes of citation. The abbreviations that Ohioans will encounter most frequently are listed below.

State Court Decisions:

Decisions of the Ohio Supreme Court:
Ohio State Reports   Ohio St., Ohio St. 2nd, Ohio St. 3d

Decisions of the Ohio Courts of Appeals:
Ohio Appellate Reports   Ohio App., Ohio App. 2nd, Ohio App. 3d

Decisions of lower state courts:
Ohio Miscellaneous Reports   Ohio Misc.

Decisions from state courts in Ohio and four other states:
Northeastern Reporter   NE., NE 2nd

Federal Court Decisions:

Decisions of the U.S. Supreme Court:
United States Reports   U.S.
Supreme Court Reporter   S. Ct.

Decisions of the U.S. Courts of Appeals:
Federal Reporter   F., F. 2nd

Decisions of the U.S. District Courts:
Federal Supplement   F. Supp.

A citation to a case from a federal court of appeals includes the circuit number in parentheses, along with the year the case was decided. So, a Sixth Circuit decision would be cited like this: *McDonald v. Verble*, 622 F. 2nd 1227 (6th Cir. 1980).

A citation to a case from a federal district court includes the name of the district in the parentheses. A decision from the Northern District of Ohio would be cited like this: *Drain v. Friedman*, 422 F. Supp. 366 (N.D. Ohio 1976).

The Judicial System

As we have seen, judges resolve disputes by interpreting and applying existing laws, and developing new ones, if necessary. The judicial system, though, is comprised of many different types of courts: Trial courts and appellate courts, federal court systems, and state court systems.

Trial Courts and Appellate Courts

The **trial** is the fundamental court proceeding in a lawsuit. The general outlines of a trial are no doubt familiar to most: Lawyers present arguments and evidence, witnesses testify, and a jury or a judge decides the case. Trials take place in a jurisdiction's lower courts, often referred to as **trial courts**.

If an individual is dissatisfied with the outcome of a trial, he generally has the opportunity to appeal at least once. On **appeal**, he asks a higher court in the same jurisdiction to reconsider the trial court's decision. A court that has the power to review the decisions of lower courts is called an **appellate court**.

Many people expect an appeal to be just like another trial, but it is a very different proceeding. To try every appealed case over again would be extremely expensive, for both the parties and the court system. Thus, the evidence is not presented again, witnesses do not testify again, and there is no jury.

Instead, the appellate court reviews the *trial record*. The **trial record** includes the pleadings, documentary, or physical evidence introduced in the trial, and a word-for-word transcript of everything the lawyers, witnesses, and trial judge said in the courtroom. In reviewing the record, the appellate court is looking for errors committed by the trial judge. An appellate court ordinarily will change a trial court's decision only if the judge committed a prejudicial error concerning a question of law.

Question of Fact Versus Question of Law

All the issues in a trial can be classified either as questions of fact or questions of law:

- A **question of fact** is any question about what actually took place: Did the landlord tell the tenant she could lease the apartment for nine months, or for a year and a half?

- A **question of law** is any question about what the law is on a particular point: Is a lease for a year and a half valid if it is not recorded in writing?

Questions of fact are decided by the **trier of fact**. In a jury trial, the trier of fact is the jury; in a non-jury trial, the trier of fact is the judge. Questions of law, on the other hand, are always decided by the judge whether there is a jury or not. The trier of fact determines the facts of the case—what actually happened based on the evidence presented—then the appropriate rules of law, as determined by the judge, are applied to the facts to reach a decision in the case.

The Appellate Process

An appellate court generally accepts the conclusions reached by the trier of fact regarding the questions of fact. The trier of fact is assumed to have had a better opportunity to assess the evidence than the appellate court. The trier of fact heard the testimony firsthand and could observe the witnesses as they were testifying. Thus, the appellate court will assume the trier of fact's conclusions are correct, unless they are completely unsupported by the evidence.

The appellate court focuses instead on the questions of law, reviewing the record to see if the trial judge ruled erroneously. If the appellate court determines that an errant ruling or interpretation was made by the judge, the appellate court considers whether the trial judge's error was prejudicial or harmless. A prejudicial error is one that may have made a difference in the outcome of the trial. The error is considered harmless if the trier of fact would almost certainly have reached the same final decision if the error had not been made.

The Appellate Decision

If the appellate court does not find any error in the record, or decides that the error was harmless, it will **affirm** the trial court's decision. If it decides there was prejudicial error, it will **modify** or **reverse** the decision. Note that the appellate court may also affirm part of the trial court's decision, while modifying or reversing another part from the same case.

When a trial court's decision is reversed, the appellate court may substitute its own ruling for the trial court's decision, or it may **remand** the case back to the lower courts. If the case is remanded, the appellate court may order the original trial judge to conduct additional proceedings, or it may order a new trial.

A Second Appeal

A litigant dissatisfied with the result of an appeal may appeal again, to a higher court. But while a first appeal is an **appeal by right**, a second appeal is usually **discretionary**. A litigant petitions the high court to hear the case, but the courts are so overcrowded that most discretionary appeals are turned down.

Federal Courts and State Courts

Just as there is a federal legislature (Congress) and 50 state legislatures, there is a federal court system and 50 state court systems. The federal court system, however, is not centralized in Washington, D.C. Rather, there are federal courts in every state, along with state courts. Jurisdictions of federal and state courts overlap.

Jurisdiction

Jurisdiction is the extent of a particular court's authority. Taking a closer look at the concept of jurisdiction will make it easier to understand the federal and state court systems and their relationship to one another.

This chapter has already discussed how a court's jurisdiction can be limited to a particular geographical area. This is known as the court's **territorial jurisdiction**. A court's jurisdiction may also be limited to a certain type of lawsuit, such as tax cases or patent cases. The types of cases that a court has authority to hear are called its **subject matter jurisdiction**.

There may also be monetary limits on a court's jurisdiction.

For Example

The Federal Court diversity minimum is $75,000. That means that the amount of money involved in the dispute (called the **amount in controversy**) must be more than $75,000 for an individual to choose federal court as a venue.

An exception to this monetary limit is where federal court is an option by statute or the issue at hand falls under federal jurisdiction (e.g., civil rights).

A court may have **exclusive jurisdiction** over a particular type of case, which means that it is the only court where that type of case can be filed. Or it may share jurisdiction with another court, so that a plaintiff can choose where to file. This shared jurisdiction is called **concurrent jurisdiction**.

The jurisdiction of each state and federal court is limited in a variety of ways. Federal courts generally may look only at cases that involve federal issues. The U.S. Supreme Court can choose to hear appeals from the federal courts or the state supreme courts. Let's take a closer look at the Ohio state court system.

The Ohio State Court System

The trial courts at the bottom of the state court hierarchy are the county courts and the municipal courts. There is a **municipal court** in each large or medium-sized city. In some cases, the municipal court's territorial jurisdiction ends at the city limits. In other places, the municipal court also has jurisdiction over neighboring areas.

For Example

The Toledo Municipal Court has jurisdiction over Toledo, Washington Township, and Ottawa Hills. Some municipal courts have jurisdiction over their entire county. The municipal court in Columbus is called the Franklin County Municipal Court, and its jurisdiction is all of Franklin County.

A **county court** has territorial jurisdiction over all the areas within a county that are not served by a municipal court.

For Example

The Lucas County Court has jurisdiction over all of Lucas County, except for Toledo, Washington Township, and Ottawa Hills.

When a municipal court has jurisdiction over the entire county (like Franklin County Municipal Court), there is no county court.

Municipal Courts

Municipal courts try all misdemeanors that occur within their territories. They also hear cases involving ordinance violations. Some municipal courts have a housing division, with exclusive jurisdiction over violations of local building codes and health and safety codes. Like county courts, municipal courts conduct preliminary hearings in felony cases that occur within their territories.

Civil matters can be tried in municipal courts when the amount in controversy is $15,000 or less, such as a broker's lawsuit against a seller for a $10,000 commission, or a dispute over a car worth $8,000.

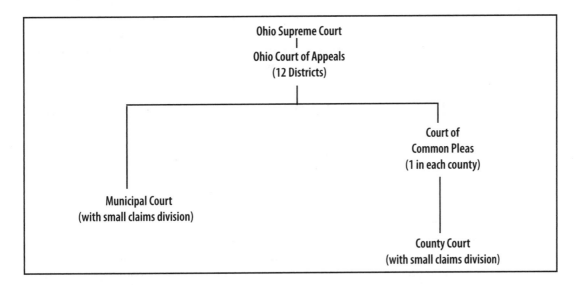

Within the $15,000 limit, municipal courts can hear any case in which the plaintiff is requesting damages only. They also have jurisdiction in a limited range of cases in which the plaintiff is asking for something other than (or in addition to) money, including any action for breach of contract, foreclosure of liens against personal property, or eviction, among other things.

The Cleveland Municipal Court has some special powers. It can hear certain actions for recovery of real property or foreclosure on real property within its territory, including foreclosure of any mechanic's lien or judgment lien. This also includes mortgage foreclosures if the mortgagee is claiming $15,000 or less. In Ohio, no other municipal court has jurisdiction over real property foreclosure or recovery actions.

Mayor's Courts. Mayor's courts have jurisdiction over cases involving violations of local ordinances in any municipality that is not the site of a municipal court. Mayor's courts also handle moving violations of traffic laws that occur on state highways within the municipality's boundaries.

The decision of a mayor's court can be appealed (by right) to the municipal or county court serving that area. Note that these are not treated like most appeals, though. The municipal or county court will conduct a new trial instead of simply reviewing a transcript from mayor's court.

County Courts

County courts can hear minor criminal cases (misdemeanors), such as shoplifting and drunk driving, for crimes that occur in areas of the county that are not served by municipal courts. It also conducts preliminary hearings in more serious criminal cases (felonies), determining whether there is sufficient evidence to send the case to the court of common pleas.

A county court's civil jurisdiction is limited to cases in which the amount in controversy is $15,000 or less. Even within that monetary limit, there are specific types of cases that cannot be heard in county court.

For Example

A county court is not allowed to decide suits concerning real estate contracts, no matter how little money is at stake. A county court also cannot hear suits for the recovery of title to real property, such as actions to quiet title or foreclosures.

Small Claims Divisions. Each municipal or county court has a small claims division for resolving minor civil disputes quickly and inexpensively. The amount in controversy must be $3,000 or less, and the plaintiff may not request any remedies other than money. To save time and expense, procedures are simplified in several respects.

For Example

The plaintiff automatically waives the right to a jury by choosing to file in small claims court. Most small claims litigants are not represented in court by lawyers (although they may be), and the trial must take place within 40 days after suit is filed.

Courts of Common Pleas

Courts of common pleas are the state's main trial courts. There is one in each county. A court of common pleas has concurrent jurisdiction over most criminal and civil cases that can be heard in the municipal or county court, and it has exclusive jurisdiction over many other cases.

All felony cases that occur in a county are tried in the court of common pleas, after a preliminary hearing in municipal or county court. The court of common pleas can also try misdemeanor cases, although most of those are taken care of in municipal or county court.

The court of common pleas hears all civil cases arising in its county that exceed the jurisdiction of the inferior courts. In an area served by a municipal court, the court of common pleas tries cases in which the amount in controversy is more than $15,000. And in an area served by a county court, the court of common pleas hears any case in which the amount in controversy is more than $15,000. The court of common pleas also hears any case involving real property foreclosure, a real estate contract, or other areas that are beyond the municipal or county court's jurisdiction.

Keep in mind, though, that the court of common pleas is not restricted to cases that exceed the $15,000 or $3,000 limit. The court of common pleas can hear almost any civil matter, as long as the amount in controversy is more than $500. Thus, many civil cases that could be filed in the municipal or county court may be filed in the court of common pleas instead. The exceptions are:

- Cases where the plaintiff is seeking $500 or less
- Code violation cases that are within the exclusive jurisdiction of the housing division of a municipal court

In addition to its trial duties, a court of common pleas also hears appeals in cases decided by a county court or an administrative agency, such as the Real Estate Commission. A court of common pleas, however, cannot take appeals from the municipal court. Appeals from municipal court decisions go directly to the state court of appeals, which is also where appeals from common pleas decisions are heard.

Ohio Court of Appeals

A litigant who is unhappy with the decision of a municipal court or common pleas court has the right to a review by the state court of appeals.

The state is divided into 12 appellate districts. The number of judges in each district depends on the population, but there are at least three in each district. A panel of three judges decides each appeal.

The decision of one of the courts of appeals is a binding precedent for all the courts of common pleas, municipal courts, and county courts within that appellate district (e.g., Ashtabula County is in the Eleventh Appellate District—the Ashtabula Municipal Court is required to follow precedents decided by the Eleventh District Court of Appeals).

The court of appeals in one district, however, is not bound to follow a precedent decided by the court of appeals in a different district.

For Example

Suppose the court of appeals in the Ninth District (Lorain, Medina, Wayne, and Summit counties) previously ruled that a home buyer does not have to climb through a trap door and inspect the attic. Now, the court of appeals in the Eighth District (Cuyahoga County) is hearing a similar case. The Eighth District court could rule that a home buyer is required to inspect the attic, even though that conflicts with the Ninth District's precedent.

When different appellate districts develop conflicting precedents, the conflict is resolved by the Ohio Supreme Court. After reaching a decision that conflicts with the Ninth District's precedent, the Eighth District court of appeals would send the case to the state's highest court.

Ohio Supreme Court

The state supreme court consists of seven judges called justices. It has appellate jurisdiction in all cases decided by state courts of appeals.

The supreme court is required to hear the conflict cases just described, where appellate courts in different districts are in disagreement. It can resolve those conflicts because its decisions are binding on all other courts in the state.

A criminal defendant who has been sentenced to death also has the right to appeal to the supreme court (after losing in the court of appeals). There is also an appeal by right in cases involving state or federal constitutional issues, and in a few other special types of cases.

In most cases, though, an appeal to the Ohio Supreme Court is discretionary. The supreme court will generally hear a discretionary appeal only if the case presents a particularly important legal question.

A Civil Lawsuit

This section will take a closer look at the litigation process. To start a lawsuit, the plaintiff's lawyer files a **complaint** in the appropriate court. The complaint outlines the dispute, explains how the plaintiff believes his legal rights have been violated by the defendant, and asks the court to grant judgment in the plaintiff's favor.

The complaint must be filed before the **statute of limitations** runs out. A statute of limitations prevents a court from hearing a case if too much time has passed since the conflict arose. It often becomes more and more difficult to prove or disprove a claim as years go by—evidence is lost and witnesses' memories fade. The time limits set by a statute of limitations vary depending on the type of case. In Ohio, written contracts have a 15 year limitation, while oral agreements are 6 years.

The kind of court in which a lawsuit takes place depends on the jurisdictional issues introduced earlier. The case must come within the court's jurisdictional limits—geographical, subject matter, and monetary limits. Most lawsuits concerning real estate are filed in the court of common pleas in the county where the property is located.

Once the lawsuit has been filed, the court sends a notice, called a **summons**, telling the defendant that the complaint has been filed, and that the defendant must file a response with the court. The summons is sent with a copy of the plaintiff's complaint to the defendant by certified mail. This notification procedure is known as **service of process**.

After receiving the summons and complaint, the defendant has 28 days to prepare an **answer**. In the answer, the defendant may challenge the court's jurisdiction, deny the plaintiff's allegations, discuss facts that the plaintiff left out of the complaint, or a combination of all of these. In some cases, the defendant may also make a **counterclaim** against the plaintiff.

The complaint, the answer, and any additional documents filed with the court are called **pleadings**.

Pretrial Discovery

The **discovery process** gives both the plaintiff and the defendant an opportunity to find out more about a given case once the lawsuit has been started. **Pretrial discovery** *uses depositions and interrogatories to learn more about the disputed facts from the opposing parties and reluctant witnesses.* The rules of discovery require each side to provide the other with information upon request.

A **deposition** is one method of acquiring information during discovery whereby one party's lawyer questions the other party or a witness about the case. The **deponent** (the person responding to the lawyer's questions) is under oath, just as if testifying in court.

Interrogatories are another important discovery tool. They are like a deposition, but are conducted by mail instead of in person. One party's lawyer sends a series of questions to the other party who answers and sends them back. Interrogatories are also answered under oath.

Settlement Negotiations

Litigation is almost always expensive, time-consuming, and unpleasant. Both parties must weigh those costs against any gain, and the likelihood of winning, if the case goes to trial.

Throughout the litigation process, the plaintiff's and defendant's lawyers negotiate to settle the case. In a **settlement**, *the defendant pays the plaintiff a sum of money (or agrees to do something or refrain from doing something) so that the plaintiff will drop the lawsuit.*

It is very likely that both sides of a dispute in a particular case will eventually reach some sort of agreement to end the lawsuit. In fact, more than 95% of all civil cases settle rather than going through to a judgment, with most cases settling even before the trial begins.

Jury or Judge

The U.S. and Ohio Constitutions guarantee litigants the right to trial by jury. That right applies in most civil cases, but some cases (and certain issues within some cases) cannot be tried by a jury. It depends on the remedies requested by the plaintiff.

The remedies awarded in civil cases are classified as:

- **Legal remedy**—Usually a damage award of money
- **Equitable remedy**—Usually involves an **injunction** (an order to do something, or to refrain from doing something)

For Example

In a boundary dispute, the court might order the defendant to move a fence to the correct boundary. Equitable remedies can only be awarded when money would not adequately correct the problem. Specific performance (Chapter 8), foreclosure (Chapter 6), and quiet title (Chapter 7) are all examples of equitable remedies.

For historical reasons, a jury is not allowed to decide equitable issues. If a plaintiff is asking only for an equitable remedy (such as foreclosure), the case cannot be heard by a jury. If a plaintiff is asking for both types of remedies (such as damages and an injunction), a jury may hear the case. The jury will decide on the legal remedy (the amount of damages), but the judge will decide on the equitable remedy (whether to issue an injunction).

Jurors are taken from a pool of citizens, chosen at random from voter registration lists and lists of licensed drivers. Both lawyers have an opportunity to question potential jurors, to learn about their backgrounds and discover their personal prejudices. Those who seem biased against, or in favor of, one of the parties may be eliminated from the jury.

When a plaintiff is requesting damages, a jury does not necessarily hear the case. Since jury trials are usually more expensive and time-consuming, both parties can waive their right to a jury and let a judge decide questions of fact and questions of law.

The Trial

The trial court proceedings follow strict rules, guidelines, and protocols for each type of case. Although the length of time can vary greatly, most trials contain an opening statement, witnesses, evidence, closing arguments, jury instructions, and a decision.

Opening Statement

The plaintiff's case is presented first, and then the defendant's. Each lawyer makes an **opening statement**, telling the client's version of events that gave rise to the lawsuit. This explanation helps the judge and jurors understand the evidence and testimony the lawyer is about to present.

Witnesses

Each party's lawyer brings in witnesses whose testimony supports the client's version of the facts. There are generally two types of witnesses called in a case:

- **Fact witness**—Someone who witnessed actual events connected with the dispute. A fact witness is supposed to only describe events that were personally observed, and usually is not allowed to offer opinions about the facts.
- **Expert witness**—Someone with expert knowledge of a subject, either through experience or education. Litigants hire expert witnesses to evaluate their claims. If an expert's opinion supports the litigant's case, the expert is paid to testify at trial.

The initial questioning of witnesses by the lawyer who called them to testify is the **direct examination**. Immediately following this, the opposing lawyer has a chance to ask the witness questions, called **cross-examination**. Here, the opposing lawyer tries to cast doubt on the witness's testimony and bring out facts that are unfavorable to the other side. The first lawyer then has a chance to repair any damage done on cross-examination by **redirect examination** of the witness. Sometimes, the opposing lawyer will cross-examine the witness a second time.

Evidence

Evidence is any testimony, documents, or objects submitted in a lawsuit as proof of facts. Court rules provide that some testimony, documents, or physical evidence may not be used in court if it is unreliable or unfair. Such testimony or evidence is **inadmissible** into the court proceedings. A lawyer can object to a witness's testimony, or to the lawyer's questioning of a witness on a variety of grounds.

For Example

A lawyer asking a witness about something that is not relevant to the issues in the case, or a fact witness giving an opinion are both grounds for objections by the opposing lawyer. If the judge agrees with the objection, the judge will order the witness not to answer the question, or instruct the jury to disregard the witness's statements.

The plaintiff has the **burden of proof** in most cases. This means the plaintiff must present evidence that a cause of action against the defendant exists before the defendant is under any duty to defend himself. This burden is fulfilled by the plaintiff through the offering of evidence in support of the claim. Since evidence attempts to furnish proof of facts in the case, anything that will buttress the plaintiff's claim would be considered evidence for the plaintiff. The defendant also has an opportunity to present evidence to support his own version of the facts.

Certain kinds of evidence are better than others. Although it is within the province of the jury to weigh the value of each item of evidence, common sense supports the value of a written document over an oral understanding, and the value of a disinterested party's testimony over that of someone close to the defendant.

For Example

A written statement signed by the defendant would be better evidence of a contract than an oral statement by the plaintiff. Likewise, a disinterested party giving testimony on the defendant's behalf is better than a sworn statement from the defendant's mother.

It is a good idea for all real estate professionals to keep accurate and complete written records of their activities. Not only is it good business practice, but it will also provide their counsel with a body of reliable evidence should they or their broker be called to testify.

Closing Arguments

Before the jury goes to make its decision, each party's lawyer gives a closing argument summarizing the evidence. Each lawyer puts the evidence in the best light for the client, trying to explain away testimony presented by the other side.

Jury Instructions

After both sides have presented their cases, the judge instructs the jury as to the applicable law. In addition to explaining the burden of proof, the judge will also instruct the jury as to what burden of proof standard they should apply in the case:

- **Greater preponderance (weight) of the evidence**—Sufficient standard of proof for most civil cases. The jury does not have to be absolutely certain the defendant was wrong. It is enough if the plaintiff has convinced the jury that, more likely than not, the defendant was in the wrong.
- **Clear and convincing evidence**—A higher standard of proof plaintiffs must meet in some civil cases.
- **Beyond a reasonable doubt**—An even stricter standard of proof applied in criminal cases where the defendant has much more at stake.

The Decision

A unanimous verdict is not necessary in a civil case in Ohio; a three-fourths vote from the jury is enough to decide. Unanimity, however, is required in criminal cases. A **hung jury** can result if the required number of jury members cannot agree on a verdict after deliberating for a long time. If this happens, the case must be tried over again before a new jury.

Appeal

Both the plaintiff and the defendant have a right to appeal the court's decision to the appropriate appellate court. A common pleas decision would be appealed to the Ohio Court of Appeals for that district. After the lower court's judgment has been entered, there is a limited period (usually 30 days) for filing an appeal. Whichever party chooses to appeal is called the **appellant**, and the other party is called the **appellee** or **respondent**.

For the most part, though, unless the trial judge committed a prejudicial error, there is no point in appealing a decision.

Alternative Dispute Resolution

Alternative dispute resolution offers a different means of settling issues and claims at stake between parties. These alternatives have become more popular, as it may take years for a case to get to trial. With the federal and state courts overflowing with litigation, alternatives have been instituted with some degree of success, especially in more populous counties.

Arbitration

Arbitration is an alternative in which both sides agree to submit the facts and evidence to an impartial third party to resolve the dispute. The process of arbitration is usually more informal than a trial (e.g., the discovery process may be limited and the rules of evidence may be relaxed). The arbitrator's decision, however, will be legally binding on the parties. The loser can appeal to the court system, but cannot just disregard the arbitrator's decision.

When an arbitration provision is included in a contract, the parties agree in advance to arbitrate if a dispute arises. These arbitration agreements are usually enforceable; one party can force the other to arbitrate instead of going to court.

In Ohio, however, an arbitration agreement is not enforceable for most disputes over title or possession of real estate.

For Example

A buyer and seller sign a purchase contract with an arbitration provision. The seller later backs out, and the buyer sues. The seller cannot force the buyer to arbitrate instead of suing.

Arbitration agreements are binding, though, for boundary disputes, controversies over the amount of rent due under a lease, and for a few other types of real property disputes.

Mediation

Mediation is the process whereby cases already filed with the court are moved forward by referring certain matters to a court referee. The referee holds a conference, not unlike a pretrial conference, to facilitate a voluntary settlement of the case. Mediation separates the cases that appear to be "settleable" from the cases with tougher issues, thus streamlining the process for all. Franklin County Common Pleas Court is the only one in the state that makes mediation mandatory.

Summary

1. The government brings a **criminal** action to punish a wrongdoer and protect society. In a **civil** action, an injured person sues for compensation. Some wrongful acts can lead to both criminal and civil penalties.

2. Contracts, torts, and property are the fundamental concepts of civil law. Contract law concerns voluntarily assumed duties; **tort** law concerns the duties of reasonable conduct imposed by law; property law concerns the duties inherent in ownership.

3. Federal and state constitutions, legislatures, courts, and administrative agencies are the sources of law in the United States. Within constitutional limits, legislative and administrative bodies issue general rules in the form of statutes, ordinances, and regulations. Courts apply those rules to resolve lawsuits. In interpreting the rules, courts develop case law. The doctrine of **stare decisis** requires judges to follow established precedents.

4. A **court system** is a hierarchy of trial courts and appellate courts. An **appeal** is not a second trial. Instead, the appellate court reviews the trial record for prejudicial error. The federal and state court systems are independent, with overlapping jurisdiction. Federal jurisdiction is limited to cases involving federal questions, citizenship, or the U.S. Government. State courts can hear any case except those Congress has reserved for the federal courts.

5. A civil suit begins when a plaintiff files a complaint with the court. The **pretrial discovery** process gives each side access to information the other might prefer to conceal. The parties' lawyers try to negotiate a settlement, to save the expense and trouble of a trial. In a trial, each side presents testimony and other evidence favorable to its case. A decision is reached by the trier of fact, but can be appealed to a higher court.

6. The result of a lawsuit can be a dismissal of claims, or a **legal** or **equitable remedy** can be awarded to one of the parties. A **legal remedy** is generally an award of money in the form of compensatory or punitive damages. An **equitable remedy** usually involves the issuing of an injunction ordering someone to do, or refrain from doing, something. Legal remedies are decided by a jury, while equitable remedies are decided by a judge. Equitable remedies can be awarded only when money damages would not adequately correct the problem.

Quiz

1. **The primary purpose of most civil lawsuits is to**
   a. compensate a person who has been harmed.
   b. deter crime.
   c. protect society.
   d. punish a wrongdoer.

2. **A person who commits a tort**
   a. has violated the standards of reasonable conduct imposed by law.
   b. must serve a jail term.
   c. will be held liable for breach of contract.
   d. will be prosecuted by the government.

3. **An unconstitutional law**
   a. can be enforced only retroactively.
   b. exceeds the powers granted to the government.
   c. may be used to modify a Supreme Court decision.
   d. violates the statute of limitations.

4. **Which would be most likely to issue an ordinance?**
   a. the Ashtabula County Court
   b. the Dayton City Council
   c. the Ohio Real Estate Commission
   d. the Ohio State Senate

5. **The main purpose of the doctrine of stare decisis is to**
   a. clarify confusing statutes.
   b. limit access to the courts.
   c. make court decisions more consistent and predictable.
   d. prevent courts from exceeding their subject matter jurisdiction.

6. **Which would LEAST LIKELY limit a court's jurisdiction?**
   a. amount of money at issue in a case
   b. geographical boundaries
   c. subject matter of the case
   d. timeframe of a case being heard

7. **Alice sued Betty for breach of contract, claiming $175,000 in damages. Which kind of state court did Alice file suit in?**
   a. Circuit Court of Appeals
   b. County Court
   c. Court of Common Pleas
   d. Municipal Court

Ohio Statutes

Between the changing environment of real estate and the increased awareness of the public regarding consumer protection, real estate law is continually changing and evolving. To address this dynamic area of law, Ohio has established both the Real Estate Commission and the Division of Real Estate and Professional Licensing within the Department of Commerce. These two bodies share the responsibility for protecting the public from unscrupulous and dishonest real estate dealers, and continuously work to elevate the positions of real estate broker and real estate salesperson to true professional status.

This chapter is entirely statutory—its content, by and large, deals with statutory law in Ohio. References to the Ohio Revised Code are presented with the abbreviation ORC followed by the section symbol (§) and the section number of the law. As future professionals in real estate, it is not important to know the code references, but it is vital to know what real estate law is and how it operates.

Key Terms

Associate Broker A licensed real estate broker with a brokerage who does not function as a principal broker or as a management level licensee.

Broker Any person, partnership, association, limited liability partnership, limited liability company, or corporation who, for a fee, sells, lists, leases, exchanges, negotiates, auctions, or otherwise deals in the real estate of others, or represents publicly that he does.

Fiduciary Someone in a position of trust and confidence, held by law to high standards of good faith and loyalty.

Foreign Real Estate Any real estate situated outside the state of Ohio.

Inactive License License status of any salesperson who returns his license to the Division of Real Estate and Professional Licensing, or whose broker does not want to maintain sponsorship of the licensee. A license may remain inactive indefinitely, as long as it is timely renewed and continuing education requirements are met.

(Continued on page 26)

Key Terms (cont.)

License on Deposit 1. A special license status that is available only to brokers who wish to return their broker's license to the Division of Real Estate and Professional Licensing in order to reactivate their license as a salesperson. Someone with a broker's license can also choose to be an associate broker, allowing the licensee to retain the broker's license without being designated a principal broker of the firm. A broker's license may remain on deposit indefinitely if timely renewed and continuing education requirements are met. 2. A special license status available to any licensee who enters the military or whose reserve military status is activated. The license remains inactive until the next renewal date following honorable discharge from the military.

Management Level Licensee A licensed broker or salesperson who is affiliated with a real estate brokerage and who has supervisory responsibility over other licensed brokers or salespersons affiliated with that brokerage.

Principal Broker A licensed real estate broker who oversees and directs the daily operations of the brokerage. A brokerage firm must have at least one principal broker but can have more.

Reactivate The process to remove a license from inactive, suspension, or deposit status (broker's license only).

Resigned The license status in which a license has been voluntarily and permanently surrendered to, or is otherwise in the possession of, the Division of Real Estate and Professional Licensing, is not renewed, and is not associated with a real estate broker.

Revocation The Real Estate Commission's permanent withdrawal of a real estate agent's license.

Salesperson Any licensed agent who is associated with a broker and, as such, may perform most of the acts of a broker, on behalf of the broker. A salesperson has the same fiduciary duty to a broker's client that a broker does.

Suspension The temporary withdrawal of a real estate agent's license for a certain and specified period of time.

Who Must Be Licensed (ORC § 4735.01)

A real estate **broker** is *any person, partnership, association, limited liability partnership, limited liability company, or corporation who, for a fee, sells, lists, leases, exchanges, negotiates, auctions, or otherwise deals in the real estate of others, or represents publicly that he so deals.* In other words, a broker is a professional who is licensed to, for a fee, represent a party in a real estate transaction. The **principal broker** is *is a real estate broker that oversees and directs the daily operations of the brokerage.* Every brokerage must have at least one principal broker. A licensed broker who is NOT a principal broker nor a management level licensee is known as an **associate broker**.

The Principal Broker. Every brokerage office must have **at least one** affiliated broker who is designated as the brokerage's **principal broker**. After the principal broker(s) is designated, all other licensed brokers at the brokerage are either management level licensees or associate brokers.

- The **principal broker** is responsible for **overseeing and directing the daily operations** of the brokerage. More specifically, the duties of the principal broker include:Ensuring compliance with the brokerage office requirements related to signage, display of licenses, and the Fair Housing Poster.

- Ensuring the timely renewal of the brokerage and branch office licenses.

- Keeping all affiliated licenses in a way that they can, and shall on request, be made immediately available for public inspection at the office or place of business of the broker.

- Keeping all affiliated licenses in a way that they can be returned until the licensee places the license on inactive or resigned status or until the licensee leaves the brokerage or is terminated.

- Ensuring the brokerage complies with all requirements to maintain trust and special accounts, including property management trust accounts if applicable.

- Maintaining complete and accurate records of all transactions.

- Maintaining complete and accurate trust account records.

- Maintaining an up-to-date Company Policy and Consumer Guide to Agency Relationships.

- Assuring that licensees are paid commissions within a reasonable time after the receipt of commission.

- Establishing practices to ensure the brokerage is not suborning unlicensed activity, e.g., only licensees are paid commission, and if paying commission to a licensee's company, that all requirements for that payment are met.

- Overseeing licensed activity to ensure licensees are providing services within their area of competency or are working with another competent agent.

The principal broker of a brokerage may assign any of these duties to a management level licensee.

With the approval of the Superintendent, one licensed broker could be the principal broker for **more than one brokerage** provided there is a commonality of **ownership** and a commonality of **name**. For example, a licensed broker might be a general partner in and the principal broker of both ABC Realty and ABC Property Management.

If there is only one principal broker in a company and that broker leaves, the company's license will be made inactive. The company must reapply to open again after hiring another broker. Any change in a brokerage's principal broker must be reported to the Superintendent of the Ohio Division of Real Estate and Professional Licensing within **15 days**.

Management Level Licensees. A **management level licensee** is *a licensed broker OR salesperson who is affiliated with a real estate brokerage and who has supervisory responsibility over other licensed brokers or salespersons affiliated with that brokerage.* A principal broker has the authority to assign duties for the brokerage's main office, a branch office, or a division within the brokerage to a management level licensee. A management level licensee could be a licensed broker or a licensed salesperson.

While the supervisory duties of the principal broker can be assigned to a management level licensee, it's important to be aware that, by law, this **does not relieve the brokerage and its principal broker(s)** from the responsibility to actively oversee and direct the operations of the business conducted on behalf of the brokerage.

A real estate **salesperson** is *a licensee who is associated with a principal broker and may perform most of the acts of a broker on behalf of the broker.* The broker is the one who charges the fee, usually a commission, and the salesperson is normally paid from the broker's funds. Property managers and rental agents who negotiate leases with tenants are also regulated by Ohio's real estate license law. Ohio also requires foreign real estate dealers to be licensed as such if they engage exclusively in sales activity in Ohio. **Foreign real estate** is *real estate situated outside the state of Ohio.*

An Ohio real estate sales license is valid only for conventional real estate transactions in Ohio. There are separate applications, requirements, and examinations for real estate auctioneers, real estate investment salespersons, and for those who sell foreign real estate outside the state of Ohio as foreign real estate salespersons or dealers.

Specific requirements must also be met in order for a salesperson to become a licensed broker in Ohio. In addition to a separate application and examination process, a licensee must have:

- Been active as a full-time (30 hours per week) salesperson for at least two of the preceding five years.

- Completed at least 20 real estate transactions.

- Completed additional education at an institution of higher education.

Exemptions

The following individuals are exempt from the licensing requirements:

1. A person who deals with **their own property,** including partnerships and corporations dealing with property through regular salaried employees

2. A **fiduciary** who is duly appointed and acting in a fiduciary capacity (e.g., executor of a will, guardian of a minor)

3. A **public official** who acts in an official capacity (e.g,. sheriff's sale)

4. An **attorney-at-law** who performs duties on behalf of clients

5. A person selling **manufactured homes** or **mobile homes** provided sales do not include the real estate on which the home sits

6. A person who engages in the **brokering of the sale of business assets**, not including the negotiation of the sale, lease, exchange, or assignment of any interest in real estate

7. An **out-of-state broker or salesperson** who engages in the sale of commercial real estate pursuant to the requirements of § 4735.022 of the Revised Code

8. A **petroleum land man**, which is someone who acquires the subsurface mineral rights from landowners for the purposes of oil and gas exploration

9. An individual who works with residential rental property **under the supervision of a broker** and whose compensation for service is primarily on a salaried or hourly basis:

May	May Not
• Perform maintenance	• Negotiate contracts or lease agreements
• Provide clerical or administrative support	• Vary or deviate from the rental price and/or other terms and conditions previously established by the owner or broker when supplying information concerning the rental of property to a prospective tenant
• Collect or accept rents and/or security deposits which are made payable to the owner or real estate brokerage	• Approve applications or lease agreements, or settle or arrange the terms and conditions of a lease on behalf of the owner or broker
• Exhibit or show residential rental units to prospective tenants	
• Furnish published information	• Offer inducements to prospective tenants unless they are previously advertised or prearranged with the owner or broker
• Supply applications and leases	
• Receive applications and leases for submission to the owner or brokerage for approval	• Interpret or provide their opinion concerning the terms or conditions of a lease agreement
	• Indicate to the public that he is in a position of authority that has the ultimate managerial responsibility of the rental property

Nonresident Commercial Brokers and Salespersons (ORC § 4735.022)

An "out-of-state" commercial broker or agent is exempt from Ohio real estate broker or salesperson licensing requirements if he does all of the following:

1. Works in cooperation with an Ohio real estate broker who holds a valid, active license issued under this chapter

2. Enters into a written agreement with the Ohio broker that includes the terms of cooperation and compensation and a statement that the out-of-state commercial broker and its agents will agree to adhere to the laws of Ohio

3. Furnishes the Ohio broker with a copy of the out-of-state commercial broker's current Certificate of Good Standing from any jurisdiction where the out-of-state commercial broker maintains an active real estate license

4. Files an irrevocable written consent with the Ohio broker, that legal actions arising out of the conduct of the out-of-state commercial broker or its agents may be commenced against the out-of-state commercial broker in the court of proper jurisdiction of any county in Ohio where the cause of action arises or where the plaintiff resides

5. Includes the name of the Ohio broker on all advertising in accordance with § 4735.16 of the Revised Code

6. Deposits all escrow funds, security deposits, and other money received by either the out-of-state commercial broker or Ohio broker in trust or special accounts maintained by the Ohio broker

7. Deposits all documentation required by this section and records and documents related to the transaction with the Ohio broker described. The Ohio broker shall retain the documentation that is provided by the out-of-state commercial broker and the records and documents related to a transaction for a period of three years after the date the documentation is provided, or the transaction occurred, as appropriate

An out-of-state commercial salesperson may perform those acts that require a real estate salesperson license with respect to commercial real estate provided that he meets all of the following requirements:

1. Is licensed with and works under the direct supervision of the out-of-state commercial broker

2. The out-of-state commercial broker with whom the salesperson is associated meets all of the requirements stated above

3. Provides the Ohio broker, who is working in cooperation with the out-of-state broker with whom the salesperson is associated, a copy of the commercial salesperson's current certificate of good standing from the jurisdiction where the out-of-state commercial salesperson maintains an active real estate license in connection with the out-of-state commercial broker

4. Collects money, including commissions, deposits, payments, rentals, or otherwise, only in the name, and with the consent, of the out-of-state commercial broker under whom the out-of-state commercial salesperson is licensed

By filing a consent-to-jurisdiction document, the person giving the consent makes and constitutes the Ohio secretary of state as an agent for service of process in this state including service of summonses and subpoenas. Service of process upon any person may be initiated by leaving with the secretary of state or an assistant secretary of state four copies of the process, an affidavit stating the address of the person given on the consent-to-jurisdiction document, and a fee of five dollars.

Upon receipt of the process, affidavit, and fee, the secretary of state immediately shall give notice of the process to the person, at the address given in the affidavit and forward to that address by certified mail, return receipt requested, a copy of the process. Service is considered to be complete upon the mailing of the notice and copy of process in accordance with this division.

A person, partnership, association, limited liability company, limited liability partnership, or corporation licensed in a jurisdiction where there is no legal distinction between a real estate broker license and a real estate salesperson license must meet the requirements of this section before engaging in any activity described in this section that requires a real estate broker license in this state.

Property Management

As indicated earlier, a person who operates, manages, or rents, or offers or attempts to operate, manage, or rent; other than as custodian, caretaker, or janitor; any building or portions of buildings to the public as tenants, needs to be licensed as a broker or be a salesperson working under the supervision of a principal broker, unless that person is performing only "ministerial duties" on behalf of the owner/landlord. The agency relationship between a property manager and an owner/landlord is created with a **property management agreement**. Among the expected duties of a property manager are:

- Selecting tenants
- Signing leases
- Setting and collecting rents
- Handling security deposits
- Initiating eviction procedures as necessary
- Hiring staff and outside vendors

Property Management Accounts

If a broker is acting as a property manager in regard to someone else's real estate, then the broker must maintain a special property management account, separate and distinct from the normal "trust account" that all brokers must maintain. This "property management" account must be used exclusively for the deposit and maintenance of all rents, security deposits, escrow funds, and other monies received by the broker in a fiduciary capacity in the course of managing real property. This account shall be separate and distinct from any other account maintained by the broker.

Unlike the broker's "trust account," this property management account *may* earn interest, which shall be paid to the property owners on a pro rata basis, unless otherwise specified in a written contract between the owner and the broker. The interest shall be paid or credited on a regular basis, but in no event less than on a quarterly basis. The property owner and broker may agree that the interest due the owner will be paid in a different manner and to a party(ies) other than the owner. Again, any such agreement must be specified in writing, signed by the owner and the broker or an authorized agent of the broker.

A separate ledger sheet shall be maintained for each owner of property managed by the brokerage identifying the following information in columnar form:

1. Name and/or address of the property
2. Parties to the transaction
3. Amount, date, and purpose of deposit(s)
4. Party from whom deposits are received
5. Amount, date, check number, and purpose of disbursements

6. Party to whom disbursements are made

7. Running balance of funds on deposit for the particular owner of property

8. Amount of interest earned on behalf of the owner(s) of the property(ies), if any

In paying expenses on behalf of an owner from a property management account, there must be enough funds credited and deposited to the owner's account to cover said expense. Security deposits received by a licensee must be deposited and maintained in the property management trust account unless the lease and property management agreement provide otherwise. Security deposits maintained in the property management account must be clearly identified and credited to the tenant.

All brokerages that engage in property management activities shall provide an accounting to each owner of property managed on a regular basis, **but in no event less than on a quarterly basis.**

Brokerages engaged in the management of property for another may, pursuant to a written contract with the property owner, exercise signatory authority for withdrawals from property management accounts maintained in the name of the property owner.

 These requirements, of course, do **not** apply to brokers who are not engaged in the management of real property on behalf of real property owners.

Requirements Necessary to Take the License Exam

There are six basic requirements that must be met before a person can take the real estate sales examination:

1. Non-education requirements

2. Prelicensing education

3. Broker affiliation

4. Submit fingerprints for a criminal background check

5. Submitting the exam application

6. Scheduling the exam

Non-Educational Requirements

Anyone wanting to become a real estate salesperson in Ohio must:

- Be at least 18 years of age.

- Be honest, truthful, and of good reputation.

- Have any criminal record *reviewed* by the Ohio Division of Real Estate and Professional Licensing.

- Have no civil rights violations within the past two years.

- Have no unsatisfied judgments from a court of law.

- Have a high school diploma or its equivalent, if born after 1950.

Prelicensing Educational Requirements

Before a person can apply to take the licensing exam, prelicensing courses must be completed at an **institute of higher learning offering at least a two-year degree program** (i.e., Associate Degree). These courses must consist of 120 hours of classroom instruction covering the following real estate topics:

- Real estate principles and practices (40 hours)

- Real estate law, civil rights, and fair housing (40 hours—waived for Ohio lawyers)

- Real estate finance (20 hours)
- Real estate appraisal (20 hours)

Brokerage Affiliation

A prospective licensee must be affiliated with a principal broker prior to being seated for the examination. There is a space on the application for a sponsoring broker's signature.

A principal broker may **terminate** sponsorship of a salesperson applicant. To do so, the principal broker must provide **written notice** to the applicant and to the Division of Real Estate and Professional Licensing. Failure to give notice is considered to be **misconduct** on the part of the principal broker.

If the principal broker withdraws sponsorship:

- An applicant who has **not yet been approved** to sit for the exam has **60 days** to submit an amended application with the name of a new sponsoring broker.
- An applicant who has **been approved** to sit for the exam will be **permitted to take the exam**. The Division of Real Estate and Professional Licensing will issue a new license only when the applicant both passes the exam and submits to the Division the sponsorship of a new principal broker.

Criminal Background Check

Applicants for an Ohio real estate license must demonstrate honesty, truthfulness, and good reputation. As evidence that an applicant has not been convicted of felony or a crime of moral turpitude, as of November 1, 2019, all applicants for a new real estate license **must submit fingerprints for a criminal history check**. This requirement applies to prospective salespersons, brokers, and reciprocal licensees.

The Ohio Real Estate Commission and the Division of Real Estate and Professional Licensing (ORC § 4735.03)

The task of regulating real estate activity in Ohio has been delegated to the **Department of Commerce**. To best address the needs of the state and real estate industry, the Department of Commerce created the **Division of Real Estate and Professional Licensing** and the **Ohio Real Estate Commission**. These two bodies share the responsibilities for implementing and enforcing the existing licensing laws.

The Ohio Real Estate Commission

The **Ohio Real Estate Commission** consists of *five members appointed by the Governor with the advice and consent of the Ohio Senate*:

- Four of the members are licensed real estate brokers who have been active as real estate brokers for no less than ten years prior to the appointment.
- The fifth member is a non-licensee, representing the interests of the public.
- These members serve five-year terms, staggered so that one appointment is made each year.
- No more than three members of the Commission may be members of the same political party.

The Commission is charged with promoting the Canons of Ethical Practice for the real estate industry in Ohio, and reviews any order issued by the Superintendent of the Division of Real Estate and Professional Licensing.

The Commission establishes the standards for licensing, including the suspension and revocation of licenses, the conduct of hearings, and examinations for licensing. Furthermore, the Commission establishes standards for continuation in business and the placing of brokers' licenses on deposit.

The Commission also reviews all educational requirements for brokers and salespersons and updates continuing education requirements. In an effort to keep all licensees informed and up-to-date, the Commission publishes a newsletter, which carries an emphasis on civil rights and fair housing laws and should be read by all brokers and salespersons.

The Education and Research Fund is administered by the Commission to help fund educational projects. One dollar of each license application fee goes into this account. A sales applicant may apply for a need-based loan of up to $2,000 to pay education costs. The application must be signed by the sponsoring broker as guarantor of the loan, which must be paid back within one year of the date of licensing. The loan bears no interest if paid on time.

Ohio Real Estate Commission	**Ohio Division of Real Estate and Prfessional Licensing**
Five Members	Superintendent
Appointed by the Governor	Appointed by Director of Commerce
Promote Canon of Ethics — Criteria/cont. business Reviews all Acts of Super. — Set licensing standards Review educ. require. — Suspension and revoc./lic. Updates C.E. require. — Rules conduct hearings Publ. civil rts. newsltr. — Sets lic. exam standards Administer educ/res accts.	Issues license AND places brokers license on deposit Administers license laws Issues comm. and other orders to enact lic. law Investigates written complaints against licensees Audits brokers' records and trust accounts May subpoena witnesses for investigations Can apply to courts for injunctions Administer Recovery Fund
May Fine up to $2,500 per Law Violation (no limit)	May issue citations $200 for certain law violations (max. total $2,500)

The Division of Real Estate and Professional Licensing (ORC § 4735.05)

The **Division of Real Estate and Professional Licensing** is run by its **Superintendent**, who is **appointed by the Director of Commerce**. The Superintendent:

- Is the administrator of the license law and is responsible for issuing any orders of the Commission or other orders necessary to implement license law.

- Investigates written complaints brought against licensees and maintains an investigations and audit bureau.

- May subpoena witnesses for these investigations and can apply to appropriate courts of jurisdiction for injunctions to stop activities that violate the law

- Administers the Recovery Fund.

Ancillary Trustee (ORC § 4735.05(C)(3))

An **ancillary trustee** is responsible for completing the business of a brokerage when a licensed broker dies or loses his license. In the case of the death of a broker, the Superintendent may recommend to the probate court, subject to the approval by that court, the appointment of an ancillary trustee. In the case of a broker who loses his license due to suspension or revocation, the Superintendent is the appointing authority but, in this case, the appointment is subject to the review of the Commission.

The ancillary trustee is put in charge of all real estate transactions that are already in the process of closing. No new listings may be taken, and listings that have not gone to contract are voided by legal impossibility. Agents who worked for the former broker must reapply to the Division of Real Estate and Professional Licensing to associate with another broker before continuing to practice real estate.

Complaint Procedure (ORC § 4735.051)

Anyone can file a written complaint against a licensee with the Superintendent. Upon receipt of the complaint, the Superintendent reviews the facts and supporting documentation for jurisdiction. If the complaint falls within the Superintendent's jurisdiction, the law provides for a voluntary informal mediation meeting to try and resolve the matter; but only if both parties agree to such an informal meeting within ten days of receiving a notice from the Division of Real Estate and Professional Licensing. If the parties fail to agree, the complaint is investigated by an investigator assigned to the case by the Superintendent.

Upon completion of an investigation, the complaint is either dismissed or placed on the docket for a formal hearing before an independent Hearing Examiner. After hearing the case, the Hearing Examiner makes a finding of facts as to whether any licensing laws have been violated. After reviewing the Hearing Examiner's finding, the Superintendent makes a recommendation to the Commission as to whether to suspend or revoke the license or take no further action. The case is then assigned to the Commission for determination on what course of action to take against the licensee, if any. The Commission would then make a decision that could result in **suspension** or **revocation** of the license, and a fine of up to $2,500 per violation, plus possible public reprimand and additional continuing education requirements.

The investigation and its results are confidential, as are all reports prepared by Division employees. Also, if more than three years have elapsed from the time the alleged facts of the incident occurred, no investigation can be commenced.

Real Estate Recovery Fund (ORC § 4735.12)

The Real Estate Recovery Fund is used to satisfy unpaid judgments against real estate licensees for activities in violation of the license law that caused financial loss to the claimant. The amount in the Fund determines what amount, if any, that the Commission may impose as a special assessment to all licensees who are renewing their licenses:

- If the Fund falls below $500,000, up to $10 may be assessed.
- If the Fund is between $500,000 and $2 million, up to $5 may be assessed.
- If the Fund is above $2 million, no amount will be assessed.

In order for a claimant to use the fund, there must be an unsatisfied court ordered judgment against a broker or salesperson for a real estate-related activity. This judgment must represent a final court order that cannot be appealed by the licensee. Furthermore, the claimant must show that the licensee has failed to pay part or all of the judgment, despite diligent efforts by the claimant to collect from the licensee. Claims against the fund must be filed within one year of the final court judgment.

The payment ceiling is $40,000 for each licensee involved in the transaction. Should more than one licensee be involved, the ceiling is multiplied by the number of licensees. If this sum is insufficient to cover the full amount of the claims from the transaction, then claimants shall be paid in proportion to their judgments.

When a payment is made from the fund in the name of any licensee, that person's license is automatically suspended and is not subject to reactivation until the amount paid on his behalf is repaid with interest. A discharge in bankruptcy will not relieve the former licensee of this obligation.

The License (ORC § 4735.13)

The broker's license (and only the broker's license) must be displayed in a public area of the broker's place of business. If there are branch offices, the principal broker must apply for and receive a **duplicate license** to be prominently displayed in each branch office. The salesperson's license is mailed to and kept on file at the broker's principal office until termination of the license or disassociation with that brokerage. The principal broker must inform the Superintendent if he changes his place of business address. All brokers and agents must keep the Division apprised of any change in their home address.

Immediately upon an affiliated licensee leaving the brokerage or termination of a real estate licensee's association with the brokerage, the principal broker shall return the license to the Superintendent of the Division of Real Estate and Professional Licensing. If the broker fails to return the license of a real estate salesperson or broker who leaves or is terminated via certified mail, return receipt requested, within three business days of receiving a request from the Superintendent, it is considered prima-facie evidence of misconduct under division (A)(6) of § 4735.18 of the Revised Code.

The failure of a broker to return the license of a real estate salesperson or broker who leaves or is terminated, via certified mail/return receipt requested, within three business days of the receipt of a written request from the Superintendent for the return of the license, is prima-facie evidence of misconduct under division (A)(6) of § 4735.18 of the Revised Code.

When a broker (and only a broker) wishes to work as a salesperson with another broker, he may apply to the Superintendent to place his broker's **license on deposit** and reactivate a salesperson's license, or he may apply for an associate broker's license. That licensee no longer needs to have a trust account, as is required of all licensed principal brokers. A broker's license may remain on deposit indefinitely, as long as it is timely renewed and the licensee meets continuing education requirements.

There is another definition for a **license on deposit**. Any licensee (broker or salesperson) may place his license on deposit when entering the armed services or upon activation in the military reserve. The license remains on deposit until the next renewal date following the licensee's honorable discharge from the military. Any licensee whose license is on deposit under this division and who fails to meet the continuing education requirements because the licensee is in the armed forces shall satisfy the Commission that he has complied with the continuing education requirements within 12 months of his discharge. The Commission shall notify the licensee of his obligations at the time he applies for reactivation of his license.

A salesperson may also wish to return his license to the Division of Real Estate and Professional Licensing so as to pursue non-real estate activities. In such case, the salesperson's license status is referred to as **inactive**. The license can remain on inactive status indefinitely so long as the licensee keeps up his continuing education requirements and renews his license in a timely manner.

Once a license is issued to a broker or salesperson, the licensee has 12 months in which to complete a required post-licensure education course. That education must consist of 10 hours of state-approved study for brokers or 20 hours of state-approved study for salespersons and is not considered part of the licensee's continuing education.

 Currently no more than eight hours of post-licensing classes can be taken in the classroom by a licensee in any one day.

Company and Trade Names

The Superintendent of the Ohio Division of Real Estate and Professional Licensing must approve any company or trade name proposed for use by a brokerage. Requirements for approval include the following:

- The name is not misleading or likely to mislead the public.

- The name is clearly distinguishable from any existing real estate brokerage, although the Superintendent may make an excep-tion with the written consent from a licensee using a similar name.

- The brokerage cannot have more than **five trade names** under which it does business, and there must be a commonality be-tween the names.

- A special or trust account is maintained in each trade name.

- The approved trade name(s) can be the only identifying name(s) used by the brokerage in all advertising.

- The approved trade name(s) must be on the brokerage license.

Trade names approved by the Superintendent must be registered with the office of the Ohio Secretary of State. If the Secretary denies the use of a trade name, the broker can appeal to the Ohio Real Estate Commission for review within 30 days of denial.

Duties of a Principal Broker

A principal broker must:

- Ensure compliance with the brokerage office requirements related to signage, display of licenses, and the Fair Housing Poster.

- Ensure the timely renewal of the brokerage and branch office licenses.

- Keep all affiliated licenses in a way that they can, and shall on request, be made immediately available for public inspection at the office or place of business of the broker.

- Keep all affiliated licenses in a way that they can be returned until the licensee places the license on inactive or resigned status or until the licensee leaves the brokerage or is terminated.

- Ensure the brokerage complies with all requirements to maintain trust and special accounts, including property management trust accounts if applicable.

- Maintain complete and accurate records of all transactions.

- Maintain complete and accurate trust account records.

- Maintain an up-to-date Company Policy and Consumer Guide to Agency Relationships.

- Assure that licensees are paid commissions within a reasonable time after the receipt of commission.

- Establish practices to ensure the brokerage is not suborning unlicensed activity, e.g., only licensees are paid commission, and if paying commission to a licensee's company, that all requirements for that payment are met.

- Oversee licensed activity to ensure licensees are providing services within their area of competency or are working with another competent agent.

The principal broker may assign any of these duties to a management level licensee.

Terminating Sponsorship

Affiliation with a licensed brokerage is required in order for a licensee to practice real estate. To terminate sponsorship of a licensee, a principal broker must:

- **Return the terminated licensee's license** to the Superintendent of the Division of Real Estate and Professional Licensing.
- Notify the licensee of the termination in writing within **three business days** of returning the license. The notice may be hand-delivered, or sent via mail, facsimile, or email.
- Maintain proof that the notice was delivered.

Failure to provide the prescribed notice is considered **misconduct** on the part of the principal broker.

Termination Notice to Salesperson. The notice of termination to a salesperson must state that the licensee's license will be placed in **inactive status** and that the licensee may submit an application to have the license reactivated if the licensee pays the required fees and is in compliance with all of the requirements for licensure. A license can remain in inactive status **indefinitely**.

Termination Notice to Broker. The notice of termination to a broker must state that the licensee's license will be placed on deposit and that the license may submit an application to have the license reactivated if the licensee pays the required fees and is in compliance with all of the requirements for licensure. A license can remain on deposit **indefinitely** as long as the broker:

- Complies with the post-licensing education requirements.
- Complies with the continuing education requirements.
- Renews the license as required.

Renewal of Licenses (ORC § 4735.14)

Each real estate broker, brokerage, or salesperson shall file a notice of renewal on or before the date the Ohio Real Estate Commission has adopted by rule. Should a broker wish to no longer sponsor a salesperson, the broker will return the license of that salesperson to the Division of Real Estate and Professional Licensing for inactivation, and send to the salesperson, via certified mail, a notice of inactivation within **three days** of the date the license was returned to the Division.

Each broker and licensee must renew his own license every three years on or before his birthday. Previously, brokers renewed a salesperson's license, but this is no longer the case. **Renewal is now the licensee's responsibility.**

The license of any real estate broker or salesperson who fails to file a Notice of Renewal prior to the filing deadline shall be suspended. A suspended license may be **reactivated** within 12 months of the date of suspension, provided that the renewal fee plus a penalty fee of 50% of the renewal fee is paid to the Superintendent. Failure to reactivate the license within this 12-month grace period shall result in automatic revocation of the license.

However, any licensee, at any time prior to the date the licensee is required to file a notice of renewal, may apply to the Superintendent of the Division of Real Estate and Professional Licensing to place the licensee's license on a **resigned status**.

The licensee pays the annual brokerage assessment fee, if applicable. If a licensee does not apply to reactivate a license, or does not satisfy the above requirements, during the 12-month period, the Superintendent shall consider that license to be in a resigned status. The Superintendent shall not reactivate a resigned license. Also, at any time during which a license has been suspended, a licensee may apply to the Superintendent, on a form prescribed by the Superintendent, to voluntarily resign his license. The resignation of a license is considered to be final without the taking of any action by the Superintendent.

If a person whose license is in a resigned status wishes to obtain an active license, the person shall apply for an active license in accordance with the requirements for new licensing, as applicable. Every license issued by the Division is valid until revoked or suspended. Specific causes of action for revocation and suspension of licenses are detailed under ORC § 4735.18, and will be covered later in this chapter.

 A licensee may transfer his license from one broker to another at any time by delivering a written notice to his present broker of the intent to transfer and then completing a transfer application with the new broker. Keep in mind when transferring from one broker to another, an agent cannot do anything on behalf of a broker once the agent has left. The agent **cannot** do any activity that requires a license on behalf of their new broker until a license is **issued** to the new broker. This includes activities such as having a sign in someone's yard, running an ad in the local newspaper, and having a live website.

Continuing Education (ORC § 4735.141)

Except for a licensee who has placed his license or resigned status, **all** active salesperson and broker licensees must meet regular continuing education (CE) requirements. All active licensees must complete 30 hours of CE every three years (those licensees who turn 70 during their current CE cycle are an exception to this rule). The 30-hours of study are broken down as follows:

- 3 hours of legal issues and recently enacted legislation (referred to as Core Law; may be satisfied with certified attendance of an entire monthly Commission meeting)
- 3 hours of civil rights updates
- A 3-hour course on "Canon of Ethics" as adopted by the Ohio Real Estate Commission
- The balance (21 hours) of CE electives must be approved by the Ohio Division of Real Estate and Professional Licensing and must be specific to real estate.

 Principal brokers, associate brokers, brokers on deposit, and management level licensees are required to take a 3-hour continuing education (CE) course on the fundamental duties of a principal broker and issues involved in operating a real estate brokerage, in addition to the 9 hours of mandated topics, leaving them with 18 hours of Division-approved electives.

Licensees may take more than 30 hours of CE, but only 10 extra hours can be counted toward future three-year periods. No more than 8 hours of CE may be taken per day.

Licensed salespersons who are **70 years old** and older (who are still active) need only complete 9 hours of CE classes, beginning with the three-year cycle in which their 70th birthday falls. The 9 hours must consist of:

- 3 hours of core law
- 3 hours of fair housing/civil rights
- 3 hours of ethics

Licensed brokers, brokers on deposit, or those acting as management level licensees who are 70 years old or older must also take the 3-hour core brokerage CE course in addition to the 9 core hours indicated above.

 All state exam questions assume everyone takes 30 hours of CE. If over age 70 and inactive, no continuing education is required.

Each licensee must submit satisfactory proof of the completion of the 30-hour CE requirement on or before the licensee's date of birth three years after the date of initial licensure, and every three years thereafter on or before the licensee's birthday. Licensees must complete all 30 hours of CE, then send copies of all the certificates of completion at one time (licensees should be sure to keep copies). The Division will send a postcard acknowledging receipt and acceptance of the submitted CE hours.

Caution: The licensee is responsible for submitting proof of completed continuing education requirements to the Division of Real Estate and Professional Licensing, and failure to submit such proof will result in license suspension. Furthermore, all programs of course study must be approved by the Division to count toward post-license or continuing education credit, but they do not need to be taken at an institution of higher learning.

Place of Business and Advertising (ORC § 4735.16)

Principal brokers must maintain a definite place of business, with a sign indicating their status as a broker. The sign must be prominently displayed outside of the brokerage office and be viewable by the public.

A brokerage office must have **at least one principal broker** who oversees and directs the daily operations of the brokerage. Any change in the principal broker must be reported to the Superintendent **within 15 days**.

With the approval of the Superintendent, one licensed broker could be the principal broker for **more than one brokerage** (no more than five) provided there is a commonality in the name of each brokerage and the principal broker is an officer, shareholder, member, or general partner of the brokerage.

Owners of a brokerage who are **not licensed** must sign an affidavit stating that they will not act as a principal broker or a management level licensee, in other words, will not oversee the real estate activities of the brokerage and its licensees.

Advertising must be made in the name of the licensed principal broker, and must clearly name and identify the brokerage. When a salesperson posts an advertisement, the principal broker's name must be at least as prominent as the salesperson's name. The salesperson must indicate his status as a licensed salesperson in any advertisement, even if selling his own property "for sale by owner."

A **real estate team** is *a group of two or more licensees associated with a brokerage and other non-licensed individuals who advertise under a team name.* A team must include the word "group" or "team" in its name and cannot use the words "realty" or "associate." When advertising under a team name, the advertisement must:

- Include the name of at least one licensee.
- Display the name of the brokerage in equal or greater prominence.
- Identify any named unlicensed team member as "unlicensed."

Each violation of any advertising rule may carry a possible citation and fine of no less than $200, but no more than $2,500. This fine imposed by the Superintendent is in addition to a fine of up to $2,500 that may be levied by the Commission, which has no limit on the amount of fines it may impose on a licensee. Three ad violation citations within a 12-month period will cause the Superintendent to initiate disciplinary action, which may result in revocation or suspension of the license by the Commission. If a licensee does not contest a citation or fine from the Superintendent within 30 days, the licensee must comply with the Superintendent's orders or face automatic license suspension.

Further, every brokerage office shall prominently display, in the same immediate area as licenses are displayed, a **Fair Housing Poster** issued by the Ohio Real Estate Commission that contains a statement that it is illegal to discriminate against any person because of race, color, religion, sex, familial status, national origin, military status, disability, or ancestry in the:

- Sale or rental of housing or residential lots.
- Advertising the sale or rental of housing.
- Financing of housing.
- Provision of real estate brokerage services.

In addition, the statement must:

- Include that blockbusting is illegal.
- Bear the United States Department of Housing and Urban Development Equal Housing logo.
- Indicate that the broker and the broker's salespersons are licensed by the Division of Real Estate and Professional Licensing and that the Division can assist with any consumer complaints or inquiries.
- Provide the Division's address and telephone number.

License Reciprocity (ORC § 4735.17)

Reciprocity of real estate licensing between states is not considered unless the licensing state has requirements similar to Ohio's. Students should refer to the Ohio Division of Real Estate and Professional Licensing's official website (www.com.state.oh.us/real) for a current list of states with which Ohio has reciprocity agreements. Under certain arrangements, license testing, course study, or other requirements may be waived or modified. These instances should be researched through the Ohio Division of Real Estate and Professional Licensing and the licensing authority in the state where the candidate was previously licensed.

Suspension or Revocation of License (ORC § 4735.18)

Ohio real estate law mandates that the Superintendent must investigate the conduct of any licensee against whom a written complaint has been filed. The Superintendent may also, on his own initiative, investigate the activities of a licensee. The Commission shall impose discipline against the licensee, which may include suspension or revocation, should such licensee be found guilty of any of the following activities:

1. Knowingly making any misrepresentation. Misrepresentation is defined as passing along false information. A misrepresentation need not be fraudulent, but the licensee must realize it is false at the time she makes the misrepresentation.

2. Making false promises with the intent to influence, persuade, or induce.

3. Making a continued course of misrepresentations or false promises through agents, advertising, salespersons, or otherwise. Note that the word "knowingly" is not part of this violation.

4. Acting for more than one party in a transaction without the knowledge and consent of all parties involved. This encompasses the problem of undisclosed dual agency, in which an agent acts on behalf of both buyer and seller without consent. However, with proper written consent from all parties, dual agency is perfectly legal.

5. Failing to account for, or remit within a reasonable time, any money coming into the licensee's possession that belongs to others.

6. Dealing dishonestly, illegally, or with gross negligence or incompetence.

7. A. A final adjudication by a court of law of any violation of any civil rights or fair housing law or any unlawful discriminatory act. The law states that this must arise out of a bona fide purchase or lease attempt, which would exclude actions by testers or checkers.

   B. A second or subsequent violation of any fair housing or civil rights law, regardless of final adjudication. This violation carries a minimum two-month suspension, with the real possibility of license revocation. Any subsequent violations mandate revocation.

8. Obtaining a license by fraud, misrepresentation, or deceit.

9. Violating or failing to comply with the laws related to agency relationships or an agent's duties after closing a transaction or willfully disregarding any other provisions of the license law.

10. Demanding unearned commissions from other persons who are not licensees.

11. Dividing commissions with non-licensees. A licensee may pay non-licensees salaries or hourly wages as telemarketers, as long as they do not enter the process of listing, selling, or leasing. However, the licensee may not pay a bonus for leads that become sales—this is referred to as **commission splitting**.

12. Misrepresenting membership in a professional association.

13. Accepting a secret profit on money or assets provided by the principal.

14. Offering anything of value not in the contract as an inducement. This includes the prohibition against using real estate or improvements thereon as prizes in games of chance.

15. Acting as an undisclosed principal. This means that the licensee is acting on her own behalf, rather than as an agent. While this is not a problem if disclosure is made immediately, the problem arises when an agent desires a property that she is listing. Without disclosure, it might appear that the broker or salesperson could under-represent the property to drive the price down.

16. Guaranteeing future profits.

17. Placing a sign on any unlisted property for sale or rent without the consent of the owner or the owner's authorized agent.

18. Inducing the breaking of a contract to enter another. This can happen when a buyer has just entered into a lease extension. Should the agent invite the buyer to enter into a purchase agreement before resolving the lease problem, the agent has violated licensing law.

19. Negotiating with an owner who has signed an exclusive agency (right-to-sell) agreement with another office.

20. Offering real estate without the consent of the owner. This includes offering unauthorized terms of sale.

21. Causing publication of inaccurate or misleading advertising. All media are covered. Intent is unimportant, and is routinely disregarded.

22. Falsifying books of account.

23. Threatening competitors with unwarranted legal action.

24. Failing to keep complete and accurate records of all transactions for three years from the date of transaction.

25. Failing to provide true copies of listings and other agreements to all parties at the time the documents are signed.

26. Failing to maintain a trust account separate from broker funds. The account must be a non-interest-bearing account with a bank in the state of Ohio. The bank and account number must be provided to the Division as part of a broker application, and are kept for inspection by the investigations and audit bureau.

27. Failing to maintain a separate and distinct account for the deposit and maintenance of rents, security deposits, and other money received in the course of managing real property. This account may be an interest-bearing account with a bank in the state of Ohio, with interest paid to the property owner. The bank and account number must be provided to the Division as part of a broker application, and kept for inspection by the investigations and audit bureau. Brokers not engaged in property management for others are exempt.

28. Failing to put definite expiration dates on all written agency agreements.

29. Having an unsatisfied judgment in any court against the licensee, arising out of conduct as a real estate licensee.

30. Failing to account on demand for funds placed into a licensee's hands by a party to a transaction.

31. Failing to pay a salesperson any due and earned commission within a reasonable time after receipt of funds.

32. Practicing law without a license to do so.

33. Having an adjudication of incompetency.

34. Allowing a non-licensee to act on her behalf.

35. Knowingly inserting any materially inaccurate term in a document, including naming a false consideration.

36. Failing to inform the licensee's client of the existence of an offer or counteroffer in a timely manner (unless otherwise instructed by the client, provided that the instruction does not conflict with any state or federal law).

37. Failing to inform the Division you were convicted of a felony.

38. Acting as a broker without authority or impeding the ability of a principal broker or a management level licensee to perform the licensee's duties.

Although not specifically listed in ORC 4735.18, it is important to point out three additional reasons for which a license may be suspended or revoked (these were previously discussed in this text):

- Putting the broker's money into the trust account (other than money required by the bank to keep the account open). This is called **commingling**, which is *illegally mixing money held in a trust on behalf of a client with personal funds*. This account can be an interest-bearing account with a bank in the state of Ohio with interest paid to the property owner. The bank and account number must be provided to the Division as part of a broker application and kept for inspection by the Investigations and Audit Bureau. Brokers that are not engaged in property management for others are exempt.

- Failing to take the required continuing education.

- Failing to renew the license regardless of its status (with the exception of *military license on deposit*).

As previously defined, **suspension** is *the temporary withdrawal of a real estate agent's license*. Suspension of a license is for a set period of time, with reactivation by application after the suspension is lifted. The licensee may also have to perform an act (e.g., completion of extra CE coursework) or pay a fine as a condition of reactivating a suspended license.

In addition to the Superintendent's and Commission's discretion to investigate conduct and cause a license to be suspended, reasons for automatic license suspension include failure to:

- Remit a disciplinary fine.
- Submit documentation for disciplinary education.
- Remit citation fees.
- Perform timely renewal of a license.
- Submit timely documentation for post-licensing education.
- Submit timely documentation for continuing education.

Revocation is *the permanent withdrawal of a real estate agent's license.* Issuance of a new license to a person with a previously revoked license is done by application, which is reviewed by the Commission and may be denied. If suspension or revocation of a license is the result of a formal hearing, the licensee has the right to appeal the decision in common pleas court. In addition to the Superintendent's and Commission's discretion to investigate conduct and cause a license to be revoked, reasons for automatic license revocation include failure to:

- Fulfill the requirements to reactivate a suspended license.
- Notify the Division of Real Estate and Professional Licensing of any felony conviction.

In addition to suspension or revocation of a license, the Superintendent may issue **citations** to a licensee in lieu of initiating a formal investigation for violations of advertising, agency, or fair housing license law. Citations may be up to $200 for each violation (up to a maximum total of $2,500), but the Superintendent must initiate a formal investigation if a licensee is cited more than three times within 12 consecutive months. A licensee may also be fined up to $2,500 by the Commission for each violation of the Ohio Revised Code. There is no limit to the amount of fines that the Commission can levy. Furthermore, a licensee may also be subject to public reprimand and be ordered to take additional CE classes as a condition for license reactivation.

Real estate professionals should take care to learn and follow these guidelines to safeguard their real estate licenses. The guidelines are important *now* because they appear frequently on the State license examination, and they are important *later* because they are the root of most of the lawsuits brought by angry clients or customers who feel they were wronged.

Any licensee shall notify the Superintendent within **15 days** if the licensee is convicted of:

- A felony or crime involving moral turpitude.
- Violation of any federal, state, or municipal civil rights law pertaining to discrimination in housing.
- Unlawful discriminatory practice pertaining to housing accommodations.
- Violation of any municipal civil rights law pertaining to housing discrimination.

If a licensee fails to notify the Superintendent within the required time, the Superintendent immediately may suspend the license of the licensee.

Common Enforcement Issues

The Ohio Division of Real Estate and Professional Licensing indicates the following as its 12 most common enforcement issues:

- Improper advertising
- Salespersons operating outside of their brokerage
- Licensees allowing unlicensed individuals or entities to perform or engage in real estate services
- Noncompliant trust accounts
- Allowing lock box access to unlicensed or unsupervised parties
- Not maintaining complete transaction files, including emails and text messages
- Brokers signing blank applications
- Not reporting convictions in a timely manner
- Improper representation in a divorce situation
- Not presenting all offers
- Not obtaining written consent to changes in a transaction
- Not disclosing material defects

Broker Lien Law (ORC § 1311.85–1311.93)

(A) Any broker that enters into a written contract for services related to selling, leasing, or conveying any interest in commercial real estate has a lien on that commercial real estate. The lien is effective only if the contract for services is in writing and is signed by the broker (or the broker's agent) and the owner of the lien property (or the owner's agent).

(B) (1) Only the broker named in the contract has a lien pursuant to this section, and a lien is not available to any employee or independent contractor for the broker.

(2) The amount of the lien is limited to the amount due to the broker pursuant to the contract. If the amount due to the broker is payable in installments, a portion of which is due after conveyance, the amount of the lien is limited to the amount due to the broker prior to, or upon, conveyance.

(3) The lien is effective only against the interest in real estate that is the subject of the contract.

Prior to the sale or lease of commercial real estate, a lien affidavit must be filed with the county recorder in order for the lien to be enforceable. If the agreed upon commission is not paid, the broker may file a complaint with the court of common pleas in the county where the commercial property is located. The complaint must be filed within two years following the recording of the lien affidavit for it to be valid.

Reporting Elder Abuse (ORC § 5101.63)

Elder abuse can take many forms, from physical harm or neglect to financial exploitation, such as when a guardian is making finan-cial decisions on behalf of a vulnerable adult that do not appear to be in that adult's best interest. Ohio law recognizes that a financial services professional is often the first person to come into contact with an elder who is being abused, neglected, or exploited. There-fore, such professionals—including real estate brokers and salespersons—**are required to report known or suspected elder abuse** to the county department of jobs and family services or by calling 1-855-OHIO-APS. Anyone who makes a report of potential elder abuse is legally protected from criminal or civil liability.

Professional Organizations

The main organization real estate licensees join is the National Association of REALTORS® (NAR). Licensees also join the state and local affiliated real estate boards. Any person who has a real estate license is called a *real estate licensee* and must abide by the Canons of Ethics.

National Association of REALTORS® (NAR)

The largest trade association in the nation. A licensee does *not* automatically become a REALTOR®. Only those who join the **National Association of REALTORS®** may use the term REALTOR® because it is a registered trademark of NAR. Members agree to voluntarily follow a Code of Ethics. Membership is not mandatory unless the licensee's sponsoring broker is also a member. Most licensees join to receive the benefits of membership, including:

- Participation in the **Multiple Listing Service** (MLS)
- The right to use the trademarked term **REALTOR®**
- A political and legislative voice at all levels of government for the interests of the real estate industry
- Education
- Training that can earn licensees professional designations
- Real estate publications
- Standardized real estate forms

The **MLS** is *a service whereby local member brokers agree to share listings, and further agree to share commissions on properties sold jointly.* The MLS generally consists of online computer services such as tools for tracking prospects and the electronic convenience of receiving listings via email. The MLS can provide invaluable assistance to agents who are planning to take a client on a tour of available properties, including a means for mapping the routes. There is even a mobile app for smart phones.

National Association of Real Estate Brokers

Another professional organization that real estate brokers can join is the **National Association of Real Estate Brokers**. Members of this organization use the term **Realtist**. This group is comprised mostly of minority brokers, since it was initially formed as a response to minorities being excluded from membership in NAR. Members voluntarily agree to follow an additional, separate Code of Ethics.

Women's Council of REALTORS® (WCR)

The **Women's Council of REALTORS®** (WCR) is an organization that female licensees can join. The organization is devoted to addressing the issues, needs, and concerns of salespeople in the real estate profession. The WCR was originally formed as a response to discrimination that kept women from full participation in NAR, but now the WCR is affiliated with NAR.

Other Professional Organizations

Other professional organizations that real estate salespeople can choose to join include:

- The Appraisal Institute
- American Society of Appraisers
- National Association of Independent Fee Appraisers
- Building Owners and Managers Association

Professional Designations

There are many designations a licensee can work to achieve as a means of keeping himself and his education current. These designations mark individuals as highly qualified specialists to other agents and the public. If a licensee wants to appear less like a new agent, getting a designation allows the licensee to advertise the designation after their name on business cards, ads, and brochures.

NAR Designations

Most of the following NAR designations are available to residential or commercial real estate agents, except ABR and CRS (residential only), and CCIM and SIOR (commercial only). All require NAR membership.

ABR—Accredited Buyer Representative can be earned by a NAR member who completes an extensive classroom training program on buyer agency practices and procedures, passes a written exam, and submits evidence of practical experience as a buyer representative.

ABRM—Accredited Buyer Representative Manager is geared to real estate firm brokers, owners, and managers who have or wish to incorporate buyer representation into their daily practice; designees have taken and passed both the ABR® and ABRMSM course and provided documentation of past management experience.

ALC—Accredited Land Consultants are the recognized experts in land brokerage transactions of five specialized types:

1. Farms and ranches

2. Undeveloped tracts of land

3. Transitional and development land

4. Subdivision and wholesaling of lots

5. Site selection and assemblage of land parcels

Licensees acquire valuable skills through educational offerings, leading to the ALC designation.

ARM—Accredited Residential Manager is given by NAR's Institute of Real Estate Management (IREM) to those specializing in managing residential properties. One must complete an IREM management course, meet experience standards, manage a sizeable portfolio, and be endorsed by the local IREM chapter.

AHWD—At Home with Diversity Certification relays to the public that those certified have been professionally trained in, and are sensitive to, a wide range of cultural issues, which invites a wider volume of business from a greater variety of cultures.

CCIM—Certified Commercial Investment Member is awarded by NAR.

CIPS—The Certified International Property Specialist network is comprised of 1,500 real estate professionals from 50 countries who deal in all types of real estate but with one common element: They are focused specifically on the "international" market. Whether traveling abroad to put deals together, assisting foreign investors, helping local buyers invest abroad, or serving an immigrant niche in local markets, CIPS designees are a consumer's best resource to ensure they are dealing with a professional skilled in the unique aspects of international real estate.

CPM—Certified Property Manager is awarded by NAR's Institute of Real Estate Management (IREM) to real estate property managers.

CRB—Certified Real Estate Brokerage Manager is given by the Real Estate Brokerage Manager's Council to those who complete required coursework. Coursework varies by experience.

CRE—Counselor of Real Estate is given by NAR's American Society of Real Estate Counselors for asset managers and others. Membership is by invitation only.

CRS—Certified Residential Specialist is given by the Residential Sales Council of NAR to those who complete CRS courses and a certain number of transactions.

e-PRO®—e-PRO® is a revolutionary training program presented entirely online to certify real estate agents and brokers as Internet Professionals. NAR is the first major trade group to offer certification for online professionalism.

GAA—General Accredited Appraiser is given by NAR's Appraisal Section to those with 1,000 hours experience and 60 hours of coursework above state mandates.

GRI—Graduate, Realtor Institute is given by state boards. In Ohio, 90 hours of coursework is required.

PMN—Performance Management Network is a new REALTOR® designation built from the ground up to bring licensees the real-world skills, the know-how, and the tools that keep their business out front and on top of a lightening-fast market. This designation is unique to the REALTOR® family designations, focusing on the idea that to enhance your business, you must enhance yourself. The curriculum is driven by the following topics:

- Negotiating strategies and tactics
- Networking and referrals
- Business planning and systems
- Personal performance management
- Cultural differences in buying and selling

RAA—Residential Accredited Appraiser is given by NAR's Appraisal Section to those with 1,000 hours of experience and 45 hours of coursework above state mandates.

RCE—REALTOR® Association Certified Executive is for association executives interested in demonstrating commitment to the field of REALTOR® association management. AEs are recognized for their specialized industry knowledge and their association achievements and experience.

REPASM—Real Estate Professional AssistantSM is a comprehensive two-day certificate course that provides an intensive introduction to the real estate business and to the specific ways support staff can become valuable assets to their employers. Every administrative employee in the brokerage office, from listing secretary to the personal assistant, benefits tremendously from this quick-start program.

RSPS—Resort and Second-Home Markets Certification is a new certification offered by NAR Resort for resort and second-home REALTORS® around the world. REALTORS® specializing in resort and second-home markets and interested in demonstrating their knowledge and expertise should pursue the RSPS certification. The RSPS core certification requirements include the NAR Resort and Second-Home Market Course and the RLI Tax-Deferred (1031) Exchange Course. RSPS applicants also choose from nine different electives including courses from the NAR Education Matrix and the NAR Resort Symposium held every 18 months.

SIOR—Society of Industrial and Office REALTORS® is a designation available to members of this NAR-affiliated organization, and is concerned primarily with the sale of factories, warehouses, and other industrial properties.

Transnational Referral Certification—The goal of this certification is to prepare real estate professionals to make and receive compensated referrals using the Transnational Referral system developed by the International Consortium of Real Estate Associations—ICREA. Students learn how to integrate international referrals, resulting in increased income, into their business plans.

When a licensee is involved in an international referral, as a referring or receiving agent, the Transnational Referral Certification demonstrates to other real estate professionals that he is well versed in the procedures of the Transnational Referral system; has pledged to follow a code of conduct in business dealings; and expects that compensation, paid in a timely manner, will be an integral part of the transaction.

Other Designations

Following are some of the designations offered in the real estate, appraisal, or property management fields.

ASA—ASA Senior Member, ASR Senior Residential Member, and **FASA Fellow** are offered by the American Society of Appraisers (ASA) to members who meet its criteria.

CSD—Commercial Specialist Designation is given to agents who successfully complete the coursework designed to give residential agents a look at the commercial side of real estate, with special emphasis on learning unique aspects of commercial real estate so agents know what it takes to succeed.

DREI—Distinguished Real Estate Instructor is awarded by the Real Estate Educators Association (REEA). The DREI designation recognizes excellence among real estate instructors. It is awarded only to those who demonstrate outstanding knowledge of their profession, experience, and classroom performance. Successful applicants must also pass a Comprehensive Real Estate Exam and a Teaching Skills Evaluation (via submission of a video tape of an actual classroom session).

IFA—IFAS Senior Member and **IFAC Appraiser-Counselor** are designations offered by the National Association of Independent Fee Appraisers (NAIFA) to members who meet its criteria.

MAI—Member Appraisal Institute is the highest designation offered by The Appraisal Institute to members who meet its criteria.

NHSD—New Home Specialist Designation is given to agents who successfully complete the coursework and is designed for those who want to make their mark in the lucrative, but increasingly competitive, field of new builds.

PMSD—Property Management Specialist Designation is given to agents who successfully complete coursework designed to enhance property management skills and knowledge of acquisitions, financing, leasing, ethics, and legal issues.

RECS—Real Estate Cyberspace Specialist Designation can be earned by becoming a member of the Real Estate Cyberspace Society by taking a Selling in Cyberspace course and completing an individual practicum. The designation distinguishes the person as a professional who is proficient in computer and Internet disciplines as well as one who stays current with industry advances and services.

RPA—Real Property Administrator is awarded to property managers for completing courses of the Building Owners and Managers Institute International, which is an independent institute affiliated with the Building Owners and Managers Association.

RSD—Residential Specialist Designation is given to agents who successfully complete coursework designed to help new agents avoid many common mistakes.

SRES—Senior Real Estate Specialist is a designation of the Senior Advantage Real Estate Council (SAREC), aimed at agents interested in the "over 55" client niche and agents looking to enhance their status from "salesperson" to that of "counselor."

Summary

1. The **licensing laws** are designed to regulate the real estate industry by setting standards for entrance into the field. Students are advised to become familiar with the licensing law. Not only does this body of law provide a definitive code of conduct, it provides the industry with the basis for true professionalism. The licensing laws further protect the public at large from fraud, misrepresentation, and deceit through imposition of a code of conduct.

2. Any person, partnership, association, limited liability partnership, limited liability company, or corporation who, for a fee, sells, lists, leases, exchanges, negotiates, auctions, or otherwise deals in the real estate of others, or represents publicly that he does so, must be licensed as a broker or salesperson. A **broker** is licensed to represent one of the parties in a real estate transaction for compensation. A **principal broker** is a broker who oversees and directs the daily operations of a brokerage firm. An **associate broker** is a licensed broker at the firm who is neither a principal broker nor a management level licensee. A real estate **salesperson** is a licensed agent who is associated with a principal broker and, as such, may perform most of the acts of a broker on behalf of the broker. A **management level licensee** is a licensed associate broker or salesperson who has supervisory responsibility over other licensed brokers and salespersons affiliated with the brokerage.

3. The following are exempt from the licensing requirement: Persons dealing with their own property (including partnerships, associations, limited liability partnerships, limited liability companies, or corporations using regular salaried employees), fiduciaries who are duly appointed and acting in a fiduciary capacity (such as the executor of a will or the guardian of a minor), public officials acting in an official capacity (such as a sheriff), attorneys-at-law in the performance of their duties on behalf of clients, persons selling manufactured homes/mobile homes (provided the sale does not include real estate), persons selling businesses (so long as no real estate is involved), an out-of-state broker under certain circumstances, petroleum "land men" who acquire the subsurface mineral rights from landowners for the purposes of oil and gas exploration, and persons performing only "ministerial duties" in regards to property management.

4. Real estate activity in Ohio is regulated by the Department of Commerce through the **Division of Real Estate and Professional Licensing** and the **Ohio Real Estate Commission**. These two bodies share responsibility for the implementation and enforcement of licensing laws. The Ohio Real Estate Commission consists of five members appointed by the Governor with the advice and consent of the Ohio Senate. The Division of Real Estate and Professional Licensing is run by its **Superintendent**.

5. A principal broker's license may be placed **on deposit** if the broker wishes to reactivate his salesperson's license. That broker's license may remain on deposit indefinitely. A principal broker may also be designated as an associate broker in lieu of putting the broker's license on deposit. Either a broker or salesperson may place a license on deposit when entering the armed services. A salesperson may **inactivate** his license to the Division of Real Estate and Professional Licensing indefinitely, as long as the license is renewed every three years and the licensee's CE is current. **Suspension** occurs when a license is temporarily withdrawn. Suspension is for set period of time, with reactivation by re-application after the suspension is lifted. **Revocation** occurs when a license is permanently withdrawn.

6. All active licensees must take 30 hours of CE classes every three years and submit proof on or before their birthdays. Of the 30 hours required, 9 hours must cover core law, civil rights, and canons of ethics. Principal brokers, associate brokers, brokers on deposit, and management level licensees must also take 3 hours on the topic of a principal broker's duties and brokerage issues. To keep an active license, licensees 70 years or older need complete only the 9 core hours of CE classes every three years (core law, civil rights, and ethics) plus the 3-hour core brokerage course only for brokers, brokers on deposit, and management level licensees. **All state exam questions assume everyone takes 30 hours of CE and is under the age of 70).**

CANONS OF ETHICS FOR THE REAL ESTATE INDUSTRY

Pursuant to the requirement of ORC § 4735.03(A), the Ohio Real Estate Commission has promulgated the Canons of Ethics for the real estate industry. All Ohio licensees are bound by the Canons of Ethics. REALTORS® and REALTISTS—that is, members of the National Association of REALTORS® and the National Association of Real Estate Brokers, respectfully, are further bound by a separate Code of Ethics.

The Canons of Ethics are reproduced in their entirety below, with emphasis added.

SECTION 1: General Duties to the Public and Industry

Article 1. Licensing as a real estate broker or salesman indicates to the public at large that the individual so designated has special expertise in real estate matters and is subject to high standards of conduct in the licensee's business and personal affairs. The licensee should endeavor to maintain and establish high standards of professional conduct and integrity in dealings with members of the public as well as with fellow licensees and, further, seek to avoid even the appearance of impropriety in any activities as a licensee.

Article 2. It is the duty of the broker to protect the public against fraud, misrepresentation, or unethical practices in real estate transactions. The licensee should endeavor to eliminate in the community, any practices which could be damaging to the public or to the integrity of the real estate profession.

Article 3. The licensee should provide assistance wherever possible to the members and staff of the Real Estate Commission and Division of Real Estate and Professional Licensing in the enforcement of the licensing statutes and administrative rules and regulations adopted in accordance therewith.

Article 4. The licensee should be knowledgeable of the laws of Ohio pertinent to the real estate and should keep informed of changes in the statutes of Ohio affecting the duties and responsibilities of a licensee.

Article 5. A licensee should represent clients competently and should promote the advancement of professional education in the real estate industry through the licensee's conduct.

Article 6. The licensee should be informed as to matters affecting real estate in the community, state, and the nation, so that the licensee may be able to contribute to public thinking on such matters including taxation, legislation, land use, city planning, and other questions affecting property interests.

SECTION II: Specific Duties to Clients and Customers

Article 7. The licensee should disclose all known material facts concerning a property on which the licensee is representing a seller or a purchaser to avoid misrepresentation or concealment of material facts.

Article 8. The licensee should recommend that title be examined and legal counsel be obtained.

Article 9. The licensee, for the protection of all parties, should see that financial obligations and commitments regarding real estate transactions are in writing, expressing the exact agreement of the parties; and that copies of all agreements, at the time they are executed, are placed in the hands of all parties involved.

Article 10. A licensee should not enter into an agency relationship with a party whose interests are in conflict with those of the licensee or another client represented by the licensee without fully disclosing the potential conflict and obtaining the informed consent of all parties.

Article 11. A licensee should not accept compensation from more than one party without the full knowledge and consent of all parties to the transaction.

Article 12. When acting as a seller's agent, a licensee should disclose to the seller if the licensee is the actual purchaser, or if the purchaser is another licensee affiliated with the same brokerage as the licensee, a business entity in which the licensee has an interest, or is a member of the licensee's immediate family.

Article 13. When asked to provide an appraisal (formal or informal), price opinion, comparative market analysis or any other task that is intended to determine the value of a property, a licensee shall not render that opinion without the careful analysis and interpretation of all factors affecting the property, and should not mislead their client as to the value of the property.

Article 14. The licensee should not undertake to provide professional services concerning a property or its value where the licensee has a present or contemplated interest unless such interest is specifically disclosed to all affected parties. Nor should the licensee make a formal appraisal when the licensee's employment or fee charged for the appraisal is contingent upon the amount of the appraisal.

Article 15. The licensee should not attempt to provide an appraisal, price opinion, comparative market analysis, or any other task that is intended to determine the value of a property, if the subject property is of a type that is outside the field of expertise of the licensee unless, the licensee obtains the assistance of another licensee or appraiser who has expertise in this type of property.

Article 16. The licensee should not advertise property without authority, and in any advertisement the price quoted should be that agreed upon with the owners as the offering price.

SECTION III: Duties to Fellow Licensees

Article 17. A licensee should respect the exclusive agency of another licensee until it has expired or until the client, without solicitation initiates a discussion with the licensee about the terms upon which the licensee might enter into a future agency agreement or one commencing upon the expiration of any existing agreement.

Article 18. A licensee should not solicit a listing that is currently listed with another broker, unless the listing broker, when asked, refuses to disclose the nature and expiration of the listing. In that event the licensee may contact the owner to secure such Canons of Ethics for The Real Estate Industry information and may discuss terms upon which the licensee might take a future listing, or one commencing upon the expiration of any existing exclusive listing.

Article 19. A licensee should not solicit a buyer/tenant who is subject to an exclusive buyer/tenant agreement, unless the broker, when asked, refuses to disclose the nature and expiration date of the exclusive buyer/tenant agreement. In that event the licensee may contact the buyer/tenant to secure such information and may discuss the terms upon which the licensee might enter into a future buyer/tenant agreement or may enter into a buyer/tenant agreement to become effective upon the expiration of any existing exclusive buyer/tenant agreement.

Quiz

1. **Who does NOT need a real estate license?**
   a. a property manager under contract by the owner
   b. a salaried employee of ABC Corporation when selling the company's own property
   c. someone selling a friend's raw land
   d. your uncle who is selling real estate options

2. **The Ohio Real Estate Commission**
   a. consists of five real estate brokers.
   b. is elected every five years.
   c. is overseen on a day-to-day basis by the Superintendent.
   d. is part of the Department of Commerce.

3. **Which authority revokes licenses?**
   a. the Department of Real Estate
   b. the Governor's task force to promote safe real estate
   c. the Real Estate Commission
   d. the Superintendent

4. **A real estate licensee may**
   a. draft deeds for sellers.
   b. keep the earnest money if the deal falls through.
   c. offer real estate to the market only on the terms allowed by the seller.
   d. use an open-ended expiration date on an open listing agreement.

5. **A sales associate**
   a. can collect commissions directly from the seller.
   b. can personally buy a listing only after disclosure to the seller that the sales associate is a principal.
   c. can sue a buyer for backing out of a deal.
   d. may take listings in his own name.

6. **All principal brokers**
   a. are bonded.
   b. are REALTORS®.
   c. must display the licenses of their salespeople.
   d. must have a place of business to operate as brokers.

7. **A real estate licensee can begin the practice of real estate when**
   a. her broker receives the license.
   b. her license has been issued by the Division of Real Estate.
   c. she finds a sponsoring broker.
   d. she passes the exam.

8. **In order to use the Recovery Fund, one must be**
   a. an attorney whose client was damaged by a licensee.
   b. damaged by a licensee in a real estate transaction.
   c. a licensee seeking commissions in a real estate transaction.
   d. seeking relief from an ancillary trustee.

9. **Continuing education for active salesperson licensees under the age of 70 requires students to take**
   a. 3 hours of core law, 3 hours of civil rights law, and 3 hours of ethics as part of the 30-hour requirement.
   b. 10 hours of post-licensing training within six months of licensure.
   c. 30 hours of education every five years.
   d. classes at a two-year college or university.

10. **Who may bring a complaint to the Superintendent?**
    a. anyone
    b. the Attorney General
    c. the local board of REALTORS®
    d. only a licensed attorney-at-law

11. **The purpose of the licensing law is to**
    a. legally separate brokers and agents.
    b. limit the number of agents to reduce competition.
    c. make it hard to get a license to discourage part-time workers.
    d. protect the public against fraudulent practice.

12. **A broker can buy property in his own name only if**
    a. he discloses his license.
    b. he places his license on deposit.
    c. his wife releases dower.
    d. the other side is properly represented.

Agency Law

Real estate agent is a common term, but few people stop to think about what the word "agent" means. An agent is a person authorized to represent another person (the principal) in dealings with third parties. Agency is a special legal relationship. The principal may be held liable to third parties for the agent's acts and the agent may be liable to the principal for failing to carry out his duties.

This chapter describes the agency relationship, how agency relationships can be created and terminated, and your duties and responsibilities to your broker, your clients, your customers, and the public.

Key Terms

Agent A person licensed to represent another (the principal) in a real estate transaction; a person authorized to represent the principal in dealings with third parties (clients or customers).

Contemporaneous Offers Offers to purchase or lease on behalf of two or more clients represented by the same licensee for the same property that the licensee knows, has known, or has reason to know will be taken under consideration by the owner or owner's authorized representative during the same period of time.

Customer A party in a transaction with whom an agent does not have a fiduciary duty or relationship, but with whom an agent must still be fair and honest.

Dual Agent A licensee who enters into any of the dual agency relationships set forth in Ohio license law; when a licensee represents both the buyer and seller in the same transaction, and all management level licensees at a brokerage. A management level licensee is not a dual agent if there is more than one management level licensee in the brokerage and that licensee either personally represents the buyer or seller or that licensee is the buyer or seller.

Estoppel A legal doctrine that prevents a person from asserting rights or facts that are inconsistent with earlier actions or statements, when he failed to object (or attempt to "stop") another person's actions.

(Continued on page 54)

Key Terms (cont.)

Fiduciary Someone in a position of trust and confidence, held by law to high standards of good faith and loyalty.

Fraud Intentional or negligent misrepresentation or concealment of material facts; making statements that a person knows, or should realize, are false or misleading.

Management Level Licensee A licensed real estate broker or salesperson who is affiliated with a real estate brokerage and who has supervisory responsibility over other licensed brokers and salespersons affiliated with that real estate brokerage.

Negligence Conduct that falls below the standard of care a reasonable person would exercise under the circumstances; an unintentional breach of a legal duty resulting from carelessness, recklessness, or incompetence. Negligence that causes harm is a tort.

Principal A person who grants another person (an agent) authority to represent him in dealings with third parties. Also referred to as the **client**.

Ratification The later confirmation or approval of an act that was not authorized when it was performed.

Split Agent A licensee assigned by a broker to represent a buyer or seller in a transaction, usually in an in-company dual agency situation.

Subagent An agent of an agent; a person an agent has lawfully delegated authority to so the subagent can assist in carrying out the principal's orders.

Transactional Brokerage An arrangement allowed in some states (not Ohio) in which a licensee serves as a facilitator to assist in the timely and accurate conclusion of a sales transaction but does not act as an agent for either party. Also called **Nonagency**.

Creating an Agency Relationship

Agency is a relationship of trust created when one person (the principal) gives another person (the agent) the right to represent the principal in dealings with third parties. An agent's authority always comes from the principal. As such, an **agent** *has the duties of good faith and loyalty (among others that we will discuss) with respect to the principal.*

When an agent acts within the scope of his authority, the principal is legally responsible for the agent's actions. Because of this, a third party may directly sue the principal instead of, or in addition to, the agent. When an agent exceeds his authority, though, a principal usually is not held liable for actions of the agent.

Authority

Depending on the scope of authority, an agent may be classified as **universal**, **general**, or **special**:

- **Universal Agent**—An agent authorized to do everything that can be lawfully delegated to a representative (e.g., a court-appointed guardian).

- **General Agent**—An agent authorized to handle all of the principal's affairs in one area or in specified areas (e.g., a property manager).

- **Special Agent**—An agent with limited authority to do a specific thing or conduct a specific transaction (e.g., a real estate broker).

Actual Authority

Actual authority is authority intentionally given to an agent by the principal, either expressly or by implication. Actual authority may be conferred by a listing agreement or a buyer broker contract.

- **Express authority** is communicated by the principal to the agent in words, either written or verbal. In some cases the principal signs a *power of attorney*. A **power of attorney** is an instrument authorizing one person (called an **attorney-in-fact**) to act as another person's agent, to the extent stated in the instrument. Note this distinction: Anyone can be an attorney-in-fact, but only a lawyer can be an attorney-at-law.

- **Incidental authority** is the authority to do everything reasonably necessary to carry out the principal's express orders. This is understood to give the agent incidental authority to tell people about the house being on the market. You cannot have incidental authority without first having express authority.

For Example

When a seller gives a real estate agent expressed written authority to list a house, he is also giving the agent incidental authority to tell people about the house being on the market. However, note that in Ohio, an agent cannot place "For Sale" signs on a property without the expresses written consent of the owner of the property.

- **Implied authority** is communicated to the agent by the principal's actions, rather than by the principal's words.

For Example

The principal hires a new property manager. Previous property managers had the authority to approve expenditures for maintenance of the property up to $100,000. Assume the principal has not given the property manager express authority (by words) to make such purchases. By the action of giving the new property manager that position, the principal has, by implication, authorized the property manager to expend company funds on maintenance items up to $100,000.

Listing Agreements. An agency relationship between a seller and a licensee in a real estate transaction is usually created with a written document referred to as a *listing agreement*. A **listing agreement** is a written agency contract between a seller and a real estate broker stipulating that the broker will be paid a commission for finding a ready, willing, and able buyer for a seller's property. A listing agreement is considered an employment agreement so the Statute of Frauds does not require it to be in writing, unless the contract is for more than one year. Though in Ohio, all listings, regardless of length, should be in writing.

Buyer Broker Contracts. An agency relationship between a buyer and a licensee in a real estate transaction can be created with a *buyer broker contract,* also called a purchaser agency agreement. A **buyer broker contract** is a written agency contract between a buyer and a real estate broker stipulating the broker will be paid a commission when the buyer purchases real estate. Ohio law does not currently require a separate buyer broker contract for a licensee to be paid, provided that the seller is willing to pay a buyer broker fee (often noted in MLS listings). It is sufficient for the licensee to be noted as representing the buyer on the signed purchase contract and agency disclosure forms. But a separate buyer broker contract is the best way to keep your buyer loyal to you, and ensure you get paid in a transaction after you have spent time helping a buyer.

Purchaser Agency Agreements. Purchaser Agency Agreements also confer actual authority in an agency relationship. In this type of agency contract a broker can negotiate a rate of commission to be paid to the broker by the buyer if the seller does not already offer compensation to the broker who brings the buyer for selling a property. An agent would not enter into a relationship with a seller without a listing agreement.

Many brokers would like for their salespeople to get Purchaser Agency Agreements signed by buyers but quite often agents and buyers enter into something called "apparent agency," also known as "ostensible agency." This is when an agent acts like a person's agent; the person does not stop them, benefits from the actions, and the outcome is that they accomplish a purpose together. It becomes difficult for the principal to say they did not have agency.

For Example

When one broker lists a property and another broker brings the buyer; the seller has an agent, the buyer has an agent, but only the listing broker had a listing agreement where the seller promised a commission and agreed to let the broker share the commission with the buyers broker.

Ratification

Ratification is *the later confirmation or approval of an act that was not authorized when it was performed.* In this way, an agency relationship can arise even without a specific agreement. If the other person later approves of these actions or accepts the benefit of the actions, she is said to have ratified them. If an agency relationship is created by ratification, the principal can be held liable for the agent's acts just as if they had been authorized in advance.

Apparent Agency

Apparent agency is when someone who has not been authorized to represent another acts as if she is that person's agent. Apparent agency can also occur when an agent acts beyond the scope of her authority—giving a third party the impression the acts are authorized. This is also called **ostensible agency.**

Because one may appear to be the agent of another, even though no agency relationship has been agreed to, third parties may be misled. There is a duty upon a would-be principal to inform these known third parties. If these parties are not so informed, the principal may be held liable for the acts of the agent, just as though there had been an agreement, under the legal doctrine of *estoppel.*

Estoppel is *a legal doctrine preventing a person from asserting rights or facts inconsistent with earlier actions or statements, when he failed to object (or attempt to "stop") another person's actions.* Estoppel makes it legally impossible for the principal to deny the agency in such a case as where a licensee's actions make him appear to be the principal's agent. The principal cannot sit back and do nothing. By accepting the rewards of the relationship, the principal must also assume the responsibilities, even though there was no formal agreement.

As a practical matter, this would never arise in the practice of real estate because of the Licensing Law. There is a duty for third parties, such as sellers, to check the bona fides (good faith credentials) of any agent or broker with whom they might deal. This is a matter of public record and can be done with a simple phone call to the Ohio Division of Real Estate and Professional Licensing.

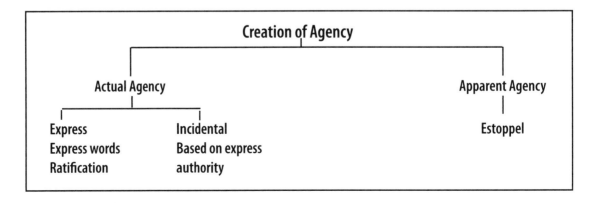

Real Estate Agency Relationships

The basic real estate agency relationship is between a broker and a seller or a broker and a buyer. *The party with whom the licensee has entered into a contract to represent*, and hence owes a fiduciary responsibility to, is referred to as the **principal** or **client.** *All third parties* are referred to as *customers.* A **customer** is a party in a transaction with whom an agent does not have a fiduciary duty or relationship, but with whom an agent must still be fair and honest.

This distinction will become important later as we define the different duties and responsibilities that a licensee has to clients and customers. As you will see, the Agency Disclosure Statement form (required by Ohio law) will help clients and customers sort out who represents them and what loyalties and responsibilities are owed to them.

It is important to understand that the promise of payment to a licensee or the source of a licensee's compensation does not necessarily establish or determine an agency relationship. In most cases, the seller is paying the commission to the real estate agents involved in the sale of a property, whether a **subagent** or a **buyer broker** is involved.

Subagents

A **subagent** is *an agent of an agent; a person that an agent has lawfully delegated authority to, so the subagent can assist in carrying out the principal's orders.* Under this definition, the broker's salespersons are agents of the broker and also technically subagents of the clients with whom their broker has entered into contracts. Subagents represent the clients through their broker, who is the agent of the client. It is illegal for a salesperson to represent a client directly, without a broker.

A broker can also represent a seller through another cooperating broker. This is what is meant by subagency in the **Multiple Listing Service (MLS)**. **MLS** is a listing service whereby local member brokers agree to share listings and to share commissions on properties sold jointly. In this subagency capacity, a salesperson licensee becomes the subagent of the seller and the listing broker. This is becoming much less common, however, due to the increase in potential liability the seller and listing broker have for any misstatements of the subagent. As a result, many MLS listings do not pay any commission to subagents in this capacity.

Buyer Brokers

A **buyer broker** is an agent representing the interests of the buyer of a property. This has become much more common and widely accepted. As such, sellers now often agree to pay commissions to buyer brokers in a transaction, even though the buyer broker does not represent the interests of the seller. Sellers want their property sold (with as little potential for liability problems as possible), so many MLS listings recognize (and pay) only buyer brokers.

Ohio law has changed to address the needs that go with these changing trends.

Ohio's Agency Law

In traditional real estate transactions, it was presumed that a real estate broker represented the seller. The buyer often did not realize that in the eyes of the law, the salesperson showing them properties represented the seller.

The law finally changed as brokers representing buyers became more common and now Ohio Agency Law no longer presumes that brokers represent sellers. Buyers like this arrangement because they now have an advocate; sellers and listing agents like this arrangement because they do not need to worry about liability for representations made by the buyer's agent or broker because that person is no longer their subagent.

Agency Relationships

Under Ohio's Agency Law, there are four types of agency relationships that may be entered into:

1. Agency relationship between a licensee and a seller
2. Agency relationship between a licensee and a buyer
3. Dual agency relationship between a licensee and both seller and buyer
4. In-company or "sub" agency relationship between two licensees in the same brokerage: One licensee and a seller and the other licensee and a buyer

These four types of agency relationships, in different combinations, offer brokers five models of business under which a brokerage may operate:

1. Brokerage practicing Split Agency and Dual Agency
2. Brokerage practicing Dual Agency for all in-house transactions
3. Brokerage practicing Exclusive Buyer Agency only
4. Brokerage practicing Exclusive Seller Agency only
5. Brokerage practicing Split Agency but no Dual Agency

The type of agency practiced by a brokerage is disclosed to customers and clients through the "Consumer Guide to Agency Relationships," which is discussed later in this chapter.

When an agency relationship is formed between a brokerage and a client under any of these arrangements, the brokerage with whom the agent is affiliated and the management level licensees in that brokerage are also considered agents of that client. A **management level licensee** is *a licensed broker or salesperson who is affiliated with a real estate brokerage and who has supervisory responsibility over other licensees affiliated with that real estate brokerage.* A management level licensee is not a dual agent if there is more than one management level licensee in the brokerage and either:

- The management level licensee personally represents the seller or buyer
- The management level licensee is the buyer or seller

Furthermore, any agent affiliated with the brokerage who receives confidential information from an agent of the client is also considered an agent of that client. This has always been true for agency relationships formed under Ohio law.

Except for these two provisions, Ohio law recognizes that another agent from the same brokerage is **not** an agent of that client, unless that agent assisted in establishing the agency relationship or is specifically appointed, with the client's consent, to represent that client. Thus, *two salesperson-level licensees in the same brokerage can represent two different parties in the same transaction, with only their broker (or other management level licensee) considered a dual agent.* This agency relationship is known as "in-company" or "**split agency.**" The agent in this case would be a **split agent**.

For Example

L and K are salespersons at Star Realty under B, who is their affiliated broker. L has a listing for a house. L and B (the broker) are both agents for the seller, who is considered a client to both of them. L and B have a fiduciary responsibility to act in the best interests of the seller.

K has been working with a buyer who likes the house that L has listed. K has a buyer broker agreement in place, so K and B (the broker) are both agents for the buyer. The buyer is considered to be a client to both of them, so both K and B have a fiduciary responsibility to act in the best interests of the buyer. Thus, B (the broker) is the only dual agent in this situation. L represents only the seller and K represents only the buyer.

Caution Regarding Teams. Care must be taken when teams exist in a real estate brokerage. The team leader may be acting as a management level licensee without thinking of themselves as management level. If they are in a supervisory position or they are privy to the confidential information being gathered in the relationship, they are considered management level. In 2011, agency law changed for the practical by forbidding any licensee to be a dual agent when they are dealing their own real estate.

Confidential Information. In the above example, B (the broker) is the only one who is in a potentially compromising position since she has access to confidential information about both the buyer and seller. Of course, the integrity of the process can be destroyed if L accidentally learns confidential information about K's buyer, or if K inadvertently stumbles across confidential information about L's seller.

To avert possible problems, Ohio's Agency Law provides that each brokerage must develop and maintain a written company policy that states:

- The types of agency relationships that its licensees may establish.
- Whether dual agency relationships as described previously are allowed.
- Specific confidential information (including how the brokerage intends to cover affiliated licensees with respect to confidential information).

This official company policy must be given to clients and customers, but only upon their request. The agency and confidentiality policies developed and maintained must comply with minimum standards established by the Superintendent of the Division of Real Estate and Professional Licensing and the Ohio Real Estate Commission.

It is important to note, though, that the development and maintenance of such a policy does not relieve the brokerage from liability for failure of the brokerage, or any affiliated licensee or employee, to keep a client's information confidential.

For Example

Here are some tips to remember concerning confidentiality: Lock your files that contain confidential information. Keep your voice down when you are on the phone. Only describe your listings at office meetings, not your seller's circumstances. Talk about what your buyers are looking for, not what is in their bank account. Agency law requires management level licensees to supervise split agents in in-company transactions. Remember to copy them when sending emails between split agents.

Ohio's Mandated Forms

Ohio law now mandates that two forms are required to be given to buyers and sellers:

- Consumer Guide to Agency Relationships
- Agency Disclosure Statement

Consumer Guide to Agency Relationships

The first form that is given to a buyer or seller is the **Consumer Guide to Agency Relationships** form. This is Ohio's consumer-friendly method of providing sellers and/or buyers with information regarding the type of agency relationships recognized in Ohio and the type of agency a particular brokerage practices. As described below, this Consumer Guide to Agency Relationships form must be provided to and acknowledged by a consumer (be they buyer or seller). The following disclosures must be included in a brokerage's Consumer Guide to Agency Relationship form:

1. Permissible types of agency relationships in Ohio

2. The brokerage's policy regarding representation of buyers and sellers, dual agency, split agency, including if the broker offers compensation to, or seeks compensation from, cooperating brokerages

3. A statement that a brokerage with a buyer as a client represents the buyer's interests, even though the seller's brokerage or seller may compensate the buyer's agent

4. The brokerage policy on customers who are not represented

5. A statement that Ohio law requires the Consumer Guide to Agency Relationships be presented to and acknowledged by the consumer

6. The brokerage's name, fair housing language, and logo

Note that the Consumer Guide to Agency Relationships form is required whether the licensee is an agent for the seller or an agent for the buyer and must be presented at the first substantive contact a licensee has with a consumer. The **first substantive contact** is defined as being no later than the occurrence of certain events, depending on whether a licensee is working with sellers, buyers, or both, in a particular transaction.

Licensees Working With Sellers. A licensee working as a seller's agent must give the seller the Consumer Guide to Agency Relationships form prior to marketing or showing the seller's property. As a practical matter, though, it is wise to take care of this disclosure requirement at the same time you are entering into a listing agreement. Check with your broker for the specific procedures established as office policy.

Licensees Working With Buyers. A licensee working with a buyer, regardless of what agency relationship may develop, must provide the buyer with the Consumer Guide to Agency Relationships form at the first substantive contact, but no later than before:

- Initiating a pre-qualification evaluation to determine whether the buyer has the financial ability to buy or lease a particular property.

- Requesting specific financial information from the buyer to determine the buyer's ability to buy or finance real estate in a certain price range.

- Showing a property to a buyer, other than at an open house.

- Discussing making an offer to buy real property with the buyer.

- Submitting an offer to buy or lease real property on behalf of the buyer.

If the agent's earliest contact with a buyer is by telephone and covers any of the above events, the licensee must make a verbal disclosure of the agency relationship the licensee may have with both the buyer and the seller. The licensee is then required to get the buyer to acknowledge receipt of the Consumer Guide to Agency Relationships form at the first meeting with that buyer following the verbal disclosure of the possible agency relationships.

Agency Disclosure Statement

The **Agency Disclosure Statement** is the second form required under Ohio law. While the first form, the Consumer Guide to Agency Relationships, provides information to consumers on the possible types of agency relationships they may encounter under Ohio law, this form discloses the actual agency relationship that will result in a property-specific transaction and lets the buyer and seller know exactly who is working for whom in a particular transaction.

The Agency Disclosure Statement form is initiated by the buyer's agent when the buyer indicates a desire to write an offer on a property, thus becoming transaction-specific. The seller's agent must present and explain the Agency Disclosure Statement form to the seller, obtaining the seller's signature consenting to the agency relationship indicated prior to presenting the offer to purchase.

The form is broken down into three sections:

1. Transactions involving two agents from different brokerages
2. Transactions involving two agents from the same brokerage
3. Transactions involving only one agent

Within each of these sections, the appropriate agency relationship resulting from an offer on one specific property can be determined. The buyer and the seller must both consent to the indicated agency relationship by signing and dating the form. The reverse side of the form explains dual agency in detail. This information includes:

*   The **minimum duties** that the agent and brokerage shall provide and things the agent and brokerage shall not do in a dual agency relationship
*   How management level licensees will function in this relationship
*   Responsibilities of the buyer and seller in the transaction
*   A statement that compensation, unless otherwise agreed upon, will be pursuant to the agency agreement
*   A statement that, by signing the form, the parties consent to dual agency
*   Information on how to contact the Division of Real Estate and Professional Licensing

Buyer's Agents Dealing With Sellers. The seller must receive a copy of a buyer's signed Agency Disclosure Statement before an offer is presented. If the agent preparing the offer does not represent the seller, the form should be given to the seller's agent.

Seller's Agents Dealing With Buyers. If the licensee is a seller's agent, he is required to give an Agency Disclosure Statement to a buyer prior to preparation of the offer for the buyer.

Changing Sides. To change the party that a licensee represents in a real estate transaction after the Agency Disclosure Statement is signed and dated, the licensee must obtain written consent from the original party represented to do so and must promptly notify anyone who knew of the original relationship what party the licensee now represents.

Exemptions. These disclosure form requirements are not required for referrals from one licensee to another, open houses (unless an offer is written), residential property that is rented or leased for a term of 18 months or less, and transactions dealing with foreign real estate or cemetery interment rights.

 Failure to comply with The Consumer Guide to Agency Relationships or the Agency Disclosure requirements will be deemed *prima facie* evidence of misconduct on the part of the licensee in violation of Ohio Agency Law. Failure to comply could also subject the licensee to a citation issued by the Superintendent of the Ohio Division of Real Estate and Professional Licensing.

CONSUMER GUIDE TO AGENCY RELATIONSHIPS

(Split Agency & Dual Agency – Model Policy)

Brokerage Name

We are pleased you have selected (brokerage) to help you with your real estate needs. Whether you are selling, buying or leasing real est ate (brokerage) can provide you with ex pertise and assistance. Because this may be the largest financial transaction you will enter into, it is i mportant to understand the role of the agents and brokers with whom you are working. Below is some information that explains the various services agents can offer and their options for working with you:

Representing the Sellers
Most sellers of real estate choose to list their home for sale with a real estate brokerage. When they do so, they sign a listing agreement that authorizes the brokerage and the listi ng agent to repre sent their int erests. A s the seller's agent, the brokerage and listing agent must: follow the seller's lawful instructions, be loyal to the seller, promote the seller's best interests, disclose material facts to the seller, maintain confidential information, act with reasonable skill and care and, account for any money they handle in the transaction. In rare circumstances a listing broker may offer "subagency" to other brokerages which would also represe nt the seller's interests an d owe the seller these same duties.

Representing Buyers
When purchasing real estate, buyers usually choose to work with a real estate agent as well. Often the buy ers want to be represented in the tr ansaction. This is referred to as buy er's agency. A brokerage and agent tha t agree to represent a buy er's interest in a transaction must: follow th e buyer's lawful instructions, be loy al to the buy er, promote the buyer's best interests, disclose material facts to the buy er, maintain c onfidential information and, account for any money they handle in the transaction.

Dual Agency
Occasionally the same agent and brokerag e who represents the sel ler also represents the buyer. This is referred to as dual agency. When a b rokerage and its agents become "dual agents", they must maintain a neutral p osition in the transaction. T hey may not advocate the position of one client over t he best interests of the ot her client, or disclose any confidential information to the other party without written consent.

Representing Both the Buyer & Seller
On occasion, the buyer and seller will each be represented by two different agents from the same brokerage. In this case the agents may each represent the best interest of their respective clients. Or, depending on com pany policy, the agents may both act as dual agents and remain neutral in the transaction. When either of the above occurs, the brokerage will be considered a dual agent. As a dual agent the brokerage and its managers will maintain a neutral position and cannot advocate for the position of one client over another. T he brokerage will also protect the confidentiality of all parties.

For more information on agency law in Ohio you can also contact the Ohio Division of Re al Estate & P rofessional Licensing at (614) 466-4100, or on their website www.com.state.oh.us.

Working With (brokerage)

(brokerage) does offer rep resentation to both buy ers and sellers. Therefore the potential exists for one a gent to represent a buyer who wishes to purchase property listed with another agent in our com pany. If this occu rs each agent will represent their own client, but (brokerage) and its managers will act as a dual agent.
This means the brokerage and its managers will maintain a neutral position and not take any actions that will favor one side over the other. (brokerage) will still supervise both agents to assure that their respective clients are being fully represented and will protect the parties' confidential information.

In the event that both the buyer and seller are represented by the same agent, that agent and (brokerage) will act as a dual agent but only if both parties agree . As a dual agen t they will treat both parties honestly, prepare and present offers at the direction of the parties, an d help the parties fulfill the terms of an y contract. They will not, however, disclose any confidential inform ation that would place one party at an advantage over the other or ad vocate or negotiate to the detriment of either party.

If dual agency occurs you will be asked to consent to that in writing. If you do not agree to your agent acting as a dual agent, you can ask that another agent in ou   r company be assigned t o represent you or   you can seek representation from another brokerage.

As a buyer you m ay also choose to represent yourself on properties (brokerage) has listed. In that instance (brokerage) will represent the seller and you would represent your own best interests. Because the listing agent has a duty of full disclosure to the seller you should not share any information with the listing agent that you would not want the seller to know.

Working With Other Brokerages

When (brokerage) lists property for sale it also cooperates with, a nd offers compensation to, other brokerages that represent buyers. (Brokerage) does reserve the right, in some insta nces, to vary the compensation it offers to other brokerages. As a seller, you should understand that just because (brokerage) shares a fee with a brokerage representing the buyer, it does not m ean that you will be represented by that brokerage. Instead that company will be looking out for the buy er and (brokerage) will be representing your interests. When acting as a buyer's agent, (brokerage) also accepts compensation offered by the listing broker. If the property is not listed with any broker, or the listing broker does not offer compensation, we will attempt to negotiate for a seller-paid fee.

Fair Housing Statement

It is illegal, pursuant to the Ohio Fair Housing Law, division (H) of Section 4112.02 of the Revised Code and the Federal Fair Housing Law, 42 U.S.C.A. 3601, as amended, to refuse to sell, transfer, assign, rent, lease, sublease or finance housing accommodations, refuse to negotiate for the sale or rental of housing accommodations, or otherwise deny or make unavailable housing accommodations because of race, color, religion, sex, familial status as defined in Section 4112.01 of the Revised Code, ancestry, military status as defined in that section, disability as defined in that section, or national origin or to so discriminate in advertising the sale or rental of housing, in the financing of housing, or in the provision of real estate brokerage services. It is also illegal, for profit, to induce or attempt to induce a person to sell or rent a dwelling by representations regarding the entry into the neighborhood of a person or persons belonging to one of the protected classes. (Effective: 9/29/11)

We hope you find this inf ormation to be helpful to you as you begin your real estate transaction. When y ou are ready to enter into a transaction, y ou will be given an Agency Disclosure Statement that specifically identifies the role of the agents and brokerages. Pl ease ask questions if there is anything you do not unders tand. Because it is important that you have this information Ohio law requires that we ask you to sign below, acknowledging receipt of this consumer guide. Your signature will not obligate you to work with our company if you do not choose to do so.

_____   _____   _____
Name   (Please Print)   Name   (Please Print)

_____   _____   _____
Signature   Date   Signature   Date

CONSUMER GUIDE TO AGENCY RELATIONSHIPS

(Dual Agency In All In House Transactions – Model Policy)

Brokerage Name

We are pleased you have selected <u>(brokerage)</u> to help you with your real estate needs. Whether you are selling, buying or leasing real estate, <u>(brokerage)</u> can provide you with expertise and assistance. Because this may be the largest financial transaction you will enter into, it is important to understand the role of the agents and brokers with whom you are working. Below is some information that explains the various services that agents can offer and their options for working with you:

Representing the Sellers
Most sellers of real estate choose to list their home for sale with a real estate brokerage. When they do so, they sign a listing agreement that authorizes the brokerage and the listing agent to represent their interests. As the seller's agent, the brokerage and listing agent must: follow the seller's lawful instructions, be loyal to the seller, promote the seller's best interests, disclose material facts to the seller, maintain confidential information, act with reasonable skill and care, and account for any money they handle in the transaction. In rare circumstances, a listing broker may offer "subagency" to other brokerages, which would also represent the seller's interests and owe the seller these same duties.

Representing Buyers
When purchasing real estate, buyers usually choose to work with a real estate agent as well. Often the buyers want to be represented in the transaction. This is referred to as buyer's agency. A brokerage and agent that agree to represent a buyer's interest in a transaction must: follow the buyer's lawful instructions, be loyal to the buyer, promote the buyer's best interests, disclose material facts to the buyer, maintain confidential information, and account for any money they handle in the transaction.

Dual Agency
Occasionally, the same agent and brokerage that represent the seller also represent the buyer. This is referred to as dual agency. When a brokerage and its agents become "dual agents," they must maintain a neutral position in the transaction. They may not advocate the position of one client over the best interests of the other client, or disclose any confidential information to the other party without written consent.

Representing Both the Buyer & Seller
On occasion, the buyer and seller will each be represented by two different agents from the same brokerage. In this case, the agents may each represent the best interest of their respective clients. Or, depending on company policy, the agents may both act as dual agents and remain neutral in the transaction. When either of the above occurs, the brokerage will be considered a dual agent. As a dual agent, the brokerage and its managers will maintain a neutral position and cannot advocate for the position of one client over another. The brokerage will also protect the confidentiality of all parties.

For more information on agency law in Ohio, contact the Ohio Division of Real Estate & Professional Licensing at (614) 466-4100, or online at www.com.ohio.gov/real.

Revised: 9/2011

Working With (brokerage)

(Brokerage) does represent both buyers and sellers. When (brokerage) lists property for sale, all agents in the brokerage represent the seller. Likewise, when a buyer is represented by a (brokerage) agent, all of the agents represent that buyer. Therefore, when a buyer represented by a (brokerage) agent wishes to purchase property listed by our company, the agent(s) involved act as dual agents. This is true whether one agent is representing both parties or two separate agents are involved.

In the event that both the buyer and seller are represented by (brokerage) agents, these agents and (brokerage) will act as a dual agent but only if both parties agree. As a dual agent, they will treat both parties honestly, prepare and present offers at the direction of the parties, and help the parties fulfill the terms of any contract. They will not, however, disclose any confidential information that will place one party at an advantage over the other or advocate or negotiate to the detriment of either party.

If dual agency occurs, you will be asked to consent to that in writing. If you do not agree to your agent acting as a dual agent, you can seek representation from another brokerage.

As a buyer, you may also choose to represent yourself on properties (brokerage) has listed. In that instance, (brokerage) will represent the seller and you would represent your own best interests. Because the listing agent has a duty of full disclosure to the seller, you should not share any information with the listing agent that you would not want the seller to know.

Working With Other Brokerages

(Brokerage) does offer representation to both buyers and sellers. When (brokerage) lists property for sale, it also cooperates with, and offers compensation to, other brokerages that represent buyers. (Brokerage) does reserve the right, in some instances, to vary the compensation it offers to other brokerages. As a seller, you should understand that just because (brokerage) shares a fee with a brokerage representing the buyer, it does not mean that you will be represented by that buyer's brokerage. Instead, that company will be looking out for the buyer and (brokerage) will be representing your interests.

When acting as a buyer's agent, (brokerage) also accepts compensation offered by the listing broker. If the property is not listed with any broker, or the listing broker does not offer compensation, we will attempt to negotiate for a seller-paid fee.

Fair Housing Statement

It is illegal, pursuant to the Ohio Fair Housing Law, division (H) of Section 4112.02 of the Revised Code and the Federal Fair Housing Law, 42 U.S.C.A. 3601, as amended, to refuse to sell, transfer, assign, rent, lease, sublease or finance housing accommodations, refuse to negotiate for the sale or rental of housing accommodations, or otherwise deny or make unavailable housing accommodations because of race, color, religion, sex, familial status as defined in Section 4112.01 of the Revised Code, ancestry, military status as defined in that section, disability as defined in that section, or national origin or to so discriminate in advertising the sale or rental of housing, in the financing of housing, or in the provision of real estate brokerage services. It is also illegal, for profit, to induce or attempt to induce a person to sell or rent a dwelling by representations regarding the entry into the neighborhood of a person or persons belonging to one of the protected classes. (Effective: 9/29/11)

We hope you find this information to be helpful to you as you begin your real estate transaction. When you are ready to enter into a transaction, you will be given an Agency Disclosure Statement that specifically identifies the role of the agents and brokerages. Please ask questions if there is anything you do not understand.

Because it is important that you have this information, Ohio law requires that we ask you to sign below to acknowledge receipt of this pamphlet. Your signature will not obligate you to work with our company if you do not choose to do so.

Name	(Please Print)	Name	(Please Print)

Signature	Date	Signature	Date

Revised: 9/2011

CONSUMER GUIDE TO AGENCY RELATIONSHIPS

(Exclusive Buyer Agency Only – Model Policy)

Brokerage Name

We are pleased you have selected <u>(brokerage)</u> to help you with your real estate needs. Whether you are selling, buying or leasing real estate, <u>(brokerage)</u> can provide you with expertise and assistance. Because this may be the largest financial transaction you will enter into, it is important to understand the role of the agents and brokers with whom you are working. Below is some information that explains the various services that agents can offer and their options for working with you:

Representing the Sellers
Most sellers of real estate choose to list their home for sale with a real estate brokerage. When they do so, they sign a listing agreement that authorizes the brokerage and the listing agent to represent their interests. As the seller's agent, the brokerage and listing agent must: follow the seller's lawful instructions, be loyal to the seller, promote the seller's best interests, disclose material facts to the seller, maintain confidential information, act with reasonable skill and care, and account for any money they handle in the transaction. In rare circumstances, a listing broker may offer "subagency" to other brokerages, which would also represent the seller's interests and owe the seller these same duties.

Representing Buyers
When purchasing real estate, buyers usually choose to work with a real estate agent as well. Often the buyers want to be represented in the transaction. This is referred to as buyer's agency. A brokerage and agent that agree to represent a buyer's interest in a transaction must: follow the buyer's lawful instructions, be loyal to the buyer, promote the buyer's best interests, disclose material facts to the buyer, maintain confidential information, and account for any money they handle in the transaction.

Dual Agency
Occasionally, the same agent and brokerage that represent the seller also represent the buyer. This is referred to as dual agency. When a brokerage and its agents become "dual agents," they must maintain a neutral position in the transaction. They may not advocate the position of one client over the best interests of the other client, or disclose any confidential information to the other party without written consent.

Representing Both the Buyer & Seller
On occasion, the buyer and seller will each be represented by two different agents from the same brokerage. In this case, the agents may each represent the best interest of their respective clients. Or, depending on company policy, the agents may both act as dual agents and remain neutral in the transaction. When either of the above occurs, the brokerage will be considered a dual agent. As a dual agent, the brokerage and its managers will maintain a neutral position and cannot advocate for the position of one client over another. The brokerage will also protect the confidentiality of all parties.

For more information on agency law in Ohio, contact the Ohio Division of Real Estate & Professional Licensing at (614) 466-4100, or online at www.com.ohio.gov/real.

Working With (brokerage)

(Brokerage) only represents buyers. It does not represent sellers or list property for sale. Therefore, (brokerage) will never act as a dual agent representing both parties in a transaction. Instead, it will only act as the buyer's agent in the purchase of real estate.

When acting as a buyer's agent, (brokerage) will seek its compensation from the listing broker. If the property is not listed with any broker, or the listing broker does not offer compensation, the brokerage will attempt to negotiate for a seller-paid fee. However, even if the listing broker or seller pays us, (brokerage) still represents only the buyer.

If (brokerage) is not compensated by the listing broker or the seller, its compensation will be paid by the buyer, pursuant to a written agreement with the buyer.

Fair Housing Statement

It is illegal, pursuant to the Ohio Fair Housing Law, division (H) of Section 4112.02 of the Revised Code and the Federal Fair Housing Law, 42 U.S.C.A. 3601, as amended, to refuse to sell, transfer, assign, rent, lease, sublease or finance housing accommodations, refuse to negotiate for the sale or rental of housing accommodations, or otherwise deny or make unavailable housing accommodations because of race, color, religion, sex, familial status as defined in Section 4112.01 of the Revised Code, ancestry, military status as defined in that section, disability as defined in that section, or national origin or to so discriminate in advertising the sale or rental of housing, in the financing of housing, or in the provision of real estate brokerage services. It is also illegal, for profit, to induce or attempt to induce a person to sell or rent a dwelling by representations regarding the entry into the neighborhood of a person or persons belonging to one of the protected classes.

We hope you find this information to be helpful to you as you begin your real estate transaction. When you are ready to enter into a transaction, you will be given an Agency Disclosure Statement that specifically identifies the role of the agents and brokerages. Please ask questions if there is anything you do not understand.

Because it is important that you have this information Ohio law requires that we ask you to sign below to acknowledge receipt of this consumer guide. Your signature will not obligate you to work with our company if you do not choose to do so.

_____   _____
Name   (Please Print)   Name   (Please Print)

_____   _____
Signature   Date   Signature   Date

CONSUMER GUIDE TO AGENCY RELATIONSHIPS

(Exclusive Seller Agency - Model Policy)

Brokerage Name

We are pleased you have selected (brokerage) to help you with your real estate needs. Whether you are selling, buying or leasing real estate, (brokerage) can provide you with expertise and assistance. Because this may be the largest financial transaction you will enter into, it is important to understand the role of the agents and brokers with whom you are working. Below is some information that explains the various services that agents can offer and their options for working with you.

For more information on agency law in Ohio, contact the Ohio Division of Real Estate & Professional Licensing at (614) 466-4100, or online at www.com.ohio.gov/real.

Representing the Sellers

Most sellers of real estate choose to list their home for sale with a real estate brokerage. When they do so, they sign a listing agreement that authorizes the brokerage and the listing agent to represent their interests. As the seller's agent, the brokerage and listing agent must: follow the seller's lawful instructions, be loyal to the seller, promote the seller's best interests, disclose material facts to the seller, maintain confidential information, act with reasonable skill and care, and account for any money they handle in the transaction. In rare circumstances, a listing broker may offer "subagency" to other brokerages, which would also represent the seller's interests and owe the seller these same duties.

Representing Buyers

When purchasing real estate, buyers usually choose to work with a real estate agent as well. Often the buyers want to be represented in the transaction. This is referred to as buyer's agency. A brokerage and agent that agree to represent a buyer's interest in a transaction must: follow the buyer's lawful instructions, be loyal to the buyer, promote the buyer's best interests, disclose material facts to the buyer, maintain confidential information, and account for any money they handle in the transaction.

Dual Agency

Occasionally, the same agent and brokerage that represent the seller also represent the buyer. This is referred to as dual agency. When a brokerage and its agents become "dual agents," they must maintain a neutral position between the buyer and the seller. They may not advocate the position of one client over the best interests of the other client, or disclose any personal or confidential information to the other party without written consent.

Representing Both the Buyer & Seller

On occasion, the buyer and seller will each be represented by two different agents from the same brokerage. In this case, the agents may each represent the best interest of their respective clients. Or, depending on company policy, the agents may both act as dual agents and remain neutral in the transaction. When either of the above occurs, the brokerage will be considered a dual agent. As a dual agent, the brokerage and its managers will maintain a neutral position and cannot advocate for the position of one client over another. The brokerage will also protect the confidentiality of all parties.

For more information on agency law in Ohio, contact the Ohio Division of Real Estate & Professional Licensing at (614) 466-4100, or online at www.com.ohio.gov/real.

Working With (brokerage)

(Brokerage) only represents seller. It does not represent buyers of real estate. Therefore, (brokerage) will never act as a dual agent representing both parties in a transaction. Instead, it will only act as the seller's agent in the sale of real estate.

Even though (brokerage) only lists properties for sellers, it can still work with buyers as customers. (Brokerage) can provide buyers with non-confidential information and write offers at the buyer's direction, but will not act as the agent of these buyers. Instead, such buyers will represent their own best interests.

It is also important for buyers to understand that because the listing agent has a duty of full disclosure to the seller, buyers should not share any information with the listing agent that they would not want the seller to know.

Working With Other Brokerages

When (brokerage) lists property for sale, it also cooperates with, and offers compensation to, other brokerages that represent buyers. (Brokerage) does reserve the right, in some instances, to vary the compensation it offers to other brokerages. As a seller, you should understand that just because (brokerage) shares a fee with a brokerage representing the buyer, it does not mean that you will be represented by that buyer's brokerage. Instead, that company will be looking out for the buyer and (brokerage) will be representing your interests.

Fair Housing Statement

It is illegal, pursuant to the Ohio Fair Housing Law, division (H) of Section 4112.02 of the Revised Code and the Federal Fair Housing Law, 42 U.S.C.A. 3601, as amended, to refuse to sell, transfer, assign, rent, lease, sublease or finance housing accommodations, refuse to negotiate for the sale or rental of housing accommodations, or otherwise deny or make unavailable housing accommodations because of race, color, religion, sex, familial status as defined in Section 4112.01 of the Revised Code, ancestry, military status as defined in that section, disability as defined in that section, or national origin or to so discriminate in advertising the sale or rental of housing, in the financing of housing, or in the provision of real estate brokerage services. It is also illegal, for profit, to induce or attempt to induce a person to sell or rent a dwelling by representations regarding the entry into the neighborhood of a person or persons belonging to one of the protected classes.

We hope you find this information to be helpful to you as you begin your real estate transaction. When you are ready to enter into a transaction, you will be given an Agency Disclosure Statement that specifically identifies the role of the agents and brokerages. Please ask questions if there is anything you do not understand.

Because it is important that you have this information, Ohio law requires that we ask you to sign below to acknowledge receipt of this pamphlet. Your signature will not obligate you to work with our company if you do not choose to do so.

Name	(Please Print)	Name	(Please Print)

Signature	Date	Signature	Date

Revised: 9/2011

CONSUMER GUIDE TO AGENCY RELATIONSHIPS

(Split Agency but No Dual Agency– Model Policy)

Brokerage Name

We are pleased you have selected (brokerage) to help you with your real estate needs. Whether you are selling, buying or leasing real estate, (brokerage) can provide you with expertise and assistance. Because this may be the largest financial transaction you will enter into, it is important to understand the role of the agents and brokers with whom you are working. Below is some information that explains the various services that agents can offer and their options for working with you.

Representing the Sellers
Most sellers of real estate choose to list their home for sale with a real estate brokerage. When they do so, they sign a listing agreement that authorizes the brokerage and the listing agent to represent their interests. As the seller's agent, the brokerage and listing agent must: follow the seller's lawful instructions, be loyal to the seller, promote the seller's best interests, disclose material facts to the seller, maintain confidential information, act with reasonable skill and care, and account for any money they handle in the transaction. In rare circumstances, a listing broker may offer "subagency" to other brokerages, which would also represent the seller's interests and owe the seller these same duties.

Representing Buyers
When purchasing real estate, buyers usually choose to work with a real estate agent as well. Often the buyers want to be represented in the transaction. This is referred to as buyer's agency. A brokerage and agent that agree to represent a buyer's interest in a transaction must: follow the buyer's lawful instructions, be loyal to the buyer, promote the buyer's best interests, disclose material facts to the buyer, maintain confidential information, and account for any money they handle in the transaction.

Dual Agency
Occasionally, the same agent and brokerage that represent the seller also represent the buyer. This is referred to as dual agency. When a brokerage and its agents become "dual agents," they must maintain a neutral position between the buyer and the seller. They may not advocate the position of one client over the best interests of the other client, or disclose any personal or confidential information to the other party without written consent.

Representing Both the Buyer & Seller
On occasion, the buyer and seller will each be represented by two different agents from the same brokerage. In this case, the agents may each represent the best interest of their respective clients. Or, depending on company policy, the agents may both act as dual agents and remain neutral in the transaction. When either of the above occurs, the brokerage will be considered a dual agent. As a dual agent, the brokerage and its managers will maintain a neutral position and cannot advocate for the position of one client over another. The brokerage will also protect the confidentiality of all parties.

For more information on agency law in Ohio, contact the Ohio Division of Real Estate & Professional Licensing at (614) 466-4100, or online at www.com.ohio.gov/real.

Working With (brokerage)

(Brokerage) does offer representation to both buyers and sellers. Therefore, the potential exists for one agent to represent a buyer who wishes to purchase property listed with another agent in our company. If this occurs, each agent will represent their own client, but (brokerage) and its managers will act as a dual agent.

This means the brokerage and its managers will maintain a neutral position and not take any actions that will favor one side over the other. However, (brokerage) will still supervise both agents to assure that their clients are being fully represented.

While it is the policy of (brokerage) to allow a buyer and seller in the same transaction to be represented by two agents in our brokerage, it does not permit one agent to represent both parties. Therefore, a listing agent working directly with a buyer will represent only the seller's interests. The agent will still be able to provide the buyer with non-confidential information, prepare and present offers at their direction and assist the buyer in the financing and closing process. However, the buyer will represent their own interests. Because the listing agent has a duty of full disclosure to the seller, a buyer in this situation should not share any information with the listing agent that they would not want the seller to know. If a buyer wishes to be represented, another agent in (brokerage) can be appointed to act as their agent or they can seek representation from another brokerage.

Working With Other Brokerages

(Brokerage) does offer representation to both buyers and sellers. When (brokerage) lists property for sale, it also cooperates with, and offers compensation to, other brokerages that represent buyers. (Brokerage) does reserve the right, in some instances, to vary the compensation it offers to other brokerages. As a seller, you should understand that just because (brokerage) shares a fee with a brokerage representing the buyer, it does not mean that you will be represented by that buyer's brokerage. Instead, that company will be looking out for the buyer and (brokerage) will be representing your interests.

When acting as a buyer's agent, (brokerage) also accepts compensation offered by the listing broker. If the property is not listed with any broker, or the listing broker does not offer compensation, we will attempt to negotiate for a seller-paid fee.

Fair Housing Statement: It is illegal, pursuant to the Ohio Fair Housing Law, division (H) of Section 4112.02 of the Revised Code and the Federal Fair Housing Law, 42 U.S.C.A. 3601, as amended, to refuse to sell, transfer, assign, rent, lease, sublease or finance housing accomodations, refuse to negotiate for the sale or rental of housing accommodations, or otherwise deny or make unavailable housing accomodations because of race, color, religion, sex, familial status as defined in Section 4112.01 of the Revised Code, ancestry, military status as defined in that section, disability as defined in that section, or national origin or to so discriminate in advertising the sale or rental of housing, in the financing of housing, or in the provision of real estate brokerage services. It is also illegal, for profit, to induce or attempt to induce a person to sell or rent a dwelling by representations regarding the entry into the neighborhood of a person or persons belonging to one of the protected classes. (Effective: 9/29/11)

We hope you find this information to be helpful to you as you begin your real estate transaction. When you are ready to enter into a transaction, you will be given an Agency Disclosure Statement that specifically identifies the role of the agents and brokerages. Please ask questions if there is anything you do not understand.

Because it is important that you have this information, Ohio law requires that we ask you to sign below to acknowledge receipt of this pamphlet. Your signature will not obligate you to work with our company if you do not choose to do so.

Name	(Please Print)	Name	(Please Print)

Signature	Date	Signature	Date

Revised: 9/2011

AGENCY DISCLOSURE STATEMENT

The real estate agent who is providing you with this form is required to do so by Ohio law. You will not be bound to pay the agent or the agent's brokerage by merely signing this form. Instead, the purpose of this form is to confirm that you have been advised of the role of the agent(s) in the transaction proposed below. (For purposes of this form, the term "seller" includes a landlord and the term "buyer" includes a tenant.)

Property Address: _____

Buyer(s): _____

Seller(s): _____

I. TRANSACTION INVOLVING TWO AGENTS IN TWO DIFFERENT BROKERAGES

The buyer will be represented by _____, and _____.
AGENT(S)   BROKERAGE

The seller will be represented by _____, and _____.
AGENT(S)   BROKERAGE

II. TRANSACTION INVOLVING TWO AGENTS IN THE SAME BROKERAGE

If two agents in the real estate brokerage _____
represent both the buyer and the seller, check the following relationship that will apply:

☐ Agent(s)_____ work(s) for the buyer and
Agent(s)_____ work(s) for the seller. Unless personally involved in the transaction, the principal broker and managers will be "dual agents," which is further explained on the back of this form. As dual agents they will maintain a neutral position in the transaction and they will protect all parties' confidential information.

☐ Every agent in the brokerage represents every "client" of the brokerage. Therefore, agents _____ and _____ will be working for both the buyer and seller as "dual agents." Dual agency is explained on the back of this form. As dual agents they will maintain a neutral position in the transaction and they will protect all parties' confidential information. Unless indicated below, neither the agent(s) nor the brokerage acting as a dual agent in this transaction has a personal, family or business relationship with either the buyer or seller. *If such a relationship does exist, explain:*
_____.

III. TRANSACTION INVOLVING ONLY ONE REAL ESTATE AGENT

Agent(s) _____ and real estate brokerage _____ will

☐ be "dual agents" representing both parties in this transaction in a neutral capacity. Dual agency is further explained on the back of this form. As dual agents they will maintain a neutral position in the transaction and they will protect all parties' confidential information. Unless indicated below, neither the agent(s) nor the brokerage acting as a dual agent in this transaction has a personal, family or business relationship with either the buyer or seller. *If such a relationship does exist, explain:* _____
_____.

☐ represent only the (*check one*) ☐ **seller** or ☐ **buyer** in this transaction as a client. The other party is not represented and agrees to represent his/her own best interest. Any information provided the agent may be disclosed to the agent's client.

CONSENT

I (we) consent to the above relationships as we enter into this real estate transaction. If there is a dual agency in this transaction, I (we) acknowledge reading the information regarding dual agency explained on the back of this form.

_____   _____
BUYER/TENANT   DATE   SELLER/LANDLORD   DATE

_____   _____
BUYER/TENANT   DATE   SELLER/LANDLORD   DATE

Page 1 of 2   Effective 02/10/19

DUAL AGENCY

Ohio law permits a real estate agent and brokerage to represent both the seller and buyer in a real estate transaction as long as this is disclosed to both parties and they both agree. This is known as dual agency. As a dual agent, a real estate agent and brokerage represent two clients whose interests are, or at times could be, different or adverse. For this reason, the dual agent(s) may not be able to advocate on behalf of the client to the same extent the agent may have if the agent represented only one client.

As a dual agent, the agent(s) and brokerage shall:
- Treat both clients honestly;
- Disclose latent (not readily observable) material defects to the purchaser, if known by the agent(s) or brokerage;
- Provide information regarding lenders, inspectors and other professionals, if requested;
- Provide market information available from a property listing service or public records, if requested;
- Prepare and present all offers and counteroffers at the direction of the parties;
- Assist both parties in completing the steps necessary to fulfill the terms of any contract, if requested.

As a dual agent, the agent(s) and brokerage shall not:
- Disclose information that is confidential, or that would have an adverse effect on one party's position in the transaction, unless such disclosure is authorized by the client or required by law;
- Advocate or negotiate on behalf of either the buyer or seller;
- Suggest or recommend specific terms, including price, or disclose the terms or price a buyer is willing to offer or that a seller is willing to accept;
- Engage in conduct that is contrary to the instructions of either party and may not act in a biased manner on behalf of one party.

Compensation: Unless agreed otherwise, the brokerage will be compensated per the agency agreement.

Management Level Licensees: Generally, the principal broker and managers in a brokerage also represent the interests of any buyer or seller represented by an agent affiliated with that brokerage. Therefore, if both buyer and seller are represented by agents in the same brokerage, the principal broker and manager are dual agents. There are two exceptions to this. The first is where the principal broker or manager is personally representing one of the parties. The second is where the principal broker or manager is selling or buying his own real estate. These exceptions only apply if there is another principal broker or manager to supervise the other agent involved in the transaction.

Responsibilities of the Parties: The duties of the agent and brokerage in a real estate transaction do not relieve the buyer and seller from the responsibility to protect their own interests. The buyer and seller are advised to carefully read all agreements to assure that they adequately express their understanding of the transaction. The agent and brokerage are qualified to advise on real estate matters. IF LEGAL OR TAX ADVICE IS DESIRED, YOU SHOULD CONSULT THE APPROPRIATE PROFESSIONAL.

Consent: By signing on the reverse side, you acknowledge that you have read and understand this form and are giving your voluntary, informed consent to the agency relationship disclosed. If you do not agree to the agent(s) and/or brokerage acting as a dual agent, you are not required to consent to this agreement and you may either request a separate agent in the brokerage to be appointed to represent your interests or you may terminate your agency relationship and obtain representation from another brokerage.

Any questions regarding the role or responsibilities of the brokerage or its agents should be directed to: attorney or to:
Ohio Department of Commerce
Division of Real Estate & Professional Licensing
77 S. High Street, 20th Floor
Columbus, OH 43215-6133
(614) 466-4100

The Agent's Duties to the Principal

The **relationship between an agent and a principal is described as a** *fiduciary relationship*. A **fiduciary relationship** is a relationship of trust and confidence, in which one party owes the other (or both parties owe each other) loyalty and a higher standard of good faith than they owe to third parties. A **fiduciary** is *someone in a position of trust, held by law to high standards of good faith and loyalty.* The fiduciary must act for the benefit of the principal, and not exploit his trust.

 Although we specifically refer to the fiduciary relationship a licensee owes to a principal with whom his broker has entered into a contract, the same fiduciary responsibilities also apply to you toward your broker. As a salesperson, you also have the duties of good faith and loyalty to your broker and must put the best interests of your broker above your own interests.

Fiduciary Responsibilities

The basic fiduciary duties are **(ACCOLD)**: **Accounting Confidentiality**, **Care**, **Obedience**, **Loyalty,** and **Disclosure**. These define the agency relationships.

Accounting

The duty of **accounting** recognizes that money received in an agency relationship belongs to the principal, not the agent. The relationship often calls for the payment of money to the broker to further, or aid, the purchase or sale of property. Since an agent or broker in any real estate transaction acts on behalf of the principal, the agent has the duty to account strictly to the principal for any amounts so received. Unless otherwise agreed to by the buyer and seller, money so received must be put, by the broker, into a separate, non-interest bearing trust account so as not to **commingle** the principal's funds with those of the brokerage. Failure to do so is a breach of the agency relationship, subject to the legal liabilities associated with this, and often loss of license.

Confidentiality

Although **confidentiality** has already been mentioned, it bears repeating. An agent has a duty to keep confidential any and all information that may harm the agent's client(s). The only instance in which such information can, and must, be relinquished is in the case of a court order. When a court orders the release of confidential information in the possession of a real estate licensee, it must be provided in accordance with the court's order, but only to the party or parties named in the order.

Care

Reasonable **care** and skill must be used by the agent at all times when acting on behalf of a client. The agent is seen and trusted as a professional and an expert. For example, an agent who fills out a purchase agreement form incorrectly or misunderstands a law may cause real problems for his client. If the client loses money as a result of the agent's incompetence or carelessness, the agent can be held liable for negligence. **Negligence** is *an unintentional breach of a legal duty. Negligence that causes harm is a tort* (see Chapter 1 for more information).

All real estate agents are held to a minimum standard of competence. An agent who claims to have expertise in a particular area (e.g., property management, appraisal) is held to an even higher standard.

Never take on tasks beyond your ability or claim expertise in areas where you have no special training or skills. When an agent does not feel qualified to give advice, he should recommend that the client seek the advice of a lawyer, accountant, appraiser, or other expert. In most cases, such a referral will protect the real estate agent from liability if problems arise.

Unauthorized Practice of Law. Many aspects of real estate transactions raise legal questions or have legal consequences. Real estate agents need to remember, and remind their clients, that they are not licensed to practice law. Agents should never give legal advice or perform any acts that require a lawyer's expertise.

In Ohio, a real estate licensee is permitted to complete standard listing forms, purchase agreement forms, and promissory note forms. A licensee should never draft an original agreement, or even add complicated clauses to the forms. That may be considered the unauthorized practice of law.

Case Example

A real estate salesperson used a standard form when the agent prepared the buyer's offer to purchase. In addition to filling in the blanks, though, she wrote in these conditions: "This contract is contingent upon Grantor acquiring Ed Lantz's property. Also upon above mentioned ground being rezoned to AR-1. If zoning is not obtained within 120 days of acceptance of this contract, then this contract is null and void unless extension is mutually agreed upon by Grantor and Grantee."

The sellers signed the contract form, but later refused to pay the broker's commission, and the broker sued to collect it. The court ruled that the salesperson's additions to the contract were an unauthorized practice of law. *Ralph R. Greer & Co. v. McGinnis*, 6 Ohio Misc. 264, 217 N.E.2d 890 (1965).

In *Ralph R. Greer & Co.*, the Franklin County Municipal Court in Columbus decided that, because of the salesperson's unauthorized practice of law, the broker was not entitled to a commission. But in a more recent case (*Foss v. Berlin*, 3 Ohio App. 3d 8, 443 N.E.2d 197 (1981)), the Tenth District Court of Appeals (Franklin County) reached a different conclusion. In *Foss*, the broker had engaged in the unauthorized practice of law by actually drafting a purchase contract from scratch. As a result, the broker was subject to disciplinary action by the Real Estate Commission. But the court ruled that the purchase contract was still valid and the broker was entitled to a commission.

Obedience

Obedience means the agent must follow the (legal) directions of the principal, obey the restrictions of the agency relationship, and not stray beyond the scope of his authority. Should the agent not follow this duty, the agent could be liable to the principal for losses sustained together with other damages.

Loyalty

The duty of **loyalty** holds that the agent must put the principal's interests above all others, including the agent's own. The principal often discloses confidential information to the agent. The agent must not reveal this information to others, nor take advantage of it for personal benefit.

Disclosure

An agent acting in good faith must make a complete **disclosure of all material information** and be sure not to keep anything from the principal. Any fact that may influence this decision should be brought to his attention. An agent should be especially careful to inform the principal of:

- True property value.
- All offers to purchase.
- Identity of the other party.
- Seller/buyer's financial condition.
- Any relationship between the other party and the broker/agent.
- Any commission splitting arrangements with other brokers.

Property Value. A real estate agent may be tempted to exaggerate the market value of the property, hoping to get an exclusive listing agreement. But that is a breach of the agent's duty to act in good faith. The agent is required to do his best to inform the seller of the property's true value. Anything about the condition of the title or the property itself that affects the value should be pointed out, as well. Sometimes inexpensive repairs can make a big difference in the selling price, and the agent should suggest these to the seller. This duty to inform the seller continues throughout the listing period. New information (e.g., new comparable sales) showing the original value was high or low must be passed on to the seller.

All Offers to Purchase. Even if an offer seems totally unacceptable, the agent must present it to the principal. The principal, not the agent, decides if an offer is acceptable. The agent must relay an offer to the principal even if its acceptance would mean a smaller commission, because the agent's first loyalty is to the principal.

Identity of Other Party and Its Financial Information. The seller's agent, for example, must tell the seller anything the agent knows about the buyer's financial position. That's especially important if the transaction would be contingent on the buyer's ability to obtain financing. The seller should be told any negative information about the buyer's assets, income, or credit rating, as well as the source of down payment (e.g., a loan from friends rather than savings), or the form of earnest money deposit.

Case Example

Mrs. Brillhart listed her home with Mr. Slusser. Mr. and Mrs. Roberts decided they wanted to buy the property, so Slusser prepared a purchase offer form for them. Brillhart accepted the offer and signed the form.

The offer stated that the Robertses had given Slusser a $1,500 deposit in cash. Actually, they had given him $200 in cash and a promissory note for $1,300.

A few weeks after accepting the offer, Brillhart changed her mind and told Mr. and Mrs. Roberts that she no longer wanted to sell her house. They bought a different house shortly afterwards.

Slusser sued Brillhart for his commission. The court ruled that if Slusser did not tell Brillhart about the promissory note before she signed the agreement, he violated his fiduciary duties. If so, he was not entitled to a commission. *Slusser v. Brillhart*, 107 Ohio App. 374, 159 N.E.2d 480 (1958).

Commission-Splitting Arrangements with Other Brokers. This goes to the heart of the agency relationship because clients have a right to know who is being paid by whom, since this goes to the issues of both accounting and loyalty. This requirement is part of the disclosures that must be made under Ohio's Agency Law.

Relationship Between the Other Party and the Broker. This also goes to the heart of the agency relationship and the issue of loyalty. Disclosing these relationships and potential conflicts of interest help prevent self-dealing and secret profits.

Self-Dealing and Secret Profits

A **secret profit** is a financial benefit that an agent takes from a transaction without authorization from the principal, nor informing the principal of the benefit retained. The most common examples involve **self-dealing**—when an agent buys the principal's property (or sells it to a relative, friend, etc.) without disclosing that fact to the principal, and then sells it again for a profit.

It is not automatically improper for an agent to buy property from the principal, but the agent must inform the seller that the agent is the buyer. The agent must also inform the seller if the buyer is the agent's relative or close friend, or a business entity in which the agent has an interest. This alerts the seller to a possible conflict of interest, so that the seller may choose to find another agent.

An agent has the duty to advise the seller of any steps that could be taken to increase the selling price of the property, such as repairs, cleanup work, or minor modifications. If the agent buys the property and carries out these improvements, the agent has used a superior knowledge of real estate for personal profit instead of the principal's. That is a breach of the duties of loyalty and good faith.

Case Example

A seller owned 12 acres of rural residential property in Oregon. He was forced to sell the property for financial reasons, so he listed it with a real estate broker for $15,000. His broker ran the following advertisement for the property:

> "**12 ACRES**—3 bedroom furnished home (needs a little work). Land is wooded and meadows. Good well. Pond. Great place for large family. $15,000. Terms."

Sometime later, the broker told the seller he could not move the property for $15,000 and asked if the seller would reduce the sale price. The seller mentioned $12,500, but the broker said he had other properties that were as good or better than the subject property that he could not even sell for $10,000.

The broker then had the seller sign a purchase agreement form in which he agreed to sell the property for $8,000. Three days later, the broker called the seller and told him that he had a buyer. When the seller arrived at the broker's office, the broker said he was the buyer. The broker said the seller had to sell him the property because he had already signed the purchase agreement form. The broker bought the property for $7,520 ($8,000, less a $480 commission).

The broker spent $1,277 on the property, cleaning it up and painting it. He then offered the property for sale in two separate parcels—one parcel with four acres and the house for $13,500, and the other eight-acre parcel of land for $6,500.

When he personally owned the property, the broker then ran the following newspaper advertisement:

> "**TAIN'T REAL FANCY**—But look what $13,500 buys—Good older (large) farm home with 4 acres fine land. The home has been recently redecorated and painted inside and out. There are 3 or 4 bedrooms. Large living room with full dining area. Big farm style kitchen with service porch. Large workshop, carport, and woodshed. Livestock shelter and poultry house. Spring-fed pond with year-round water. Magnificent place to raise your children. Keep ponies, calves, sheep, chickens, etc. School bus at front gate. Also thrown in free of charge is some furniture including a good heating stove; washer and dryer; dining room table and chairs; several dressers; davenport; farm and garden tractor. This charming big family farm home is located about 12 miles from town on a paved road. More land is available if needed. Owner will carry paper with modest down payment for responsible party."

Within three months, the broker sold both parcels for a total of $19,900. He made a profit of $12,380. The seller found out what had happened and sued the broker. The court ruled that the broker had breached his fiduciary duties to the seller and ordered the broker to pay damages. *Starkweather v. Shaffer*, 262 Or. 198, 497 P.2d 358 (1972).

Other Fiduciary Responsibilities to a Client

In addition to the basic fiduciary duties detailed previously, Ohio Agency Law states that a licensee should use his best efforts to further the client's interests by:

- Performing the terms of any written agency agreement.

- Following the lawful instructions of the client.

- Disclosing any material facts of the transaction that the licensee becomes aware of and are not considered confidential information.

- Advising the client to obtain expert advice related to material matters when necessary or appropriate.

- Keeping all confidential information confidential.

Specific Duties of a Licensee Representing a Buyer

In addition to the basic fiduciary duties and disclosure requirements discussed, Ohio's Agency Law requires a licensee representing a buyer in an agency relationship to promote the interests of the client by:

- Seeking a property at a price and with terms acceptable to the client.

- Presenting any purchase offer to the seller or seller's agent in a timely manner.

- Disclosing to the licensee representing the seller, or directly to the seller if unrepresented, that the buyer is being represented by him or her.

- Disclosing verbally during the first contact with an unrepresented seller if there is any intention of seeking compensation from the seller.

Purchase offers from the buyer must be presented to a seller, even if the property is subject to a pending contract of sale, lease, or letter of intent. The licensee is not obligated to seek additional purchase or lease possibilities if the buyer is party to a contract of sale, lease, or letter of intent, unless directed to do so by the client.

A licensee does not breach any duty or obligation to a buyer with whom an agency relationship exists by showing the same property to other buyers, or by acting as an agent or subagent for other buyers or sellers, but any dual agency must be disclosed.

Specific Duties of a Licensee Representing a Seller

In addition to the basic fiduciary duties and disclosure requirements discussed previously, Ohio's Agency Law requires a licensee representing a seller in an agency relationship to promote the interests of the client by:

- Seeking a purchase offer at a price and with terms acceptable to the client.

- Presenting any purchase offer to the client in a timely manner.

- Providing the seller with a copy of an Agency Disclosure form signed by the buyer prior to presenting any purchase offers to the seller.

Unless a seller waives the specific duty, purchase offers must be presented to the seller, even if the property is subject to a pending contract of sale, lease, or letter of intent; but the licensee is not obligated to seek additional purchase offers unless directed to do so by the client.

A licensee does not breach any duty or obligation to a seller with whom an agency relationship exists by showing alternative properties to a prospective buyer, or by acting as an agent or subagent for other sellers.

Assisting a Non-Client

A licensee may assist a party who is not the licensee's client in a real estate transaction by providing:

- Information regarding lenders, inspectors, attorneys, insurance agents, surveyors, draftspersons, architects, schools, shopping facilities, places of worship, and other similar information.

- Market information or other information obtained from a property listing service or public records.

A licensee who assists a customer in any of these permissible areas is not violating the agency relationship with his client, and provision of the services for that party neither forms nor implies any agency relationship with that party. **However, an agent must be diligent in this area to ensure that assistance is strictly confined to the permissible activities.**

Transactional Brokerage

Some states allow what may be called transactional brokerage or nonagency. This is an arrangement in which the licensee simply assists in the completion of the sale by performing the administrative tasks necessary to ensure that each step of the sale process is concluded in an accurate and timely manner. Such limited representation allows a licensee to act as a facilitator by working with the buyer and seller equally, but it does not obligate the licensee to the fiduciary duties owed to a client. This type of relationship is NOT recognized in Ohio. An Ohio licensee representing a client in a transaction may work with an unrepresented party as a customer, however.

Acts That Require a Client's Consent

Ohio's **Agency Law does not** permit licensees representing buyers or sellers to do either of the following without the knowledge and consent of their clients:

- Extend an offer of subagency to other licensees

- Offer compensation to, or accept compensation from, a broker representing another party in a transaction

Often, both of these issues are addressed in listing agreements. Your broker can provide additional guidance, as necessary, to ensure compliance with consent issues.

Waiver of Duties—"Limited Service Agents"

Ohio's Agency Law separates fiduciary duties into two categories. The first category of fiduciary duties must be performed by a real estate licensee for each client and may **not** be waived, even with the client's approval. This first group of responsibilities an agent owes to the principal and other fiduciary responsibilities was discussed earlier in this chapter. The second category includes those duties that, at the client's discretion and with the client's written agreement, may be waived.

 The Waiver of Duties Statement is available at the Division's website: www.com.state. oh.us/real.

	WAIVER OF DUTIES STATEMENT
Ohio Department of Commerce Division of Real Estate & Professional Licensing	Pursuant to ORC 4735.621
	To Be Used when Certain Duties are Waived by the Client

REQUIRED DUTIES:

After entering into an agency relationship, a real estate licensee (meaning a licensed broker or salesperson) is considered a "fiduciary" of the client. This means the licensee will use his or her best efforts to further the interests of the client. Under Ohio law, these fiduciary duties <u>may not</u> be waived. The client's real estate licensee must:

- Exercise reasonable skill and care in representing the client and carrying out the responsibilities of the agency relationship;
- Perform the terms of any written agency agreement;
- Follow any lawful instructions of the client;
- Be loyal to the interest of the client;
- Comply with all requirements of Ohio real estate licensing laws and other applicable statutes, rules, and regulations, including state and federal fair housing laws;
- Disclose any material facts of the transaction of which the licensee is or should be aware;
- Advise the client to obtain expert advice related to material matters when necessary or appropriate;
- Account in a timely manner for all moneys and property received in which the client has or may have an interest; and
- Keep all confidential information confidential, unless permitted to disclose the information pursuant to ORC 4735.74(B). This includes the duty to not disclose confidential information to any licensee who is not an agent of the client.

DUTIES THAT <u>MAY</u> BE WAIVED:

Under Ohio law, a real estate licensee is required to perform additional duties for his or her client <u>unless these duties are waived by the client</u>. By signing below, the client agrees that the real estate licensee will <u>not</u> perform the duties initialed (only initial the duties waived)

Sellers may waive:	**Initial If Waived:**
• Seeking a purchase offer at a price and with terms acceptable to the seller	_____ _____
• Accepting delivery of and presenting any purchase offer to the seller in a timely manner, even if the property is subject to a contract of sale, lease, or letter of intent to lease	_____ _____
• Answering the seller's questions and providing information to the seller regarding any offers or counteroffers	_____
• Assisting the seller in developing, communicating, and presenting offers or counteroffers	_____
• Answering the seller's questions regarding the steps the seller must take to fulfill the terms of any contract (within the scope of knowledge required for real estate licensure)	_____
Buyers may waive:	
• Seeking a property at a price and with purchase or lease terms acceptable to the buyer	_____
• Presenting any offer to purchase or lease to the seller or the seller's agent in a timely manner and accepting delivery of and presenting any counteroffers to the buyer	_____
• Answering the buyer's questions and providing information to the buyer regarding any offers or counteroffers	_____
• Assisting the buyer in developing, communicating, and presenting offers or counteroffers	_____
• Answering the buyer's questions regarding the steps the buyer must take to fulfill the terms of any contract (within the scope of knowledge required for real estate licensure)	_____

Agreement to Waive

By signing below, I agree that the real estate licensee who represents me will not perform the duties that are initialed above. I also understand that in any proposed real estate transaction, no other real estate licensee is required to perform the waived duties unless I subsequently hire them to do so, and realize that I may need to hire other professionals such as an attorney.

_____   _____   _____   _____
Seller or Buyer   Date   Real Estate Broker or Salesperson   Date

When a seller or buyer waives certain duties that would normally be owed to them by an agent, that agent may be termed a "**limited service agent**."

Duties that may be waived by a **seller** include:

- Seeking a purchase offer at a price and with terms acceptable to the seller
- Accepting delivery of any purchase offer and presenting it to the seller in a timely manner, even if the property is subject to a contract of sale, lease, or letter of intent to lease
- Answering the seller's questions and providing information to the seller regarding any offers or counteroffers
- Assisting the seller in developing, communicating, and presenting offers or counteroffers
- Answering the seller's questions regarding the steps the seller must take to fulfill the terms of any contract (within the scope of knowledge required for real estate licensure)

Duties that may be waived by a **buyer** include:

- Seeking a property at a price and with purchase or lease terms acceptable to the buyer
- Presenting any offer to purchase or lease to the seller or the seller's agent in a timely manner and accepting delivery of presenting any counteroffers to the buyer
- Answering the buyer's questions and providing information to the buyer regarding any offers or counteroffers
- Assisting the buyer in developing, communicating, and presenting offers or counteroffers
- Answering the buyer's questions regarding the steps the buyer must take to fulfill the terms of any contract (within the scope of knowledge required for real estate licensure)

Authority to Negotiate

When a buyer or seller enters into an exclusive agency agreement with a broker but waives any of the responsibilities listed above, it may require an agent representing the other principal to deal directly with the other broker's client. Prior to 2006 changes in Agency Law allowing duties to be waived, doing so would have automatically constituted "crossing the sign," (ignoring the "For Sale" sign in the front yard and the fact that a seller is already under an exclusive listing with a different broker and trying to talk directly to the seller) resulting in a license law violation.

A broker who has the exclusive authority to represent a client under a written exclusive agency agreement, exclusive right to sell agreement, or exclusive purchaser agency agreement (discussed in the next chapter) may authorize other licensees to negotiate directly with that client. The authorization shall be in writing and the broker shall comply with the requirements of section 4735.621 of the Revised Code.

Under Ohio law, the definition of "negotiate" includes:

- Delivering or communicating an offer, counteroffer, or proposal
- Discussing or reviewing the terms of any offer, counteroffer, or proposal
- Facilitating communication regarding an offer, counteroffer, or proposal and preparing any response as directed

Under the revised law, a broker who has an exclusive right to represent a client may give written authorization to other licensees to negotiate directly with that client.

For Example

Broker A has an exclusive right to sell agreement with S. S waives the duty for Broker A to answer his questions and provide information to him regarding any offers or counteroffers. When Broker B delivers an offer to purchase directly to Smith, per the MLS, Broker B can request and receive written authority to negotiate with S from Broker A. Under the authority to negotiate, Broker B is not violating license law nor is she creating or implying an agency relationship with S.

Dual Agency

Traditionally, **dual agency** is *when a licensee represents both buyer and seller in a transaction.* Ohio's Agency Law has expanded this traditional definition, making it clear that a licensee does not breach any duty to the clients by acting as a dual agent in a transaction as long as proper dual agency disclosure has been made and all parties consent before entering into any form of dual agency.

As we have discussed, real estate licensees have certain fiduciary obligations to their clients. This entails:

- Putting the client's interests before those of all others.
- Maintaining confidentiality.
- Giving the client all information necessary to protect his interests.

A **dual agent** *owes fiduciary duties to both buyer and seller.* Thus, an agent must be careful not to disclose any confidential information to the other party, especially with regard to price, so as to balance the ability to represent opposing parties with an understanding of the ethical considerations involved. Furthermore, when an agent has an ongoing relationship with one party (friend, relative, or established client) in a dual agency relationship, that ongoing relationship must be disclosed in writing and both the buyer and seller must consent to it.

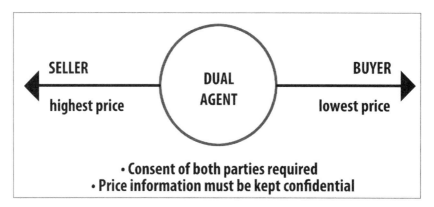

Critics of dual agency point out that there is an inherent conflict of interest in the dual agency arrangement. They argue it is not possible to maintain all fiduciary obligations to two separate clients with opposing interests because a seller is looking for the highest price, while the buyer is looking for the lowest price. Although it is difficult, if not impossible, to adequately represent these two opposing interests, Ohio's Agency Law has addressed some of these issues.

Dual Agency under Ohio's Agency Law

A dual agency relationship may be entered into by a brokerage firm in Ohio only after the brokerage has **established a procedure to safeguard confidential information** during the transaction, and provided that the licensee for each client in the dual agency relationship fulfills the licensee's duties exclusively to that client.

Ohio's Agency Law allows these three forms:

1. One licensee may represent both the buyer and seller (or lessor and lessee) as clients in the same real estate transaction

2. Two licensees affiliated with the same brokerage, one representing the buyer or lessor while the other represents the seller or lessee, where the broker and management level licensees are dual agents (unless a management level licensee falls under the exemption below)

3. Two licensees affiliated with the same brokerage, one has the buyer or lessor as a client and the other has the seller or lessee as a client, where every licensee in the brokerage represents every client, therefore, both agents are dual agents

In other words, depending on the brokerage's policy on agency relationships, two different dual agency relationships can exist in an in-company (split agency) transaction. Two salesperson-level licensees in the same brokerage can represent two different parties in the same transaction, and either their broker (and other management level licensees, depending on the situation) is considered a dual agent **or** their brokerage policy states that every licensee in the brokerage will function as a dual agent. A licensee assigned by a broker to represent a buyer or seller in a transaction, usually in an in-company dual agency situation, is referred to as a **designated agent**.

A dual agency situation can be entered into only if both the seller and buyer have full knowledge of the dual representation and consent to it in writing. If the buyer and seller are represented in an in-company (split agency) transaction by two different agents who are non-management level licensees affiliated with the same brokerage, the appropriate statement in Section II of the original Agency Disclosure form must be completed after it is determined that a dual agency situation exists. However, if both buyer and seller are represented by the **same** agent in a transaction, the first statement in Section III of the Agency Disclosure form must be completed.

 Caution: Ohio law forbids any licensee from acting as a dual agent when they are dealing their own real estate.

Dual Agency Disclosures

In addition to providing the dual agency disclosure information, which is found on the reverse side of the Agency Disclosure Statement and details the exact implications of the dual agency relationship and options available to the client, the licensee must first disclose to both the buyer and seller all relevant information necessary to enable each party to make an informed decision as to whether to consent to the dual agency relationship. If after consent is obtained there is a material change in the information disclosed to the buyer and seller, the licensee must disclose the change of information and give each party a chance to revoke their consent.

The brokerage must make the dual agency disclosure to both buyer and seller **as soon as practical** after it is determined that a dual agency may exist. Usually, this will occur when the buyer asks the licensee to write an offer on a property listed by the licensee's brokerage. The seller must be informed of, and consent to, the dual agency prior to receipt of the offer. The parties to the transaction must sign and date the Agency Disclosure Statement indicating dual agency in a timely manner, but the form must be signed and dated prior to the signing of any offers.

Duties of the Brokerage and Management Level Licensees

The brokerage and management level licensees in a dual agency situation must objectively supervise the affiliated licensees in the fulfillment of their duties and obligations to their respective clients, refrain from advocating or negotiating on behalf of either the buyer or seller, and from disclosing confidential information to other agents, clients, or parties. This includes a duty to see that confidential information is not used by anyone to benefit one party or client over the other.

 Remember: A management level licensee is *not* a dual agent if the brokerage has more than one management level licensee and the management level licensee either personally represents the seller or buyer, or he is the buyer or seller.

Duties of Two Non-Management Level Licensees

When two non-management level licensees affiliated with the same brokerage represent clients in the same transaction, each licensee must serve as the agent of only the party in the transaction that the licensee agreed to represent, and must fulfill duties owed to the respective client as agreed in the agency agreement and set forth in the Agency Law. This agency relationship is known as **split agency**.

A licensee who obtains confidential information concerning another client of the brokerage in a dual agency relationship must not, under any circumstances, disclose that information to, or use that information for the benefit of, the licensee's client. If a brokerage determines that confidential information of one client in a split agency relationship has become known to any licensee who is representing the other client in the split agency, the brokerage must notify both clients of the situation. Such notification must include an offer of resignation of the agency relationship. If a client chooses to accept the resignation option, the brokerage may not receive compensation from that client.

Contemporaneous Offers

A licensee who represents **multiple buyers** interested in the same property simultaneously does not breach a duty of confidentiality or other obligation to a client by showing properties in which the client is interested to other prospective buyers or tenants. A licensee can legally prepare and present **contemporaneous offers**, which are *any offers to purchase or lease on behalf of two or more clients represented by the same licensee for the same property that the licensee knows, has known, or has reason to know will be taken under consideration by the owner or owner's authorized representative during the same period of time.* A licensee cannot, however, disclose the names of the other interested buyer or the terms of any offer.

Since the Canon of Ethics provides that a licensee should not enter into an agency relationship with a party whose interests are in conflict with those of the licensee or another client of the licensee, it may seem that presenting contemporaneous offers would present a conflict of interest. If the licensee makes the required disclosure of contemporaneous offers, however, clients have the opportunity to request referral to another licensee if so desired. This disclosure should occur **prior to preparing a contemporaneous offer**. The disclosure of contemporaneous offers should be in writing unless written disclosure cannot be delivered in a timely manner, in which case the licensee must provide the disclosure verbally.

Note: This is **not** a dual agency situation unless the same licensee (or licensee's brokerage) represents both buyer and seller.

The Agent's Duties To Third Parties

In addition to having a duty to the principal, an agent owes third parties a duty of good faith and fair dealing. Although, an agent is not a fiduciary in relation to a third party, the agent is not required to advance the third party's interests. In fact, the agent's duty of loyalty to the principal will often prohibit that.

In a real estate transaction, fair dealing basically means the seller's agent must:

- Disclose certain information to prospective buyers.
- Avoid misrepresentation.

Disclosure to the Buyer

Caveat emptor means *"Let the buyer beware"* in Latin. This rule says that a buyer is expected to examine property carefully, instead of relying on the seller to point out problems. That warning applies to real estate transactions in Ohio. Buyers have to look after themselves, instead of relying on the seller or the seller's agent. This is another reason why buyer brokerage is becoming more and more popular: Buyers desire an agent to look after their interests during the real estate transaction.

In Ohio, a buyer is always supposed to inspect the property before agreeing to buy it. Although the seller and the seller's agent must tell the buyer about any **latent defects** (defects that are not visible or apparent), the seller and the seller's agent generally are not required to tell the buyer about **patent defects** (defects that are visible and would be discovered in a reasonably thorough inspection). This is true even if the buyer never actually inspected the property, as long as the buyer was given the opportunity to do so. The rule also applies if the buyer inspects the property and sees the defect but does not recognize that it is a problem.

Case Example

Mr. and Mrs. Binns hired contractors to build a house for them. When the structure was almost finished and earth was backfilled around the foundation, the foundation gave way in one place, causing the basement wall to bow in. The contractors installed steel beams to support the wall, but the bowing was still visible.

Six years later, the Binnses put their house up for sale. They told the listing broker about the problem with the basement wall, but he did not mention it in the information sent to the multiple listing service.

Mr. and Mrs. Layman were interested in buying the Binns' property. The Laymans inspected the house, including the basement. Although Mr. Binns was home at the time, he did not accompany the Laymans into the basement, and did not tell them about the bowed wall. Mr. Layman noticed the steel beams, but he did not ask Mr. Binns about them because he assumed that they were a normal part of the structure.

The Laymans bought the house. They did not discover there was anything wrong with the wall until they tried to resell the property a few years later. A real estate agent pointed out the defective wall to them, and the Laymans learned it would cost anywhere from $32,000 to $49,000 to fix.

The Laymans sued the Binnses for failing to disclose the wall problem. The court ruled the Binnses did not have a duty to disclose the problem since it was unconcealed and open to observation. Mr. Binns had not prevented the Laymans from inspecting the property; the Laymans' inspection simply had not been thorough enough. Thus, the Binnses were not required to pay the Laymans' damages. *Layman v. Binns*, 35 Ohio St. 3d 176, 519 N.E.2d 642 (1988).

Remember, though, *the seller and seller's agent are required to tell the buyer about any latent defects they are aware of.* Ohio law says a licensee must disclose any material facts pertaining to the physical condition of the property that the buyer would not discover by a reasonably thorough and diligent inspection, including material defects in the property, environmental contamination, and information that any statute or rule requires be disclosed. Also, knowledge of facts is inferred if a licensee acts with reckless disregard for the truth.

Case Example

Ms. Maylone listed her house with Mr. McSwegin. He showed the house to the Mileses. They decided to buy it and applied for a mortgage.

According to its standard practice, the lender had the property inspected for termites. The inspector discovered an infestation. Maylone and McSwegin were informed of the problem, but the Mileses were not. McSwegin told Maylone she would have to treat the problem. The extermination cost her $460.

At closing, the Mileses were given settlement papers that stated a termite inspection had been performed. But the papers did not mention the infestation or the extermination, and no one told the Mileses about it.

The Mileses found evidence of the termites shortly after moving into the house. They learned the termites had caused severe structural damage, and repairs would cost almost $6,000. They sued McSwegin and Maylone.

The case against Maylone was dismissed by the buyer, but McSwegin was held liable. The court ruled that McSwegin had a duty to disclose the termite problem to the Mileses. It was a latent defect; one that prospective buyers would not discover in a reasonably thorough inspection of the property. *Miles v. McSwegin*, 58 Ohio St. 2d 97, 388 N.E.2d 1367 (1979).

Ohio law says a licensee must disclose any material facts of which the licensee has actual knowledge pertaining to the physical condition of the property that the buyer would not discover by a reasonably thorough and diligent inspection, including material defects in the property, environmental contamination, and information that any statute or rule requires be disclosed. Also, knowledge of facts is inferred if a licensee acts with reckless disregard for the truth.

Lead paint disclosure laws also require the agent and/or seller to disclose any known lead paint hazards. For houses built before 1978, the buyer must be given a lead paint booklet and a chance to perform a lead paint inspection. In addition to the lead paint notification language included in many standard board real estate contracts, many brokers and licensees also use Lead-Based Paint Disclosure forms as a way to prove compliance with the lead paint disclosure requirements of HUD and the EPA, since the penalty for failure to disclose lead hazards is a fine of up to $16,380 and up to one year in jail, plus treble damages.

Disclosure by the Seller

For residential real estate purchase contracts involving one- to four-dwelling units, Ohio Real Estate Law (ORC § 5302.30) requires the delivery of a Residential Property Disclosure Form to the buyer, prior to an offer to purchase the property by the buyer. While there are thirteen exceptions to this requirement, they are not important to the purposes of this text. However, it is important that real estate agents are familiar with the official disclosure form, which was created by the Ohio Department of Commerce.

The form allows for a detailed description of the property's condition (water, sewer, roof, etc.) and is signed by both the seller and the buyer. While the owner's statements are to be based only on his "actual knowledge" of the property's condition, the form also has a catchall space for "known material defects" (non-observable physical conditions or problems). Updates to the form in 2004 added items such as:

- Whether the property has been inspected for mold
- If there has been any smoke damage to the property
- Whether the property is located in a flood plain
- Disclosure of problems and defects with mechanical systems, water quality and intrusion, and nonconforming uses of the property

Lead-Based Paint Disclosure
Housing Sales

Property Address _____

LEAD WARNING STATEMENT

Every buyer of any interest in residential real property on which a residential dwelling unit was built prior to 1978 is notified that such property may present exposure to lead from lead-based paint that may place young children at risk of developing lead poisoning. Lead poisoning in young children may produce permanent neurological damage, including learning disabilities, reduced intelligence quotient, behavioral problems, and impaired memory. Lead poisoning also poses a particular risk to pregnant women. The seller of any interest in residential real property is required to provide the buyer with any information on lead-based paint hazards from risk assessments or inspections in the seller's possession and notify the buyer of any known lead-based paint hazards. A risk assessment or inspection for possible lead-based paint hazards is recommended prior to purchase.

Intact lead-based paint that is in good condition is not necessarily a hazard. See the EPA pamphlet **"Protect Your Family From Lead in Your Home"** *for more information.*

Seller's Disclosure (Please initial where indicated):

[ ]   **(a) Presence of lead-based paint and/or lead-based paint hazards** (check one):

[ ] Known lead-based paint and/or lead-based paint hazards are present in the housing. (explain)

[_____]

[ ] Seller has no knowledge of lead-based paint and/or lead-based paint hazards in the housing.

[ ]   **(b) Records and reports available to the seller** (check one):

[ ] Seller has provided the buyer with all available records and reports pertaining to lead-based paint and/or lead-based paint hazards in the housing (list documents below).

_____

[ ] Seller has no reports or records pertaining to lead-based paint and/or lead-based paint hazards in the housing.

Buyer's Acknowledgment (Please initial where indicated):

[ ]   **(c) Buyer has received copies of all information listed in (b) above.**

[ ]   **(d) Buyer has received the pamphlet** *Protect Your Family from Lead in Your Home.*

[ ]   **(e) Buyer has** (check one below):

[ ] Received a 10-day opportunity (or mutually agreed upon period) to conduct a risk assessment or inspection for the presence of lead-based paint and/or lead-based paint hazards; or

[ ] Waived the opportunity to conduct a risk assessment or inspection for the presence of lead-based paint and/or lead-based paint hazards.

Agent's Acknowledgment (Please initial where indicated):

[ ]   **(f) Agent has informed the seller of the seller's obligations under 42 U.S.C. 4852d and is aware of his/her responsibility to ensure compliance.**

Certification of Accuracy: The following parties have reviewed the information above and certify, to the best of their knowledge, that the information provided by the signatory is true and accurate.

By:

Seller	*Date*	*Buyer*	*Date*
Seller	*Date*	*Buyer*	*Date*
Agent	*Date*	*Agent*	*Date*

STATE OF OHIO

DEPARTMENT OF COMMERCE

<u>2013</u>

RESIDENTIAL PROPERTY DISCLOSURE FORM

Purpose of Disclosure Form: This is a statement of certain conditions and information concerning the property actually known by the owner. An owner may or may not have lived at the property and unless the potential purchaser is informed in writing, the owner has no more information about the property than could be obtained by a careful inspection of the property by a potential purchaser. Unless the potential purchaser is otherwise informed, the owner has not conducted any inspection of generally inaccessible areas of the property. This form is required by Ohio Revised Code Section 5302.30.

THIS FORM IS NOT A WARRANTY OF ANY KIND BY THE OWNER OR BY ANY AGENT OR SUBAGENT REPRESENTING THE OWNER. THIS FORM IS NOT A SUBSTITUTE FOR ANY INSPECTIONS. **POTENTIAL PURCHASERS ARE ENCOURAGED TO OBTAIN THEIR OWN PROFESSIONAL INSPECTION(S).**

Owner's Statement: The statements contained in this form are made by the owner and are not the statements of the owner's agent or subagent. The statements contained in this form are provided by the owner only to potential purchasers in a transfer made by the owner. The statements are not for purchasers in any subsequent transfers. The information contained in this disclosure form does not limit the obligation of the owner to disclose an item of information that is required by any other statute or law to be disclosed in the transfer of residential real estate.

OWNER INSTRUCTIONS

Instructions to Owner: (1) Answer ALL questions. (2) Report known conditions affecting the property. (3) Attach additional pages with your signature if additional space is needed. (4) Complete this form yourself. (5) If some items do not apply to your property, write NA (not applicable). If the item to be disclosed is not within your actual knowledge, indicate Unknown.

2013

**STATE OF OHIO DEPARTMENT
OF COMMERCE**

RESIDENTIAL PROPERTY DISCLOSURE FORM

Pursuant to section 5302.30 of the Revised Code and rule <u>1301:5-6-10</u> of the Administrative Code.

TO BE COMPLETED BY OWNER (*Please Print*)

Property Address: _____

Owners Name(s): _____

Date: _____, 20_____

Owner ☐ is ☐ is not occupying the property. If owner is occupying the property, since what date: _____

If owner is not occupying the property, since what date: _____

THE FOLLOWING STATEMENTS OF THE OWNER ARE BASED ON OWNER'S ACTUAL KNOWLEDGE

A) WATER SUPPLY: The source of water supply to the property is (check appropriate boxes):

☐ Public Water Service ☐ Holding Tank ☐ Unknown
☐ Private Water Service ☐ Cistern ☐ Other_____
☐ Private Well ☐ Spring _____
☐ Shared Well ☐ Pond _____

Do you know of any current leaks, backups or other material problems with the water supply system or quality of the water? ☐ Yes
No ☐ If "Yes", please describe and indicate any repairs completed (but not longer than the past 5 years): _____

Is the quantity of water sufficient for your household use? (NOTE: water usage will vary from household to household) ☐ Yes ☐ No

B) SEWER SYSTEM: The nature of the sanitary sewer system servicing the property is (check appropriate boxes):

☐ Public Sewer ☐ Private Sewer ☐ Septic Tank
☐ Leach Field ☐ Aeration Tank ☐ Filtration Bed
☐ Unknown ☐ Other_____

If not a public or private sewer, date of last inspection: _____ Inspected By:_____

Do you know of **any previous or current** leaks, backups or other material problems with the sewer system servicing the property?
Yes ☐ No ☐ If "Yes", please describe and indicate any repairs completed (but not longer than the past 5 years):_____
_____

Information on the operation and maintenance of the type of sewage system serving the property is available from the department of health or the board of health of the health district in which the property is located.

C) ROOF: Do you know of **any previous or current** leaks or other material problems with the roof or rain gutters? ☐ Yes ☐ No
If "Yes", please describe and indicate any repairs completed (but not longer than the past 5 years):_____
_____

D) WATER INTRUSION: Do you know of **any previous or current** water leakage, water accumulation, excess moisture or other defects to the property, including but not limited to any area below grade, basement or crawl space? ☐ Yes ☐ No
If "Yes", please describe and indicate any repairs completed: _____
_____

Owner's Initials _____ Date _____   Purchaser's Initials _____ Date _____
Owner's Initials _____ Date _____   Purchaser's Initials _____ Date _____

(Page 2 of 5)

Property Address_____

Do you know of any water or moisture related damage to floors, walls or ceilings as a result of flooding; moisture seepage; moisture condensation; ice damming; sewer overflow/backup; or leaking pipes, plumbing fixtures, or appliances? ☐Yes ☐No
If "Yes", please describe and indicate any repairs completed: _____
_____

Have you ever had the property inspected for mold by a qualified inspector? ☐Yes ☐No
If "Yes", please describe and indicate whether you have an inspection report and any remediation undertaken: _____
_____

Purchaser is advised that every home contains mold. Some people are more sensitive to mold than others. If concerned about this issue, purchaser is encouraged to have a mold inspection done by a qualified inspector.

E) STRUCTURAL COMPONENTS (FOUNDATION, BASEMENT/CRAWL SPACE, FLOORS, INTERIOR AND EXTERIOR WALLS): Do you know of **any previous or current** movement, shifting, deterioration, material cracks/settling (other than visible minor cracks or blemishes) or other material problems with the foundation, basement/crawl space, floors, or interior/exterior walls?
☐Yes ☐No   If "Yes", please describe and indicate any repairs, alterations or modifications to control the cause or effect of any problem identified (but not longer than the past 5 years):_____
_____

Do you know of **any previous or current** fire or smoke damage to the property? ☐Yes ☐No
If "Yes", please describe and indicate any repairs completed: _____
_____

F) WOOD DESTROYING INSECTS/TERMITES: Do you know of **any previous/current** presence of any wood destroying insects/termites in or on the property or any existing damage to the property caused by wood destroying insects/termites? ☐Yes ☐No
If "Yes", please describe and indicate any inspection or treatment (but not longer than the past 5 years):_____
_____

G) MECHANICAL SYSTEMS: Do you know of **any previous or current** problems or defects with the following existing mechanical systems? If your property does not have the mechanical system, mark N/A (Not Applicable).

	YES	NO	N/A			YES	NO	N/A
1) Electrical	☐	☐	☐	8) Water softener		☐	☐	☐
2) Plumbing (pipes)	☐	☐	☐	a. Is water softener leased?		☐	☐	☐
3) Central heating	☐	☐	☐	9) Security System		☐	☐	☐
4) Central Air conditioning	☐	☐	☐	a. Is security system leased?		☐	☐	☐
5) Sump pump	☐	☐	☐	10) Central vacuum		☐	☐	☐
6) Fireplace/chimney	☐	☐	☐	11) Built in appliances		☐	☐	☐
7) Lawn sprinkler	☐	☐	☐	12) Other mechanical systems		☐	☐	☐

If the answer to any of the above questions is "Yes", please describe and indicate any repairs to the mechanical system (but not longer than the past 5 years): _____
_____

H) PRESENCE OF HAZARDOUS MATERIALS: Do you know of the **previous or current** presence of any of the below identified hazardous materials on the property?

	Yes	No	Unknown
1) Lead-Based Paint	☐	☐	☐
2) Asbestos	☐	☐	☐
3) Urea-Formaldehyde Foam Insulation	☐	☐	☐
4) Radon Gas	☐	☐	☐
a. If "Yes", indicate level of gas if known _____			
5) Other toxic or hazardous substances	☐	☐	☐

If the answer to any of the above questions is "Yes", please describe and indicate any repairs, remediation or mitigation to the property: _____
_____

Owner's Initials _____ Date _____   Purchaser's Initials _____ Date _____
Owner's Initials _____ Date _____   Purchaser's Initials _____ Date _____

Property Address_____

I) UNDERGROUND STORAGE TANKS/WELLS: Do you know of any underground storage tanks (existing or removed), oil or natural gas wells (plugged or unplugged), or abandoned water wells on the property? ☐ Yes ☐ No
If "Yes", please describe: _____
_____

Do you know of any oil, gas, or other mineral right leases on the property? ☐ Yes ☐ No

Purchaser should exercise whatever due diligence purchaser deems necessary with respect to oil, gas, and other mineral rights. Information may be obtained from records contained within the recorder's office in the county where the property is located.

J) FLOOD PLAIN/LAKE ERIE COASTAL EROSION AREA:

	Yes	No	Unknown
Is the property located in a designated flood plain?	☐	☐	☐
Is the property or any portion of the property included in a Lake Erie Coastal Erosion Area?	☐	☐	☐

K) DRAINAGE/EROSION: Do you know of **any previous or current** flooding, drainage, settling or grading or erosion problems affecting the property? ☐ Yes ☐ No
If "Yes", please describe and indicate any repairs, modifications or alterations to the property or other attempts to control any problems (but not longer than the past 5 years):_____
_____

L) ZONING/CODE VIOLATIONS/ASSESSMENTS/HOMEOWNERS' ASSOCIATION: Do you know of any violations of building or housing codes, zoning ordinances affecting the property or any nonconforming uses of the property? ☐ Yes ☐ No
If "Yes", please describe: _____

Is the structure on the property designated by any governmental authority as a historic building or as being located in an historic district? (NOTE: such designation may limit changes or improvements that may be made to the property). ☐ Yes ☐ No
If "Yes", please describe: _____
_____

Do you know of **any recent or proposed** assessments, fees or abatements, which could affect the property? ☐ Yes ☐ No
If "Yes", please describe: _____
_____

List any assessments paid in full (date/amount)_____
List any current assessments: _____ monthly fee _____ Length of payment (years _____ months _____)

Do you know of any recent or proposed rules or regulations of, or the payment of any fees or charges associated with this property, including but not limited to a Community Association, SID, CID, LID, etc. ☐ Yes ☐ No
If "Yes", please describe (amount)_____
_____

M) BOUNDARY LINES/ENCROACHMENTS/SHARED DRIVEWAY/PARTY WALLS: Do you know of any of the following conditions affecting the property?

	Yes	No		Yes	No
1) Boundary Agreement	☐	☐	4) Shared Driveway	☐	☐
2) Boundary Dispute	☐	☐	5) Party Walls	☐	☐
3) Recent Boundary Change	☐	☐	6) Encroachments From or on Adjacent Property	☐	☐

If the answer to any of the above questions is "Yes", please describe: _____
_____

N) OTHER KNOWN MATERIAL DEFECTS: The following are other known material defects in or on the property:
_____
_____

For purposes of this section, material defects would include any non-observable physical condition existing on the property that could be dangerous to anyone occupying the property or any non-observable physical condition that could inhibit a person's use of the property.

Owner's Initials _____ Date _____   Purchaser's Initials _____ Date _____
Owner's Initials _____ Date _____   Purchaser's Initials _____ Date _____

Property Address_____

CERTIFICATION OF OWNER

Owner certifies that the statements contained in this form are made in good faith and based on his/her actual knowledge as of the date signed by the Owner. Owner is advised that the information contained in this disclosure form does not limit the obligation of the owner to disclose an item of information that is required by any other statute or law or that may exist to preclude fraud, either by misrepresentation, concealment or nondisclosure in a transaction involving the transfer of residential real estate.

OWNER: _____   DATE: _____

OWNER: _____   DATE: _____

RECEIPT AND ACKNOWLEDGEMENT OF POTENTIAL PURCHASERS

Potential purchasers are advised that the owner has no obligation to update this form but may do so according to Revised Code Section 5302.30(G). Pursuant to Ohio Revised Code Section 5302.30(K), if this form is not provided to you prior to the time you enter into a purchase contract for the property, you may rescind the purchase contract by delivering a signed and dated document of rescission to Owner or Owner's agent, provided the document of rescission is delivered prior to all three of the following dates: 1) the date of closing; 2) 30 days after the Owner accepted your offer; and 3) within 3 business days following your receipt or your agent's receipt of this form or an amendment of this form.

Owner makes no representations with respect to any offsite conditions. Purchaser should exercise whatever due diligence purchaser deems necessary with respect to offsite issues that may affect purchaser's decision to purchase the property.

Purchaser should exercise whatever due diligence purchaser deems necessary with respect to Ohio's Sex Offender Registration and Notification Law (commonly referred to as "Megan's Law"). This law requires the local Sheriff to provide written notice to neighbors if a sex offender resides or intends to reside in the area. The notice provided by the Sheriff is a public record and is open to inspection under Ohio's Public Records Law. If concerned about this issue, purchaser assumes responsibility to obtain information from the Sheriff's office regarding the notices they have provided pursuant to Megan's Law.

Purchaser should exercise whatever due diligence purchaser deems necessary with respect to abandoned underground mines. If concerned about this issue, purchaser assumes responsibility to obtain information from the Ohio Department of Natural Resources. The Department maintains an online map of known abandoned underground mines on their website at www.dnr.state.oh.us.

I/WE ACKNOWLEDGE RECEIPT OF A COPY OF THIS DISCLOSURE FORM AND UNDERSTAND THAT THE STATEMENTS ARE MADE BASED ON THE OWNERS ACTUAL KNOWLEDGE AS OF THE DATE SIGNED BY THE OWNER.

My/Our Signature below does not constitute approval of any disclosed condition as represented herein by the owner.

PURCHASER: _____   DATE: _____

PURCHASER: _____   DATE: _____

(Page 5 of 5)

Finally, the form includes notification to the purchaser of how to obtain information on Ohio's Sex Offender Registration and Notification Law, known as "Megan's Law."

The form is required to be delivered by any method (including fax) and applies to each and every prospective transferee. The form must be delivered prior to entering into a purchase agreement. If the disclosure form is not delivered before this deadline, the purchaser may rescind the purchase contract by delivering to the seller a signed and dated recession letter prior to all three of the following:

1. The date of closing
2. 30 days after the seller accepted the purchase contract
3. Within three business days following the purchaser's (or his agent's) delivery of the disclosure form, or an amendment to it

If the disclosure statement is delivered on time, no additional right to cancel the contract (other than the conditions of the contract) is created.

Also, as the disclosure form itself clearly states, it is **not** a warranty statement, nor does it create any additional liability for the agent or broker as to the property's condition. Furthermore, it is not intended to replace a professional inspection.

Fraud

Fraud is *intentional or negligent misrepresentation or concealment of material facts.* Failing to disclose required information can be a form of fraud. Fraud also includes actively concealing information and making false or misleading statements. Fraud falls into two categories:

- Actual fraud
- Constructive fraud

Actual Fraud

Actual fraud (also called **deceit** or **intentional misrepresentation**) is an intentional misrepresentation or concealment of a material fact. Actual fraud is also when a person actively hides information, or makes statements known to be false or misleading. When any of these is done with intent to deceive, it constitutes actual fraud.

Case Example

The Fousts were considering buying a house listed with Mr. Mandell. Mandell told the Fousts the house currently used a septic tank, but they would have the option of tapping into the new city sewer for $500.

In fact, tapping into the new sewer was mandatory, and it would cost more than $1,100. There was also a $2,200 special assessment levied against the house to pay for the new sewer. Mandell did not tell the Fousts about the assessment.

The Fousts found out about these extra expenses after they bought the property, so they decided to sue Mandell and the sellers.

The court held that Mandell had misrepresented facts he knew regarding the sewer tap-in and intentionally failed to disclose the assessment in order to close the sale. The court ordered Mandell to pay damages to the Fousts. The court ruled that the sellers were also liable since Mandell was their agent. *Foust v. Valleybrook Realty Co.,* 4 Ohio App. 3d 164, 446 N.E.2d 1122 (1981).

Constructive Fraud

Constructive fraud (also called **negligent misrepresentation**) is a negligent misrepresentation or concealment of a material fact. When information is not disclosed or false statements are made unintentionally, it may be considered constructive fraud. Here, the false statements or failure to disclose are the result of carelessness or negligence, rather than intent to deceive.

Case Example

The McCoys' farm had serious water problems. There was not enough water pressure to run the washing machine and flushing the toilet three times would make the pump go dry. When the McCoys listed the property with Mr. Goodman, they explained these problems to him. Goodman noted the problems on his listing form but neglected to mention them on the information card he sent to the multiple listing service.

The Crums were shown the property by Mr. Jones (an agent from the MLS) when the McCoys were not home. The Crums inspected the house but did not notice that the washing machine was not hooked up. Mr. Crum turned on the water faucets, flushed the toilet twice, and everything seemed to work fine. The Crums decided to buy the property.

The McCoys did not meet the Crums until closing and did not realize the Crums had not been told about the water problem. Goodman never spoke to the Crums.

The Crums discovered the water problem when they moved in and sued the McCoys and Goodman. The court held that the McCoys had not intended to conceal the problem, but Goodman's failure to mention it in the MLS was negligent and, thus, constructive fraud. The McCoys were liable to the Crums for their agent's fraud, and Goodman was liable to the McCoys for breach of his fiduciary duties. *Crum v. McCoy*, 41 Ohio Misc. 34, 322 N.E.2d 161 (1974).

Actionable Fraud

Fraud is said to be **actionable** when certain elements are present. To sue for actual or constructive fraud, the plaintiff must be able to prove *all five* of the following elements:

1. A person makes a false statement of a material fact, or conceals a material fact, that he has a legal duty to disclose.

2. The person making the statement knows, or should know, it is false.

3. The statement or concealment is made with the intent of inducing another to enter into a transaction.

4. The other person relies on the statement, or lack of knowledge of the concealed information, and is induced to enter the transaction.

5. The other person is harmed as a result of entering the transaction.

Note that #2 encompasses both actual fraud (knows the statement is false) and constructive fraud (should know the statement is false). A real estate agent is not required to verify everything the seller says before passing it on to prospective buyers. But if there was something to suggest that the seller's claims might be false, an agent who did not investigate further could be considered negligent and held liable.

Fraud

Failure to disclose
Active concealment
False statements
Misleading statements or actions

| **Actual Fraud** | **Constructive Fraud** |
| Intentional | Negligent |

Opinions, Predictions, and Puffing

As a general rule, a seller or agent cannot be sued for misrepresentation if the agent's statements were merely opinions, predictions, or puffing:

- **Opinion:** "Compared to the sale prices for other homes in the neighborhood, this one appears to be an excellent buy."

- **Prediction:** "Historically, property values have gone up 4% a year, and there currently is no reason to believe this will change for this area."

- **Puffing:** "Look at this back yard!" (Even though you know the house really backs up to a park, but you do not mention this.)

To prove fraud based on a false statement, it is necessary to show the person relied on the statement. Because of their non-factual or exaggerated nature; opinions, predictions, and puffing are not considered the type of statements a reasonable person would rely on in making a decision to buy property. As such, they do not generally fall under the fraud category.

However, a real estate agent should be very cautious about stating unsubstantiated opinions. In special circumstances, opinions may be actionable. A court may allow recovery based on opinions stated by an expert hired to give advice, or a person who has superior knowledge and is acting in a fiduciary relationship. Someone who states an opinion that he does not actually believe may also be held liable.

"As Is" Clause

An **"as is" clause** is a provision in a purchase agreement stating the buyer accepts the property in its present condition. The implication is that the buyer has inspected the item and agrees to accept it just the way it is.

In summary, Ohio law states that an "as is" clause does not protect the seller from liability for nondisclosure of a latent defect. Also, an "as is" clause can never protect the seller or agent if they deliberately conceal a defect from the buyer. An "as is" clause is not a defense to fraud.

Exceptions to Fraud Rules

A licensee is not liable to any party for false information that the licensee's client provided to the licensee, which the licensee in turn provided to another party in the transaction, unless the licensee had actual knowledge that the information was false or acted with reckless disregard for the truth.

From the client's standpoint, no cause of action may be brought against a client for any misrepresentation a licensee made while representing the client unless the client had actual knowledge of the licensee's misrepresentation.

Penalties for Breach of Duty

When a real estate agent breaches a duty to the principal or to a third party, there are a number of possible consequences:

- Disciplinary action by professional associations
- Action by the Ohio Division of Real Estate and Professional Licensing
- Civil lawsuits filed by injured parties
- The filing of criminal charges against the agent (in very serious cases)

Action by Professional Associations

A code of ethics is a system of moral standards and rules of conduct adopted by many real estate professional organizations to set standards for members' conduct toward the public, clients, and other members. This should not be confused with the Canon of Ethics—standards of conduct put forth by Ohio Real Estate Commission.

The most widely recognized code is the National Association of REALTORS'® Code of Ethics. Although not legally binding, all NAR members voluntarily agree to follow it. A member who violates the code may be expelled from NAR, which may force the agent to change brokers as he must be a NAR member if his broker is one.

Action by the Division of Real Estate and Professional Licensing

As we have seen, a real estate agent's breach of duty is often a violation under the License Law. As such, the Superintendent can investigate the conduct of an agent even without a complaint. These remedies are cumulative and, thus, may be imposed in addition to civil and/or criminal penalties.

The Commission often suspends or revokes the broker's license when an agent has engaged in disreputable conduct. This occurs when the broker knew of the agent's activities and did nothing to stop the conduct.

Civil Lawsuits

A real estate agent may be sued by a client or customer for breach of duty. If the plaintiff is able to prove that he suffered harm as the result of the breach of duty, the agent will be liable. An agent found liable for breach of duty may have to pay **compensatory damages**, compensating the injured party for any monetary loss resulting from the breach. If the injured party was a client, the agent may be required to pay back the commission. A client can also use breach of duty as a defense if a broker sues to collect a commission. In a case involving secret profits, the court may order the agent to give up the profits earned unjustly.

In addition to compensatory damages, a court may award **punitive damages**; these punish the wrongdoer and attempt to deter others from similar acts. Generally, punitive damages are awarded only when the act was intentional or malicious.

Criminal Charges

Sometimes, a serious breach of duty is a crime (e.g., acting as a real estate agent without a license). And, under certain circumstances, fraud or misappropriation of trust funds may result in felony prosecution. Remember that criminal penalties—fines and jail sentences—may be imposed in addition to, not instead of, civil liability.

Terminating an Agency

An agent's powers end when the agency ends. There are several ways an agency may be terminated, including:

- Accomplishment of purpose
- Expiration of the agency agreement
- Operation of law
- Mutual agreement
- Renunciation by the agent
- Revocation by the principal

Accomplishment of Purpose

Perhaps the most common reason for termination of an agency relationship is that the purpose of the agency has been accomplished. The agency relationship between a seller and a real estate broker ends when the reason for the agency relationship ends—usually when a buyer is found and the sale closes.

Expiration

If an agency agreement specifies the agency is for a limited term (either a certain period of time or with a set expiration date), the agency ends automatically when the term expires. Note that a real estate agency agreement is required by Ohio Licensing Law to have an expiration date. This ensures the agency relationship is brought to a conclusion, either through accomplishment of purpose or expiration.

Operation of Law

An agency relationship ends automatically, as a matter of law, if certain events occur. An agency is terminated by operation of law if:

- Either party dies or becomes incapacitated.
- Either party goes bankrupt.
- The property that is the subject of the agency is destroyed or condemned.
- The agent loses his license.

Mutual Agreement

An agency is a consensual relationship, meaning it is based on the consent of both parties. If both the principal and the agent want to end the agency, they can agree to terminate it at any point. When an agency is terminated by mutual consent, neither party is liable to the other for breach of contract (see Chapter 8). This is considered the best way to terminate an agency (outside of accomplishment of purpose), since it is mutually voluntary.

Renunciation

Renunciation is when someone who has been granted something, or has accepted something, later gives it up or rejects it. With a normal agreement, which is left open-ended without a specific termination date, a party may renounce the contract at any time with no further obligation. But, if there was a termination date, such as with a typical real estate listing agreement, the renunciation may be a breach of contract—making one party liable to the other party for damages.

Revocation

Revocation is when someone who granted or offered something withdraws it. A principal may revoke the grant of agency powers at any time. In effect, the principal is firing the agent. Some examples are when a principal withdraws the authority granted to an agent, an offeror withdraws the offer, or the Real Estate Commission cancels a real estate agent's license.

In the case of an agreement that was open-ended, the principal will have to reimburse the agent only for expenses already incurred. If the agreement had a specific termination date, though, the principal may be required to pay the agent damages for breach of contract.

For Example

C is planning to sell his house. He signs a 90-day exclusive listing agreement with A, a real estate broker. Two weeks later, C starts dating a real estate agent and decides to change the listing to her brokerage. C tells A that her agency is revoked because he is changing to a different broker.

Once C revoked the agency, A is no longer authorized to represent him, and C cannot be held liable for A's acts. But the revocation was a breach of contract, so C will have to pay A damages. That might mean paying A the full commission she would have earned.

If an offeror revokes an offer before it is accepted, there is usually no compensation that must be paid. The Real Estate Commission may also revoke a license for misconduct or other breach without payment of compensation, since the rules of conduct and other requirements to keep a license are agreed to by the license recipient when the license is granted by the Commission.

Agency Coupled With an Interest

There is an exception to the rule allowing a principal to revoke an agency agreement. A principal does not have the right to revoke an agency agreement if it is an **agency coupled with an interest** (when the agent has a personal interest in the subject of the agency).

For Example

Agency coupled with an interest occurs when one co-owner has been authorized by the others to sell the property. Another example of personal interest is if the agent has a financial or security interest in the property that's the subject of the agency. Thus, if a listing agreement states the real estate broker will invest money to improve the property, the seller cannot revoke the broker's agency.

It is also important to note that an agency coupled with an interest is **not** terminated by the death, incompetency, or bankruptcy of the principal.

Summary

1. **Agency** is a relationship of trust created when one person (the **principal**) gives another person (the **agent**) the right to represent the principal in dealings with third parties. Agency creates a **fiduciary** relationship. A principal may be liable for an agent's acts. An agent is universal, general, or special, depending on the authority given. **Actual authority** is given to an agent by a listing agreement; this gives express authority to find a buyer and **incidental authority** to tell people the home is available (but not the right to put a "For Sale" sign in the front yard; that requires expressed written authority in Ohio). An agent cannot have incidental authority without **express authority**.

2. Basic real estate agency is between a broker and seller or broker and buyer. The individual a broker enters into a contract with to represent (and owes a fiduciary responsibility to) is the **client** or **principal**; all third parties are **customers**. Salespersons are broker's subagents. **Dual agency** is when a licensee represents both buyer and seller in the same transaction, *and* all management level licensees at a brokerage. Two non-management licensees can represent different parties in a transaction, with only the broker as a dual agent. Parties must sign the **Consumer Guide to Agency Relationship** form at the first substantive contact, and an **Agency Disclosure Statement** form must be signed when an offer is prepared or presented for or to a party. Brokerages must have a **company policy** that addresses the acceptable agency relationships and provides procedures for handling various situations that can arise during a transaction.

3. An agent owes fiduciary duties to the principal. These basic fiduciary duties are **accounting**, **confidentiality**, **care**, **obedience**, **loyalty**, and **disclosure**. Disclosure is a key responsibility. An agent must be careful to inform the principal of the true property value, all offers to purchase, identity of the buyer, buyer's financial condition, any commission splitting with other brokers, and the relationship between the buyer and broker. A real estate agent must not conceal material information from the principal, or take any secret profits from a transaction. However, a party may consent and waive certain duties that normally would be owed to them by an agent. This arrangement is often called "**Limited Service Agent**." Licensees do not breach a fiduciary duty by presenting **contemporaneous offers** from two or more buyer clients on the same property as long as proper disclosure has been made and the identities of the clients and the terms of their offers remain confidential. With disclosure of contemporaneous offers, buyer clients have the opportunity to request referral to a different licensee.

4. Agents have duties of good faith and fair dealing to third parties. Sellers and sellers' agents must tell buyers about **latent (hidden) defects**, but because of the caveat emptor rule, they usually do not have to tell buyers about **patent defects** that could be discovered through a reasonably thorough inspection. Intentional misrepresentation or concealment of material facts is **actual fraud**. Negligent misrepresentation or concealment of material facts is **constructive fraud**. Opinions, predictions, and puffing are not fraud since they are non-factual and exaggerated—a reasonable person would not rely on them to buy property. Agents must never guarantee anything, and make only statements they believe.

5. Penalties for breach of duty to principals or third parties include disciplinary action by professional associations, action by the Ohio Division of Real Estate and Professional Licensing, civil lawsuits filed by the injured parties and, in particularly serious cases, the filing of criminal charges against the agent.

6. Agency can be terminated by accomplishment of purpose, expiration of agency agreement, operation of law, mutual agreement (best way), renunciation by agent, or revocation by principal. Agency ends by operation of law if a party dies, becomes incapacitated, goes bankrupt, property is destroyed or condemned, or the agent loses his license. Agency coupled with an interest cannot be revoked, nor terminated by death, incapacity, or bankruptcy of the principal.

Quiz

1. **In relationship to their brokers, real estate licensees are usually considered**
   a. general agents.
   b. inadvertent agents.
   c. special agents.
   d. universal agents.

2. **An apparent agent is one who**
   a. appears to be the agent of another but does not have actual authority.
   b. appears to be working for the buyer instead of the seller.
   c. has actual authority from the principal.
   d. has implied authority from the principal.

3. **A real estate agency agreement**
   a. is required by Ohio's Statute of Frauds to be in writing.
   b. must be ratified by the principal.
   c. must have an expiration date.
   d. should be created by estoppel.

4. **The agent may terminate the agency relationship by renouncing it**
   a. as long as the agency agreement did not specify an expiration date.
   b. at any time.
   c. only if it is coupled with an interest.
   d. only if the principal consents.

5. **Under which circumstance is a real estate agency relationship NOT terminated by operation of law?**
   a. The listing salesperson dies.
   b. The broker loses his real estate license.
   c. A seller is in bankruptcy proceedings.
   d. A property was destroyed due to a fire.

6. **A real estate salesperson working for the listing broker is the**
   a. buyer's agent.
   b. buyer's subagent.
   c. cooperating agent.
   d. seller's subagent.

7. **The real estate broker who works with a buyer must provide the buyer with the Consumer Guide to Agency Relationships form**
   a. at the first substantive contact.
   b. only if the buyer requests one.
   c. only if it is a residential transaction.
   d. when the seller directs the broker to provide one.

8. **A real estate agent representing the seller is a fiduciary in relation to the**
   a. buyer.
   b. buyer's agent.
   c. seller.
   d. seller's subagent.

9. **A seller's real estate agent drafted a purchase contract for the transaction instead of using a form. This is**
   a. completely legal; although, it is discouraged by the Ohio Bar Association and the National Association of REALTORS®.
   b. legal as long as the buyer does not object.
   c. standard practice in rural communities in Ohio.
   d. the unauthorized practice of law.

10. **Broker X takes the seller's listing, but later decides he wants to buy the property himself. Which statement is TRUE?**
    a. It is legal for X to buy the property only if he agrees not to resell it for two years.
    b. It is legal for X to buy the property only if he turns the listing over to another broker before making an offer.
    c. It is legal for X to make an offer only if the seller understands that X himself is the prospective buyer.
    d. It is not legal for a broker to buy a client's property.

11. **Which statement regarding dual agency is TRUE?**

    a. It is listed as unethical conduct in the Ohio Real Estate Commission's regulations.

    b. It must be disclosed in writing and consented to by the parties when the agent has an ongoing business relationship with one party and not the other.

    c. It requires the agent to reveal everything one client tells him to the other client.

    d. It was recently made illegal in Ohio.

12. **In Ohio, for all real estate purchase contracts, the seller is required to**

    a. disclose all known latent defects in the property to the buyer, whether or not the buyer asks about them.

    b. disclose negative information about the property only if the buyer asks a direct question about a problem.

    c. disclose negative information about the property only if the buyer has not signed an "as is" clause as part of the purchase contract.

    d. make no statements regarding the condition of the property.

13. **Which statement describes the difference between actual fraud and constructive fraud?**

    a. Actual fraud is actionable and constructive fraud is not.

    b. Actual fraud is intentional and constructive fraud is unintentional.

    c. False statements are actual fraud and failure to disclose information is constructive fraud.

    d. False statements are constructive fraud and misleading actions are actual fraud.

14. **A listing broker knew a termite infestation had caused structural damage but told the buyer, "You don't have to worry about termites here. This house is solid." The buyer signed a contract that included an "as is" clause. He discovered the termite damage when he moved in and sued. The broker**

    a. can be held liable because the "as is" clause is void in all real estate transactions.

    b. can be held liable because her statements to the buyer were fraudulent.

    c. cannot be held liable because her statements were merely an opinion.

    d. cannot be held liable because of the "as is" clause.

15. **Punitive damages**

    a. are awarded in addition to compensatory damages in some tort suits.

    b. are awarded only in criminal cases.

    c. may be awarded instead of exemplary damages in some tort suits.

    d. must be paid out of the Real Estate Recovery Fund.

16. **Under Ohio Agency Law, which form of dual agency is NOT permitted?**

    a. A management level licensee may represent a client in an in-company real estate transaction.

    b. One licensee may represent both the buyer and seller (or lessor and lessee) as clients in the same real estate transaction.

    c. Two licensees affiliated with the same brokerage, one representing the buyer or lessor while the other represents the seller or lessee, may be involved in the same real estate transaction.

    d. A listing licensee may negotiate the sale of the listed property for a buyer client without disclosing to the seller that they represent the buyer.

Fair Housing

The United States Congress and the Ohio General Assembly have made it clear that ensuring everyone equal access to housing is an important goal for our society. To avoid potential liability, real estate agents need to know what conduct is in direct violation of anti-discrimination laws. They play an important role in combating discrimination and have a responsibility to explain these laws to their clients. In this chapter, we discuss federal and state anti-discrimination laws that affect real estate transactions.

Key Terms

Blockbusting The illegal practice of inducing owners to sell their homes (often at a deflated price) by suggesting the ethnic or racial composition of the neighborhood is changed, with the implication that property values will decline as a result. Also called **panic selling**.

Disparate Impact A law that is not discriminatory on face value but has a greater impact on a minority group than on other groups.

Exclusionary Zoning A zoning law that effectively prevents certain groups (such as minorities or poor people) from living in a community.

Familial Status A protected class under the Federal Fair Housing Act and the Ohio Civil Rights Act, which make it illegal to discriminate against persons who are the parent or guardian of a child under 18 years of age.

Mrs. Murphy Exemption An exemption to the Federal Fair Housing Act for an owner-occupied dwelling of four units or less provided the owner occupies one unit, does not use discriminatory advertising, and does not use a real estate agent. Ohio does not recognize this exemption.

Redlining Refusing to make loans secured by property located in certain neighborhoods for discriminatory reasons.

Steering Channeling prospective buyers or tenants to particular neighborhoods based upon their race, religion, national origin, or ancestry.

Title VIII Another name for the Federal Fair Housing Act, which is Title VIII of the Civil Rights Act of 1968.

Historical Background

The first civil rights laws in the United States were passed more than 120 years ago. The Thirteenth, Fourteenth, and Fifteenth Amendments to the Constitution were adopted right after the Civil War. They abolished slavery, guaranteed equal protection of the laws, and established that citizens of all races have the right to vote. During the same period, Congress enacted the Civil Rights Act of 1866.

Early civil rights laws were originally interpreted only to prohibit discrimination that involved **state action**—that is, action by a federal, state, or local governmental body (see Chapter 1). So, although it was illegal for a city government to enact discriminatory ordinances and for the police to enforce the laws in a discriminatory way favoring one group over another, the laws were interpreted in such a way that it was not illegal for private citizens to discriminate.

The landmark case concerning discrimination in connection with real estate was decided by the U.S. Supreme Court in 1948. At that time, it was not unlawful for a deed to include a covenant restricting ownership of the property to members of a particular race or religion. But in *Shelley v. Kraemer*, 334 U.S. 1 (1948), the Court held that it was unconstitutional for a court to enforce discriminatory restrictions. The court reasoned that a court order enforcing the restrictions would constitute discriminatory state action.

So, even though restrictive covenants (private action) were legal, a court order enforcing them (state action) was illegal. Without court enforcement, however, a restrictive covenant was not very effective. The *Shelley v. Kraemer* decision was an early step toward eliminating housing discrimination by private parties, but the Shelley rule still depended on state action.

Court decisions and legislation have extended laws against discrimination to purely private activities involving no state action. In 1968, the landmark Supreme Court decision of *Jones v. Alfred H. Mayer Co.*, 392 U.S. 409 (1968) prevented discrimination by private parties as well. Today, federal and state laws make it illegal to include discriminatory covenants in deeds or other documents, or to honor such provisions already in existing documents. Many other forms of discrimination by private parties are also against the law and are discussed in greater detail in this chapter.

Federal Legislation

The two federal anti-discrimination statutes that have the greatest effect on real estate transactions are the Civil Rights Act of 1866 and Title VIII of the Civil Rights Act of 1968, commonly referred to as the Federal Fair Housing Act.

The Civil Rights Act of 1866

The Civil Rights Act of 1866 prohibits racial discrimination in *any property transaction* in the United States. Section 1982 of the Act states:

> *"All citizens of the United States shall have the same right, in every State and Territory, as is enjoyed by white citizens thereof to inherit, purchase, lease, sell, hold, and convey real and personal property."*

Because of the reference to "white citizens," the 1866 Act was interpreted to prohibit only racial discrimination (as opposed to religious or sex discrimination, for example). In 1987, the Supreme Court held that the Act applies to discrimination based on ancestry as well as race (see *Shaare Tefila Congregation v. Cobb*, 481 U.S. 615 (1987)).

Unlike the 1968 Federal Fair Housing Act that applies only to housing and vacant land sold or leased for residential purposes, the 1866 Civil Rights Act applies to **all** property: Real or personal, residential or commercial, improved or unimproved. The constitutionality of the 1866 Act was challenged in a landmark case decided by the Supreme Court in 1968.

Case Example

Mr. and Mrs. Jones, a black couple, attempted to buy a home in a subdivision being developed near St. Louis by the Mayer company. When their offer was refused, they filed a lawsuit against the Mayer Company based on the 1866 Civil Rights Act. They claimed they were turned down because of their race. Ruling in favor of the Joneses, the Supreme Court held that the 1866 Act was constitutional. *Jones v. Alfred H. Mayer Co.*, 392 U.S. 409 (1968).

The ruling in favor of the Joneses established that the 1866 Act prohibited racial discrimination by private parties, even without state action. The Supreme Court reasoned that the right to buy or lease property could be impaired just as effectively by those individuals who place property on the market as by government actions.

Enforcement

A person who has been unlawfully discriminated against under the 1866 Act can sue only in federal district court. The Act does not specify a time limit for filing an action, but the lawsuit must be filed within the time limit specified by state law for similar claims. In Ohio, action must be filed within one year after the discriminatory incident occurred.

Since the statute does not specifically prescribe remedies, the court fashions the remedies it finds necessary. Case law shows that a claimant who proves discrimination that violates the 1866 Act may be entitled to an injunction, compensatory damages, and punitive damages.

An **injunction** is a court order requiring the defendant to do or refrain from doing a particular act (see Chapter 1). In a discrimination case, a court might order the defendant to sell her house to the plaintiff, for example.

An award of **compensatory damages** in a discrimination suit may include reimbursement for expenses caused by the discrimination—extra rent or transportation, storage, and moving costs, for instance. The award may also include compensation for emotional distress (humiliation, stress, and anger) that results from being discriminated against. In many discrimination cases, the compensatory damages total thousands of dollars; in exceptional cases, hundreds of thousands of dollars have been awarded.

Punitive damages may also be awarded if the acts of the defendant are deliberate or particularly egregious. Recall from the discussion of damages in Chapter 1, **punitive damages** are intended to punish the wrongdoer and discourage others from engaging in similar behavior. There is no limit on the amount of punitive damages that may be awarded for claims under the 1866 Act and awards have exceeded $100,000 in some cases.

The Federal Fair Housing Act

Title VIII of the Civil Rights Act of 1968 is commonly called the Federal Fair Housing Act. The first section of Title VIII states:

> *"It is the policy of the United States to provide, within constitutional limitations, for fair housing throughout the United States."*

To that end, the Act prohibits discrimination based on **race, color, religion, sex, national origin, disability, or familial status in the sale or lease of residential property.** The law also prohibits discrimination in **advertising, real estate brokerage, lending,** and **some other services associated with residential transactions.**

The law applies to most sales, rentals, and exchanges of residential property. This includes vacant land, if it is offered for the construction of residential buildings.

Exemptions

Although the Federal Fair Housing Act covers the majority of residential transactions in the U.S., there are four specific exemptions as follows:

1. The law does not apply to a single-family home sold or rented by a private individual owner, provided that:

   - The owner owns no more than three such homes.
   - No discriminatory advertising is used.
   - No real estate broker (or any real estate professional) is used.

If the owner is not the occupant or most recent occupant, he may use this exemption only once every 24 months. **Ohio does not recognize this exemption.**

2. The law does not apply to the rental of a room or unit in a dwelling with no more than four units, provided that:

   - The owner occupies one unit as his residence.
   - No discriminatory advertising is used.
   - No real estate broker or agent is used.

This exemption is referred to as the "**Mrs. Murphy exemption.**" **Ohio does not recognize this exemption.**

3. In dealing with their own property in noncommercial transactions, religious organizations or affiliated nonprofit organizations may limit occupancy, or give preference, to their own members—provided membership is not restricted on the basis of race, color, or national origin.

4. Private clubs with lodgings not open to the public and not operated for a commercial purpose may limit occupancy, or give preference, to their own members.

Even the limited exemptions listed above are available in far fewer situations than it first appears. Remember, under the 1866 Civil Rights Act, discrimination based on race or ancestry is prohibited in any property transaction, regardless of any exemptions available under the Fair Housing Act. **No transaction involving a real estate licensee is exempt.**

 The exemptions listed above in #1 and #2 are **not** exempt from Ohio's fair housing laws. So, even though the Federal Fair Housing Act does not prevent discrimination in those transactions, the Ohio Civil Rights Act does.

Familial Status. As mentioned earlier, the Fair Housing Act prohibits discrimination on the basis of **familial status**, making it *illegal to discriminate against a person because she is a parent or guardian with custody of a child under 18 years old*—but that rule does not apply to "housing for older persons." The Act defines housing for older persons as any housing that is:

- Provided under a state or federal program designed to assist the elderly.
- Intended for and solely occupied by persons 62 or older.
- Designed to meet the physical or social needs of older persons, if management publishes and follows policies and procedures demonstrating an intent to provide housing for persons 55 or older, and at least 80% of the units are occupied by at least one person 55 or older.

A condominium, apartment building, subdivision, or other development that qualifies as housing for older persons **can** have a "no kids" rule; other housing developments cannot.

Disability. Under the Fair Housing Act, a disability is defined as a physical or mental impairment that substantially limits or curtails one or more major life activities. Discrimination would include refusal by a landlord or rental agent to permit, at the expense of the disabled person, reasonable modification of the premises. Furthermore, under the Federal Fair Housing Act, discrimination also encompasses the building of new multi-family dwellings for first occupancy on or after April 1, 1991 that do not include certain accommodations for the disabled (e.g., wheelchair-width doorways, accessible common areas, modified light switches, electrical outlets, thermostats, kitchen fixtures, and bathroom facilities).

While most disabilities are covered under the Federal Fair Housing Act, there are minor exceptions, such as addiction to a controlled substance, which are not part of the protected class.

Americans with Disabilities Act (ADA). This federal regulation, signed into law July 26, 1990, requires compliance in five general areas of service or operation and provides a standard for the application of the requirements found in the Act. The five areas, or Titles, set out are:

1. **Employment**—Any employer with 15 or more employees must comply with the provisions of this Title for accessibility in the workplace for disabled individuals.

2. **Public services**

3. **Public accommodations**—Requires accessibility in commercial facilities and private entities that offer certain educational courses. Since 1993, all new builds have to comply with the Act.

4. **Private Entities**

5. **Telecommunications**

The Standard of Application requires reasonable accommodations be made for disabled employees without placing an undue financial burden on the employer, entity, or enterprise. Accommodations considered reasonable by the Act include:

- Handicap parking spaces
- Wheelchair ramps
- Accessible bathrooms
- Widened doorways and hallways
- Elevators
- Lowered workspace counters
- Repositioned shelves

An exemption exists for historic buildings where adaptation could destroy the building's historic significance.

Further, accommodations and/or modification to a rental housing unit must be made if they are "reasonable" accommodations or modifications and if the tenant is willing to pay for the modification. The tenant may be required to post a security deposit of up to twice the amount it would cost to remove the modification from the premises once the lease has expired.

Ohio adopted requirements of ADA into the Ohio Basic Building Code, so standards may be enforced by local (in addition to state or federal) building departments throughout Ohio.

Requirements

The Federal Fair Housing Act requires all real estate brokers, salespeople, banking personnel, and all others associated with housing to treat all persons equally with regard to housing choice, services provided, and all other facets of their real estate activities.

The Federal Fair Housing Act further requires all real estate brokers and lenders to display fair housing posters in their offices and to use the fair housing logo in their advertising. If a broker or lender is investigated for alleged discriminatory acts, failure to display the poster and use the logo may be considered prima facie evidence of discrimination.

Prohibited Acts

The following practices and activities violate the Federal Fair Housing Act if they are based on a person's race, color, religion, sex, national origin, disability, or familial status:

1. Refusing to rent or sell residential property after receiving a good faith offer

2. Refusing to negotiate for the sale or rental of residential property

3. Taking any action that would otherwise make residential property unavailable or deny it to any person (this general clause prohibits **steering** and **redlining** along with many other discriminatory practices and marketing methods)

4. Discriminating in the terms or conditions of any sale or rental of residential property, or in providing any services or facilities in connection with such property

5. Using discriminatory advertising or any other notice that indicates a limitation or preference, or intent to make any limitation, preference, or discrimination

6. Making any representation that property is not available for inspection, sale, or rent when it is in fact available

7. Inducing or attempting to induce, for profit, any person to sell or rent property based on representations made regarding entry into the neighborhood of persons of a particular race, color, religion, sex, or national origin (**blockbusting**)

8. Discriminating against anyone by a commercial lender in making a loan for buying, building, repairing, improving, or maintaining a dwelling, or in the terms of such financing (includes **redlining**)

9. Denying access to a multiple listing service or any similar real estate brokers' organization, or discriminating in terms or conditions for access to the organization

10. Coercing, intimidating, threatening, or interfering with anyone because of his enjoyment, attempt to enjoy, encouragement, and assistance to others in their enjoyment of the rights granted by the Federal Fair Housing Act

As you can see, most discriminatory behavior in connection with residential transactions would violate federal law. Three of these terms come up frequently in discussions of fair housing laws: Steering, blockbusting, and redlining.

Steering. Steering relates to buyers or renters and is *defined as channeling prospective buyers or renters to specific neighborhoods based on their race (or religion, national origin, or other protected class) to maintain or change the character of a neighborhood.* For instance, white customers might be shown homes only in white neighborhoods and black customers shown homes only in black neighborhoods.

EQUAL HOUSING OPPORTUNITY

It Is Illegal To Discriminate Against Any Person Because of Race, Color, Religion, Sex, Familial Status, National Origin, Military Status, Disability or Ancestry

- **In the sale or rental of housing or residential lots**
- **In advertising the sale or rental of housing**
- **In the financing of housing**
- **In the provision of real estate brokerage services**

Blockbusting is also illegal.

The Broker and Sales Associates are licensed by the Ohio Department of Commerce, Division of Real Estate & Professional Licensing. The division may be contacted for inquiries and complaints and for information on the Real Estate Recovery Fund (Section 4735.12 of the Revised Code) as a source of satisfaction for unsatisfied civil judgments against a licensee.

Ohio Department of Commerce Division of Real Estate & Professional Licensing

77 S. High Street, 20th Floor
Columbus, OH 43215-6133
(614) 466-4100

www.com.ohio.gov/real

PROVIDED BY THE OHIO REAL ESTATE COMMISSION

Effective 3/25/2008

Case Example

Mr. Mayfield, a sales agent for a real estate brokerage in Cleveland, met Ms. Tufts, a black woman, in 1977 at an open house on Maple Road in Cleveland Heights. She told him she was looking for a home in Cleveland Heights or South Euclid in the $20,000 to $30,000 range.

While Mayfield showed Tufts the Maple Road house, he told her that a white woman who looked at it earlier had decided against it because there were too many black people in the area. He pointed out various houses on the street and told Tufts which ones were owned by white families and which were owned by black families. Mayfield called Tufts several days later and offered to show her another home. It happened to be in a predominantly black neighborhood—one that Tufts had expressed no interest in. He also invited her to another open house in Cleveland Heights. This house was located on a street right next to East Cleveland (where the population was 77% black at that time).

Ms. Pap, a white woman, also met Mayfield at the open house on Maple Road. She told him she was interested in houses in the eastern suburbs for $25,000 to $30,000. She later went to his office to look at listings. He told her she was lucky to be white because she could get a better deal. According to Pap's later testimony, Mayfield said, "It was just human nature, owners prefer selling to whites." He also said, "...they sold to whites 80% of the time and that was the way it should be."

A few days later, Mayfield showed Pap three homes in Cleveland Heights, on Monticello Boulevard, Englewood Road, and Revere Road. After they looked at the Englewood Road house, Mayfield commented that the neighborhood was not very integrated. He told Pap there was "a high demand for white buyers and that all agents knew this and showed them the neighborhood first." When they looked at the house on Revere Road, Mayfield said he "preferred the Englewood area... it wasn't as integrated as the area around Revere and never would be."

Mayfield had given Pap a computer printout of listings. It showed three homes in Pap's price range that Mayfield did not take her to. He told her she would not be interested in them. She asked why not and he said, "Those neighborhoods weren't integrated anymore...they were black, and...even blacks were reluctant to buy in the neighborhood."

The brokerage Mayfield worked for was sued for racial discrimination. The court held that Mayfield's remarks to Tufts and Pap were intended to influence their choice of homes on racial grounds. In addition, Mayfield showed Tufts homes in black neighborhoods only and did not show Pap any homes in black neighborhoods. The remarks and the selective showings amounted to steering and violated the Federal Fair Housing Act. *Heights Community Congress v. Hilltop Realty, Inc.*, 629 F. Supp. 1232 (N.D. Ohio 1983), *aff'd in part, rev'd in part*, 774 F.2d 135 (1985).

The *Heights Community Congress v. Hilltop Realty, Inc.* case involved the use of **checkers** or **testers**. Ms. Tufts and Ms. Pap were not actually planning to buy homes; they were volunteers from a fair housing organization, posing as home buyers to check on the practices of real estate agents in the area. The lawsuit against Mayfield's brokerage was based on their tests and other similar tests, as well as on incidents involving actual home buyers. Note that it was always Mayfield who brought up the issue of race, not the checkers. A real estate agent's good faith answer to a question from a prospective buyer about the racial or ethnic composition of a neighborhood probably would not violate the law, as long as the agent did not intend to discriminate or encourage discrimination. However, anything beyond a very simple, factual answer could be considered steering. It is safest to avoid any discussion of race or ethnic background.

Blockbusting. Blockbusting (also called **panic selling** or **panic peddling**) relates to selling and *is defined as the practice of predicting the entry of minorities into a neighborhood and stating or implying this will result in lower property values, higher crime rates, or other undesirable consequences.* The purpose is to induce property owners to list properties for sale or to sell properties at a reduced price, so the individual making the predictions (usually a real estate agent) can profit.

A wide variety of blockbusting "techniques" appear in the case law. Here are some examples of illegal blockbusting activities:

- Distributing pamphlets stating that a member of a minority group has purchased a home nearby

- "Wrong number" phone calls in which the callers indicate they thought they were calling, for example, "the Asian family that just moved in"

- Purchasing a home in the area and selling it on contract to a minority buyer, then suggesting to owners that it is time to move

Redlining. Redlining relates to lenders and is *defined as refusal to make loans on property located in a particular neighborhood, for discriminatory reasons.* In the past, many lenders assumed that an integrated or predominantly black neighborhood was automatically a neighborhood where property values were declining. Based on that assumption, they refused to make loans in those neighborhoods. In many cases, this worked as a self-fulfilling prophecy. Since it was almost impossible to obtain purchase or renovation loans, it was extremely difficult to market, maintain, or improve homes in those neighborhoods and that caused values to decline.

Lenders may still deny loans in neighborhoods with declining property values, but that action must be based on objective economic criteria concerning the condition and value of the particular property or surrounding neighborhood, without regard to the racial or ethnic composition of the neighborhood. A lender may not simply equate an integrated or minority neighborhood with declining property values.

Enforcement

A person who has been discriminated against in violation of the Federal Fair Housing Act may file a written complaint with the Office of Equal Opportunity (OEO) of the Department of Housing and Urban Development (HUD). HUD may also file a complaint on its own initiative. A complaint requesting a hearing has to be filed with HUD within one year after the discriminatory incident occurred.

In states like Ohio, where there is a state fair housing law substantially equivalent to the federal law, HUD may refer complaints to the state or local agency with similar responsibilities (e.g., the Ohio Civil Rights Commission). Otherwise, when HUD receives a complaint, the agency itself investigates the incident. If the investigation reveals evidence of a violation, the agency uses negotiation and conciliation in an effort to obtain voluntary compliance with the Federal Fair Housing Act.

If efforts at voluntary resolution to the problem are unsuccessful, the parties may have the dispute decided by one of HUD's administrative law judges. In the administrative hearing (just as in a lawsuit), the person who filed the complaint (the **complainant**) has the burden of proof. It is up to the complainant to prove the accused person (the **respondent**) violated the law. Proof of discriminatory intent is not necessary since the Federal Fair Housing Act is to be construed expansively to implement the goal of eliminating housing discrimination.

If the complainant is not able to prove an act of discrimination, the respondent is found innocent of the allegation. In some cases, the administrative law judge will order the complainant to pay the respondent's attorney's fees.

If the administrative law judge rules in favor of the complainant, the judge can award compensatory damages to the complainant, issue an injunction against the respondent, impose civil penalties (fines ranging from a maximum of $11,000 for a first offense and up to $55,000 for a third offense), and order the respondent to pay the complainant's attorney's fees.

Court Option. Either the complainant or respondent may choose to have the dispute decided in a civil lawsuit instead of by an administrative law judge. In that case, HUD refers the matter to the Attorney General's office, which will file suit in U.S. district court against the respondent on behalf of the complainant.

A Fair Housing Act violation does not have to be handled through HUD. A person who has been discriminated against can file a civil suit directly instead. The lawsuit may be filed in U.S. district court or a state trial court of general jurisdiction (in Ohio, the common pleas court) within two years after the discriminatory incident or after the conclusion of a HUD hearing. The court may grant an injunction, compensatory damages, punitive damages, and attorney's fees. Punitive damages awarded under the Federal Fair Housing Act are no longer limited (previous limit was $10,000).

In addition, the U.S. Attorney General may bring a civil suit in federal district court against anyone engaged in an ongoing pattern or practice of discriminatory activities. These are referred to as "**pattern and practice lawsuits**." The Attorney General may request an injunction to ensure that all persons are able to exercise the rights granted under the Fair Housing Act. The court may also award damages to the victims of the discriminatory activities and impose civil penalties of up to $100,000.

Federal Fair Housing Act

- **Prohibits discrimination based on:**
  Race   Color   Religion   Sex   Disability
  National Origin   Familial Status

- **Applies only to residential transactions**
- **Exemptions:**
  1. Certain single-family home sales and rentals
  2. Rental of a unit in an owner-occupied residence
  3. Nonprofit religious organizations
  4. Private clubs
  5. Housing for older persons (familial status only)

The Ohio Civil Rights Law

The Ohio Civil Rights Law prohibits housing discrimination on the basis of **race, color, religion, sex, ancestry, national origin, disability, familial status, or military status**.

 Familial status and disability were added to Ohio's law, effective June 30, 1992. Military status was added March 24, 2008.

The state law applies to the sale or lease of any building used or intended to be used as a residence. It also applies to any vacant land offered for sale or lease (not just land offered specifically for residential purposes).

Prohibited Acts

Ohio's statute covers most of the same ground as the Federal Fair Housing Law. The state law makes it illegal to discriminate by refusing to sell or rent, refusing to negotiate for sale or rental, or otherwise make housing unavailable. The law also makes it illegal to discriminate in the terms or conditions of a sale or lease, or in furnishing facilities and services in connection with housing. The Ohio Civil Rights Law outlaws all of the following with regard to housing:

- Blockbusting
- Steering
- Discriminatory advertising
- Discriminatory restrictive covenants
- Interference with a person's enjoyment of his civil rights
- Discrimination by multiple listing services
- Discrimination by insurance companies (concerning homeowners insurance and fire insurance)
- Redlining and other lending discrimination

The state law also generally prohibits asking questions (either in person or on an application) about race, color, religion, sex, ancestry, disability, military status, or national origin in connection with the sale or lease of housing. However, there is an exception to this rule: It is permissible to ask questions and keep records about race, religion, and so forth to monitor compliance with the Ohio Civil Rights Law.

Exemptions

Like the Federal Fair Housing Act, the fair housing provisions of the Ohio Civil Rights Law allow a religious organization to limit use of its noncommercial housing accommodations to its own members, unless membership in the religious organization is restricted on the basis of race, color, or national origin. Similarly, a private or fraternal organization may limit use of its noncommercial lodgings to its members, as long as the operation of the lodgings is incidental only to the organization's primary purpose.

 Remember: The Ohio Civil Rights Law does not recognize the "Mrs. Murphy exemption" or allow the seller or lessor of a single-family home to discriminate.

Enforcement

The procedures for enforcing the fair housing provisions of the Ohio Civil Rights Law are very similar to those for enforcing the Federal Fair Housing Act. A person who has been discriminated against in violation of the Ohio Civil Rights Law may file a charge with the Ohio Civil Rights Commission. The charge must be in writing, under oath, and filed with the Commission within one year after the discriminatory incident occurred.

If a preliminary investigation appears to support the charge, the Commission may ask the court of common pleas to issue a temporary restraining order to prevent the respondent from selling or renting the property until the dispute is resolved. In any case, the Commission (like HUD) uses negotiation and conciliation to try to persuade the respondent to comply with the law voluntarily. If that is unsuccessful, the Commission holds a formal hearing.

If the hearing confirms there has been a violation, the Commission may issue a **cease and desist order**, ordering the respondent to stop the discriminatory activities. The respondent may also be ordered to take affirmative steps to rectify the situation.

For Example

The respondent may be ordered to sell or rent the property (if it is still available), or a similar property, to the complainant.

In addition, the respondent may be required to pay the complainant compensatory damages, attorney's fees, and punitive damages up to $11,000 for the first violation and up to $55,000 for two previous unlawful discriminatory practices in the last seven years.

Court Option. Instead of filing a charge with the Commission, a victim of housing discrimination may file a civil lawsuit in the court of common pleas within one year after the discriminatory incident. The court can apply the same remedies as the Commission: Temporary restraining orders, injunctions, compensatory damages, attorney's fees, and punitive damages.

If the Commission finds that anyone is engaged in a pattern or practice of housing discrimination, it may ask the Ohio Attorney General to file a lawsuit in the court of common pleas. The Attorney General may ask the court for a restraining order or an injunction.

Ohio Civil Rights Law

- Prohibits discrimination based on race, color, religion, sex, ancestry, national origin, disability, familial status, and military status
- Applies only to transactions involving residential property or any vacant land
- Exemptions: Accommodations operated by nonprofit religious, fraternal, or charitable organizations

---

Fair Housing and Ohio's License Law

When an Ohio real estate broker or salesperson has violated a local, state, or federal civil rights law pertaining to real estate transactions, the Ohio Real Estate Commission will suspend or revoke that person's real estate license. If it is the licensee's first offense, the licensee must have been found guilty of a violation by a court. However, this is not a requirement in the case of later offenses. For a second offense, the Commission must suspend the license for a minimum of two months or revoke it. If there are any subsequent offenses, the license must be revoked.

These rules about suspension or revocation of an agent's license apply only if the violation occurred in "a situation wherein parties were engaged in bona fide efforts to purchase, sell, or lease real estate" (ORC § 4735.18(A)(7)). In other words, the rules do not apply if the case involves checkers from a fair housing organization instead of real buyers, sellers, or renters.

Case Examples of Discrimination

The overall effect of federal and state legislation is to outlaw discrimination based on race or ancestry in all property transactions, with no exceptions.

Discrimination based on religion, national origin, sex, or disability is prohibited in the sale or lease of vacant land or housing, except that nonprofit religious or charitable organizations and private clubs can limit use of their noncommercial accommodations to their own members.

Discrimination based on familial status is generally prohibited, but there are exemptions in the Fair Housing Act for certain sales or rentals of single-family homes, for the rental of a unit in an owner-occupied residence, and for the sale or rental of housing for older persons.

Following are case examples that illustrate different forms of discrimination in real estate transactions. These examples also show how courts interpret and apply anti-discrimination laws in real estate cases. Although some cases are from other states, similar results would be reached in decisions by Ohio courts in applying civil rights laws to ensure fair and equal housing opportunity for all.

Discrimination in Renting

Sometimes discrimination is blatant. In rejecting a prospective tenant, a landlord may make very little effort to conceal the fact that racism (or some other form of prejudice) is the reason for not accepting the person.

Case Example

Mr. Pecsok owned an apartment building in Cleveland. He received a call from Mr. Bishop who looked at a vacant apartment in the building and wanted to rent it. Pecsok arranged to meet Bishop and his wife so they could give him a deposit and sign a lease.

When Pecsok met the Bishops, he discovered that Mr. Bishop was white, and Mrs. Bishop was black. Pecsok told the Bishops he had decided against renting to them because they did not meet his financial criteria. Mrs. Bishop asked Pecsok if her race had anything to do with his decision. At first Pecsok said, "Not necessarily," but during the discussion that followed, Pecsok told the Bishops that blacks were responsible for most crime in the U.S. and that he did not allow them in his building "because their friends would hang around and terrorize the other tenants."

The Bishops sued Pecsok under the Civil Rights Act of 1866 and the Federal Fair Housing Act. At trial, evidence was introduced to show that the Bishops would have been able to pay the rent and that Pecsok did not apply the same financial criteria to the Bishops that he applied to his other tenants. Another black woman testified that when she called Pecsok about an apartment, he said he did not rent to blacks because it would upset the other tenants.

The court ordered Pecsok to pay the Bishops a total of $10,000: $1,500 in compensatory damages (for emotional distress), $5,000 in punitive damages because he acted wantonly and maliciously, and $3,500 in attorney's fees. *Bishop v. Pecsok*, 431 F. Supp. 34 (N.D. Ohio 1976).

It is very likely the court would have found Mr. Pecsok guilty of discrimination even if he actually had legitimate financial reasons for rejecting the Bishops as tenants. When race, color, religion, sex, national origin, or disability is a factor in a refusal to sell or rent—even if it is not the only reason for the refusal—it is a violation of fair housing laws.

Blatant discrimination has become less common over the past few decades. Today, discrimination tends to be veiled. The landlord finds other ways to avoid minority applicants or pretends all applicants are being treated equally.

Case Example

The Marshalls, a black couple, wanted to rent an apartment in a building managed by Miller Properties in Columbus. The Marshalls completed an application for a certain apartment and left a $50 deposit with the rental agent.

The next morning, an employee of Miller Properties called Mr. Marshall and told him the apartment he had chosen was subject to an earlier oral application that had priority over his written application. So, Marshall returned to the complex and chose another apartment. Again, he was informed that someone else had already orally reserved that apartment. Marshall picked a third apartment and ran into the same problem.

After that, Marshall tried to contact the rental agent at least six times. Each time, he was told the agent was busy or out of the office. The agent never returned Marshall's calls.

The Marshalls filed a charge with the Ohio Civil Rights Commission, which found that Miller Properties had violated the fair housing provisions of the Ohio Civil Rights Law and issued a cease and desist order against the management company. *Miller Properties v. Ohio Civil Rights Comm'n*, 34 Ohio App. 2d 113, 296 N.E.2d 300 (1972).

In another case, it was the property management company's policy to process only rental applications accompanied by a deposit. The rental agents told white applicants about that policy and, accordingly, the white applicants all made a deposit. Black applicants were not informed that a deposit was required, so they did not make one and their applications were never processed. These are just some of the many examples of discrimination in the rental of housing.

Discrimination in Selling

Discrimination in selling property may be relatively simple: Salespeople in a model home may go out the back door when a prospective buyer drives up, or a developer might discourage minority buyers by making them pay higher closing costs. Sometimes, however, discrimination entails an elaborate scheme as in the following case that took place near Chicago.

Case Example

A home in an exclusive residential community (with private roads and a security entrance) was listed for sale. The asking price was $850,000 but, after some negotiation, the seller and a black couple signed an agreement with a purchase price of $675,000. The buyers made an earnest money deposit of $75,000.

News spread that a black couple had bought the home, upsetting a number of the community residents. Restrictive covenants required all sales in the community to be reported to the homeowners association. The covenants also gave the association a 30-day assignable option to buy the property on the same terms that had been offered. In an unprecedented action, the president of the association called a special meeting to discuss the situation. In 16 or 17 previous sales, the option right had been routinely waived without discussion.

At the meeting, talk centered on the buyer's race and occupation (the husband operated a chain of car washes), and on ways to prevent the sale. Although the seller was a member of the board of governors and vice president of the association, he was not told of the meeting.

(Continued on next page)

Case Example *(cont.)*

The association's attorney suggested that it might not be advisable for the association itself to buy the property to frustrate the sale, but perhaps they could form a separate syndicate or find another buyer. Shortly before the 30-day option period was to expire, the association contacted another buyer (a white woman) who had viewed the home earlier. She agreed to buy the association's option.

The black couple filed a lawsuit, alleging that the homeowners association and the white buyer had conspired to deny them housing based on their race. The court ruled in favor of the black couple.

The white buyer claimed she was not aware of the race of the other prospective buyers, but the court did not believe her. The court also did not believe the failure to notify the seller of the meeting was an oversight, or the association's claim that its main concern was that the low sale price would lessen the value of other properties in the community. The price was not discussed at all at the meeting (no one there even knew what the price was), and the white buyer had agreed to pay exactly the same price.

The court concluded that the only difference between the second deal and the first was that the second buyer was a white professional and the first was a black car wash operator.

The court entered judgments in favor of both plaintiffs (the husband and the wife) against the homeowners association and the white buyer: $2,675 in compensatory damages for storage expenses and other out-of-pocket expenses occasioned by the delay and the additional move, $25,000 for each plaintiff for emotional distress and other compensatory damages, $50,000 for each plaintiff against each defendant for punitive damages ($200,000 total), $35,000 in attorneys' fees, and $1,016 in costs. The total judgment was $288,691. *Phillips v. Hunter Trails*, 685 F.2d 184 (7th Cir. 1982).

Following is a case that shows what can happen when a real estate agent goes along with a client's discrimination.

Case Example

Mr. and Mrs. Verble, a white couple, owned a four-unit apartment building in the McArthur Park neighborhood in Sandusky and advertised the property for sale in the newspaper. The McDonalds, a black couple, saw the ad and called the Verbles to find out more about the property. The Verbles said the purchase price was $26,500, and they arranged to meet the McDonalds at the property that evening.

When the McDonalds looked over the property, Mr. McDonald told Mr. Verble they were interested in buying it. Verble asked McDonald to call him at home that evening. McDonald called, but Verble was not home. McDonald asked Mrs. Verble to have her husband call him back, but Verble never called.

A few days later, Mrs. McDonald called the Verbles again. Mr. Verble told her two men were going to buy the property. Mrs. McDonald said she and her husband were still very interested in it and asked Verble to call them if it turned out the two men could not finance the purchase.

Then, Mr. Holderness, a real estate broker, contacted the Verbles and persuaded them to list their property with him for $29,500. The Verbles did not tell Holderness about the McDonalds.

In his first conversation with Holderness, Mr. Verble said he would prefer not to sell the property to a black person. Holderness explained he had to show the property to any interested buyer and the Verbles would have to sell it to a black person who offered $29,500 (or, if there were competing offers, to whomever made the highest offer).

(Continued on next page)

Case Example *(cont.)*

The McDonalds had not heard from the Verbles, but they noticed the ad was still running in the newspaper. They got in touch with a white friend, Mr. Owens, and asked him to try buying the property. Owens called and arranged to have one of Holderness's sales agents show him the property.

The day after Owens visited the property, Mr. McDonald went to Holderness's office. He told Holderness he was interested in buying some investment property. Holderness suggested a number of properties but did not mention the Verbles' apartment building. McDonald specifically asked if there was anything available in McArthur Park. At first Holderness said that there was nothing available there, but McDonald persisted, and Holderness finally brought up the Verbles' property. He said he had been reluctant to tell McDonald about the property because he was thinking of buying it himself.

Holderness asked McDonald if he would like to see the property, but McDonald said it would not be necessary. If it was good enough for Holderness, it was good enough for him. He asked Holderness to prepare an offer to purchase. Holderness told McDonald the listing price was $29,500, but McDonald offered $26,500 (the price the Verbles originally quoted to him). Mr. and Mrs. McDonald both signed the offer and gave Holderness an earnest money deposit.

Holderness called Mr. Owens and told him a couple made an offer on the Verbles' property. Holderness explained that the Verbles might be willing to accept less than their listing price from Owens, because they did not want to sell to the couple who made the offer.

After consulting with McDonald, Owens offered $27,500 for the Verbles' property. Although it would have been Holderness's standard practice to call the buyers who made the lower offer and ask them to top the other bid, he did not call the McDonalds about Owens's offer. The Verbles accepted Owens's offer and rejected the McDonalds' offer that same day.

The McDonalds took their story to the Sandusky NAACP. An NAACP representative got in touch with the Verbles and Holderness to discuss the McDonalds' discrimination claims. Holderness replied that if the current buyer was unable to complete the purchase, the Verbles were willing to sell their property to the McDonalds for $27,500.

Owens then withdrew his offer to purchase. Holderness promptly informed the McDonalds and they submitted another offer for $26,500, which the Verbles rejected. The McDonalds raised their offer to $27,500, but the Verbles stated they would not take anything less than $29,500.

The McDonalds filed a lawsuit in federal court, claiming the Verbles and Holderness discriminated against them because of their race, in violation of the Civil Rights Act of 1866 and the Federal Fair Housing Act. Holderness then notified the McDonalds that the Verbles would accept their offer of $27,500 on the property. A purchase contract was signed by the parties and the McDonalds finally took possession of the property.

The trial court then dismissed the McDonalds' case, since the sale of the property was no longer an issue. But the McDonalds appealed the decision, and the appellate court ruled in their favor. The appellate court held that even though the Verbles ultimately sold the McDonalds the property the McDonalds were still entitled to collect damages and attorney's fees, both from Verble and from Holderness. *McDonald v. Verble*, 622 F.2d 1227 (1980).

Discrimination in Advertising

Both federal law and Ohio law prohibit any advertising that indicates a limitation, preference, or intent to discriminate based on race or other protected class. Discriminatory advertising may be subtle; seemingly innocent statements are sometimes intended or interpreted as discriminatory.

For Example

In some areas of the country an advertisement that describes a home as "near schools and churches" may be taken to mean that it is in a gentile neighborhood and that those of Jewish faith (who attend temples or synagogues, not churches) are not welcome.

Under certain circumstances, even the newspapers a broker chooses for advertising may be held to have the effect of racial **steering**.

Case Example

A large real estate brokerage in Detroit (with more than 20 offices and over 300 salespeople) advertised its listed properties in two newspapers distributed over the entire metropolitan area, a number of smaller newspapers circulated primarily in certain neighborhoods, and a weekly newspaper circulated mainly in black neighborhoods.

Whenever the brokerage took a listing in one of the "changing areas" of the city (a neighborhood becoming more integrated or becoming predominantly black), its standard practice was to advertise that home in the black newspaper and not in the newspapers of general circulation.

Because of the brokerage's advertising policy and some of its other policies, the U.S. Attorney General filed a pattern and practice lawsuit against the brokerage. The court held that the advertising policy had an impermissible steering effect. It brought homes in the integrated and black neighborhoods only to the attention of the readers of the black newspaper, and most of those readers were black. As a result, the advertising policy was likely to contribute to changing an integrated neighborhood into a predominantly black neighborhood. This violated the government's policy of fostering integrated neighborhoods and it violated the Federal Fair Housing Act.

The court ordered the brokerage to maintain the same level of advertising in the black newspaper, but also advertise those same homes in the two newspapers of general circulation, plus do advertising in smaller community newspapers. *U.S. v. Real Estate One, Inc.*, 433 F. Supp. 1140 (E.D. Mich. 1977).

Exclusionary Zoning and Other Municipal Actions

Exclusionary zoning laws are defined as *any laws that have the effect of denying housing to minorities or other protected classes.* The clause "make otherwise unavailable or deny" in anti-discrimination legislation has been interpreted to prohibit such exclusionary zoning.

Since it is unlikely that a municipality would enact an openly racist ordinance, these cases usually involve arguments based on the concept of *disparate impact*. A law with **disparate impact** *may be neutral on its face, but it has a discriminatory effect since it has a greater impact on one group than it has on others.*

For Example

With regard to employment, there have been a number of cases alleging that height restrictions for police or fire departments had a discriminatory effect. Women and certain minorities tend to be shorter than white males, and there was no evidence to indicate that the height restrictions were related to job requirements.

Exclusionary zoning cases usually involve ordinances that prohibit or unreasonably restrict multi-family or low-income housing. In comparison to the white population, members of minority groups are much more likely to fall into the low-income demographic. As a result, it has been successfully argued in a number of cases that ordinances limiting low-cost housing have a disparate impact on minority groups, in effect excluding them from certain communities.

Case Example

Arlington Heights, a city near Chicago, refused to rezone and permit the construction of multi-family dwellings within its boundaries. The population of the Chicago metropolitan area was approximately 18% black, but Arlington Heights had only 27 black residents out of a population of approximately 65,000 (0.04%).

A developer sued the city, claiming the city's actions violated fair housing laws. Since a greater percentage of the occupants of multi-family dwellings were black rather than white, the court ruled that the city's zoning ordinance had the effect of excluding black people from living there. *Metropolitan Housing Develop. Corp. v. Arlington Hts*, 517 F.2d 409 (7th Cir. 1975).

Several years ago in another exclusionary zoning case, the U.S. Attorney General successfully sued Parma (a suburb of Cleveland) for violations of the Fair Housing Act (see *U.S. v. City of Parma*, 661 F.2d 562 (1981)). According to the 1970 census, Parma's population was 100,216, but only 50 of its residents were black. Cleveland's population, by contrast, was 16% black at that time.

The court ruled that certain actions by city officials had the purpose and the effect of maintaining Parma as a segregated community. These actions included the refusal by city officials to enact a fair housing resolution welcoming "all persons of good will," refusal to participate in public low-income housing programs, denial of building permits for a privately sponsored low-income housing development, and the adoption of an ordinance requiring voter approval for subsidized housing projects.

To correct the problem, the court issued a wide variety of remedial injunctions. These included ordering Parma to establish an educational program for its officials, advertise its non-discriminatory policies (to counteract the city's reputation as a closed community), permit construction of public housing, and organize a fair housing committee as part of the city government. The court also invalidated the community's ordinance that required voter approval for subsidized housing projects.

Liability for Discrimination

A civil lawsuit can be filed only by someone who has **standing to sue.** That generally means the plaintiff must have been personally injured by the defendant's actions in order to bring a cause of action against him in court. In other words, if an individual has not been injured by another, he does not have the right to sue the other person—even on behalf of others who have been injured. The injured parties are the ones with standing to sue, so it is up to them to decide whether they want to sue.

For the purposes of the Fair Housing Act, however, the U.S. Supreme Court interpreted the concept of standing to sue quite broadly. The Court held that it is not only actual buyers and renters who can sue for violation of the Act. In some cases, a fair housing organization also has standing to sue, as do the individual checkers from a fair housing organization, since it is said to be the whole community that is injured by housing discrimination. This is illustrated in the following Supreme Court case.

Case Example

Mr. Coles, a black man, inquired about renting an apartment in a complex near Richmond, Virginia and was told there were no vacancies. Mr. Coles was suspicious and complained to a local nonprofit fair housing organization.

The organization sent two checkers, one black and one white, to the apartment complex. On four different occasions the black checker was told there were no vacancies, yet the white checker was shown vacant apartments.

The property management company and one of its employees were then sued by Mr. Coles (the actual rental applicant), the black checker, the white checker, and the fair housing organization. The defendants challenged the checkers' and the organization's standing to sue and the case went all the way to the U.S. Supreme Court.

The Court held that all of the plaintiffs were entitled to sue because, in effect, they all had been injured by the defendants' discriminatory practices.

The actual rental applicant's claim was based on straightforward allegations of denial of housing and racial steering. The black checker's claim was based on a provision of the Fair Housing Act that makes it unlawful for anyone to misrepresent that housing is not available when, in fact, it is. To recover under that provision, it is not necessary to be seeking housing. Even checkers who expect they will be lied to still have a right to sue. The white checker's claim was based on a general right to enjoy the benefits of an integrated society; the defendants' practices interfered with that right. Finally, the fair housing organization had a right to sue on the theory that the defendants' practices interfered with the organization's housing counseling and referral services, with a resulting drain on its financial resources. *Havens Realty v. Coleman*, 455 U.S. 363 (1982).

So, just about everyone affected by unlawful discrimination can sue under the Fair Housing Act. And just about everyone connected with the violation can be held liable, either because of their own actions or because they are legally responsible for the actions of their agents (e.g., property managers, real estate brokers, real estate salespeople, property owners).

 Remember: If a seller refuses to go through with a transaction because of the buyer's race, religion, ethnic background, etc., the broker may sue the seller for the commission.

Who Can Sue for Violation of Anti-Discrimination Laws

- Prospective buyer/tenant
- State Attorney General
- Checker
- HUD
- Ohio Civil Rights Commission
- Fair Housing Organization
- U.S. Attorney General

Who Can Be Held Liable for Unlawful Discrimination

- Seller/landlord
- Property manager
- Resident manager
- Real estate broker
- Real estate salesperson
- Multiple Listing Service
- Rental agent
- Lender
- Loan officer
- Homeowners association

One final point: Refusing to deal with someone who has sued you for discrimination may be considered unlawful retaliation and make you liable to be sued again under the Federal Fair Housing Act. This is illustrated in the following case.

Case Example

Several black brokers wanted to join a multiple listing service operating in a suburb of Gary, Indiana. Only members of the suburb's Board of REALTORS® were allowed to join the MLS and a broker could not join the board unless he had an office in the suburb. The brokers tried to rent office space in the suburb but could not, apparently because of widespread prejudice against black people there.

The brokers filed a complaint against the MLS, the suburban Board of REALTORS®, and eight individual brokers, who were white. They claimed the board's membership requirements had the effect of excluding them from the MLS because of their race. The U.S. Attorney General filed a lawsuit on behalf of the black brokers. That lawsuit was settled when the board agreed to waive its requirement that members maintain an office in the suburb.

After that lawsuit was filed, some of the white brokers who were defendants refused to split commissions or work as cooperating brokers in any transactions with the plaintiffs (the black brokers). The black brokers then sued the white brokers in a separate lawsuit, alleging that their refusal to cooperate was in retaliation for the discrimination suit.

The white brokers freely admitted that their refusal to cooperate was because of the lawsuit. They did not want to work with anyone who was suing them. However, the court held that the white brokers' refusal to cooperate interfered with the black brokers' exercise of their rights under the Fair Housing Act. *U.S. v. South Suburban MLS,* No. H 80-307 (N.D. Ind. March 1, 1984) (order granting partial summary judgment).

Summary

1. The **Civil Rights Act of 1866** prohibits discrimination based on race or ancestry in any personal or real property transaction in the United States.

2. The **Federal Fair Housing Act** (**Title VIII** of the **Civil Rights Act of 1968**) prohibits discrimination based on race, color, religion, sex, national origin, disability, or familial status in the sale or lease of residential property. It also prohibits discrimination in advertising, lending, and brokerage in residential transactions. Steering, blockbusting, and redlining are among the practices outlawed by the act. **Steering** is channeling prospective buyers or tenants to particular neighborhoods based on race, religion, or ethnic background. **Blockbusting** is trying to induce owners to sell their homes by suggesting the ethnic or racial composition of the neighborhood is changing, with the implication that property values will decline. This is also called **panic selling**. **Redlining** is refusing to make loans on property located in a particular neighborhood for discriminatory reasons. The Federal Fair Housing Laws are enforced by HUD or through a civil lawsuit in state or federal court.

3. Certain transactions are **exempt** from the Federal Fair Housing Act, but a person who has been discriminated against on the basis of **race** or **ancestry** in any of those transactions can still sue under the Civil Rights Act of 1866. Most of the Fair Housing Act's exemptions are not relevant in Ohio, because those transactions are **not** exempt from the Ohio Civil Rights Law.

4. The **Ohio Civil Rights Law** prohibits discrimination based on race, color, religion, sex, ancestry, national origin, disability, familial status, or military status. Ohio's fair housing provisions apply to the sale or lease of housing and any vacant land. The law also covers residential advertising, lending, and brokerage. The only exemptions from the fair housing provisions allow religious groups, charitable organizations, and private clubs to limit use of their own accommodations to their own members. The law can be enforced by the **Ohio Civil Rights Commission** or through a civil lawsuit in state court.

5. A seller or landlord who rejects a prospective buyer or tenant has violated **anti-discrimination laws** if the person's race (or religion, sex, etc.) was a factor in the rejection. That's true even if there were legitimate reasons for the rejection. Almost anyone associated with a real estate transaction can be held liable for fair housing violations and the Supreme Court has held that even **checkers** and **fair housing organizations** have **standing to sue** for violations of the fair housing laws.

6. A law that is neutral on its face value may have a **disparate impact** on a minority group, thus making it a violation of the fair housing laws. **Exclusionary zoning** ordinances violate fair housing laws because they tend to have a greater impact on minorities and other protected groups. Exclusionary zoning and disparate impact cases usually involve ordinances that prohibit or unreasonably restrict the construction of multi-family or low-income housing, effectively excluding minorities and low-income individuals from some communities.

Fair Housing Laws Summarized			
	Civil Rights Act of 1866	Federal Fair Housing Act	Ohio Civil Rights Act
Race	X	X	X
Color	X	X	X
Religion		X	X
Sex		X	X
National Origin		X	X
Ancestry	X		X
Disability		X	X
Familial Status		X	X
Military Status			X
Age			
Marital Status			
All Property (Real+Personal)	X		
Only Housing+Land for Housing		X	
Housing and ANY Vacant Land			X
Exceptions (FSBO= For Sale By Owner)	NONE	1. FSBO 2. FSBO, 4-Plex 3. Religious Groups 4. Private Clubs	1. Religious Groups 2. Private Clubs
Statute of Limitations	Same as State (1 Year in Ohio)	1 Yr—HUD Hearing 2 Yrs—Lawsuit	1 Yr—Hearing 1 Yr—Lawsuit

Quiz

1. **The Civil Rights Act of 1866 prohibits**
   a. all housing discrimination.
   b. any discrimination in the provision of government services.
   c. only discrimination in lending.
   d. racial discrimination in the sale or lease of any property.

2. **Title VIII of the Civil Rights Act of 1968 is also called the**
   a. Equal Opportunity in Housing Act.
   b. Federal Fair Housing Act.
   c. HUD.
   d. Ohio Civil Rights Law.

3. **The Federal Fair Housing Act declares that it is the policy of the United States to**
   a. build public housing for minority groups throughout the U.S.
   b. eliminate prejudice throughout the U.S.
   c. guarantee separate but equal housing in all states.
   d. provide for fair housing throughout the U.S.

4. **The Federal Fair Housing Act prohibits discrimination against**
   a. families with children.
   b. people more than 55 years old.
   c. students.
   d. unmarried couples.

5. **HUD's Office of Equal Opportunity handles complaints based on the**
   a. Civil Rights Act of 1866.
   b. Federal Fair Housing Act.
   c. Ohio Civil Rights Act.
   d. Panic Selling Act of 1975.

6. **Under the Federal Fair Housing Act, who can legally refuse to rent to a couple because they have a ten-year-old daughter? Assume no real estate agent is involved and no discriminatory advertising is used.**
   a. the owner of five-unit apartment house in Akron
   b. the owner of a large apartment complex in Cincinnati, who has a long, established policy of not renting to young couples with children
   c. the owner of a single-family home in Canton, who owns one other single-family home
   d. the female owner-occupant of a duplex who advertises "only women accepted"

7. **Blockbusting is an acceptable practice**
   a. only if the buyer and seller are notified and agree to participate.
   b. only when approved by HUD or the Ohio Real Estate Commission.
   c. under federal law but not under Ohio law.
   d. under no circumstances.

8. **The term "steering" refers to**
   a. directing customers to different listings based on their race or ancestry and the racial or ethnic composition of the neighborhoods.
   b. directing customers toward affordable property, based on their income and assets.
   c. giving minority customers special treatment as a form of affirmative action.
   d. refusing to accept listings from members of a particular minority group.

9. **X owns a retail office building in Springfield. He puts the property up for sale and Z makes an offer to buy it. X refuses to sell the property to Z because she is a born-again Christian who wants to open a daycare. This action violates**
   a. the Civil Rights Act of 1866 prohibition against discrimination in commercial property transactions.
   b. the Federal Fair Housing Act prohibition against discrimination based on familial status.
   c. the Ohio Civil Rights Law prohibition against discrimination based on religion.
   d. none of these laws, since this is a commercial transaction.

10. **Under the Ohio Civil Rights Law, complaints relating to housing discrimination are handled by the**

    a. Ohio Board of REALTORS®.
    b. Ohio Civil Rights Commission.
    c. Ohio Fair Housing Council.
    d. U.S. Department of Human Rights.

11. **To sue someone for violating the fair housing provisions of the Ohio Civil Rights Law, the plaintiff has to file suit in the court of common pleas within _____ after the violation.**

    a. 60 days
    b. 90 days
    c. 120 days
    d. 1 year

12. **V, a Japanese American, tries to rent an apartment in a four-unit building. The real estate broker who manages the building rejects V's application because her credit rating is not very good and also because she is Japanese. Does the real estate broker's refusal violate the Federal Fair Housing Act?**

    a. No, because a poor credit history is a legitimate reason for rejecting a rental applicant.
    b. No, because residential buildings with four units or less are exempt from the Fair Housing Act.
    c. Yes, because credit history is a protected class under the Federal Fair Housing Act.
    d. Yes, because V's race was a factor in the manager's decision, even though it was not his only reason for rejecting her.

13. **Nowhere City's new zoning ordinance contains no discriminatory language but has the effect of keeping minority families out of the city. Does this ordinance violate the Fair Housing Act?**

    a. No, because the Act does not prohibit discrimination against poor people.
    b. No, because the ordinance does not express intent to discriminate.
    c. Yes, because the Act prohibits discrimination based on income.
    d. Yes, because the ordinance has a disparate impact on minority groups.

14. **Which transaction, exempt from the Federal Fair Housing Act, is also exempt from the fair housing provisions of the Ohio Civil Rights Law?**

    a. J owns a duplex and lives in one of the units; he refuses to rent the other half to because she is female.
    b. The Qs refuse to sell their single-family home to Y because he is of Iranian ancestry.
    c. The Travelers Club (a private club that admits only men) refuses to let M stay in its lodgings because he is not a club member.
    d. W refuses to rent the spare room in his house to T because he is Jewish.

15. **This is the second time that B, an Ohio real estate broker, has been held liable for violating fair housing laws. As a result, the Real Estate Commission is required to**

    a. issue a restricted license to the broker.
    b. revoke his license.
    c. suspend his license for at least two months, or else revoke his license.
    d. suspend his license for at least one year, or else revoke his license.

5

The Nature of Real Property

This chapter explains the distinction between real property and personal property, with an in-depth discussion of the rights of ownership that go along with real property. These rules are important to everyone involved in the sale of real estate because they determine exactly what is being sold.

Key Terms

Appropriative Rights Water rights allocated by government permit, according to an appropriation system. It is not necessary to own property beside the body of water to apply for an appropriation permit.

Appurtenance A right that goes with ownership of real property; usually transferred with the property but may be sold separately.

Constructive Annexation Personal property associated with real property in such a way that the law treats it as a fixture, even though it is not physically attached to the real property.

Doctrine of Emblements The rule that allows an agricultural tenant to re-enter land to harvest crops if the lease ends (through no fault of the tenant) before the crop can be harvested. This rule applies only to the first crop.

Fixture An item of personal property that may or may not be attached to real property but is closely associated with real property in such a way that it has legally, and is intended to, become part of real property.

Fructus Industriales Plants sowed and cultivated by people ("fruits of industry").

Fructus Naturales Naturally occurring plants ("fruits of nature").

Natural Attachments Plants growing on land (e.g., trees, shrubs, crops)—considered real property.

Riparian Rights The water rights of a landowner whose property is adjacent to, or crossed by, a river (or more generally, any body of water).

Rule of Capture A legal principle that grants a landowner the right to all oil and gas produced from wells on her land, even if it migrated from land belonging to someone else.

Trade Fixture Articles of personal property annexed to real property by a tenant for use in her trade business.

Real and Personal Property

The law classifies all property as either:

- **Real property**—Land and everything attached to it

- **Personal property**—Any property that is moveable and not affixed to land (sometimes referred to as **chattel** or **personalty**)

The distinction between the two becomes important whenever the ownership or possession of land is transferred. Unless otherwise agreed, all the real property is included in the transfer, but personal property that happens to be on the land is not included. Because of this rule, buyers and sellers, landlords and tenants, and owners and foreclosing lenders often disagree about whether property is real property or personal property.

However, real property law is technical and precise, and the terminology has an exact meaning. The real estate laws value tradition, precision, and precedent. Normally, there is a well-defined law to cover a given situation. Change in real property law has been slow and evolutionary, usually in response to commercial and business needs.

Real Property Rights

Real property rights are defined in terms of a **bundle of rights** that are conferred by ownership:

- **Right of use**—Confers to the owner the right to make the land productive. The owner may make use of the land in any way seen fit, as long as that use does not interfere with the rights of others.

- **Right of enjoyment**—Confers to the owner the freedom to use the land without undue interference from the outside (also includes the responsibility to ensure that neighbors' enjoyment of their land is not adversely affected).

- **Right of disposal**—Confers to the owner the ability to transfer all or some of these rights to others. The landowner normally has the right to sell, divide, and retain part of the land while selling the rest, leasing the land, giving it away, or disposing of the land by will or intestate transfer.

If one secures the entire bundle of rights from another, that person is said to be the owner.

Trespass, Encroachment, and Nuisance

Certain activities interfere with a property owner's bundle of rights. These activities can be categorized as trespass, encroachment, and nuisance.

Trespass

Trespass is defined as *a physical invasion of the land by another person who has no lawful right to enter the land*. Trespass interferes with the owner's possessory interest in the land, diminishing the owner's right of use and right of enjoyment, since during the trespass the owner of the land has less than full possession of the land. However, in order for an action in trespass to ensue, the act of trespass must cause direct, rather than consequential, damage.

Encroachment

Encroachment, which is *a legal synonym for trespass*, is *used in reference to objects* (e.g., buildings) whereas trespass refers to people. If a neighbor's building is constructed over the property line, that neighbor's building encroaches on another person's land. Legal steps can be taken to force the encroaching landowner to either remove the encroachment by tearing down the building or buy the land on which the encroachment sits. In another case, if a tree grows over the property line, it may be trimmed by the owner encroached upon to the property line with the full support of the law.

Nuisance

A **nuisance** *involves interference with the quiet enjoyment of the land from the outside;* thus, it does not involve interference with possessory rights. In order to be actionable, a nuisance must be more than a single occurrence. It must be a condition that constitutes an unreasonable use of the land by the offending landowner, extending over a period of time. Should the complaining landowner prevail in court, he may collect damages as well as obtain an injunction from a court of law to stop the unreasonable use of the land through an injunction.

Normally, courts take a dim view of actions in nuisance when the offended landowner moved into the area knowing of the nuisance (e.g., a landowner offended by the smells of the stockyard situated a few blocks away will find it hard to sustain action in nuisance). Furthermore, where the common good would be better served by *not* disturbing the offending use, the offended landowner may not win in court (e.g., a factory built in an area of high unemployment would probably be protected against landowners claiming smoke to be a nuisance).

The Land Itself

Land is legally considered to include the surface of the earth, the subsurface to the center of the earth, and the atmosphere above the land. In common law, property rights in land (in theory) extend into the heavens above. However, commercial air travel and the practical necessity for limiting air rights have severely curtailed the common law rule. In general, the rights of landownership include the surface, subsurface, and reasonable air rights.

When describing the land as in a legal description, only the surface is detailed; the law implies the subsurface and air rights are included. The description consists of the land's boundaries and does not include any buildings or other improvements to the land. As you will see, these would be included in any transfer of the land, regardless of their absence from the legal description.

People tend to think of the land itself when they hear the term "real property;" however, the term refers to much more than rocks and dirt. Real property also encompasses items and property attached to the land (**attachments**) and rights that go with ownership of the land (**appurtenances**).

Attachments

Attachments are things connected to the land, whether natural or man-made. Attachments can be grown on the land (trees and shrubs) and built on the land (houses and fences). All attachments are generally considered real property.

Natural Attachments

Natural attachments are *plants growing on land.* There are two types of natural attachments:

- **Fructus naturales** ("fruits of nature")—Naturally occurring trees and plants
- **Fructus industriales** ("fruits of industry")—Cultivated plants

Originally, different legal rules applied to the two types of natural attachments but today they are treated essentially the same. Both types are ordinarily considered part of real property while they are growing but become personal property when they are severed from the land.

For Example

A tree growing on the land is part of the real property. Once the tree is cut down, however, it is personal property.

The same rule applies to crops (as opposed to the plants or trees themselves). Until harvested, crops are part of the real property.

Case Example

Mr. and Mrs. Herron owned some farmland. Mr. Herron sowed wheat on the property after his wife filed suit for divorce. In the divorce decree, the court awarded the farmland to Mrs. Herron and did not mention the wheat.

When the wheat crop ripened some months later, Mr. Herron re-entered the property and harvested it. His ex-wife sued him for trespassing.

The court ruled in favor of Mrs. Herron. When she took title to the land through the divorce decree, she also took title to the wheat crop. The court ruled that the wheat crop was part of the real property. *Herron v. Herron*, 47 Ohio St. 544, 25 N.E. 420 (1899).

In the same way, an unharvested crop would be treated as part of the real property in a sale of the land. The buyer would take title to the grains, fruits, or vegetables unless it had specifically been agreed that the crop was excluded from the sale.

There are some exceptions to the general rule:

- When land is assessed for tax purposes, the market value of an unharvested crop is not included in the assessed value of the real property. In this case, an unharvested crop is treated as personal property.

- Natural attachments (e.g., crops) sold separately from the land are treated as personal property even before they are actually severed from the land.

For Example

A farmer sells the timber on his east 40 acres to a lumber company. The sale contract states the trees are to be cut next year, but the lumber company owns the trees as of the contract date. They are considered personal property from that date forward, although they are still attached to the land.

There is also a special rule that applies to crops planted by tenant farmers. A tenant farmer's crops are referred to as **emblements**. Under the legal theory of the **doctrine of emblements**, *a tenant farmer is allowed to re-enter the land to harvest crops that were planted by the tenant farmer even after the tenancy ended.* This doctrine applies if the tenancy was for an indefinite period of time and the tenancy is terminated (through no fault of the tenant) before the crop is ready for harvest. If the crops are an annual product of perennial plants (e.g., apples), the right to re-enter and harvest applies only to the first crop that matures.

Fixtures

A **fixture** is *an item of personal property that may or may not be attached to real property but is closely associated with real property in such a way that it has, and is intended to, become part of the real property.*

For Example

An air-conditioner is personal property but becomes a fixture when permanently installed in a building. A pile of lumber is personal property but is turned into a fixture when used to build a barn. A major fixture that significantly increases the value of the property, such as a building, is commonly called an **improvement**.

Annexation is the *legal term for attaching or affixing personal property to real property.* Since fixtures and improvements are part of the land, they need not be mentioned in the purchase agreement; they are included by implication in the description of the real estate. Although, trouble can arise when an agent encounters questionable items that could be classified differently depending on who he asks.

Real estate agents must constantly deal with the question of what constitutes personal property and what items are fixtures and, therefore, are real property:

- Are a built-in washer and a dryer fixtures?

- Is a tool shed an improvement?

- Is a chandelier personal property?

- What about a satellite dish?

To avoid trouble, a real estate agent should discuss any questionable items with the seller and buyer before they sign a contract, making sure everyone understands what is and is not included in the sale.

For the arguments that end up as lawsuits, the courts take a variety of factors into account in determining whether an item is a fixture. In *Masheter v. Boehm*, 37 Ohio St. 2d 68, 307 N.E.2d 533 (1974), the Ohio Supreme Court listed these criteria:

- The nature of the item

- The manner in which the item is annexed to the realty

- The purpose for which the item was annexed

- Whether the annexer intended to make the item part of the realty

- How difficult it would be to remove the item

- Any economic loss removal of the item would cause

- Whether removal would damage the item

Intention and Purpose

The Ohio Supreme Court indicated that one of the most important considerations are the intention of the **annexer** (the person who owned the item as personal property and brought it onto the real property) and the purpose of the annexation:

- Did the annexer intend for it to become part of the real property or to remain personal property?

- Did the annexer acquire the item to improve the real property or simply for personal use?

In answering these questions, the court will look for objective evidence of the annexer's intention. It is not enough for the annexer to claim that he always intended to remove the item. The other considerations the court listed, such as the nature of the item and the manner of annexation, are viewed as objective evidence of intent.

For Example

Embedding a birdbath in concrete indicates an intention to make it a permanent feature; simply setting one out on the lawn does not.

Manner of Annexation

The manner of annexation was the key factor in many early court decisions about fixtures. If the item was securely attached to the real property (e.g., nailed or bolted down), then it was considered a fixture. If it was not physically attached and could be moved easily, then it was not a fixture.

That test is not rigidly applied today. Physical attachment is still taken into account, but it is not decisive. An item may be physically attached and still be personal property if none of the other criteria are met.

For Example

A Persian carpet in the front hall is attached to the floor with fine tacks. When the homeowner acquired the carpet, the homeowner tacked it down to prevent it from sliding—not to make it a permanent part of the house. The tacks could be easily removed without damaging the carpet and it would not cost much to repair the tiny holes made in the floor by the tacks. A modern court would probably rule that the carpet was personal property, not a fixture, in spite of the physical attachment.

Actual annexation is *when a fixture is physically attached to the real property.* On the other hand, an item may be considered a fixture without being physically attached to the property in any way. It is called **constructive annexation** *when personal property is associated with real property in such a way that the law treats it as a fixture, even though it is not physically attached to the real property.* In other words, any item that is essential to the use of the real property (e.g., the key to the front door of a house) is a fixture. Items specially designed or adapted for the property are also likely to be considered fixtures (e.g., wall-to-wall carpeting cut to fit a particular room even if not tacked down, a set of storm windows made for a particular building even if they are being stored in the basement).

The rule that an item may be a fixture even though it is not physically attached is often referred to as "**the doctrine of constructive annexation**." Along with the previous examples, the doctrine covers fixtures that have been temporarily removed from the real property for servicing (e.g., a homebuyer takes title to the built-in dishwasher even though it was at the repair shop on the day the sale closed).

Here is a case that illustrates how a court weighs various factors in deciding what is a fixture and what is not.

Case Example

Mr. Long owned a large, elegant home built on 97 acres in Indian Hill in the style of an English manor house with vaulted ceilings, stone stairways, a marble fireplace, a pipe organ, and formal gardens.

Mr. Long died in a plane crash. In his will, he left all his personal property to his adult children. The executor of the estate was directed to sell the Indian Hill house and place the proceeds in a trust.

The executor sold the house to Mr. Paul for $575,000. When Mr. Paul took possession of the property, he discovered Mr. Long's children removed many things that had been in the house when he agreed to buy it.

Mr. Paul sued, and the court had to sort out whether each missing item was personal property or a fixture. The Longs had the right to take personal property, but not fixtures.

The court considered the characteristics of each missing item and ruled that most were fixtures. For example, the lights around the swimming pool had been easy to remove—simply unplugged and unhooked from the poles they were hanging from—but the court held that the lights were fixtures because they had been specially designed for the house and the poles looked bare and incomplete without them.

(continued on next page)

_____
Case Example (cont.)
_____

The Longs had taken four statues off pedestals in the garden. These statues were not just sitting on the pedestals—each statue had a hole in its base and was held in place by a pipe projecting out of the pedestal into the hole. The court ruled that these statues were "permanent emplacements, intended to be part of the continuing visual effect of the estate."

Another statue in the garden was not attached to the property in any way. Even so, the court decided it also was a fixture, since it was part of the elegant character of the house and grounds. And though the walnut organ bench was not physically attached to the property, it belonged with the pipe organ, which was built in.

On the other hand, the court found that the large stove was personal property. Although it was enclosed in a cabinet, it could be pulled out without being damaged or damaging the house. There was nothing special about the stove and it could easily be replaced.

The Longs were ordered to pay damages to Mr. Paul to compensate him for the fixtures they wrongfully removed. *Paul v. First Nat'l Bank of Cincinnati*, 52 Ohio Misc. 77, 369 N.E.2d 488 (1976).

Relationship of the Parties

Another factor a court often takes into account in fixture disputes is the relationship of the parties.

Between *a seller and a buyer* of real property, the rules for determining whether an item is a fixture are usually interpreted *in favor of the buyer.*

For Example

S, a homeowner, screws a chandelier into the dining room ceiling. Several months later, she sells the house to C. The chandelier is likely to be considered a fixture, even though it would be easy to remove.

Between *a landlord and a tenant*, the rules tend to be interpreted *in favor of the tenant.* A tenant who installs a chandelier (or some other ornamental item) usually has the right to remove it at the end of the lease.

These rules tie in with considering the annexer's intention: The law presumes that a homeowner intends to improve real property, but that a tenant installs things only for personal use.

This rule does not mean a tenant is invariably allowed to remove everything he installed. If a tenant built a deck onto the back of a rented house, for instance, it would almost certainly be considered a fixture and part of the landlord's real property. As usual, the court would look at the nature of the item, the manner of annexation, how difficult it would be to remove, etc.

However, there is a special rule for trade fixtures. **Trade fixtures** are *articles of personal property annexed to real property by a tenant for use in her trade business.* A tenant is always allowed to remove trade fixtures at the end of the tenancy.

For Example

A tenant who operates a salon could remove the shampoo basins, lighted mirrors, and adjustable chairs, even though they were attached to the walls or floors. The tenant would be responsible for repairing any damage to the premises caused by the removal.

Written Agreement

Regardless of any of the previously discussed considerations, if there is a written agreement between the parties stipulating how a particular item is to be treated, a court will enforce the agreement.

When a seller wants to remove things that might be considered fixtures, he should inform the buyer and include a statement in the purchase agreement specifying what items are excluded from the sale. Natural attachments (e.g., rosebushes) can be excluded in the same way.

On the other hand, the seller might agree to include items that could be considered personal property in the sale. In that case, it is a good idea for the buyer to ask for a **bill of sale**, which transfers title to personal property, just as a deed transfers title to real property. The buyer should always make sure the purchase agreement lists the personal property the seller has agreed to leave behind.

Mobile Homes

A mobile home is classified as personal property until it is permanently attached to real estate by removing the wheels and mounting the unit on a foundation. As personal property, mobile homes may be sold without a real estate license.

In the Practice of Real Estate

Two problems face the real estate agent:

* Fixtures the owner wishes to remove

* Personal property items the buyer wishes to include in the sale

Regarding fixtures, suggest to the seller that the item be removed and replaced prior to showing. This eliminates the situation in which a buyer sees the beautiful crystal chandelier in the dining room and resolves all issues regarding whether the buyer saw the item and assumed it would transfer. This situation can even occur when "red tagging" items. The tag may be accidentally removed, or the buyer may misunderstand the meaning of the tag and assume that he is getting an item the seller never intended to be sold as part of the real property transaction.

Regarding personal property to be included in the sale, resolve the issue by including a list of the items in the offer to purchase. That way, there are no assumptions regarding whether something will or will not be included in the sale. In either case, an agent should recommend that everything be put in writing—this will allow an agent to more genuinely assist his client or customer should a dispute arise.

The Impact of the Uniform Commercial Code

The **Uniform Commercial Code (UCC)** is a *body of statutory law that governs transactions involving personal property*. As previously explained, personal property becomes realty when any of the tests for fixtures are met. The UCC and its procedures protect the vendor of the personal property, the new owner of the real estate, and the seller by fixing the rights of each at the time of the sale of the item to be affixed.

For Example

M purchases a home with a new furnace. It is clear from any test that this furnace is a fixture; that is, it is part of the house. At one time, however, it stood on a showroom floor or was crated in a box in a warehouse as personal property. Let's assume at the time the furnace was purchased A, the owner, entered into an installment contract to pay for the furnace and that it was not completely paid off when he sold his home to M. A would assume M would have to pay for the furnace since she bought the furnace as part of the real estate. The vendor's contract, however, is with A, the seller. But A moved and is no longer in the area. The vendor then attempts to seek satisfaction from M. However, M can successfully defend against the vendor, claiming never to have been a party to the vendor's contract. So, the vendor would be out the money.

The UCC solves all these problems by making the vendor file, within ten days of installation, a financing statement with the office of the county recorder in the county within which the land is situated. This fixture filing includes a legal description of the land as well as the name and address of the landowner. In this way, all parties are protected. Since the home buyer would be on notice of the debt, the seller might not be able to convey marketable title without paying off the furnace. The vendor will likely be paid and not have to chase the parties in litigation. Vendors who fail to file in a timely manner lose their rights against the owner in cases like in the previous example.

Appurtenances

Appurtenances are *rights that go along with real property*. When real property is sold, appurtenant rights are ordinarily sold along with it. However, they can be sold separately and may be limited by past transactions. In addition to knowing the boundaries of a piece of property and what items are considered part of the real property, an agent also needs to understand what rights are transferred along with that property.

One way to understand the rights that accompany real property is to imagine the property as an inverted pyramid, with its tip at the center of the earth and its base extending out into the sky. An owner has rights to the surface of the land within the property's boundaries, plus everything under or over the surface that falls within the pyramid. This includes rights to oil and minerals beneath the surface and certain air and water rights.

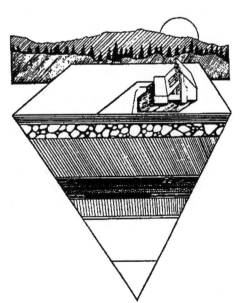

The Inverted Pyramid:

A Summary of Appurtenant Rights

Limited Air Rights

Some Water Rights

Surface Rights

Access Rights

Sub-Surface Rights

Mineral Rights

Oil Rights

Air Rights

According to the inverted pyramid concept, a property owner's rights extend to the upper limits of the sky. When air travel became established, however, Congress gave the federal government complete control over U.S. airspace. Property owners still have the exclusive right to use the lower reaches of airspace over their property, but they may not interfere with air traffic.

On the other hand, owners have the right *not* to be harmed by use of the airspace above their property.

For Example

An airport is built near a chicken farm. If the noise of the airplanes flying over the farm causes the chickens to stop laying eggs, the farmer may be able to recover damages for the resulting loss of income.

A property owner may also sell rights to the airspace over a property separately from the land.

For Example

The New York Central and New Haven Railroads have tracks running across real estate in a prime location. They sold rights to the airspace above the tracks, along with an easement to allow for the construction and support of buildings. A large complex of commercial buildings was later built above the tracks.

A more common example is an ordinary condominium sale. Someone who buys a condominium unit in a high rise building purchases not just the physical apartment, but also the airspace in which the unit is situated.

Water Rights

There are two main types of water rights that can be acquired:

- **Riparian rights**—Obtained through land ownership
- **Appropriative rights**—Obtained by government permit

Riparian Rights

Riparian rights are *the water rights of a landowner whose property adjoins a river, lake, or other body of water.* Any land adjacent to water or crossed by water is riparian land. The terms "**riparian rights**" and "**riparian land**" also encompass the terms "**littoral rights**" and "**littoral land**." Technically, riparian rights are associated with rivers and littoral rights are associated with lakes, but the term riparian rights is most commonly used and usually refers to both types of water rights.

The owner of riparian land has the right to make reasonable use of the water. Keep in mind that having the right to use the water is not the same thing as owning the water. All the riparian landowners on a river or lake share the right to use the water for recreational purposes. They also share the right to take water for domestic purposes (e.g., drinking, washing, watering a garden).

Riparian owners can also take water for other purposes (e.g., irrigation, power). These uses, however, must not be wasteful or interfere with other riparian owners' use of the water. An upstream owner also may *not* unreasonably diminish the flow or the quality of the water, which would prevent downstream owners from using it to their full and rightful advantage.

Case Example

Mr. Elsea owned property upstream from Mr. and Mrs. Montelious on Scippo Creek in Pickaway County. The Monteliouses used the creek to water their livestock.

In the spring, Elsea pumped water from the creek to irrigate two acres of strawberries. The Monteliouses claimed Elsea's pump caused the water level in the creek to drop and muddied the water so it was not fit for their livestock to drink. They sued Elsea to make him stop using the pump.

At trial, expert testimony established that Elsea's irrigation did not make a significant difference in the amount or the quality of the water flowing past the Monteliouses' property. Instead, their water problems were due to natural causes. The court ruled that Elsea had the right to continue pumping water from the creek for his strawberries. *Montelious v. Elsea*, 11 Ohio Op. 2d 57, 161 N.E.2d 675 (1959).

As a general rule, a riparian landowner is not allowed to divert water for use on non-riparian land. This is because when the water is used on riparian land, all of the excess flows back into the river or lake; when water is transported out of the watershed, it does not return, and the river or lake is diminished. So, in the previous example, Mr. Elsea would not have been allowed to take water from Scippo Creek to irrigate strawberries planted on non-riparian land, but what he did was acceptable.

Appropriative Rights

Appropriative rights are *water rights granted by government permit, and do not depend on ownership of riparian land.* The government grants a permit to give the holder the right to take water from a particular body of water for a specified use.

Appropriated water does not have to be used on riparian land. The appropriation system is particularly important in western states, where there are vast tracts of arid land. To make that land habitable and productive, water has to be transported from other areas for irrigation and public consumption.

The rights of the riparian landowners on a lake or river are taken into account when permits to appropriate water from that lake or river are issued. Appropriative rights generally are not allowed to interfere with riparian rights.

Navigable Waters and Ownership of Submerged Land

All navigable waterways in the U.S. are controlled by the federal and state governments. The landowners beside navigable waters have riparian rights, subject to a public easement. That means the public has the right to use the waterways for transportation and recreation.

In many states, the government has title to all lands submerged under navigable waters. In Ohio, however, a riparian landowner has title to the riverbed out to its midpoint, even if the river is navigable. The exception to this rule is that the state of Ohio has title to the land submerged beneath Lake Erie, held in trust for its citizens.

A non-navigable lake is considered private property. If a small lake is completely within the boundaries of one person's land, that landowner also owns the lake bed. If several people own lots around a non-navigable lake, ownership of the lake bed is generally divided among the riparian landowners by tracing lines from each lot boundary to the center of the lake. Each owner has title to the piece of the bed adjoining his lot.

Mineral Rights

Solid mineral rights are straightforward. A landowner owns all the solid minerals located in or under his land. Minerals are considered real property until they are extracted from the earth. A landowner may sell or lease mineral rights separately from the surface land. Since most landowners do not have the necessary skill or equipment to mine or drill, they usually sell or lease their rights to a mining, oil, or gas company.

But while solid mineral rights are easy to quantify, there is a different rule for oil and gas. In their natural state, oil and gas lie trapped beneath the earth's surface under great pressure. Once an oil or gas reservoir has been tapped, the oil and gas flow toward the point where the reservoir was pierced by the well (since that is the area of lowest pressure). By drilling a well, a landowner can drain oil or gas not only from beneath his own land, but also from beneath the neighboring land.

Because of their fugitive nature, oil and gas are governed by the rule of capture. The **rule of capture** says that *whoever drills a well on his land owns all the oil or gas the well produces, even though it may have migrated from under a neighbor's land*. This rule is designed to stimulate oil and gas production, since the only way landowners can prevent the oil or gas under their property from migrating to a neighbor's well is by drilling their own offset wells.

Dormant Mineral Interests

The Ohio legislature passed a statute to terminate certain unused mineral interests, where these mineral interests are held by someone other than the surface owner of the property. As of 1992, mineral interests are considered abandoned if they have been completely inactive for more than 20 years. In most cases, an interest will terminate 20 years after the mineral deed or lease was recorded, unless the interest holder actually extracted minerals or was issued a drilling or mining permit during that period. The holder can prevent termination by recording a notice of intent to preserve his or her mineral interest.

This statute applies to oil, gas, and most solid minerals but it does not apply to coal. When mineral interests are abandoned under the terms of this statute, the mineral rights return to the surface owner.

Support Rights

A piece of land is supported by other land surrounding it. A landowner has a right to the natural support provided by land beside and beneath his property.

Lateral Support

Lateral support is *support from adjacent land*. This lateral support may be affected by certain occurrences which may be negligence on the part of an individual.

For Example

S's excavations made his neighbor's land shift and settle. In some cases, S can be held liable for the resulting damage. Usually that liability depends on negligence. The neighbor must prove S did not use reasonable care in carrying out the excavations. Reasonable care includes warning adjacent landowners about the planned excavations far enough in advance so they can take steps to protect their property.

Ohio has a special rule for excavations that take place within a city and go deeper than nine feet. Under those circumstances, the excavating landowner will be held liable for any resulting damage to the neighbor's buildings, no matter how carefully the excavations were performed.

Subjacent Support

Subjacent support is *support from the underlying earth*. The right to subjacent support is important when a landowner transfers mineral rights to someone else. Generally, the mining party is liable for surface damage caused by underground mining even if excavations were carefully performed.

Accession

When an item or additional land is added to a parcel of real property, the owner acquires title to the addition by **accession**. This can occur by annexation or by the forces of nature.

Annexation

As a general rule, **annexation** *transforms personal property into a fixture that becomes part of the real property*; the owner of the real property also becomes the owner of the annexed property. When someone builds a house or installs a swimming pool or plants a tree, personal property is annexed to real property. If a person plants or builds something on someone else's land, knowing that the land is not his, that person will lose title to the personal property he annexed to the land. The plants or structures now belong to the landowner. Special rules apply, however, if the person believed in good faith that he had title to the land.

For Example

Suppose that after inheriting some land from her great-uncle, C built a house on it. Later, it turns out her great-uncle did not actually have title. The true owners of the land file an action to recover the property and the court rules in their favor. At that point, the true owners can evict C from the property and pay her the value of the house she built, or they can demand that she pay them the value of the unimproved land.

The previous example illustrates the **occupying claimant law**. However, C may have a claim of "**adverse possession**" if she had used the property openly and notoriously for 21 years or more.

Forces Of Nature

The land itself can move or change shape and sometimes, this results in an involuntary transfer of title.

Erosion. Erosion is the gradual wearing away of land by wind, rain, and other natural forces. Eroded soil may end up moving across a property line from A's land to B's land. When this happens, A loses title to the eroded soil, and B acquires title.

Accretion. Accretion is when waterborne silt is deposited in a river or lake bed or on the shore. These deposits are called **alluvion** or **alluvium**. Riparian or littoral property is increased by alluvium, and the riparian or littoral landowner acquires title to the newly deposited silt. Like erosion, accretion is a gradual process that may significantly increase or decrease an owner's property over a very long period.

Avulsion. Avulsion occurs when land is violently torn away by flowing water. Avulsion is not a gradual process and does not necessarily result in a transfer of title. If it is possible to identify the severed land, the original owner can reclaim it.

Avulsion can also refer to a sudden change in a watercourse.

For Example

A river has always marked the boundary line between two properties. Flood waters tear away some land and, when the flood subsides, the river flows in a different channel. The boundary between the two properties does not change, even though the river has moved. In other words, the river no longer marks the boundary.

Reliction. Reliction is when a body of water recedes slowly, exposing more of the riverbed or lake bed. This is also called **dereliction.** In Ohio, since a riparian landowner already has title to the bed out to the midpoint of the body of water, reliction does not increase a landowner's property. In other states, where a landowner's property ends at the water's edge, reliction can add to the property.

Summary

1. **Real property** is defined as land and everything attached or appurtenant to it. Real property rights are defined in terms of a **bundle of rights** that are conferred by ownership. These rights are the *right of use*, the *right of enjoyment*, and the *right of disposal*. If one secures the entire bundle of rights from another, that person is said to be the owner. **Trespass, encroachment**, and **nuisance** are three kinds of interference with these rights.

2. **Attachments** to real property are part of the real property. The two types of attachments are **natural attachments** (e.g., plants, trees) and **man-made attachments** (e.g., fences, buildings). Man-made attachments are called **fixtures**. A major fixture (e.g., a building), is called an **improvement**. Unless otherwise agreed, attachments are transferred with the land; personal property is not. Difficulties can arise over what is considered real property versus personal property.

3. A **fixture** is an item of personal property that may or may not be attached to real property; it is either intended to remain with, or is so closely associated with, real property in such a way that it has legally become part of the real property. In deciding whether an item is a fixture, a court tries to determine the intention of the **annexer**. The court also takes into account the nature of the item, the manner of annexation, the purpose for which it was annexed, the difficulty and cost of removal, potential damage from removal, the relationship of the parties, and any written agreement. **Written agreements** always take precedence. **Trade fixtures** are an exception to the general fixture rules. Since they are installed by a tenant for use in the business, trade fixtures may be removed by the trade tenant before the lease period is over.

4. An **appurtenance** is a right that goes with or relates to real property, including **air, water, mineral**, and **support rights**. These rights are ordinarily transferred with the land but may be severed from it and sold separately. This is often the case with mineral rights where the owner does not have the skill or equipment necessary to tap these mineral resources. **Mineral rights** are straightforward in that the landowner owns all solid minerals beneath his land. Oil and gas, however, are governed by the **rule of capture,** which states whoever drills a well owns all of the oil and gas it produces.

5. The right to use water is either a **riparian right** or an **appropriative right**. All landowners whose property adjoins a body of water have riparian rights to use the water for recreation or personal use on their own land. To acquire an appropriative right, one must obtain a permit from the government, which then allows the permit holder to use water for irrigation or other special uses.

6. A real property owner acquires title by **accession** when something is added to the property, either by **annexation** or by **forces of nature**. Annexation transforms personal property into a fixture, which becomes part of the real property. The forces of nature can *add* to an owner's land through **accretion** or *subtract* land from an owner's holding through **erosion** or **avulsion**.

Quiz

1. **If a tenancy is terminated before a crop is ready to harvest, a tenant farmer has the right to re-enter the land later to harvest the crop. This rule is known as the doctrine of**

   a. appurtenance.

   b. constructive annexation.

   c. emblements.

   d. fructus industriales.

2. **L is in the process of selling her house. On the closing date, the built-in microwave is at the repair shop. As a result, the microwave**

   a. is L's personal property and will not be considered part of the sale.

   b. will be considered part of the sale under the doctrine of constructive annexation.

   c. will have to be conveyed under a separate contract, since it was not actually in the house at the time of the sale.

   d. is the property of the first person to retrieve it from the repair shop.

3. **In determining whether an item is a fixture, the most important test is**

   a. the intention of the annexer.

   b. the relationship of the parties.

   c. the size of the item.

   d. whether it is physically attached to the realty.

4. **Trade fixtures**

   a. are considered the landlord's personal property.

   b. are considered real property and cannot be removed by the tenant.

   c. can be removed by the tenant before the lease expires.

   d. cannot be removed unless the lease specifically states they are personal property.

5. **A candy maker has a five-year lease. The lease states that any improvements the tenant makes to the premises will become part of the real property and pass to the landlord at the end of the lease. The candy maker installs a marble counter on which to roll the candy. When the lease is up, the candy maker may**

   a. not remove the counter because he did not ask the owner if he could install it.

   b. not remove the counter because of the written agreement.

   c. remove the counter because it is not a fixture.

   d. remove the counter because it is a trade fixture.

6. **The Erie Railroad's tracks run through downtown Lumpington. The railroad owns the property around its tracks. The Colossus Corporation wants to buy the airspace above the tracks to build a shopping complex. Which statement is TRUE?**

   a. Colossus can buy the air rights from the railroad.

   b. Colossus must buy the air rights from the federal government, since it has control over airspace.

   c. Unlike other appurtenant rights, air rights cannot be sold separately from the property.

   d. Colossus cannot refuse to sell the air rights if the development would not interfere with operations.

7. **T owns two tracts of property. Fierce Creek runs through one tract, but the other tract is across the road and does not adjoin the creek. T uses water from the creek to irrigate his crops on both tracts. This use of the water is**

   a. illegal.

   b. illegal, unless Fierce Creek is navigable.

   c. legal, if T has an appropriation permit.

   d. legal, since T has a riparian right to the use of the water.

8. ***J owns property along a navigable river in Ohio. Which statement is TRUE?***

   a. The federal government owns the riverbed.

   b. J is not entitled to use the water because it is owned by the federal government.

   c. J owns the section of the riverbed adjoining her property out to the middle of the river.

   d. The state government owns the riverbed.

9. ***The rule of capture provides that***

   a. oil and gas remain real property even after being captured.

   b. oil and gas rights cannot be sold separately from the land.

   c. a property owner who drills a well owns all of the oil or gas it produces, even though some migrated under a neighbor's land.

   d. all of the above

10. ***Ohio's statute concerning abandoned mineral interests***

   a. applies only to unused coal rights.

   b. applies only when the holder of the mineral interest is someone other than the owner of the surface property.

   c. does not apply to oil and gas rights.

   d. terminates interests that have been inactive for five years or more.

Interests in Real Property

A person who has a property right or a claim against property is said to have an interest in the property. An interest might be an ownership right (e.g., life estate), a right to use the property (e.g., easement), or a financial claim against the title (e.g., mortgage). This chapter explains the various types of interests, how they are created and terminated, and how they affect the property.

Key Terms

Adverse Possession When someone acquires title to real property by openly occupying it without the owner's permission for more than 21 years.

Dower In Ohio (and some other states), the interest held by a married person in the real property his or her spouse owns in fee simple during their marriage. (At common law, dower referred only to the wife's interest in her husband's property, while the husband's interest in his wife's property was called **courtesy**—also spelled **curtesy**. Now, dower refers to either spouse's interest in the other's property.)

Easement A right to use part of another person's real property for a particular purpose. An easement is irrevocable and creates an interest in the property.

Encumbrance A nonpossessory interest in property (such as an easement, lien, or restrictive covenant), which burdens the property owner's title.

Estate 1. A possessory interest in real property; either a freehold estate or a leasehold estate. 2. The real and personal property left by someone who has died.

Fee Simple An inheritable, transferable, perpetual ownership interest.

Foreclosure When a lienholder causes property to be sold so unpaid debt secured by the lien can be satisfied from the sale proceeds.

Freehold Estate An ownership estate in real property; either a fee simple or a life estate. The holder of a freehold estate has title.

Leasehold Estate An interest that gives the holder (tenant) a temporary right to exclusive possession of the estate, but without having title.

Lien A nonpossessory interest in property, giving a lienholder the right to foreclose if the owner does not pay a debt owed the lienholder; a financial encumbrance on the owner's title.

Life Estate A freehold estate (ownership interest) that lasts only as long as a specified person (the **measuring life**) lives.

Possessory Interest An interest in property that includes the right to possess and occupy the property, either now or in the future.

Possessory Interests: Estates

An **estate** is *a possessory interest in real property*. A **possessory interest** *entitles the holder to possession of the property, either now or in the future*. A person who has an estate has either the right to possess the property now, will have that right in the future, or may have that right in the future. A right to immediate possession is called a **present interest**. A right to possession in the future is called a **future interest**. In addition to being classified according to the time of enjoyment (present or future), interests are either **freehold estates** or **leasehold estates**.

Freehold Estates

A **freehold estate** is *a possessory interest of uncertain duration*. Although the estate may end, no one knows exactly when it will. There are two main categories of freehold estates:

- Fee simple estates
- Life estates

Fee Simple Estates

Fee simple estates (also referred to as **fee simple absolutes**) are *the fullest freehold estate interest that can exist in real property*. When a person is referred to as the "owner" of property, it usually means he holds a fee simple absolute. Since the fee simple estate is absolute, this implies there are no conditions on the property title—it is inheritable, transferable, and perpetual. The owner of a fee simple absolute has the right to possess the property for an unlimited period of time and it will pass to the owner's heirs after death. The owner may also choose to sell the property, give it away, or transfer a lesser interest in it.

When a fee simple absolute owner deeds an interest in property to someone else, it is presumed that the entire estate is transferred, unless the deed specifies that it transfers something less.

For Example

If A owns land in fee simple absolute and deeds it "to B" without any limiting language, B will then own the land in fee simple absolute.

Fee Simple Defeasible

A **fee simple defeasible** (or **defeasible fee**) is *a type of real property ownership that may be defeated or undone if certain events occur or certain conditions are not met*.

For Example

The grantor (A) could choose to qualify B's title by including a condition or requirement in the deed language that may transfer property "to B, so long as the house is used as a Civil War museum." If B uses the house for some other purpose, B might forfeit title to the property and title would revert to A (or if A is no longer alive, to A's heirs).

One type of defeasible fee interest is known as a **fee simple determinable**, which is *a defeasible fee estate terminated automatically if certain conditions occur*. This is also known in the law as a **fee simple conditional**, which is slightly different in that it is a defeasible fee that *may be* terminated by the owner if conditions stated in the deed are not met.

Since a fee simple determinable terminates automatically and immediately if the condition in the deed is not met, the former owner who set up the condition can seek recovery of the land through an **action in forcible entry**. The land will once again belong to the former owner. No consideration is given in law for money paid for the land or any improvements on the land. Until the condition is met, however, the former owner has merely a contingent future interest in the land, which is called a *possibility of reverter*.

This **possibility of reverter** is a reversionary interest, since, if the condition is met, title to the land reverts back to the former owner who set the condition. It may be of interest to note the harsh result that completely divests the owner from property in this way is avoided wherever possible in today's legal system. Courts strain to find remedies that will give the landowner an interest that is to be protected at law. However, they will use a literal interpretation of the language in a properly prepared deed, especially in the case of property dedicated to a public purpose, which is qualified in a reasonable and technically correct way.

In the case of private sale, rather than gift, the court will attempt to find the second type of defeasible fee: The **fee simple subject to a condition subsequent.** A fee simple subject to a condition subsequent differs from a fee simple determinable in that there is no automatic reversion of title upon breaking of the condition. The former owner has a **power of termination**, meaning the former owner can take steps to re-enter the land legally and force possession away from the landowner. This right of re-entry must be exercised within a reasonable period of time or forfeited. A reasonable period of time differs on a case-to-case basis, but the action the former owner files would be an **action to recover real estate**, rather than forcible entry.

Thus, with a fee simple determinable, the grantor (or his heirs) has a possibility of reverter. With a fee simple subject to a condition subsequent, the grantor (or his heirs) has a power of termination. These interests in real property are called **future possessory interests** since they do not represent present possessory interests in the property and may, in fact, never ripen into fee simple title. How do you tell the difference between a fee simple defeasible and a fee simple subject to a condition subsequent? The distinction between the two types of defeasible fees is very technical and depends on the exact language in the deed. Most real estate agents will not have to worry about it since defeasible fees are rare today. If an agent encounters one, he should refer his client or customer to a real estate lawyer.

 People commonly refer to "fee simple title" without specifying which kind of fee simple. If this is the case, they virtually always mean a fee simple absolute.

Life Estates

Life estates are *freehold estates that last only as long as a specified person lives.*

For Example

If A owns property in fee simple, she could deed it "to B for life." B would have the right to occupy and use the property for the rest of his life. But when B died, the life estate would terminate.

The holder of a life estate is called the **life tenant**. When A grants property "to B for life," the life estate's duration is measured by the lifetime of the life tenant—B. This is referred to as an **ordinary life estate**, as this is the way most life estates are set up (e.g., the life tenant and the measuring life are the same person).

A life estate may also be based on the lifetime of someone other than the life tenant. The grantor could deed the property "to B for the life of C." B's life estate would terminate when C died. This is called a life estate **pur autre vie** (for another's life). While B has the right to occupy the property and, thus, is called the life tenant, the length of the life estate is measured by C's life. In this case, C is called the **measuring life**.

Life estates are created for a variety of reasons.

For Example

A property owner may grant a life estate to another person to simplify the division of property in a will. Or, an owner may transfer property to someone else and reserve a life estate for himself so the property will not have to be probated after he dies. Occasionally, a life estate is created involuntarily, when a spouse's dower rights become vested (**dower** is explained later in this chapter).

A life tenant owns an interest in the land that can be sold, mortgaged, or leased. But a person can transfer only the interest that he owns. So, if a life tenant sells the property, the buyers have purchased only a life estate. The buyers' interest ends when the life tenant dies in a regular life estate, or at the death of the measuring life in a life estate pur autre vie. A mortgage signed by a life tenant becomes an invalid lien when the life estate ends. Similarly, a lease signed by a life tenant terminates when the life estate ends, regardless of its terms.

Case Example

Mr. Waters owned some land in fee simple. In 1936, he deeded the land to his children, but reserved a life estate for himself.

In 1972, Waters signed a mineral lease, giving a coal company the right to mine his land. The document stated, "The term of this lease is until the merchantable coal is fully worked out."

Waters died in 1974, which terminated his life estate. His children then owned the land in fee simple and wanted to stop the mining company's operation on the land. The court held that Mr. Waters' death also terminated the mineral lease, even though there was still plenty of coal left to be mined. *Waters v. Monroe Coal Co.*, 54 Ohio Misc. 37, 376 N.E.2d 977 (1977).

Future Interests

As with defeasible fee estates, life estates also create **future interests**. The life tenant holds the present possessory interest, and the one who will possess the land upon the expiration of the measuring life holds the future possessory interest. This future interest is either **reversionary** or **remainder,** depending on who holds the future interest.

If the grantor deeds the property "to B for life," title reverts to the grantor or the grantor's heirs (if the grantor has already died) upon the death of the life tenant. The grantor's interest is always called a **reversionary interest**, even if it passes through the grantor's estate. If the grantor deeds the property "to B for life, then to C," C has a **remainder interest**, and C is known in law as the **remainderman**. When the life estate ends, the remainderman takes title in fee simple.

 This was the situation with the heirs in the previous *Waters v. Monroe Coal Co.*, case example. The heirs were remaindermen.

If the remainderman dies before the life estate ends, the future interest in the estate in remainder passes to the remainderman's heirs. Then, when the life estate ends, the remainderman's heirs take title in fee simple. It works the same way for an estate in reversion: If the grantor dies before the life estate ends, the grantor's heirs acquire the future interest.

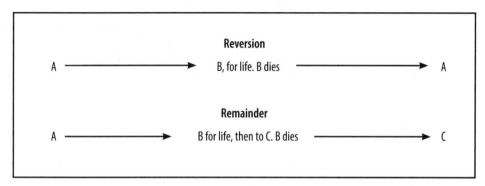

A life tenant may not use the property in any way that would permanently damage it or reduce its market value. Such abuse is called **waste**. A life tenant has to allow the holder of the future interest (the remainderman or grantor) to inspect the property at reasonable times. If the remainderman or grantor discovers waste, she may sue the life tenant for damages.

A life tenant has a severely restricted right of use. If he cuts timber, he must plant trees. He cannot lease the mineral rights, since this would permanently devalue the land. It is the duty of the life tenant to preserve the land for the benefit of the remaindermen or reversionary interest holder. Furthermore, the life tenant has almost no practical rights of disposal. A life tenant can sell or transfer the life estate to another, but this person would then have the life tenant's limited right of use. Since a life tenant cannot transfer more rights than those held, a life tenant transfers a life estate in her life, not for the life of the new owner. Thus, a subsequent transfer of a life estate creates a life estate pur autre vie.

Dower

Dower is *a special real property interest that the law provides as a statutory life estate to a spouse when a married person owns real property in Ohio and attempts to sell or otherwise transfer an interest in that real property.* A person has dower rights in any realty a spouse owns as an **estate of inheritance** at any time during their marriage. A couple that owns property together has mutual dower interests in each other's share. Regardless of whether property was acquired during the marriage or brought into the marriage, dower interests attach with marriage. Note that the land must be held as an **estate of inheritance** (property that can be willed or descend to heirs). Thus, life estates do not carry dower rights since life estates terminate on the death of the measuring life and the life tenants cannot pass their interest to heirs.

As long as the married person owns the property, or remains alive, the spouse's dower rights are contingent or incomplete. This is referred to in the law as **inchoate** (pronounced in-koe-it) **dower rights**. These contingent rights are not possessory—merely potentially possessory. The dower rights become active or complete, referred to as **choate** dower, if and when two things happen:

1. The owner spouse sells the property without benefit of dower release; and

2. The owner spouse dies before the innocent spouse.

If and when these two events happen, the innocent surviving spouse acquires a life estate amounting to an undivided one-third interest in any real property so transferred.

The law grants dower rights to recognize the sanctity of marriage and discourage interspousal fraud and deceit. The law affords this protection not so much as a penalty to the guilty spouse, who is dead at the time dower interests vest and cannot be hurt further, but rather as security to the deceived surviving spouse, whose support and contribution to the maintenance of the property should not be ignored.

As a real estate agent, always secure an agreement to provide a dower release in the case of married clients. In short, get the spouse to join the owner on the listing agreement because by signing the listing, they agree to provide marketable title if a buyer is found. There is a serious issue of marketable title should the spouse not sign an agreement to provide dower release. Also, find out if there is a possibility that a client will be married in the near future and get the future spouse to sign the listing. This creates no liability for the person if the marriage never takes place, but should the marriage occur, dower attaches immediately, creating the need for dower release.

Dower must be released in virtually every real estate transaction involving married sellers. The consequences for the buyer of the land if dower is not released involve, at best, a potential legal battle and could result in a serious compromise of valid title. One example that may render a dower release unnecessary would be where the parties to a marriage have executed a valid ante-nuptial agreement. However, many title insurance companies will still insist on a release of dower regardless of the ante-nuptial agreement, citing the possibility that the agreement could be set aside at some time in the future. An action by a court in attempting to seek an equitable solution for the parties may void such an agreement that attempts to keep the parties' property rights separate.

There is also the problem of dower with common law marriages. Ohio passed a law outlawing common law marriages effective October 10, 1991. After that date, no common law marriages may be formed, but the law did not invalidate common law marriages entered into before October 10, 1991. Now, to be recognized as legal, a marriage must be solemnized by a legally-authorized person and a certificate of marriage issued. This may solve some future problems. Regardless, real estate professionals still need to be familiar with the nuances and potential problems that can result from common law marriages.

Common law marriages were created when two persons of the opposite sex held themselves out to the world as being married to each other. This often took the form of a "Mr. and Mrs." checking account, or a similar application for credit, school registration, life insurance policies, or the like, which announced to the community at large that the couple was announcing they were legally married. The problem with common law marriages, however, is that there is no such thing as a common law divorce.

Although one could create a marriage by announcement, it could not be ended the same way. In order to end a common law marriage, one must seek and obtain a decree of divorce, annulment, or dissolution of marriage through a court. Until then, one remains married. There are many cases of people being in the legal state of marriage without realizing it. The real estate agent is in no position to render legal advice on the issue. An agent must know that one is legally in married common law if the announcement of marital status (legally known as "holding oneself out to be married") occurred prior to October 10, 1991 and no decree of divorce, annulment, or dissolution of marriage has been issued.

Dower rights can be terminated by divorce and by the innocent spouse's death, since dower represents a life estate interest. Dower **cannot** be terminated by a post-nuptial agreement.

Dower is also an issue when a creditor forecloses on a married person's real property. The court can order the property sold without dower release, but the spouse is entitled to receive a share of the proceeds from the sale as compensation for lost dower rights. This is true even though those dower rights were inchoate (contingent, inactive, or incomplete).

Sometimes, to avoid the dower issue, a seller will form a corporation and title real property in the name of a corporation prior to marriage. When the corporation sells the real estate, the spouse of the shareholder need not be called upon to release dower, since the spouse owns shares of stock, not real estate. Absent fraud in the transfer, and as long as the transfer occurred prior to the marriage, this appears to be perfectly legal. Again, the parties should seek legal advice if confronted with this type of situation.

Leasehold Estates

Leasehold estates are *interests that give the holder a **temporary** right to possession of the estate, without title.* A leasehold estate is a more limited interest in property than a freehold estate; thus, a leasehold estate is also called a **less-than-freehold estate.** The holder of a leasehold estate is called the **lessee** or, more familiarly, the **tenant.** A tenant has the right to exclusive possession of the property, but only for a limited time. An owner who leases property to a tenant is called the **lessor** or **landlord.** Possession will revert to the landlord when the lease ends.

The rules that govern landlord/tenant relationships are presented in Chapter 11. Here, the basic characteristics of leasehold estates are described. The three main types of leasehold estates are:

- Estate for years
- Periodic tenancy
- Tenancy at will

Estate for Years

Estate for years is *any leasehold estate for a fixed time period.* In spite of the name, the term does not have to be a period of years. The tenancy may last ten days, ten months, or ten years—any fixed period with a specific beginning and ending date. Estates for years are sometimes called **term tenancies.**

An estate for years terminates automatically at the end of the specified rental period. Usually, neither the landlord nor the tenant can terminate the lease sooner, unless both parties agree. Ending a lease by mutual consent is called **surrender.**

Periodic Tenancy

Periodic tenancy is *a leasehold estate for a duration of time, not a specific date.* It continues from period to period until the landlord or tenant gives the other party notice of termination. The period may be any length of time on which the parties agree. Month-to-month tenancies are the most common. A month-to-month tenancy automatically renews itself at the end of each month, unless one of the parties terminates it (for notices of termination, see Chapter 11).

Tenancy at Will

Tenancy at will is *a leasehold estate with no specified termination date or specified period of time.* Either party can end it at any time. The tenancy also has no regular rental period and, in some cases, no rent is paid (e.g., when the tenant is a caretaker), or the rent owed has no reference to periods of time (e.g., "35% of all profits from the tenant's sales of timber").

Sometimes, a tenancy at will arises after an estate for years ends. The original lease has expired, but the tenant stays on with the landlord's permission and without signing a new lease.

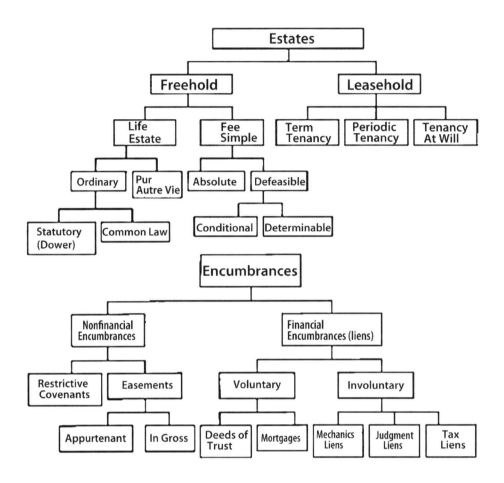

Unlike a term tenancy or a periodic tenancy, a tenancy at will *cannot* be assigned to someone else. Also, a tenancy at will automatically ends on the death of either the landlord or tenant, which is not true of the other leasehold estates.

 If the tenant continues to pay the landlord rent at regular intervals, a periodic tenancy is created instead of a tenancy at will.

Tenancy at Sufferance

Tenancy at sufferance is the term used to describe *possession of property by a holdover tenant*. A **holdover tenant** is *someone who came into possession of property under a valid lease, but stays on after the lease expires, without the landlord's permission*.

As such, a tenancy at sufferance is not actually a leasehold estate. A tenant at sufferance is not very different from a trespasser, except the tenant at sufferance, unlike a trespasser, originally had a right to be on the property.

A landlord is not required to give a tenant at sufferance notice of termination, but the landlord cannot use force to regain possession of the property. The landlord has to use the legal eviction process (explained in Chapter 11) to remove the tenant.

Nonpossessory Interests: Encumbrances

Nonpossessory interests are also called **encumbrances**, since they encumber or burden the title or use of the land. Someone who holds a nonpossessory interest has a claim or right concerning the property, but does not have the right to possess the property.

Two types of nonpossessory interests discussed here are **easements** and **liens**. (Restrictive covenants also create nonpossessory encumbrances on land—see Chapter 10.)

Easements

Easements are *rights to use another's real property for a particular purpose*. That right can be limited in a number of ways. An easement is classified as either an **appurtenant easement** or an **easement in gross**.

Appurtenant Easements

Appurtenant easements *burden one piece of land for the benefit of another piece of land.* The land benefited by an appurtenant easement is called the **dominant tenement**. "Tenement" is an old legal term that refers to the land and all the rights that accompany it. The land burdened by that easement is the **servient tenement**. The owner of the dominant tenement and thus, the person who benefits from the easement, is referred to as the **dominant tenant**. The owner of the servient tenement and thus, the person whose land is burdened by the easement, is referred to as the **servient tenant.**

For Example

D has an access easement across neighbor S's property. The easement permits D to cross S's land to get to D's own property. The easement burdens S's land for the benefit of D's land. Therefore, D's land is the dominant tenement and S's land is the servient tenement; D is the dominant tenant and S is the servient tenant.

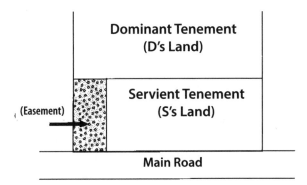

The term "appurtenance" was introduced in Chapter 5. It is a right that goes along with ownership of real property (like water rights or mineral rights). An appurtenant easement is appurtenant to the dominant tenement—it is a right that goes along with ownership of the dominant tenement.

If the dominant tenement is transferred (sold, willed, or given away), the easement is also transferred. Whoever owns the dominant tenement also owns the easement. If the servient tenement is transferred, the new owner takes title subject to the burden of the easement. An appurtenant easement *runs with the land*—in other words, it benefits and burdens the same two pieces of property, no matter who owns the land.

Easements in Gross

Easements in gross *benefit a person only and not a piece of land.* Therefore, there is a dominant tenant (person benefiting from the easement), but no dominant tenement (because there is no land benefiting from the easement). And since an easement in gross, like all easements, is a right that burdens another's land, there is still both a servient tenement (land burdened by the easement in gross) and a servient tenant (person owning the land burdened by the easement).

For Example

F lives five miles away from G. G grants F an easement in gross to enter G's property and fish in the small lake.

F's easement is not appurtenant to his land. If F sells his property, the new owner does not gain the right to fish on G's land. The easement belongs to F personally, wherever he lives. But the easement in gross does run with G's land: If G sells his land to someone else, F still has the right to fish in the lake.

An easement in gross belonging to an individual (like F's right to fish in the previous example) is called a **personal easement in gross**. Someone who holds a personal easement in gross cannot assign it to someone else and it is extinguished when the easement holder dies.

Most easements in gross belong to commercial enterprises rather than individuals.

For Example

A utility company has an easement right that allows its employees to enter private property to install and service lines. Unlike a personal easement in gross, a commercial easement in gross can be assigned. When Mega Electric Corporation buys the Smalltown Electric Company, it also buys the company's easements in gross.

Creation of Easements

Easements can be created in a number of ways; either voluntarily or involuntarily. In addition to creation of easements through agreement of the parties involved, there are also several ways to establish easements by operation of law.

Easements by Express Reservation

Easements by express reservation are created in a deed when a landowner divides property and includes language in the deed that transfers a servient tenement to the buyer, but retains a dominant tenement for the seller. Thus, the seller keeps an easement across his former property.

For Example

X owns a large tract of land and sells part of it to Z. In the deed, X might reserve the right to cross Z's parcel to reach his own land.

Easements by Express Grant

Easements by express grant are created in a deed or other document. Here, the easement can be granted in the original deed or at a future date, and either party may request the easement. Thus, the original deed might state that Z has the right to cross X's land to reach Z's parcel. Or, the easement might be conveyed later in a separate document that conveys only the easement. For example, several years after Z bought her parcel from X, Z might ask X to grant Z an easement across X's land.

In any case, easements created by express reservation or express grant **must be in writing to be valid**—oral agreements are not enough. Ohio law requires any transfer of real property interests to be in writing, and easements are real property interests.

For Example

D and S are neighbors. D asks S for an access easement allowing D to cross S's property. S agrees, but the easement agreement is never put in writing. Six months later, S changes his mind and tells D to keep off his land. D cannot enforce her easement right because it was only an oral agreement.

But, suppose S signed a document granting D the easement. Now, if S changes his mind, D has an enforceable right.

A document granting an easement should be drawn up and signed just like a deed (see the requirements for a valid deed in Chapter 7). The document should also be recorded to make sure anyone who buys the servient tenement has notice of the easement. If the purchaser does not have notice, the easement probably will not run with the land.

Easements by Implication

Easements by implication are *easements created by operation of law when a parcel of land is divided if there is a long-standing, apparent use that is reasonably necessary for the enjoyment of the dominant tenement.* This is also called an **implied easement**. Generally, implied easements arise when a tract of land was originally held by one owner, then divided into two or more parcels. The original owner would keep an **ingress** or **egress**—a means onto or off of land. At the time of the division, the use giving rise to the easement must have been in place for a long time and must be apparent from a visual inspection of the property. The use must also be reasonably necessary for the enjoyment of the dominant tenement.

For Example

X owned a large piece of land with a long driveway leading from the main road to her house. X sold the south half of her land (the part beside the main road) to Y, and kept the north half (the part with her house on it).

X did not reserve an easement for herself in the deed to Y. Although she could reach her property by a winding back road, the driveway across Y's parcel was much more direct, so X just went on using the driveway as she always had. Y filed a lawsuit to prevent X from using it.

The court ruled that X had an easement by implication across Y's parcel. X's use of the driveway was obvious and well-established when the land was divided. Although the driveway was not the only access to X's parcel, it was reasonably necessary for the enjoyment of her property.

Easements by necessity are *special easements by implication that occur when a piece of property would be completely useless without an easement against another property, even if there is not a long-standing, apparent use.* In such a case, a court will hold that there is an easement by necessity. The claimant does not have to prove the use was long-established and obvious at the time of the sale, but must prove the easement is strictly necessary (not just reasonably necessary) for use of the land. A person cannot claim an easement by necessity when there is another way to his property, even if that alternative route is much less convenient than the easement route.

Easements by Prescription

Easements by prescription are created by three conditions:

1. **Open and notorious use of the land**: Use must be obvious and unconcealed so that if the landowner keeps reasonably well informed about the property, he is aware of the use.

2. **Hostile and adverse use of the land**: Use is without the permission of the owner and against the owner's interests. If the owner gives permission, an easement cannot develop by prescription.

3. **Continuous use for 21 years**: Required in Ohio, but the use does not have to be constant; it can be just regular use—normal for the type of property in question. The user does not have to be the same person for all 21 years, either. If the property is used in the same way by two or more people in succession, their periods of use can be added together to equal the required 21 years. This is called **tacking**.

For Example

D and S own adjoining property. For ten years, D drives across a corner of S's property without S's permission. Then, D sells his property to M. For another six years M drives across the same corner. Then M sells to J. J drives across S's property for another five years.

Now J can claim an easement by prescription. Added together, D's ten years, M's six years, and J's five years make up the necessary 21 years of continuous use.

You will see that the requirements for prescription are similar to those for adverse possession of property (explained later in this chapter). Adverse possession results in a transfer of ownership, however, not just the creation of an easement.

 An easement by prescription can *never* be acquired against government property.

Termination of Easements

An easement can be terminated in several ways—some voluntary, some involuntary. There are also a number of ways to terminate an easement through operation of law.

Release

A **release** is *a document in which a legal right is given up* and, in this case, a document that relinquishes the easement holder's interest in the servient tenement. The easement holder may be willing to give up the easement (with or without compensation). An easement release should always be recorded.

Merger

Merger is *the uniting of two or more separate properties by transferring ownership of all to one person.* When one person becomes owner of both the dominant tenement and the servient tenement, the easement is extinguished by merger. A person cannot have an easement in his own property, since an easement is defined as an interest in another's land. Even if the land is later divided and all or part is sold again to different persons, the easement no longer exists and must be recreated, if desired.

Abandonment

Abandonment is *the failure to occupy and use property, which may result in a loss of rights.* An easement ceases to exist if the owner abandons it. Non-use alone, however, is not enough for abandonment. There must be an act or statement that clearly expresses the owner's intention to abandon the easement.

Prescription

Loss of easement by **prescription** *occurs after 21 years of non-use.* Just as easements can be created by prescription, they can be terminated by prescription. If the owner of the servient tenement prevents the dominant tenant from using the easement for 21 years, the easement is lost by prescription.

Case Example

In 1849, Mr. Lusk conveyed a 70-foot strip of his land to the Cleveland & Pittsburgh Railroad. The railroad laid its tracks along the strip.

The strip divided Lusk's property in two, so he acquired an easement across the strip at a particular point. The easement allowed him to cross the tracks and go from one part of his land to the other.

Lusk's property changed hands many times over the years. Most owners used the easement, and wood was put down to make crossing the tracks easier.

In the early 1950s, the tracks were temporarily relocated to permit construction of the Ohio turnpike. When the turnpike was completed, the tracks were put back in their original location, but the wood crossing was not replaced and a fence was built along both sides of the track in 1955.

Mr. Szaraz acquired the Lusk property in 1965. He asked the railroad to replace the crossing, but the railroad did not comply with his request. In 1979, (24 years later) Szaraz sued to establish his right to use the easement.

The court ruled the easement had been terminated by prescription. The fence along the tracks prevented the owners of the Lusk property from using the easement since 1955—more than 21 years—so the easement was lost. *Szaraz v. Consolidated R.R. Corp.,* 10 Ohio App. 3d 89, 460 N.E.2d 1133 (1983).

Destruction

The involuntary destruction (e.g., fire) of a building would end an easement that allows the dominant tenant to use the building. If the building is rebuilt, the easement does not automatically revive. This is called termination by **destruction.**

Failure of Purpose

An easement terminates when the purpose for which it was created no longer exists (e.g., an electric company's easement for power lines across a farmer's property would end if the company removed the lines). This is called termination by **failure of purpose.**

Easements versus Licenses

A **license** is *a revocable, non-assignable permission to enter another person's land for a particular purpose*; thus, a license is similar to an easement in that it grants permission to use another's property. However, unlike an easement, a license does not create an interest in the property and is not considered an encumbrance.

There are other differences:

- Easements are normally for an indefinite period of time; licenses are usually temporary.

- Easements are created by written agreement or by action of law (implication or prescription); licenses may be created by oral agreement.

- Easements must run with the land; licenses do not have to.

Perhaps the most important distinction is that an easement cannot be revoked, whereas a license, usually, may be revoked at any time. However, if the licensee makes a substantial financial commitment in reliance on the license, the financial commitment may limit the licensor's power to revoke it. A court may allow the licensee to continue using the licensor's property long enough to get a fair return from his expenditures.

Also, like a personal easement in gross, a license cannot be assigned. It becomes invalid if the licensee dies.

Easements and Encroachments

An **encroachment** is a *physical object intruding onto a neighbor's property* (e.g., a tool shed that is two feet over the property line, a tree branch growing over a fence). Although most encroachments are unintentional, the law sees them as a form of trespassing. If a neighbor sues, the court can order an encroachment removed; if removal is unfeasible, the encroacher may be ordered to pay damages.

An encroachment is not an encumbrance because it is not a right or interest held by the encroacher. Sometimes, though, the encroacher will purchase an easement from the neighbor, allowing the encroachment to continue. If the neighbor ignores an encroachment for 21 years, it could ripen into easement by prescription.

Liens (Financial Encumbrances)

Liens are nonpossessory *financial interests in property*. A lien provides security for a debt, giving the creditor (the **lien holder**) the right to foreclose on the debtor's property if the debt is not paid. **Foreclosure** is *when a lien holder causes property to be sold so unpaid debt secured by the lien can be satisfied from the sale proceeds*.

The fact that there are liens against a property does not prevent its transfer, but transfer will not eliminate the liens. The new owner takes the property subject to the liens. In most real estate transactions, the seller is required to clear the title of liens before closing by paying off the underlying debts.

Voluntary Liens

Voluntary liens are *liens placed against property with consent of the owner*. The most common are **mortgages** and derivatives, such as home equity credit lines.

Mortgages

Mortgages are *written instruments, which are signed by the owner (the **mortgagor**) and given to the lender (the **mortgagee**), that use real property to secure the payment of a debt*. Without the existence of a debt, there can be no mortgage.

The debt is created by a separate instrument called a **note**, or *promissory note*. A **promissory note** is *a written, legally binding promise to repay a debt*. The note creates the debt and the mortgage secures its payment. Since the note creates the liability for payment, the mortgage is only one protection the mortgagee (lender) has to insure payment. But it holds a powerful incentive for the landowner to pay, since the mortgage represents a potential transfer of title to the land in favor of the mortgagee in case of *default*.

Default is *the failure to fulfill an obligation, duty or promise, as when a borrower fails to make payments*. The mortgage instrument itself defines what constitutes a default. The most common reason for default is non-payment of principal and interest by the due date, but other factors may result in default:

- Failure to pay real estate taxes

- Committing waste to the property

- Failure to adequately cover the property with insurance

The lender is a *secured creditor*. A **secured creditor** is *a creditor with a lien on specific property*, in this case holding the mortgage as security. This is an obvious advantage since the lender can obtain a judgment against the debtor and institute foreclosure if default occurs. Should the foreclosure sale not yield enough to pay the debt, a *deficiency judgment* could result. A **deficiency judgment** is granted by the courts and can allow the creditor to go after other property owned by the debtor. It is enforceable and collectable in the same manner as any other judgment at law.

Foreclosure. Foreclosure actions arose out of inequities that existed in the law. Historically, mortgages transferred title to a lender. This still occurs in some states today (**title theory** states). A **defeasance clause** in a mortgage *stated that if a mortgage was paid as agreed and the mortgage conditions met, transfer of title to the lender was voided and title returned to the debtor*. But if a debt was not paid when due, the lender's title became absolute, reserving no rights to the debtor.

This harsh rule gave way, in most jurisdictions, to the thinking that a debtor be given a chance to bring payments up-to-date or to redeem equity in the property. Courts began to allow a reasonable period of time after the due date for debtors to make up payments and regain title to property, but the courts placed a time limit on this. After that date, a debtor was foreclosed from asserting any right of redemption. This is called **strict foreclosure** and is prohibited in Ohio by statute (ORC § 2323.07).

Most states, including Ohio, refer to mortgages as liens on real estate (**lien theory** states). Some Ohio case law allows a mortgagee to eject a mortgagor upon default, as though the mortgagee had title; but other case law is consistent with lien theory thinking. **Ohio is referred to as a lien theory state.**

Foreclosure Procedure. Foreclosure by **judicial sale** is the most common form of foreclosure and is also used in Ohio:

- When a borrower **defaults** on a loan, the lender **accelerates** the due date of the debt to the present, giving the debtor a **notice of default** demanding the entire loan balance be paid at once.

- If the debtor fails to do so, the lender starts a lawsuit, called a **foreclosure action**, in the common pleas court where the land is located.

- If the court finds the lender is owed the money, an **order of execution** is issued directing an officer of the court to seize and sell the land.

- An officer of the court, usually a sheriff, has the property appraised and notifies the public of the place and date of the sale by **advertising** for three consecutive weeks in a newspaper circulated in the county.

- On the sale date, a **public auction** is held in which anyone can bid on the property.

- The minimum bid is two-thirds of the sheriff's appraised value, as determined by three disinterested appraisers living in the county.

- The land is sold to the highest bidder, with proceeds used to: First, pay costs of the sale; second, pay property taxes; and third, pay off the mortgage(s) and other liens on the property. Any surplus funds go to the debtor. If the property does not bring enough money to pay off the mortgage, the creditor may bring a separate court action to obtain a **deficiency judgment** against the debtor for the rest of the debt.

- After the sale, a **confirmation of sale** is filed to finalize the sale.

- A **sheriff's deed**, made out to the buyer, is executed, acknowledged, and recorded like any deed.

A debtor can redeem property from the time a foreclosure action is brought until the confirmation of sale. This is done by paying the court what is due, which may include court costs and attorneys' fees. *The right to redeem property prior to confirmation of sale* is called **equitable right of redemption.** Once the redemption is made, the court will set aside the sale, pay the parties, and the debtor has title to the property again. After the confirmation of sale, though, the transfer of property is final. The debtor no longer has the right to redeem the property by paying what is due.

Some states (but not Ohio) have *statutory redemption.* This lets a mortgagor redeem property for a set period of time after foreclosure sale, regardless of the timing of other events. Time frames for **statutory right of redemption** vary by state.

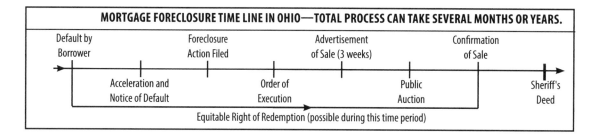

| MORTGAGE FORECLOSURE TIME LINE IN OHIO—TOTAL PROCESS CAN TAKE SEVERAL MONTHS OR YEARS. |

Default by Borrower · Foreclosure Action Filed · Advertisement of Sale (3 weeks) · Confirmation of Sale

Acceleration and Notice of Default · Order of Execution · Public Auction · Sheriff's Deed

Equitable Right of Redemption (possible during this time period)

Requirements for a Valid Mortgage. The requirements for a valid mortgage in Ohio include the usual requirements for the formation of contracts in general:

- Meeting of the minds

- Legal capacity

- Legally sufficient consideration.

 The requirements for a valid contract will be explained in detail in Chapter 8.

Additional requirements for a valid mortgage include:

- Language indicating that the instrument is given as security for a debt.

- A legal description, unless another instrument containing a description of the land (e.g., deed) is incorporated into the instrument by reference.

- Identification of the debt instrument, since without the debt, there is no security.

- Mortgage must be in writing, executed before a notary, and recorded with the county recorder in the county where the land is located to be effective.

The mortgage takes effect as to third parties from the time it is recorded. Between the parties (the owner and the mortgagee), the mortgage is valid even if unrecorded. An unrecorded mortgage, however, has no effect as to third parties, even if the third party actually knew of the existence of the mortgage. Across the country, this view is a minority position. Most states will conclude that **actual notice** (meaning the person actually knew) of the mortgage's existence is sufficient to alert the third party to the prior interest of a mortgagee.

The owner of mortgaged real estate may sell that real estate, subject to the mortgage. This means the mortgage does not affect the owner's ability to sell. Normally the mortgage is paid off at the closing, when the buyer tenders the balance of the proceeds to the seller. In some instances, however, the purchaser may wish to assume the seller's mortgage. Absent any provision in the mortgage to the contrary, this is perfectly legal. A mortgage or note, though, may contain a provision that calls for the acceleration of both principal and interest in the event the property is sold. This is called a **due-on-sale clause** or, more recently, a **transfer of interest clause,** which effectively prohibits the assignment of the mortgage to the purchaser.

Involuntary Liens

Involuntary liens, also referred to as **statutory liens**, arise through operation of law without the consent of the property owner. These liens are created to protect creditors of the landowner. These liens can be *general* or *specific*:

- A **general lien** attaches to all property owned in the county by the debtor.
- A **specific lien** attaches to specific property.

Obviously a mortgage is a specific lien, but it is voluntary. Let's look at some involuntary liens and see whether they are general or specific.

Vendor's Liens

Vendor's liens are *involuntary, specific liens that secure payment of the balance of the purchase price of a piece of real estate, if a real estate buyer does not pay the seller in full at closing.* In such a case, the seller automatically has a lien against the property for the balance of the purchase price. It is called a vendor's lien because "vendor" is another term for seller and the two terms are interchangeable. A vendor's lien does not attach, however, if the seller accepts a mortgage from the buyer for the amount owed.

When property is subject to a vendor's lien, the seller should state that in the deed (or another recorded document). Otherwise, the lien will be effective only against the buyer—not against third parties. If the buyer sells the property to someone else, the vendor's lien of the original seller will be void.

Mechanic's Liens

Mechanic's liens are *involuntary, specific liens claimed by someone who performed work on real property—construction, remodeling, repairs, or demolition—and has not been paid.* In such a case, the property serves as security for payment of the labor and material costs. Each person who works on a project, or supplies materials for it, can obtain a mechanic's lien. If the owner does not pay the bills, the holder of a mechanic's lien can force the sale of the property and collect the debt from the proceeds.

In legal terms, anyone who performs labor on real property is a **mechanic** (e.g., landscaper, builder, subcontractor). Anyone who supplies building materials, machinery, or fuel for a project is a **materialman** (e.g., trucking or lumber company). A **materialman's lien** is usually referred to, and treated the same, as a mechanic's lien.

Note that a mechanic's lien attaches only to the interest of the person who contracts to have the work done. If the contracting party is only a part owner, and the other owners did not authorize the project, the mechanic's lien generally will not affect the other owners' interests in the property.

Claiming a Mechanic's Lien. Before any work is begun or any materials are furnished for improving property, the landowner (or lessee, if he is contracting the work) must record a notice of commencement of work with the county recorder's office. The notice requires:

- A legal description of the property.
- The type and nature of the improvement to be made.
- The name, address, and capacity of the person filing the notice.
- The name and address of the contractor.
- If applicable, the names and addresses of a lender or other party with an interest in the project.

The notice states that claimants may preserve their lien rights by providing notice of furnishing labor and/or materials to the party named, together with the timely filing with the county recorder of an affidavit (sworn statement) making a claim for the exact amount owed.

If the property is a one-, two-, or three-family dwelling, or condominium, the affidavit must be filed within 60 days after the claimant last worked on the project. Otherwise, with a minor exception for oil and gas wells, the time limit is 75 days.

If an affidavit is not recorded within these time limits, the lien rights are forever lost. The mechanic or materialman can still sue the property owner for breach of contract, but that is a more complicated and lengthy process than foreclosing on a lien.

The lien holder must serve a copy of the affidavit for a mechanic's lien on the property owner within 30 days after recording it. Ordinarily, the lien will last six years, unless the owner pays the debt or the lien holder forecloses.

Removing a Mechanic's Lien. Sometimes, an owner does not believe the holder of the mechanic's lien is entitled to the amount claimed. If the owner intends to challenge the claim, he can post a bond. The bond insures that the money will be available to pay the debt if the claimant wins the dispute. Once a bond is posted, the lien is void.

Alternatively, the owner may choose to send the lien holder (and record with the court) a **notice to commence suit**. Unless the lien holder files a foreclosure suit within 60 days after receiving the notice, the lien will be void.

If the owner pays off the debt, posts a bond, or wins the foreclosure suit, the lien holder must record a release of the lien within 30 days. If that deadline is not met, the lien holder is liable to the owner for damages that result from the "cloud" on the title.

Homeowner's Protection. The Ohio mechanic's lien statute has a provision that protects homeowners. It applies when a general contractor handles work on a single-family home, duplex, or condominium unit that the owner uses as a personal residence. Once the homeowner pays the general contractor in full, the subcontractors cannot claim a lien against the property. Even if the general contractor runs off without paying the subcontractors, the homeowner is in the clear.

Tax Liens

Tax liens are *liens on real property to secure the payment of real estate taxes.* Counties, cities, and certain non-political entities (such as school districts and utility districts) raise revenue by taxing real property according to its value. In Ohio, real property tax liens automatically attach to the property on the first day of each year and the property can be foreclosed on if payment is delinquent. Annual real property taxes create an involuntary, specific lien against the property.

Special assessments are *taxes used to pay for public improvements (e.g., paving roads, installing sewer lines) in a particular neighborhood.* Property owners who benefit from an improvement are required to pay their share of its cost. Special assessments create an involuntary, specific lien against the owners' properties.

Unpaid **federal income taxes** create another type of tax lien. When payment is overdue, liens attach to all of the taxpayer's personal and real property. Income tax liens are involuntary, general liens.

NOTE: Ad Valorem – tax based upon the assessed value of the property.

Judgment Liens

Judgment liens are *involuntary, general liens that attach to a person's property as a result of court action.* At the end of a civil lawsuit, if the judge or jury determines that one party owes money to the other, a judgment is entered against the losing party. The winner (the **judgment creditor**) may claim a lien against the loser's (the **judgment debtor's**) real property.

To claim a lien, the judgment creditor obtains a **certificate of judgment** from the clerk of the court that issued the judgment. The creditor then files the certificate with the clerk of the court of common pleas in the county where the judgment debtor owns real property. The creditor must also have the certificate recorded with the clerk in that county. If the debtor owns real property in more than one county, the creditor may file and record the certificate in each of those counties.

A judgment lien attaches to all of the debtor's real property in each county where the certificate was recorded.

In Ohio, a judgment lien is valid for only five years after the date the judgment was entered. Recording another certificate renews the lien for five additional years.

Attachment Liens

Attachment liens are *liens intended to prevent transfer of property, pending the outcome of litigation.* When a plaintiff files a lawsuit there is a danger that, by the time a judgment is entered, the defendant will have sold all of his property and left the jurisdiction. That would make the plaintiff's judgment a worthless piece of paper.

To prevent this, at the outset of a lawsuit, the plaintiff can ask the court to issue an **order of attachment**. The order directs the sheriff to seize enough of the defendant's property to satisfy the judgment the plaintiff is seeking. In the case of personal property, this may involve an actual physical seizure. For real property, the order simply creates an involuntary lien, called a **lis pendens**, which is a recorded notice stating there is a lawsuit pending that may affect title to the defendant's property.

Broker Lien law (ORC § 1311.85-1311.93)

(A) Any broker that enters into a written contract for services related to selling, leasing, or conveying any interest in commercial real estate has a lien on that commercial real estate. The lien is effective only if the contract for services is in writing and is signed by the broker (or the broker's agent) and the owner of the lien property (or the owner's agent).

(B) (1) Only the broker named in the contract has a lien pursuant to this section, and a lien is not available to any employee or independent contractor for the broker.

(2) The amount of the lien is limited to the amount due to the broker pursuant to the contract. If the amount due to the broker is payable in installments, a portion of which is due after conveyance, the amount of the lien is limited to the amount due to the broker prior to, or upon, conveyance.

(3) The lien is effective only against the interest in real estate that is the subject of the contract.

Prior to the sale or lease of commercial real estate, a lien affidavit must be filed with the county recorder in order for the lien to be enforceable. If the agreed upon commission is not paid, the broker may file a complaint with the court of common pleas in the county where the commercial property is located. The complaint must be filed within one year following the recording of the lien affidavit for it to be valid.

Classification of Liens				
	Voluntary	Involuntary	General	Specific
Property Tax Lien		X		X
Special Assessment		X		X
Mortgage	X			X
Vendor's Lien		X		X
Mechanic's Lien		X		X
IRS Lien		X	X	
Judgment Lien		X	X	
Broker Lien		X		X

Lien Priority

It is not unusual for property to have several liens against it at the same time. It may be subject to a mortgage, a mechanic's lien, and a property tax lien, for example. In some cases, the total amount of the liens is more than the property will bring at a forced sale. If so, then all liens cannot be paid in full, so there is an established order of priority for paying off liens after foreclosure.

As a general rule, liens are given priority according to the order in which they attached to the property. For most liens, the attachment date is the date the lien was recorded; so, the lien recorded first has first priority for payment.

There are important exceptions to this rule:

• The state's lien for delinquent property taxes is superior to all other liens against the property, so the property tax lien has priority over liens that are attached before it. (If taxes are not delinquent, though, the lien's priority is established by the attachment date of January 1.)

• A vendor's lien attaches automatically as soon as title to the land is transferred. However, the lien will lose its priority unless the deed or other recorded document stated the property was subject to a vendor's lien (giving notice to other lien claimants).

For Example

A mortgage recorded long after the sale would have priority over the vendor's lien, because the mortgagee had no notice of the other lien.

The priority of a mechanic's lien depends on whether first work on the project occurred before or after the filing of the work commencement notice. If work started, or materials were delivered before filing of the notice, the date of first work controls priority. Otherwise, the filing date of the notice establishes priority. As a general rule, all mechanics' liens from the same project have the same priority, regardless of when the individual mechanic or materialman performed work or recorded a lien claim. If the proceeds from the foreclosure sale are not enough to cover all the mechanic's liens, the mechanic's lien holders receive prorated shares of the money.

With other liens, however, there is no proration. If the sale proceeds are enough to pay off only the highest priority lien, the other lien holders get nothing.

For Example

X's property has the following liens against it:	If X's property is sold at foreclosure, the liens will be paid in the following order:
November 6—First mortgage recorded	1. Property tax lien (always due)
December 15—Judgment lien recorded	2. First mortgage
January 1—Property tax lien attached	3. Both mechanic's liens (prorated shares, if necessary)
January 8—Second mortgage recorded	4. Judgment lien
January 10—Mechanic's lien recorded (work began December 15, notice of commencement filed December 1)	5. Second mortgage
January 19—Mechanic's lien recorded (from previous project)	

If the sale brings enough to pay off only the first mortgage (or part of it), the other lien holders will receive nothing. If there is enough to pay off only the first mortgage and part of the two mechanics' liens, the rest will receive nothing, and so forth.

Homestead Laws

Homestead laws give owner-occupied residences some protection from lien foreclosure. A certain amount of the homeowner's equity in the property is exempt from foreclosure. This means if a lien holder forecloses, the exemption amount will be set aside for the homeowner out of the sale proceeds—even if there is not enough left to pay off all the liens.

In Ohio, homestead protection is very limited. Only $136,925 of the homeowner's interest in the property is exempt from foreclosure. If the property is co-owned by a married couple, $273,850 is exempt. The exemption applies only to foreclosure of a judgment lien or attachment lien. The $136,925 or $273,850 exemption is not protected from foreclosure of a vendor's lien, mechanic's lien, mortgage, or property tax lien.

Adverse Possession

Adverse possession is *acquiring title to someone else's real property by possession of it.* The main purpose of adverse possession laws is to encourage productive use of property. The idea is that it is better to give title to someone who actively uses the property than to leave title with someone who ignores the property for a long time.

In Ohio, possession and use of property can mature into title if the claimant's possession is:

- Open and notorious.
- Hostile or adverse.
- Exclusive.
- Continuous for more than 21 years.

Open and notorious

This means the adverse possessor must use the property openly, in a way that will put the owner on notice that his title is threatened. A person cannot sneak around on someone's property and then claim adverse possession. His use must be open enough so the owner would be aware of his presence, if she were paying reasonable attention to the property.

Hostile or Adverse

The nature of the possession must conflict with the owner's interest. If the owner gave someone permission to use the property, that person's use is not hostile and can never develop into adverse possession. The adverse possessor must treat the property as if he owns it.

Exclusive

An adverse possessor must be the exclusive user of the property; possession cannot be shared with the owner.

Continuous

The adverse possession must be continuous for more than 21 years. Possession is considered continuous if the property is used as constantly as an owner would ordinarily use that type of property. For example, a person could adversely possess a summer cabin by occupying it every summer for 21 years.

The period of exclusive possession must not be interrupted by the owner. If an adverse possessor has been living on the land for 19 years and the owner unexpectedly visits the property that year, the adverse possession is broken. The adverse possessor would have to start counting the 21 years all over again after the owner left.

It does not necessarily have to be the same person adversely possessing the property for all 21 years, either. A court may add the periods of possession from a series of adverse possessors so they total 21 years. This is called **tacking**.

Case Example

Mr. Craig and Mr. Schaffner were neighbors. There was a ditch on Craig's land near the boundary between his property and Schaffner's. In 1950, Craig put up a fence to keep his sheep from wandering into the ditch. He placed the fence several yards to the west of the property boundary, leaving a strip of his land unenclosed. That strip was about a third of an acre.

After the fence went up, Schaffner began using that strip, even though he knew it was not part of his property. He grew alfalfa and hay on it, and his hogs grazed on it. In 1959, when Schaffner rebuilt his house, he installed a leach field that extended into that strip of land. Craig did not use the strip in any way.

In 1963, Craig sold all of his land (including the strip) to the McClellans. The McClellans never used the strip, nor objected to Schaffner's use. In 1968, Schaffner died and his son Karl inherited his land. Karl continued using the strip as his father had. He also did some work on the ditch to prevent erosion.

In 1972, Karl sold Schaffner's land to the Demmitts who assumed the strip was part of their property and continued to use it.

Finally, in 1981, the McClellans sold their property to the McMillans. At first they thought their property ended at the fence, but a survey showed that the legal description in their deed also included the strip beyond the fence. They took down the fence and told the Demmitts to stop using the strip.

The Demmitts sued claiming they had acquired title to the strip by adverse possession, and they won in court. Tacking together Schaffner's, his son Karl's, and the Demmitts' periods of use, the strip had been used openly, notoriously, adversely, exclusively, and continuously for more than 21 years (1950-1981). *Demmitt v. McMillan*, 16 Ohio App. 3d 138, 474 N.E.2d 1212 (1984).

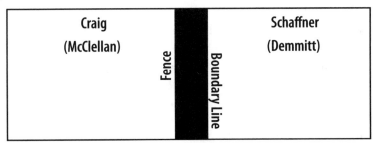

Note that the requirements for adverse possession are very similar to those for easement by prescription, which were discussed in the beginning of this chapter. But while the easement claimant's use does not have to be exclusive, the adverse possessor's use must be. Also, the adverse possessor actually acquires title to the property, not just an easement.

Exceptions

Most property can be adversely possessed, but there are a few important exceptions:

- Property owned by the federal or state government
- Land registered in the Torrens system (explained in Chapter 7)
- In Ohio, a local government's property is not necessarily immune, but a municipal street cannot be adversely possessed

Summary

1. An **estate** is a possessory interest in real property, entitling the holder to possession now or in the future. There are **freehold estates**, which have a possessory interest of uncertain duration, and **leasehold estates**, which give tenants a temporary right to exclusive possession. Freehold estates include **fee simple estates**, which are inheritable, transferable, and perpetual ownership, and **life estates**, where ownership lasts as long as a specified person lives.

2. A **fee simple absolute** is the fullest interest in property. A person referred to as "owner" usually holds a fee simple absolute. The duration of a **fee simple defeasible** is also unlimited, but a defeasible estate can be defeated or undone if certain conditions are not met, with title reverting back to the grantor. A **life estate** lasts only as long as someone's lifetime. During a life estate, the grantor holds an estate in reversion, or a remainderman holds an estate in remainder. When the **measuring life** dies, title to the property passes to the reversionary owner, or to the remainderman with a life estate pur autre vie. **Dower** is an interest held by married persons in each other's real property. Dower is **inchoate** (inactive or incomplete) when both spouses are alive, but becomes a statutory life estate for the surviving spouse when the other dies. Spouses should sign a dower release when property is sold.

3. The leasehold estates are the **estate for years**, **periodic tenancy**, and **tenancy at will**. A leasehold tenant has a temporary possessory interest, but does not hold title. Remember that an estate for years can be any fixed period of time. Tenancy at sufferance describes possession by a holdover tenant.

4. **Easements** are the right to use another's property for a particular purpose. Easements are nonpossessory interests (encumbrances) that are **appurtenant** or **in gross**. They are created by *express grant, express reservation, implication, necessity,* or *prescription*. Easements are terminated by *release, merger, abandonment, prescription, destruction,* or *failure of purpose*. Easements are normally for an indefinite period of time, created by written agreement or action of law, cannot be revoked, and must run with the land. **Licenses** are a revocable, non-assignable permission to enter a person's land for a particular purpose. Licenses are often temporary and can be verbal.

5. **Liens** are nonpossessory interests, which are financial encumbrances. Lien holders can **foreclose** on property in the event of default, forcing it to be sold so unpaid debt can be paid from the sale proceeds. Debtors have the **equitable right of redemption** until the confirmation of sale. The most common liens are **mortgages**, **tax liens**, **mechanics' liens**, and **judgment liens**. Most liens are prioritized (and thus paid out in foreclosure) in the order they are recorded, but tax liens always have priority. Later liens may get nothing.

6. **Adverse possession** is acquiring title to someone else's real property by possession of it. A claimant's possession must be **open and notorious**, **hostile or adverse**, **exclusive**, and continuous for more than 21 years (**tacking** is okay). Federal, state, and Torrens system land may not be adversely possessed.

Quiz

1. **The fullest and most complete real property ownership interest is called a**
   a. defeasible fee.
   b. fee simple absolute.
   c. leasehold estate.
   d. life estate.

2. **X granted R a life estate in some property. When R dies, the property will pass to B or B's heirs. B is called the**
   a. measuring life.
   b. primary owner.
   c. remainderman.
   d. reversionary owner.

3. **T rents a house. The lease gives T the right to occupy the house from August 1, 2010 through December 31, 2010. This is called a(n)**
   a. estate for years.
   b. periodic tenancy.
   c. tenancy at will.
   d. tenancy pur autre vie.

4. **A nonpossessory interest in real property is also called a(n)**
   a. encumbrance.
   b. leasehold estate.
   c. license.
   d. servient tenement.

5. **An easement allows the present and any future owner of Lot D to drive across a neighbor's (Lot S) property to reach her own. This is a(n)**
   a. appurtenant easement.
   b. defeasible easement.
   c. easement in gross.
   d. encroachment.

6. **B's property has an easement appurtenant that allows B to hunt on the neighbor's land. When the neighbor sells his land to B, the easement terminates through**
   a. abandonment.
   b. destruction of the dominant tenement.
   c. failure of purpose.
   d. merger.

7. **Which is an involuntary, specific lien?**
   a. easement created by express agreement
   b. judgment lien
   c. mechanic's lien
   d. mortgage

8. **When liens are paid off out of the proceeds of foreclosure sale,**
   a. a judgment lien generally has lowest priority.
   b. a lien for delinquent property taxes always has highest priority.
   c. a mortgage always has highest priority.
   d. priority depends on the amount of the lien.

9. **The proceeds of a foreclosure sale did not yield enough money to pay off the first mortgage holder. The mortgage holder**
   a. can file a mechanic's lien or a materialman's lien, depending on why the original lien was granted.
   b. can seek a deficiency judgment against the debtor by filing a separate court action.
   c. could choose to transfer the mortgage interest to another piece of property owned by the debtor.
   d. has absolutely no recourse against the debtor because only the piece of property with a lien on it was subject to foreclosure.

10. **Y owns some land in Ohio. X started living on Y's land in 2000. The soonest that X could acquire the title by adverse possession is**
    a. 2015.
    b. 2016.
    c. 2021.
    d. 2025.

Deeds

Ownership of real property is transferred from one person to another in many ways. Sometimes, an owner voluntarily transfers title by deed or in a will. In other cases, title is transferred involuntarily, as in a foreclosure sale. Alienation is the legal term that includes all the various methods of transfer—voluntary and involuntary.

This chapter describes the requirements for the various types of transfers and their effects, the various forms of ownership that title may be held in, and the recording system, which plays an essential role in the transfer of real property.

Key Terms

Acknowledgment When a party signing a document formally declares to an authorized official (usually a notary public) that he signed voluntarily. The official certifies that the signature is voluntary and genuine.

Actual Notice Having actual knowledge of a fact, as opposed to knowledge imputed or inferred by law.

Consideration Anything of value (e.g., money, services, goods, promises) given to induce another person to enter into a contract.

Constructive Notice Knowledge of a fact imputed to a person by law. A person is held to have constructive notice of a fact because it was a matter of public record, even if the person was not actually aware of it.

Deed An instrument that conveys the grantor's interest, if any, in the real property.

Donative Intent A grantor's intent to transfer title immediately and unconditionally.

Inquiry Notice Having notice of a problem because circumstances should have alerted a person to a problem that needed to be investigated further, even if actual knowledge of a particular fact does not exist.

Ownership in Severalty Ownership by a single individual as opposed to a co-ownership.

Title The actual lawful ownership of real property. This is not a document, but rather a concept or theory dealing with ownership.

Undivided Interest A co-tenant's interest, giving him the right to possession of the whole property rather than a fraction of it.

Deed versus Title

A **deed** is *an instrument that conveys the grantor's interest, if any, in the real property*. The deed is the document used by the owner of real property to transfer all or part of his interest in the property to another. A deed is evidence of title.

Title is *the actual lawful ownership of real property* and refers to holding the bundle of rights conveyed. The deed is written proof of the rights conveyed to the owner; having title to the land means the person actually owns it.

This distinction is important because, although rare, it is possible to possess a deed to property, yet not have title to that property. Suppose the *seller* (known as the **grantor**) does not own the land. The grantor may think he owns a piece of land as part of a larger tract, or may have already conveyed part of the land to someone else in a prior transaction and forgot. Can this grantor pass good title by merely giving the *buyer* (the **grantee**) a deed to the land? Of course not. Examples of this will be discussed later in this chapter, as well as other ways in which a perfectly innocent looking deed might be invalid.

It is important for agents to know, in their practice of real estate, that much of the discussion in this chapter involves the practice of law and is out of bounds as far as advising their clients or customers. It is necessary, however, for their professional development and overall knowledge that they read and understand the contents of this chapter, since the culmination of a real estate transaction is the delivery and acceptance of a properly-drafted deed.

Requirements for a Valid Deed

In order for a deed to be valid in Ohio, the deed must be in writing and contain necessary information on its face. These requirements include:

1. **Competent grantor's signature**

2. **Last recorded instrument number**

3. **Identifiable grantee** to whom title will pass, named in such a way so as to reasonably separate this person from all others

4. **Words of conveyance** stating the grantor's intent to convey the land

5. **Description** of the property being conveyed, adequate enough to distinguish it from all other parcels of land

6. **Consideration** recited to prove that a sale of land took place

7. **Acknowledgment** of the grantor before a notary public, stating that the sale of land is a free and voluntary act

8. **Delivery and acceptance** of the deed during the grantor's life to the grantee

 In many other states (but not Ohio), a grantor must also sign the deed in front of two witnesses.

Competent Grantor's Signature

A **competent grantor** is *a person wishing to grant or convey land, who is of sound mind for the purposes of entering a contract, and who has reached the age of majority (18 years of age in Ohio)*. A competent grantor's signature (and the grantor's spouse, if married) is vital for a valid deed to transfer title.

In order for a deed to be binding and valid, there must be a grantor who can be bound by the deed. There are five possible problem areas:

1. Mental capacity
2. Minors
3. Married persons
4. Corporations
5. Partnerships

Mental Capacity

The term "competent grantor" presumes a sound mind. The test for mental capacity in Ohio is whether the grantor can formulate an intention to convey his property. This capacity is measured at the time of signing the deed. Capacity is presumed to exist, and the burden of proof falls to the one asserting the invalidity of the deed on this ground. The signing of a deed by a mentally incapable grantor results in a transaction voidable at the option of the incapacitated person, or the person's representatives.

Minors

The term "competent grantor" also refers to the legal ability of a person to enter into a valid contract. In Ohio, a person must be at least 18 years old, the **age of majority**, to enter into a legally binding contract. A person younger than 18 is referred to as a **minor** and a deed executed by a minor results in a voidable transaction at the option of the minor, within a reasonable period of time after he reaches the age of majority.

Married Persons

A married grantor must be joined by his spouse in signing the deed to release the dower interest the law allows the spouse. Without this release, marketable title is severely compromised.

Corporations

A corporation is a competent grantor, and the deed must recite the grantor's corporate status on its face. However, it is imperative that the person representing the corporation has the power and authority to carry out the transaction. Prior to listing corporately-owned property, the listing broker must obtain a *corporate resolution* allowing the corporation to sell the asset. This resolution should appoint the broker as agent, and grant the authority to one of the officers or directors to sign the purchase agreement and deed.

Partnerships

A partnership is also a competent grantor, and the deed must recite the status of partnership on its face. Again, agents need to make sure they are dealing with the correct person who has the power and authority to complete the transaction. The issue of dower interest in partnership property is unclear so the safe course is to obtain dower releases from the partners' spouses.

Identifiable Grantee

An **identifiable grantee** is *the person to whom the interest in real property is to be conveyed; identified in such a way so as to reasonably separate this person from all others in the world.* This would include getting proper and complete full names for the grantee(s), as well as any generational designations (e.g., Jr., Sr.). Furthermore, a deed must name an identifiable grantee in existence at the time of conveyance.

For Example

Conveyance to an unincorporated business reciting corporate status would fail for lack of a grantee in existence at the time of conveyance.

Since the burden of grantee identification often falls to the agent on the buying side of the transaction, it is important to get the correct information to the person preparing the deed. Any unclear situations or peculiarities should be investigated first.

Words of Conveyance

Words of conveyance is *a clause in the deed that states the grantor intends to convey title to the land*. Also called the **granting clause**, these words identify the document as one that involves the transfer of interest from one person to another. The wording of the deed must be such that it communicates a definite and clear intent by the grantor to part with the subject land. The words "give," "grant," "bargain," "sell," and "convey" leave no doubt as to the intent of the grantor. The **habendum clause**, included after the granting clause in many deeds, begins "to have and to hold" and describes the type of estate granted.

Description

Description of the property being conveyed should be thorough and complete, and based on one of the following:

- The rectangular survey method
- The metes and bounds method
- The lot and block method using a recorded plat

The test of a property's valid description is the ability to identify and distinguish that property from any and all other parcels of land.

Rectangular Survey Method

The **rectangular survey method** is *a legal description for land referencing principal meridians and base lines designated throughout the country*. This is also known as the **government survey system** and **fractional designation**.

Metes and Bounds Method

The **metes and bounds method** is *a legal description that starts at an easily identifiable point of beginning, then describes the property's boundaries in terms of compass directions and distances, ultimately returning to the point of beginning (POB)*.

Lot and Block Method

The **lot and block method** is *a legal description used for platted property*. The description states only the property's lot number and block number in a particular subdivision. To find the exact location of the property's boundaries, the plat map for that subdivision must be consulted.

Consideration

Consideration is *anything of value* (e.g., money, goods, services, promises) *given to induce another person to enter into a contract*. Consideration recited on the deed is necessary to prove that a sale of land took place and that the transfer was not a gift, since a gift may be attacked by creditors as a fraudulent transfer of assets. The actual price paid need not be recited, but the full consideration must be stated in cases involving public sale (e.g., at foreclosure).

If the property is truly being given as a gift, then the consideration may just state "For the love and affection given to me by my daughter, I hereby deed to her the following real property." This would be called "**good consideration**."

Acknowledgment

Acknowledgment is *when a party signs a document before a notary public, stating it was signed voluntarily.* In the case of a deed, the grantor acknowledges before the notary public that the act of selling the land is an act of free will. After a formal declaration before the authorized official (the notary), the official then certifies the signature is voluntary and genuine.

Delivery and Acceptance

Even when a deed has been properly executed, it has no legal effect until:

- **Delivery**—The grantor actually places the document in the grantee's possession, or gives it to a third party with instructions to turn it over to the grantee.

- **Acceptance** by a grantee—The law presumes the deed has been accepted as long as the grant is beneficial to the grantee.

Once a deed has been effectively delivered, the grantee holds title to the property and it cannot be reconveyed simply by destroying the deed or returning it to the grantor. The grantee would have to execute a new deed transferring title back to the original grantor. A deed must also be delivered to the grantee while the grantor is alive, or it has no legal effect.

Doctrine of Relation Back

Doctrine of Relation Back (also known as **Delivery in Escrow**), *a legal doctrine establishing the effects of the grantor's death or title impairment on an escrow transaction.* In a valid escrow, there is an irrevocable deposit of the executed deed, purchase money, and instructions into the escrow pending performance of the escrow conditions. (Usually Grantee conditions that need to be completed) Under this doctrine, death of the grantor does not terminate the escrow or revoke the escrowee's authority to deliver an executed deed. When the escrow conditions are performed, title passes to the grantee, and the deed can be formally delivered to the grantee without any probate court approval.

Delivery of deed to the grantee relates back to the date it was originally deposited with the escrow agent, and it is as if the grantor made delivery to the grantee before the grantor's death.

Additionally, the delivery of the deed into escrow eliminates the rights of any potential sellers creditors (after the first delivery) and thus passing clear title as of the date of the escrow.

Donative Intent

Donative intent is *intent by the grantor to transfer title immediately and unconditionally.* This is also vital for a valid deed. Even when a deed is given to the grantee while the grantor is alive, it is not effective unless the grantor intends to surrender control over the property and transfer title immediately. If the grantor retains any power to recall the deed, or intends for it to take effect only under certain conditions or at some other time in the future, the deed does not transfer title to the grantee.

Case Example

Mr. Adams, a widower, owned a duplex and lived in one half of the house and rented the other half to his son, Calvin. In 1939, Adams executed a deed conveying the entire property to Calvin.

Adams gave Calvin the deed but instructed Calvin not to record it until after he (Adams) was dead. Adams explained that he intended to go on living on the property for the rest of his life, and it would be Calvin's after his death.

Calvin continued to pay Adams rent and Adams continued to pay the taxes, insurance premiums, and repair expenses for the property that was the subject of the deed.

A few months after giving Calvin the deed, Adams remarried. Four years later, in 1943, Adams executed a deed conveying a one-half interest in the property to his wife, Helen. That deed was recorded right away. Ten years after that, Adams conveyed the other one-half interest to Helen, and that deed was also promptly recorded.

Adams died in 1955. Calvin recorded his 1939 deed a few days after his father's death. When he found out about the earlier deeds to Helen, Calvin sued to determine who owned the property.

The court ruled that the property belonged to Helen. When Adams gave Calvin the deed in 1939, Adams did not intend to transfer title immediately. Since Adams lacked donative intent, the deed was ineffective and did not actually transfer title to the property. The property still belonged to Adams, until he deeded it to Helen later on. *Adams v. Adams*, 107 Ohio App. 1, 150 N.E.2d 81 (1958).

Types of Deeds

There are three general classifications of deeds in Ohio:

- Warranty deeds
- Deeds without warranties
- Transfer on death deeds

Warranty Deeds

Warranty deeds *carry warranties of clear title and the grantor's right to convey title.* They transfer title in real property, with the grantor making certain guarantees (also called warranties or covenants) to the grantee regarding status of the title.

For Example

If the grantor is married and fails to obtain a dower release from his spouse, that is a breach of warranty under a warranty deed.

The guarantees that go with a deed differ depending on whether a **general warranty deed** or a **limited warranty deed** is used. The Ohio legislature created a statutory form for both types of warranty deeds. An example of a general warranty deed is provided on the next two pages. If the statutory form is followed, it is not necessary to actually state the warranties on the face of the deed. Instead, the warranties are incorporated into the deed by reference to the statute.

When a warranty is breached, the grantee has the right to sue the grantor for compensation. But the grantor may have left the jurisdiction, or may be judgment-proof, so the grantee cannot collect. Title insurance protects the grantee much more reliably than deed warranties.

Example of a General Warranty Deed: Note that in addition to being a written document, this sample contains 6 of the 7 requirements for a valid deed—delivery and acceptance cannot be illustrated here.

WARRANTY DEED 2922 PAGE 561

FUTURE TAX BILLS TO THE SALMON P. COULTER CO.

COLUMBUS BLANK BOOK CO., COL., O.
FORM NO. L12-9

Know all Men by these Presents

That Ralph B. S. Mowery, Widower 19096

5. Consideration

of the City of Columbus, County of Franklin and State of Ohio Grantor in consideration of the sum of One Dollar ($1.00) and other good and valuable considerations to him paid by William A. Thompson and Helen Thompson

2. Grantee

of the City of Columbus, County of Franklin and State of Ohio Grantees the receipt whereof is hereby acknowledged, does hereby **grant, bargain, sell and convey** to the said Grantees

William A. Thompson and Helen Thompson

3. Words of Conveyance

following **Real Estate** situated in the County of Franklin in the State of Ohio, and in the City of Columbus and bounded and described as follows:

4. Description

Being Lot Number Eighty-five (85) of CHARLES R. CORNELL'S SUBDIVISION in the said City of Columbus, Ohio, as the same is numbered and delineated upon the recorded plat thereof, of record in Plat Book No. 5, page 48, Recorder's Office, Franklin County, Ohio.

TRANSFERRED
AUG 28 1968
ARCH J. WARREN
AUDITOR
FRANKLIN COUNTY, OHIO

TRANSFER TAX
PAID
$10.80 By RM
ARCH J. WARREN
FRANKLIN COUNTY, AUDITOR

Last Transfer: Deed Record Volume 734 *, Page* 67

To have and to hold *said premises, with all the privileges and appurtenances thereunto belonging, to the said Grantees*

their *heirs and assigns forever.*

And the said Grantor

does hereby covenant with the said Grantee s for himself and his heirs,

their *heirs and assigns, that* he is *lawfully seized of the premises aforesaid; that the said premises are* **Free and Clear from all Incumbrances whatsoever** Except taxes and assessments due and payable hereafter and all conditions, easements and restrictions of record.

VOL ___ PAGE ___

and that   he   will forever **Warrant and Defend** the same, with the appurtenances, unto the said Grantee s

their heirs and assigns

against the lawful claims of all persons whomsoever

In Witness Whereof the said Grantor

      Ralph B. S. Mowery, Widower

###, ha s hereunto set his hand, this 27th day of August in the year of our Lord one thousand nine hundred and sixty-eight (1968)

Signed and acknowledged in presence of

C. Richard O'Neil   _Ralph B S Mowery_
Robert H. Moore   Ralph B. S. Mowery

1. Grantors' Signatures

The State of OHIO   FRANKLIN **County** ss.

Be it Remembered That on this   27th   day of   August   , A.D. 19 68 , before me, the subscriber, a   Notary Public   in and for said county, personally came the above named   Ralph B. S. Mowery

6. Acknowledgment

the Grantor in the foregoing Deed, and acknowledged the signing of the same to be his voluntary act and deed, for the uses and purposes therein mentioned.

In Testimony Whereof, I have hereunto subscribed my name and affixed my official seal on the day and year last aforesaid.

C. Richard O'Neil
C. RICHARD O'NEIL
ATTORNEY-AT-LAW
NOTARY PUBLIC, STATE OF OHIO

             C. RICHARD O'NEIL
             ATTORNEY-AT-LAW
This instrument was prepared by ___ 2346 N. HIGH ST.
             COLUMBUS 2, OHIO

Warranty Deed 19096

MAIL TO

Transferred _____ 19___
COUNTY AUDITOR

STATE OF OHIO
COUNTY OF FRANKLIN ss
RECEIVED FOR RECORD ON THE
AUG 28 1968 19___
day at 9:45 o'clock ___ M
and RECORDED AUG 30 1968 19___ in
DEED BOOK ___ PAGE ___
James A. Schafer
COUNTY RECORDER
RECORDERS FEE $ 2.50

COLUMBUS BLANK BOOK CO.

General Warranty Deeds

General warranty deeds are *deeds in which the grantor warrants the title against defects that might have arisen before or during his period of ownership.* They are also called **standard warranty deeds** or simply **warranty deeds**.

A general warranty deed gives the grantee the broadest possible protection. Most real estate transfers in Ohio are carried out with a general warranty deed. With this type of deed, the grantor specifically guarantees the following covenants:

- **Covenant of seizen**—The grantor warrants that he owns the estate conveyed and has the right to convey.

- **Covenant against encumbrances**—The grantor warrants that the property is free of all encumbrances not recited as exceptions in the deed.

- **Covenant of quiet enjoyment**—The grantor warrants that the grantee shall possess the land undisturbed by claims of title from others.

- **Covenant of warranty forever**—The grantor warrants that he shall defend the grantee's interest against all lawful claims of title.

Limited Warranty Deeds

Limited warranty deeds are *deeds in which the grantor warrants the title only against defects arising during the time that he owned the property, and not against defects arising before that time.* They are also called **special warranty deeds.** This type of deed is not so broad. With this type of deed, the grantor guarantees only the following covenants:

- Grantor guarantees there are not any encumbrances he created.

- Grantor promises to defend title against anyone claiming under him.

Deeds without Warranties

Deeds without warranties can also transfer title to real property, but with them the grantor makes no warranties regarding title, nor does the grantor guarantee that he even has the right to convey title. There are three kinds of deeds without warranties:

- Quitclaim deeds
- Bargain and sale deeds
- Fiduciary deeds

Quitclaim Deeds

Quitclaim deeds *convey any interest in real property the grantor has at the time the deed is executed.* A quitclaim deed makes no warranties whatsoever regarding the title, if any, held by the grantor. It conveys whatever right, title, or interest the grantor holds in the property without representation that there is any interest at all. Often, quitclaims are used to clear up problems with the title, known as **clouds on the title**.

For Example

A spouse may use a quitclaim deed to release any dower interest he may have in conveyed property. It may also be used in the case of a life estate to deed the remainder interest to the life tenant, thus creating marketable title by **merger**.

Bargain and Sale Deeds

Bargain and sale deeds *imply the grantor owns the property and has a right to convey it, but there are no warranties that go with it.* This type of deed is rarely used in Ohio.

Fiduciary Deeds

Fiduciary deeds are *executed by a trustee, executor, or other fiduciary, conveying property that the fiduciary does not own but is authorized to manage.* A fiduciary is one who is in an appointed position of trust and is acting on another's behalf. The fiduciary cannot give general warranty provisions, since the fiduciary is merely acting on behalf of someone else. The only warranties fiduciaries can give, by law, involve their role as fiduciaries, not the state of the title to land. Fiduciaries warrant that they have been duly appointed by a court of competent jurisdiction as fiduciaries and that the act of selling the subject land falls within the duties, as outlined, in their fiduciary relationships.

Transfer on Death Deed or Affidavit

A **Transfer on Death Deed** (now called a **Transfer in Death Designation of Beneficiary Affidavit**), established in Ohio law in 2000, can be *a deed/affidavit with or without a warranty and works like a payable on death bank account.* One present owner of the real property may designate one or more death beneficiaries and may also name contingent beneficiaries.

The beneficiary may be a person, trust, charity, business, or other entity, but must be specifically named.

For Example

To list a beneficiary on a transfer on death deed as "my grandson" is not sufficient; it must read "my grandson, Kevin Smith." A named beneficiary or contingent beneficiary has only a future interest in the real estate. No present interest exists.

The property owner may change the transfer on death deed beneficiary at any time while the owner is alive, but the original transfer on death and any subsequent deeds must be recorded to establish transfer of the property on death. The sale or other conveyance of the property terminates the transfer on death provision.

Additionally, a lien or foreclosure action may be taken against the present property owner, not against the beneficiary's interest.

Ownership

There are two basic kinds of ownership of real property:

- **Ownership in severalty**—Ownership by a single individual or corporation, where one person's interests are severed (cut) from the interests of all others.

- **Co-ownership**—Any form of ownership in which two or more people share title to a piece of real property.

Ownership by Associations

Ownership in severalty and co-ownership can also be further categorized into ownership by associations or by individuals. Associations include businesses, non-profit groups, and other organizations. Depending on its form, an association may be:

- A legal entity separate from its individual members or owners (e.g., a corporation where property is owned by the corporation in severalty).

- Informal (e.g., a general partnership where partnership property is co-owned by the partners).

Title to property can be held in an association's name.

Corporations

A **corporation** is *a legal entity in which individuals hold ownership shares of stock. A corporation is regarded by the law as an artificial person, separate from the individual stockholders.* A corporation is the most sophisticated form of association. To establish a corporation in Ohio, the organizers (incorporators) must file articles of incorporation with the Secretary of State's Office.

A corporation is owned by **shareholders**, *individuals who purchase shares of stock in the company as an investment.* Since the law treats the corporation as an artificial individual, it can enter contracts, incur debts, sue and be sued, and own property. When a corporation owns property, it owns it in severalty, just like a natural person. The shareholders do not own the corporation's property, and they are not personally liable for the corporation's debts. A shareholder's spouse has no dower rights in property owned by the corporation. This is true even when a married person is the corporation's sole shareholder.

A corporation is managed by a board of directors. The board appoints corporate officers to run the business on a day-to-day basis. In most cases, the officers are not automatically authorized to convey or encumber the corporation's real property. Those actions must be expressly authorized by a resolution of the board.

The chief drawback to a corporation is double taxation. With a standard "C" corporation, the corporation first pays corporate income taxes on its profits. Then, if profits are distributed to shareholders as dividends, the same money is taxed again as the shareholders' personal income. There are special tax benefits for a Subchapter "S" corporation, but legal counsel should be sought for the special requirements.

General Partnerships

A **general partnership** is simply *an association of two or more individuals as co-owners of a business run for profit.* It does not have to be formally organized like a corporation. A group of people running a business may be a partnership without even realizing it.

For most purposes, the law does not recognize a general partnership as an entity independent from the individual partners. Unlike corporate shareholders, general partners have unlimited liability for the acts of the partnership. Each partner can be made to pay the partnership's debts out of his own pocket. The partners have to pay taxes on the income they receive from the business, but the partnership itself does not pay taxes.

Partnership Property. *All property that general partners bring into the business at the outset, and all that they later acquire for the business,* is **partnership property**. Anything purchased with partnership funds is also presumed to be partnership property.

The partners own the partnership property as **tenants in partnership**. This is a form of co-ownership, giving each partner an equal, undivided interest in the property. Each partner has an equal right to possess the partnership property for partnership purposes—that is, in carrying on the partnership's business. They do not, however, have the right to possess the property for any other purpose, without the other partners' consent.

A partner cannot sell his undivided interest in partnership property to someone outside the partnership, and a judgment against an individual partner will not create a lien on the partnership property. A lien will attach only if the judgment is against the partnership.

A married partner's spouse does not have dower rights in the partnership property. When a partner dies, his interest in the partnership property passes to the surviving partners. The deceased partner's family has no claim on it.

Title in the Partnership Name. For title to real property to be held in the partnership's name, a **business name certificate** or **"fictitious name certificate"** must be recorded in the county where the partnership's principal office is located, and also in the county where the real property is located. The certificate lists the names and addresses of all partners.

When property is held in a partnership's name, it can be conveyed or mortgaged by any of the partners. They do not all have to sign the deed or mortgage. In fact, the deed or mortgage may be valid even if the partner's action was unauthorized (unless the grantee or mortgagee knew it was unauthorized, or acted in bad faith).

Title to partnership property does not have to be held in the partnership's name.

For Example

X, Y, and Z own XYZ Enterprises and, using partnership funds, X buys some land for the partnership. The land is partnership property even if the deed names only X as grantee.

Limited Partnerships

A **limited partnership**, like a general partnership, is *an association of two or more persons as co-owners of a business.* A limited partnership differs from a general partnership in that a limited partnership has one or more general partners, plus one or more limited partners. The rights and duties of general partners in a limited partnership are the same as in a general partnership. The limited partners, however, have limited liability for partnership debts and a limited role in management of the business.

To create a limited partnership, a **certificate of limited partnership** must be recorded in the county where the partnership's principal place of business is located. The certificate lists the names and addresses of all the general and limited partners.

A limited partnership combines some advantages of a corporation with some advantages of a general partnership. Limited partners are protected from liability (e.g., corporate shareholders and profits are taxed only once as partners' personal income).

Limited Liability Companies

A **limited liability company (LLC)** is a new form of association being used in Ohio. *It is structured similarly to a corporation, thus the limited liability, but has tax benefits of a partnership* (e.g., no double taxation of profits).

Real Estate Investment Trust (REIT). A **Real Estate Investment Trust (REIT)** is a real estate investment business with at least 100 investors, organized as a trust. This form of real estate ownership was created by the Federal Real Estate Investment Trust Act of 1960 to give tax benefits to real estate investors who organize their business as a trust. Here, one or more trustees manage property for the benefit of the beneficiaries. A trust document vests title to the property in the trustees, who have only power expressly granted to them in the trust document. The beneficiaries have no legal interest in the property; they have only the power to enforce performance of the trust.

As previously mentioned, an REIT must have at least 100 investors, who are the beneficiaries of the trust. If an REIT distributes over 90% of its income to its investors, it pays corporate taxes only on the income it retains. So, 90% (or more) of the earnings are taxed only as the investors' personal income, and not as the REIT's income. The investors, like corporate shareholders, are shielded from liability for the REIT's debts.

An REIT can transact real estate business in Ohio only if a special report has been filed in the Secretary of State's Office. The report includes the names and addresses of the trustees and a copy of the trust document. Title to property may be held in the REIT's name or in the name of one of the trustees.

Syndicates

A **syndicate** is not a recognized legal entity. Like "company," the term "syndicate" can refer to almost any business organization.

For Example

The XYZ Syndicate may be a corporation, partnership, or REIT, and can hold title to property accordingly.

Condominiums and Cooperatives

As cities have grown more crowded, single-family homes have become harder to find and more expensive to buy and maintain. Condominiums and other multi-family housing have become popular ownership alternatives. They are structured (physically and legally) to combine individual ownership with co-ownership.

Condominiums

Condominiums are *properties developed for co-ownership, where each co-owner has a separate interest in an individual unit and an undivided interest in the **common areas** of the property.* Office buildings and retail centers can be developed as condominiums but most condominiums are designed for residential use. Typical condominiums look like apartment buildings, but condominiums are not owned by landlords who rent units to tenants. Instead, residents own their units.

Each resident (or family of residents) has exclusive ownership of one unit. The other parts of the property—the grounds, the recreational facilities, the building's lobby, and hallways—are called the **common areas**. These are owned by all of the residents as tenants in common. Thus, each condominium owner owns his unit in severalty and has an undivided interest in the common areas.

There are common areas and limited common areas. A **limited common area** *is part of the condominium project owned by all of the members but used exclusively by one member.*

For Example

A porch outside of a unit may be in the common area owned by all members but may be limited exclusively in use to the member whose property it adjoins.

Property can be developed as a condominium or an existing building can be converted to a condominium. In either case, the developers establish condominium status by filing a **condominium declaration** with the county auditor and having it recorded. The declaration describes the project in detail. It also includes a set of drawings that show the land and floor plans of the building(s).

Along with the declaration, the developers file and record **bylaws** for the **unit owners association**. These bylaws are *the rules that govern the condominium association and owners*. The developers are required to turn over management of the condominium to the association once a certain number of units have been sold. The association is made up of all the unit owners who elect a **board of managers** from among themselves. The board is responsible for the common areas of the condominium:

- Maintenance
- Utilities
- Insurance
- Repairs
- Taxes

Some issues are referred back to the association as a whole for a vote. Under the condominium bylaws, the association has the power to levy assessments to pay for common area expenses. If a unit owner fails to pay his share of an assessment, the association may claim a lien against that unit by recording a certificate of lien.

Encumbrance and Transfer. Each owner may give a lender a mortgage on his unit and its accompanying undivided interest in the common areas. Each owner's creditors can claim a lien against an individual's unit and undivided interest in the common areas. If a lien holder forecloses, only that unit and its undivided interest are affected. A lien holder cannot foreclose on the entire condominium complex. Property taxes are also levied against each unit separately, so a tax lien foreclosure will not affect the whole property.

When a condominium unit is conveyed, an undivided interest in the common areas and membership in the unit owners association are automatically transferred, too. An owner cannot sell his unit without transferring his interest in the common areas, or sell his interest in the common areas separately from his unit.

Timesharing. In a timesharing arrangement, co-owners have the exclusive right to possession of the property for specified periods each year. Each timeshare owner purchases an interest for a fraction of the total cost of the unit. A timesharing arrangement could be developed for any kind of housing, but it is most commonly used for resort condominiums.

Cooperatives

Cooperatives are *buildings owned by corporations. Residents are shareholders in the corporation and each shareholder receives a proprietary lease on an individual unit in the cooperative building and the right to use the common areas.* Title to a cooperative building is held by a corporation formed for that purpose.

A person who wants to live in the building buys shares in the corporation, instead of renting or buying a unit, and is given a *proprietary lease* for a unit in the building. The **proprietary lease** has a longer term than most ordinary leases and gives the shareholder more rights than an ordinary tenant would have. A cooperative shareholder pays a prorated share of the building's expenses. Since each apartment is not separately owned, they are not separately financed. Instead, the corporation gives the lender a **blanket mortgage** that covers the whole building. The expenses also include property taxes levied against the whole building. If any resident fails to pay his share of the expenses, the entire cooperative may be threatened with foreclosure.

To transfer an interest in a cooperative, a shareholder conveys his stock and assigns the proprietary lease to the new shareholder. Since financial instability of one person can jeopardize the whole cooperative, an agreement may provide that a shareholder cannot transfer an interest in the cooperative without the other shareholders' consent.

Co-Ownership by Individuals

Co-ownership between individuals is *any form of ownership in which two or more people share title to a piece of real property.* This is also called **co-tenancy** or **concurrent ownership**. **Undivided interest** *gives each co-owner the right to possession of the whole property, not just a fraction of it.*

Under the law, any number of people may join in the ownership of realty, but the relationship these people share depends on the deed language, which is evidence of their right to title to the land. Legal title to real estate is held by more than one person in one of the following ways:

- Tenancy in common
- Statutory survivorship tenancy
- Joint tenancy
- Tenancy by the entireties

As we examine each of these forms of co-ownership, there are four additional key concepts that will be introduced. They are referred to as the "**four unities**:"

1. Unity of possession
2. Unity of interest
3. Unity of time
4. Unity of title

Each of these unities defines the relationship that exists between the various co-owners of a piece of real property.

Tenancy in Common

Tenancy in common is *a form of co-ownership in which two or more persons each have an undivided interest in the entire property, but no right of survivorship.* Tenancy in common is the most common form of co-ownership. A court will set up a tenancy in common if there is no wording in the deed regarding the intent of the parties. No special words or terms are necessary to create a tenancy in common.

Each tenant in common may own equal shares or shares of different proportions—it does not matter. The deed will set up the fractional interests of the parties. Should the deed be silent as to the interests of the parties, the shares will be equal.

Unity of Possession

A key concept in a tenancy in common is **unity of possession**, which means *each co-owner is entitled to possession of the entire property, because the ownership interests are undivided.* Each tenant in common, no matter what fractional interest he holds, has a right to possess the whole land. This means there are no boundary lines within the land itself separating the co-tenants' interests from each other. All co-tenants under tenancy in common enjoy unity of possession.

Each tenant in common:

- Has the right to share proportionately in the profits of the land, whether those profits are generated through use of the land itself (e.g., farming, mining) or through leasing the land to another.
- Has, in proportion to their share of ownership, the burden of maintaining the land (paying taxes and other expenses incident to land ownership).
- Must not commit waste to the land or he will be responsible for reimbursing the innocent tenants for the damage.

A tenant in common is free to transfer ownership of his or her interest at any time without the consent of the other co-tenants. However, to sell the entire parcel, or to encumber the land with a mortgage, all tenants in common must sign the deed, note, or mortgage.

Case Example

Mr. Uckotter and his sister owned some property as tenants in common, each with an undivided one-half interest. Uckotter wanted to sell the property, and his sister agreed, so Uckotter listed it with a real estate broker for $45,000.

A prospective buyer offered $37,500 for the property. Uckotter accepted the offer and signed a purchase contract, agreeing to convey the property for that price.

However, Uckotter's sister did not think $37,500 was enough, so she refused to sign the contract. Uckotter could sell his own interest without his sister's consent, but not the whole property. The buyer, who wanted all or nothing, withdrew from the transaction. *Cincinnati M & M Realty, Inc. v. Uckotter*, 14 Ohio St. 2d 31, 235 N.E.2d 719 (1968).

When a tenant in common dies, the fractional interest the tenant held passes to her heirs, through the probate estate, to be distributed according to probate laws. The other tenants in common have no independent claim to the deceased's share. This may cause difficulties for listing agents who attempt to take a listing from a surviving tenant in common. In order to sell the entire parcel, the probate court must approve the sale. This is the major disadvantage to tenancy in common.

Termination

A tenancy in common can be terminated by the agreement of all the tenants. They can agree to change to another form of co-ownership or they can agree to divide their property so that each owns a portion of it in severalty. This division by agreement is called **voluntary partition.**

A tenancy in common can also be terminated by the unilateral action of one of the tenants, without the others' consent. If X wants to end the tenancy in common and the other tenants do not, X can file a **partition action** in the court of common pleas. The court may order the property physically divided, or order it to be sold. Each former co-tenant receives a share of the property or the sale proceeds proportionate to his fractional interest.

Statutory Survivorship Tenancy

Statutory survivorship tenancy is *a form of co-ownership in which each co-tenant has an equal undivided interest in real property, and the right of survivorship.* This is also called **joint tenancy with the right of survivorship**. Statutory survivorship tenancy is the other main form of co-ownership used in Ohio. It was created by the Ohio General Assembly to replace joint tenancy and tenancy by the entireties for Ohio property.

Any language that clearly sets up a survivorship interest is sufficient to create one. If the language in the deed is unclear, or would lead reasonable minds to different conclusions, the courts can be asked to impose a tenancy in common as the form of co-ownership. There is no question, however, if the statutory form for the survivorship tenancy deed is used.

Statutory survivorship tenancy represents a completely different set of legal relationships than those found in a tenancy in common. The chief feature to the statutory survivorship tenancy allows the co-tenants to take the ownership share of a deceased co-tenant without having to go through the probate process. Since survivors take ownership equally and simultaneously, a person cannot will or inherit a survivorship estate.

Because probate is avoided, the issue of whether a surviving co-tenant may immediately sell a property interest is resolved. However, the value of the survivorship interest is included in the evaluation of the estate for federal and state estate tax purposes.

Unity of Interest

The first key concept with a statutory survivorship tenancy is *unity of interest.* **Unity of interest** means that *each co-owner has an equal interest (equal share of ownership) in a property.* This makes a statutory survivorship tenancy less flexible than a tenancy in common, because each survivorship tenant must hold a share equal to other tenants, even if their financial contributions to the purchase were unequal.

Unity of Time

The second key concept to understand, **unity of time,** means that *each co-owner acquired title at the same time.* This says that all co-tenants take equal rights of survivorship to the land by taking title at the same time and by the same deed, in order to preserve the survivorship tenancy. In this way, the right to sell survivorship real estate differs from a tenancy in common. Should a survivorship tenant sell his interest in the land, the grantee's title is conditioned upon the survivorship of the grantor.

For Example

John, Chris, and Sam are survivorship tenants. John sells his interest to Pat, so Pat's interest is conditioned upon John's survival. If John dies before either Chris or Sam, Pat loses title to the land. Remember, John cannot sell more than he already has. He owns a survivorship interest, which is what he would sell to Pat. Should he sell that interest to Pat, Pat buys that survivorship interest. Thus, if John dies, Pat loses title.

Pat could defeat this problem if he could get Chris and Sam to join John in the transaction. Thus, if John, Chris, and Sam would deed the property to Chris, Sam, and Pat, Pat's interest would be safe, and not contingent on John's survival.

Unity of Title

The third key concept, **unity of title,** means that *each co-owner acquired title through the same instrument, whether that instrument was a deed, will, or court order.* Taking title on a survivorship basis differs from tenancy in common in that the title a person has is wrapped up in the other survivorship co-tenants. As seen in the previous example, the only way that Pat can guarantee a right to possession and use of the land is to have the other co-tenants join the selling co-tenant on the deed. The fact that a survivorship co-tenant cannot convey all of the bundle of rights by his signature alone indicates a unity among the co-tenants that assures survivorship among them, as a whole, will not be compromised by any one of them. With this unity of title, one co-tenant cannot fully divest himself of ownership without the consent of the rest of the co-tenants. One co-tenant's rights of disposal are limited by the other co-tenants.

Conversion to Tenancy in Common

Additionally, there are two important ways that a **survivorship tenancy** may convert to **tenancy in common**:

1. If the entire title to a parcel of land is held by two survivorship tenants married to each other, and the marriage is terminated by divorce, annulment, or dissolution of marriage, the survivorship tenancy becomes a tenancy in common. Unless the decree states otherwise, the tenants each hold an undivided one-half interest in the property.

2. A creditor of one survivorship tenant may enforce a lien against the survivorship interest of that co-tenant. Upon the proper showing of valid lien holder's rights, the court will convert the survivorship interest of the debtor into a tenancy in common in order to allow foreclosure. Thus, a purchaser at foreclosure would be on equal footing with the other co-tenants since the interest conveyed at foreclosure would be a tenancy in common.

Joint Tenancy

Joint tenancy is not as well established in Ohio as in other states. It is very similar to a statutory survivorship tenancy: Each joint tenant has an equal undivided interest in the property and the right of survivorship. There is an important difference, however, between the two forms concerning what happens when one co-tenant conveys his interest without the consent of the other(s).

When one joint tenant conveys his interest, it simply terminates the right of survivorship as to that interest. The new co-owner is a tenant in common in relation to the others.

For Example

A, B, and C are joint tenants. A sells his undivided 1/3 interest to X. X is a tenant in common in relation to B and C, but B and C are still joint tenants in relation to one another. So, if X dies, her 1/3 interest passes to her heirs. But if B dies, C automatically acquires B's 1/3 interest by right of survivorship.

Remember, if the previous example was a statutory survivorship tenancy, X's interest would have been conditioned on whether A outlived both B and C. With a joint tenancy, that rule does not apply. X's interest is a fee simple absolute right from the start and will not be affected by A's death.

Tenancy by the Entireties

Tenancy by the entireties was abolished by the Ohio General Assembly in 1985. However, many of the tenancies by the entireties that were created between 1971 and 1985 still exist, so a real estate agent should be familiar with the concept.

When the Ohio General Assembly passed a statute establishing tenancy by the entireties in 1971, the statute did not go into detail about the characteristics of the tenancy. Thus, when legal disputes arose, Ohio courts determined the parties' rights by looking at the case law concerning tenancy by the entireties in other states. Some of the resulting court decisions were very controversial, leading to the 1985 abolition of tenancy by the entireties in Ohio.

A **tenancy by the entireties** was *a form of co-ownership in which a married couple owned the property with right of survivorship, and neither spouse could convey or encumber his or her interest without the consent of the other spouse.* Only a husband and wife could be tenants by the entireties. Since each spouse owned an undivided one-half interest in the property, when either spouse died, the other would take title to the whole property by right of survivorship.

The key characteristic of a tenancy by the entireties was that neither spouse could convey his or her interest without the other's consent.

For Example

H and W own some land as tenants by the entireties. If W tried to sell her undivided one-half interest in the land to a third party without H's consent, the transaction was void. W could sell her interest only if H agreed to terminate the tenancy by the entireties.

In the same way, neither spouse could encumber his or her interest without the other's consent. As a result, an involuntary lien against only one spouse did not attach to property held as a tenancy by the entireties.

For Example

H and W own their home as tenants by the entireties. H is involved in a car accident. An injured pedestrian sues and is awarded a judgment against H. The judgment creditor records a certificate of judgment in the county where H and W's home is located. But the judgment lien will not attach to the home, since the judgment was only against H, not against both H and W.

The feature illustrated in the previous example made tenancy by the entireties an extremely popular form of co-ownership for married couples. But the tenancy was extremely unpopular among creditors, and that was what eventually made the general assembly decide to abolish it. If H and W own their home as a statutory survivorship tenancy, the judgment lien against H will attach to his one-half interest in the property.

Recording

Just because someone offers to sell real property does not necessarily mean she has title to it. The seller may be lying or (more commonly) there may be some problem with the title of which the seller is not aware. To limit these risks, every state has a recording system. By making it possible to determine who holds an interest in any property, the recording system protects real estate buyers and lenders against secret conveyances and encumbrances.

Any legal document that affects title to real property can be recorded, and almost all should be, including:

- Deeds
- Easements
- Restrictive covenants
- Court orders
- Long-term leases

Certain documents have no legal effect unless they are recorded (e.g., mortgages, mechanics' liens). Other documents are binding on the parties even if they are not recorded.

For Example

A deed does not have to be recorded in order for title to transfer from the grantor to the grantee. The purpose of recording the deed is to provide *notice* to others.

There are different kinds of **notice**, and different rights and responsibilities that go along with each, but basically the concept of notice with regard to deeds is to announce to the world that the grantee now owns the property. The importance of notice will be explained in this chapter, but first let's take a brief look at the mechanics of the recording process.

The Recorder's Office

To have a document recorded, a person must file it at the county recorder's office and pay the recording fee. The document is said to be "filed for record." The recorder then places the document in the public record.

Long ago, a clerk actually transcribed the document into a record book; as technology became more advanced, the document was photographed into microfilm or microfiche. Today, many counties utilize electronic systems to scan, or digitize, documents for storage as pictures or text documents. These images can be viewed and printed from computers in the recorder's office or online.

Documents are processed *in the order they were filed for record*. This is extremely important, since deed priority or lien priority often depends on when the competing documents were filed. Each document is numbered so it can be located in the public record.

The recorder keeps an index of all recorded documents. Counties using the multiple index system usually divide the index into two parts:

1. The **direct index** (also called the **grantor/grantee index)** lists all documents in alphabetical order under the grantor's last name

2. The **reverse index** (also called the **grantee/grantor index)** lists all documents under the grantee's last name

The index lists the volume and page where the document is located in the public record. A person can then look at the document and obtain a copy.

The recorder may also maintain a **sectional index**, which lists documents under the tax parcel number of the property they apply to. In that way, it groups together all recorded documents affecting a particular property. This type of index is also called a **tract index**.

Many counties have now moved to a single index system, called an **official index**, in which all documents are recorded and accessible by computer.

Notice

When two people have conflicting claims, sometimes their rights and liabilities depend on whether one had notice of the other's claim:

- One has **actual notice** of something if he actually knows about it.

- One has **constructive notice** of something he ought to know about, even though he does not actually know about it.

The law holds that everyone has constructive notice of recorded documents. Even if someone did not know about a particular recorded document, he could have found out about it by searching the public record. The law expects a buyer or lender to take that step for his own protection. The law will not look after a buyer or lender who does not bother to check.

For Example

S grants an easement across his property to J and J records the easement document. S then sells his property to K.

K claims she does not have to honor the easement because she could not tell that it existed simply by looking at the property and S never told her about it.

However, the easement is still valid because K is deemed to have constructive notice of it. Even though she did not have actual notice, she could have found out about the easement granted to J by checking the public records.

It is possible, however, for a recorded document to fall outside the *chain of title*. The **chain of title** is the chain of deeds (or other documents) passing title for a property from one owner to the next, as disclosed in the public records. A deed outside the chain of title is considered a "wild deed," and buyers and lenders are not held to have constructive notice of it.

For Example

A buys a house and records her deed. Later she sells the property to B, but B does not record his deed.

B sells the property to C, and C records his deed promptly. Now there's a break in the chain of title: The record shows only A's deed and C's deed, but the link between them (B's deed) is missing. That makes C's deed a wild deed.

A is aware that B never recorded his deed and she decides to sell the same property a second time. This time she sells it to D.

D does not know about B or C, so he has no reason to look up those names in the grantee/grantor index. He looks up A's name in the grantor/grantee index, and as far as he can tell from the record, she is still the owner of the property. So D goes ahead with the purchase.

D does not have constructive notice of C's interest in the property, because C's deed was outside the chain of title. Thus, a court would probably determine that D is the owner of the property since he had neither actual or constructive notice of the other deeds.

In addition to actual notice and constructive notice, there is **inquiry notice**. A person is said to have inquiry notice when *there is some indication of a claim or other circumstance that would lead a reasonable person to be alerted to a possible problem, and cause further inquiry into the condition of the title.* If a person does not find out about the claim because he fails to investigate any further, he may still be held to have had inquiry notice of the claim.

When someone is in possession of the property, a buyer is held to have inquiry notice of the possessor's claim—even if the buyer never visited the property. This is why it is a bad idea to buy real estate sight unseen.

Race/Notice Rule

What happens when an owner sells property to one person and then sells the same property to another person? Ohio follows the **race/notice rule**. Figuratively speaking, the two grantees race each other to the recorder's office and whoever records a deed first wins. The first to record the deed has title to the property, unless he had notice of an earlier conveyance.

Case Example

Storer owned a large tract of property. Campbell purchased a small piece of the tract from Storer in 1965. Campbell received a warranty deed, but never recorded it.

In 1970, Storer accidentally sold the same piece of property again as part of a larger parcel. This time, the grantees recorded their deed promptly.

These later grantees did not have actual notice of the earlier sale to Campbell. They did not have inquiry notice, because Campbell was not occupying the property at the time of the second sale. They could not be deemed to have constructive notice, since Campbell's deed was not recorded. The later grantees were **subsequent good faith purchasers without notice**. As a result, they had valid title to the land even though Campbell bought it first.

Campbell was entitled to recover damages from Storer, but had no claim against the property or against the later grantees. *Campbell v. Storer*, 52 Ohio App. 2d 103, 368 N.E.2d 301 (1975).

The race/notice rule protects only subsequent good faith purchasers. In the previous example, if Storer had given the later grantees the property as a gift, Campbell's title would still have prevailed over theirs.

 Ohio does not apply the race/notice rule to mortgages. A recorded mortgage has priority over all unrecorded or subsequently recorded interests, even if the mortgagee had actual notice of those interests. With mortgages, Ohio follows a pure race rule: Notice does not matter—winning the race is all that counts.

The Marketable Title Act

Ohio became a state in 1803, and, as such, its public records go back a long way. Tracing a property's history back to its first deed to discover all possible claims against the title would be a time-consuming process.

The **Marketable Title Act** is intended to improve the marketability of title and simplify the title search process. It does so by extinguishing certain old, dormant claims against a title. The Act usually makes it unnecessary to search back much further than 40 years.

Under the Act, an owner with an unbroken chain of recorded title going back at least 40 years has a **marketable record title.** The **root of title** is the deed (or other document of transfer) that, 40 years ago, was the most recently recorded.

For Example

It is 2010, and D is the current owner of Lot 6. D acquired the property from C, by a deed recorded in 1995. C acquired it from B, by a deed recorded in 1979. B acquired it from A, by a deed recorded in 1966.

The 1966 deed from A to B is D's root of title. Forty years ago (1970), it was the most recently recorded deed transfer in the chain of title.

When an owner establishes a marketable record title (as D has in the previous example), any claims are extinguished that arose before the root of title, unless they have been preserved.

An easement, use restriction, or other interest is preserved if it has been specifically mentioned in a deed (or other transfer document) recorded sometime after the root of title.

For Example

Suppose an easement was recorded against Lot 6 in 1961, before D's root of title. If the 1979 deed from B to C said, "Subject to the access easement granted July 6, 1961, and recorded at Vol. 168, page 35," that preserved the easement. D still has to allow the easement to be used.

Even if none of the deeds mentioned the easement, it would be preserved if the easement holder recorded a notice preserving it, within 40 years after the root of title. The notice must:

- Be in the form of an affidavit (a sworn statement).

- Include a full description of all property affected by the preserved interest.

- State the names of the property's current owners.

But the easement would be extinguished if no transfer document recorded since the root of title specifically mentioned the easement, and no affidavit was filed. (A general reference in a deed, such as "Subject to all easements and restrictions of record," is not enough to preserve those interests. The reference must be specific.) Once an interest is extinguished, it is gone for good. It cannot be revived by recording an affidavit after the 40-year deadline has passed.

Certain types of interests can be preserved only by affidavit—mentioning them in a deed will not suffice. These interests include possibilities of reverter, rights of entry, and powers of termination (see Chapter 6).

There are several exceptions to the Marketable Title Act. An easement cannot be extinguished if there is clearly observable physical evidence of its use or if it involves pipes, cables, or other physical objects on or embedded in the land. Furthermore, none of these interests can be extinguished under the Act:

- A lessor's right to possession at the end of a lease

- A railroad or public utility easement

- Any interest in coal

- A mortgage

- Any interest held by the federal, state, or local government

The Torrens System

Not all documents affecting title to real property in Ohio are recorded. At the beginning of this century, Ohio adopted the **Torrens system** of title registration. It is an alternative to the recording system.

To use the Torrens system:

- A landowner registers her property with the state Torrens registrar.

- A careful title search and survey of the property are performed.

- The registrar issues a Torrens certificate; the original is kept in the registrar's office and the property owner receives a duplicate certificate.

- When the owner sells the property, she must surrender the duplicate certificate to the registrar.

Once the property has been registered ("Torrenized"), no deed, mortgage, lien, easement, or other encumbrance pertaining to it can be legally effective unless it is registered with the Torrens registrar. If someone has a lien against the property recorded instead of registered, the lien will have no effect. A prospective buyer or lender can determine the status of the title by consulting the Torrens register, without having to search the public record.

Despite its convenience, the Torrens system is rarely used, primarily because the initial registration process is expensive. In 1991, Ohio law was revised to allow counties to abolish the land registration system, based on an evaluation of the cost of initially registering the property and maintaining the system at the county level. Property may be removed from the system by notifying the recorder of the intent to remove, and then recording a deed to evidence the conveyance.

Summary

1. The **deed** is the most important document in a typical real estate transaction—it is an instrument that conveys ownership in real property. The deed is mere evidence of title. **Title** is the actual lawful ownership of real property. Title refers to holding the rights conveyed in a transfer. For a deed to be valid in Ohio, it must be in writing and contain these elements: Competent grantor's signature, identifiable grantee, words of conveyance, description of property, consideration, acknowledgment, delivery, and acceptance.

2. **Warranty deeds** include general warranty deeds and limited warranty deeds. Deeds without warranties include quitclaim deeds, bargain and sale deeds, and fiduciary deeds. **General warranty deeds** have guarantees obligating the grantor to defend the grantee from claims against the title. General warranty deeds give the grantee the best possible protection, and are most used for real estate transfers in Ohio. The most common deeds without warranty are **quitclaim deeds**, where the grantor conveys only the interest he may have in the property, without warranty that he has an interest. Quitclaim deeds are mostly used to clear up **clouds on title** (e.g., a spouse releasing dower).

3. Ownership can be held in **severalty** (one person), or **co-owned** by two or more people with each having an undivided interest. Undivided interest means each co-owner has a right to possession of the whole property, not just part of it. Forms of co-ownership are: **Tenancy in common**, **statutory survivorship tenancy**, **joint tenancy**, or **tenancy by the entireties**. If title is severable between co-tenants, then title is a tenancy in common. In Ohio, two or more people can set up a survivorship estate by deed language. Since 1985, tenancy by the entireties is not an option in Ohio. Joint tenancy is not well established in Ohio.

4. Title to real property can be held by associations of individuals: **Corporations**, **general** and **limited partnerships**, or **REITs**. Corporations own property in severalty; general partners own property as tenants in partnership. The owner of a **condominium** unit owns the unit in severalty, and has an undivided interest in the common areas. A **cooperative** is owned by a corporation, with each shareholder having a proprietary lease for one unit.

5. Deeds and other documents are recorded to give notice of ownership or other claimed rights. One has **actual notice** if he knows a fact to be true. One has **constructive notice** of all filings in public records. Real estate buyers have a duty to check public records for filings about the subject property. Possession or use of land by another puts buyer on **inquiry notice**. Ohio follows **race/notice rule**, meaning the first to record gets title to property. This is true except for subsequent good faith purchasers who record a deed (they are not held to prior non-recorded interests unless they had actual notice of them) and mortgage (Ohio follows a pure race rule giving them priority regardless of notice).

6. The **Marketable Title Act** says that the chain of title deeds transferring ownership need only be traced back 40 years. An unbroken chain of documents going back 40 years to the **root of title** is sufficient to establish proper title. A deed that falls outside the **chain of title** because it was not recorded is called a wild deed. **Torrens System** registration could solve chain of title problems since all things must be recorded with a Torrens registrar to be valid, but this system is rarely used due to cost.

Quiz

1. **The deed that offers the grantor the greatest protection against claims is the**
   a. fiduciary's deed.
   b. general warranty deed.
   c. limited warranty deed.
   d. quitclaim deed.

2. **The warranty that allows the grantee to seek recovery from the grantor on the basis of a secret lien is the covenant**
   a. against encumbrances.
   b. of highest authority.
   c. of quiet enjoyment.
   d. of seizen.

3. **If a grantor is 17 years old, the only type of deed presented at close would be a**
   a. deed of trust.
   b. fiduciary's deed.
   c. general warranty deed.
   d. nefarious deed.

4. **All are requirements for a valid deed EXCEPT**
   a. an acknowledgment before a notary public.
   b. an adequate description of the property conveyed.
   c. the signature of a competent grantee.
   d. the signatures of two competent witnesses.

5. **Title to real estate generally passes from grantor to grantee with**
   a. delivery and acceptance of the deed.
   b. the payment of the broker's commission.
   c. the recording of the deed.
   d. Words of Conveyance.

6. **When a grantee asks a real estate licensee for advice on how to hold title to property, the agent should**
   a. advise an estate in common to allow the estate to be severed in case of trouble.
   b. advise a survivorship interest to avoid probate.
   c. advise a tenancy at will, which can be terminated by any of the parties without notice.
   d. not offer advice of this kind because it involves the practice of law.

7. **How many persons may share ownership in severalty?**
   a. one
   b. two, as long as they are married to each other
   c. two or more persons, as long as there is unity of title
   d. any number, regardless of unity of title

8. **Who should prepare the deed?**
   a. buyer's attorney
   b. buyer's broker
   c. escrow agency
   d. listing broker

9. **Tenancies by the entireties**
   a. are illegal in Ohio.
   b. automatically confer dower rights.
   c. cannot exist in common law marriage.
   d. may be formed by two consenting adults.

10. **Title to real estate CANNOT pass from grantor to grantee without**
    a. an attorney's letter of opinion.
    b. a policy of title insurance for the bank.
    c. present donative intent of the grantor.
    d. recording the deed.

11. **Company X is a general partnership. Partnership funds were used to purchase a building for the company's offices. The building is partnership property**
    a. as long as the partners are not married.
    b. even though the title is in one partner's name alone.
    c. only if the title is in the partnership's name.
    d. only if the title lists all partners and expressly states they are tenants in partnership.

12. **In most cases, which statement about condominiums is FALSE?**
    a. A blanket mortgage covers the entire condominium property.
    b. Each unit owner has an undivided interest in the common areas.
    c. Property taxes are assessed separately for each unit.
    d. The unit owners association can levy assessments to pay for maintenance of the common areas.

Contracts

A contract is an agreement to do, or not do, something. It does not have to be a long legal document—a spoken promise, a bus pass, and a movie ticket are all examples of contracts. To be enforced by a court, an agreement must be made according to the rules of contract law. This chapter explains those rules and discusses some of the types of contracts used in real estate transactions: Listing agreements, purchase agreements, and options.

Key Terms

Acceptance When parties agree to the terms of an offer to enter into a contract, thereby creating a binding contract.

Assignment When a person transfers her interests under a contract to another.

Consideration Anything of value (e.g., money, services, goods, promises) given to induce another person to enter into a contract.

Counteroffer A response to an offer to enter into a contract changing some terms of the original offer. It is a rejection of the original offer (not a form of acceptance) and does not create a binding contract unless the new counteroffer is accepted by the original offeror (the counter-offeree).

Liquidated Damages A sum of money agreed to in advance by parties to a contract (at the time of entering into the contract), which will serve as compensation in the event of a contract breach.

Material Breach An unexcused failure to perform according to the terms of a contract, important enough that the non-breaching party is not required to perform his contractual obligations.

Mitigation When the non-breaching party takes action to minimize the losses resulting from a breach of contract.

Offer When one person proposes a contract to another; if the other person accepts the offer, a binding contract is formed.

Rescission When a contract is terminated, and each party gives back to the other party anything acquired under the contract.

Specific Performance A legal remedy in which a court orders the breaching party of a contract to perform as agreed, rather than simply paying monetary damages.

Statute of Frauds A law that requires certain types of contracts to be in writing and signed in order to be enforceable.

Contract Classifications

A **contract** is an agreement between two or more parties to do, or not do, something. Contracts can be classified several different ways. A contract is either:

- Express or implied
- Unilateral or bilateral
- Executory or executed

Express versus Implied

An **express contract** is *an agreement that has been expressed in words, whether spoken or written* (e.g., offering a kid $20 to cut your grass). An **implied contract** is *an agreement that has not been put into words but is implied by the actions of the parties.* Going to the doctor is an implied contract. It is understood that the patient agrees to pay the doctor's fee, even if they do not actually discuss it.

Unilateral versus Bilateral

A **unilateral contract** occurs when only one party makes a legally binding promise to the other party. A **bilateral contract** occurs when each party makes a binding promise to the other.

For Example

A says to B, "I'll pay you $100 if you paint my fence this week. Will you do it?" B says, "Sure, I'll start tomorrow morning." They have a bilateral contract: B has promised to paint the fence, and A has promised to pay.

Offering a reward—$100 for the return of a lost necklace—is a unilateral contract. An *option* and an *open listing agreement* (explained later in this chapter) are two more examples of unilateral contracts. A *purchase contract* and an *exclusive right to sell listing agreement* are examples of bilateral contracts.

Executory versus Executed

An **executory contract** is *a contract in which one or both parties have not yet completed performance of their contractual obligations.* They may be in the process of carrying out their duties. An **executed contract** is *a contract in which both parties have completely performed their contractual obligations.* Most contracts start out executory and end up executed.

 Do not confuse an **executed contract** with *executing* a contract, which is merely the act of signing a contract.

Status of Contracts

In addition to the six classifications just discussed, a contract is also one of the following:

- Valid
- Void
- Voidable
- Unenforceable

Valid. A **valid contract** is *a binding, legally enforceable contract*. It meets items 2, 3, and 4 of the legal requirements for contract formation outlined next. If one of the parties does not fulfill his side of the bargain, the other party can sue to have the contract enforced.

Void. A **void contract** is *a contract that is not enforceable because it lacks items 2, 3, and/or 4 for contract formation, or is defective in some other respect*. In the eyes of the law, it is not a contract at all. If both parties fulfill their promises, fine; but if one party does not perform and the other party sues, a judge will rule there was no contract.

For Example

A contract is contingent upon financing and the buyer is unable to get a loan; thus, the contract would be void.

Voidable. A **voidable contract** is *a contract that one of the parties can disaffirm, without liability, because of a lack of legal capacity or a negative factor* (e.g., fraud, duress). This generally happens when one of the parties is a minor or has been taken advantage of in some other way. The injured party can choose whether to go through with the contract. If he decides against it, the injured party can **disaffirm** the contract by taking some action that notifies the other party the contract is terminated.

Unenforceable. An **unenforceable contract** is *a contract that a court would refuse to enforce*.

For Example

A contract may be unenforceable because its contents cannot be proven (a problem with an oral contract), it is not in writing (such as a real estate contract), or the statute of limitations has run out (even though the contract was valid at one time). Vaguely worded contracts may also be unenforceable.

Contract Formation

There are five essential elements for a valid and enforceable contract:

1. Contractual capacity
2. Offer
3. Acceptance (with Delivery)
4. Consideration
5. Lawful and possible objective

These requirements apply to all contacts. Also, certain contracts—such as those for the sale of real property—must be in writing and signed to be enforceable.

 Only items 2, 3, and 4 are necessary for a valid contract; items 1 and 5 make the contract enforceable in a court of law.

Contractual Capacity

Contractual capacity (also called **contractual ability**) is *the legal ability to enter a contract.* To make a valid contract in Ohio, a person must be at least 18 years old and mentally competent. This requirement protects minors and the mentally ill who otherwise might enter into contracts without understanding the consequences. When an adult enters into a contract with a minor, that contract is voidable by only the minor at any time before turning 18 or within a reasonable time thereafter. The minor, though, may choose to enforce the contract and require the adult to perform. The adult does not have the power to disaffirm the contract.

For Example

M is only 17. He signs a contract to buy a house from S, an adult, who does not realize M is underage. A few weeks later, when the sale is ready for closing, M changes his mind. He tells S their deal is off. S cannot sue to enforce the contract. However, if the tables were turned and S wanted to back out, M would have the right to sue S to enforce the contract.

An adult who is incapable of understanding the nature and consequences of a contract also does not have capacity to contract. After a person has been declared incompetent by a court (because of mental illness, disability, or senility), any contract he enters into is considered void. Neither the incompetent person nor the other party can have it enforced. To be enforceable, the contract would have to be signed by the incompetent person's court appointed guardian or power of attorney.

Even if a person has not been declared legally incompetent, in some cases, it can be proven that he was not of sound mind when he signed the contract. When that occurs, a court may rule in different ways, depending on the circumstances in each case. The contract may be voidable by the incompetent person but, if the other party acted in good faith without notice of the incompetency, a court might decide to enforce the contract.

Offer

For a contract to be a binding obligation, all parties must consent to its terms. This is achieved through *offer* and *acceptance.* An **offer** occurs when one party proposes a contract to another party. A contract is formed only if the other party accepts the offer.

Requirements of an Offer

The process of forming a contract begins when one party (the **offeror**) makes an offer to another party (the **offeree**). For this to serve as the basis for a contract, there are two basic requirements of an offer:

- It must express an intent to contract.
- It must have definite terms.

Intent to Contract. The intent requirement is concerned with **objective intent** (what the offeror says and does) rather than **subjective intent** (what the offeror is actually thinking). If a person says or does something that a reasonable person could interpret as a serious expression of the intention to make a contract, that may be a legally binding offer—even if the person was just kidding.

Definite Terms. The offer must also have definite terms. An offer is not binding if it is too vague. The offer should state at least such basic items as the subject matter, the time for performance, and the price. In some cases, a court will fill in the blanks with a reasonable time or a reasonable price, but if too many terms are left unspecified, no contract is formed.

Offers Regarding Real Estate

Note that a **real estate listing** is *not* considered a property owner's offer to sell. By listing the property, the seller is merely soliciting offers from potential buyers. A buyer does not create a contract by accepting the seller's listing. Instead, a buyer makes an offer to purchase and the seller accepts or rejects the offer. The listing is considered an independent contract between the seller and a real estate broker, not part of a purchase contract between the seller and buyer.

Termination of an Offer

To create a binding contract, an offer must be accepted before it terminates. An offer can be terminated by:

- Lapse of time.
- Death or incapacity of one of the parties.
- Revocation.
- Rejection.

Lapse of Time. Many offers state they will expire at a certain time (e.g., "after five days" or "on March 31"). When an offer does not specify an expiration date, it expires after a reasonable time. Even when an offer has an expiration date, it may be terminated sooner by death or incapacity, revocation, or rejection.

Death or Incapacity. The death or incapacity of one of the parties often makes it impossible to form a contract. This would also terminate an offer before a stated expiration date.

For Example

An offer made on March 1 states it will expire on March 31. If the offeror dies on March 23, before the offer has been accepted, the offer terminates on that date—it does not continue until March 31. The offeree cannot create a contract by accepting the contract on March 24.

Revocation. An offer is terminated if the offeror revokes or withdraws it before the offeree accepts it. At the point that the offer is revoked, the offeree has lost the chance to accept it. This is true even if the offer stated it was irrevocable, or that it would not expire until a particular date.

For Example

On March 1, B submits a written offer to buy S's house for $150,000. The offer states that it will remain open until March 9. While S is making up his mind, B finds a different house she wants instead of S's. She calls S on March 6 and revokes her offer. Now, even if S sends B an acceptance before March 9, it will not create a binding contract.

It is a different matter if an offeree pays the offeror a sum of money to keep the offer to purchase open: The offer cannot be revoked during the specified period. A preliminary contract has been formed in this situation. The offeree can still choose to accept or reject the original offer to purchase, but at least the offeror cannot withdraw the offer to purchase before the agreed time period has elapsed.

Rejection. An offer is also terminated when it is rejected by the offeree.

For Example

If G rejects the offer on Monday, he cannot change his mind and call R, the offeror, back on Tuesday to accept it. If G is still interested in the deal, G and R can start the process of offer and acceptance over again, but the original offer was terminated by G's rejection. If R lost interest, G can no longer hold him to his offer.

Acceptance

Acceptance is *when a party agrees to the terms of an offer to enter into a contract.* When an offer is accepted, a contract is formed. At that point, the parties are legally bound, and neither can back out unless the other is willing to call off the contract.

Requirements of Acceptance

There are four basic requirements for acceptance:

1. May be made only by the offeree
2. Must be communicated to the offeror
3. Must be made in the manner specified
4. Must not vary the terms of the offer

Acceptance of an Offer Can Be Made Only by the Offeree. This may sound obvious, but there is an important distinction. It means that if A makes an offer to B, and B decides not to accept it, C cannot accept the offer and force A to deal with him. Of course, A may be willing to work with C but, in legal terms, any contract between A and C is based on a new offer, not on the offer A made to B.

Acceptance Must Be Communicated to the Offeror. An offeree may already have decided to accept an offer, but until he lets the offeror know he has accepted it, the offeror can still revoke it.

Case Example

On February 15, Mr. Toro submitted a written offer to buy Mr. Geyer's property. He gave Geyer a check for $5,000 as an earnest money deposit. The offer stated that if it was not accepted on or before March 1, the check was to be returned to Toro.

Although Geyer cashed Toro's check on February 23, he did not notify Toro that he was accepting the offer. Toro decided he did not want to go through with the purchase, so on March 1, he withdrew the offer and asked Geyer to return the earnest money. Geyer refused and Toro sued.

The court ruled that no binding contract had been created since Geyer had not communicated his acceptance to Toro before the offer was revoked. Cashing the check was not enough; he had to express his intention to Toro. *Toro v. Geyer*, 66 Ohio Law Abs. 497, 117 N.E.2d 620 (1951).

"The mailbox rule" says when an acceptance is not communicated directly, either in person or over the phone, it is effective as soon as it is sent in the mail to the offeror, even though the other party has not received it yet.

For Example

Suppose B drops a letter accepting A's offer into the mailbox at 1:00 p.m. At 1:30 p.m., A calls B and tells her the offer is revoked. A's revocation has come too late—a binding contract was formed when B put her acceptance in the mail, even though A had not received it yet.

Note that the mailbox rule applies only to acceptances and not to revocations. If an offeror mails a revocation to the offeree, it is not effective until the offeree actually receives it. Until the offeree has received notice of the revocation, he can still create a binding contract by accepting the offer.

Acceptance Must Be Made in the Manner Specified. Many offers specify a particular manner of acceptance, such as "in writing," or "by delivering a cashier's check." The offeree's acceptance will not be effective unless those instructions are followed. Suppose the offer states that acceptance must be in writing but the offeree calls and accepts over the phone. That does not create a binding contract—the offeror can still revoke the offer.

When an offer does not specify how it is to be accepted, any reasonable method of acceptance will effectively bind the offeror and prevent revocation. This rule applies to all contracts—even those that are required by law to be in writing and signed, such as real estate purchase agreements.

Acceptance Must Not Vary the Terms of the Offer. To create a contract, the offeree must accept exactly those terms that he was offered. The offeree cannot modify them or add any new terms. If an offeree makes changes, his response to the original offer technically is not an acceptance; it is a *counteroffer*, which represents a change. A **counteroffer** is *essentially a rejection and a new offer*. The original offeror has become the counterofferee, and the original offeree is now the counterofferor. A binding contract is not created unless the counterofferee accepts the counteroffer.

Since a counteroffer is a rejection, it terminates the original offer. If a counteroffer is rejected, it is too late to go back and accept the original offer. The counterofferor can start again with a new offer identical to the original one, but if the original offeror has had a change of heart, he can no longer be held to the original offer.

Sometimes, an offeree rewords the offer slightly, or adds a phrase to clarify or emphasize a particular provision. As long as these revisions or additions do not materially change the terms of the offer, the response is still an acceptance, not a counteroffer.

Case Example

The Brogans offered to sell their farm to the Karases. The offer stated that the title would be "free and clear of all liens and encumbrances." When the Karases accepted the offer, they added the phrase, "Oil lease has to be cancelled."

The Brogans ended up selling the farm to someone else and the Karases sued to enforce their contract. The Brogans claimed no contract had been formed. They argued that since the Karases had added that phrase about the oil lease, their response was a counteroffer, not an acceptance. The Brogans did not accept the counteroffer, so they did not have a contract with the Karases.

The court disagreed. Since the oil lease was an encumbrance, the Brogans would have been required to cancel it under the original terms of their offer. The court held that the Karases' addition did not actually change the terms of the offer. Their response was effective as an acceptance, not just a counteroffer. The court ruled that the Karases had an enforceable contract with the Brogans. *Karas v. Brogan*, 55 Ohio St. 2d 128, 378 N.E.2d 471 (1978).

Consideration

Consideration is *something of value (e.g., money, services, goods, promises) given to induce another to enter into a contract*. This is also called **valuable consideration**. A contract cannot be a one-way street, though. Each party must give something to the other.

 A deed may be supported by either valuable or good (e.g., love and affection) consideration; however, a contract must be supported by valuable consideration.

The exchange of consideration is what distinguishes a contractual promise from the promise of a gift. The courts will not enforce a gift (although it may not be socially acceptable to promise someone a gift and then break the promise, the law will not get involved). A promise is not enforceable unless it is a contractual obligation, and it is not a contractual obligation unless both parties exchange consideration.

Valuable consideration can be anything of value (e.g., a hat, $20, a split-level home). The consideration for most contracts is a promise to give something of value. For this reason, the parties to a contract are sometimes referred to as the **promisor** (the one making a promise) and the **promisee** (the one receiving the benefit of a promise).

In a typical real estate contract, the buyer promises to pay the seller money, and the seller promises to transfer title to the buyer. By exchanging promises, they create an executory contract; when they fulfill their promises (i.e., when the buyer pays the seller and the seller gives the buyer the deed), the contract is executed.

Something already done cannot be consideration.

For Example

If A says to B, "Because you quit smoking, I'm going to buy you a yacht," a contract is not created. Since B already quit smoking, he did not give A anything (or give up anything) in exchange for A's promise.

Also, promising to do something that one is already legally obligated to do (or promising to refrain from doing something that the law does not allow one to do) is not consideration.

For Example

Suppose A contracts to build B a house for $200,000. When the house is more than half completed, A says, "You're going to have to pay me another $30,000 if you want me to finish this project." B meekly agrees. This is not an enforceable contract. A cannot sue B for the additional $30,000 because A was already obligated to finish the house.

Adequacy

It is important to understand that the value of the consideration one party gives does not have to be equal to the value of what the other gives. In other words, even though one party struck a bad bargain, they still have an enforceable contract.

For Example

X's house appraised at $200,000. He is eager to sell it quickly because he thinks he may have to leave the country in a hurry. When Z offers $75,000 for the house, X accepts, and they execute a written contract.

As it turns out, X will not have to leave the country. He wants to back out of the sale, but Z will not let him. Although X's consideration is worth more than twice what Z is giving, their contract is binding.

Of course, when the consideration is grossly unequal, that may be a sign that there was fraud, undue influence, duress, or mistake involved. But unless one of those negative factors is proven, the contract is enforceable.

Lawful and Possible Objective

Lawful and possible objective means *the purpose or objective of a contract must be lawful at the time the contract is made.* When one person promises to pay someone for committing an illegal act, their contract is void. A court may also refuse to enforce a contract that is not strictly illegal, if its objective violates public policy.

Many contracts have more than one purpose and they are often *severable*. **Severable** means *one part or provision of a contract can be held unenforceable without making the entire contract unenforceable.* The unenforceable part is severed, or cut, from the rest of the agreement. When part of a contract is lawful and part is unlawful, a court may set aside the unlawful part and enforce the rest.

In addition to being lawful, the objective of a contract must be possible. But that does not necessarily mean possible for the person who promised to do it; it means possible for anyone.

For Example

S contracts to sell a house to B, but S does not actually own the house. This contract is not void because of impossibility. Although it is impossible for S to perform as promised (since she does not own the house), it is not impossible for anyone to perform—the true owner could sell the house. S may be required to buy the house and sell it to B, or to pay B damages for breach of contract.

The Statute of Frauds (ORC § 1335)

The **statute of frauds** is *a law that requires certain types of contracts to be in writing and signed in order to be enforceable.* The same name is used for similar laws in other states because the term was adopted from English law. As the name suggests, the writing requirement is intended to prevent fraudulent claims and perjury (false testimony). The parties to an unwritten contract are likely to later disagree about exactly what each agreed to do—or whether they agreed to do anything at all.

Contracts That Must Be in Writing

In Ohio, the statute of frauds applies to any contract:

- That cannot be performed within one year from the time it is made.
- For the sale of goods for $500 or more.
- For the sale of personal property for $5,000 or more.
- Made in exchange for a promise of marriage, a promise to guarantee payment of another's debt, and a lease where the term is longer than one year.

All of these kinds of contracts must be in writing and signed.

Real Estate

Most importantly for the purposes of this text, Ohio's statute of frauds applies to any contract or document that conveys an interest in real property (e.g., purchase contracts, options, mortgages, deeds). A written contract or document is needed to enforce these agreements.

In addition, the statute of frauds applies to any *power of attorney* authorizing another person to sell another's real estate. A **power of attorney** is an instrument authorizing one person (called an attorney-in-fact) to act as another's agent, to the extent stated in the instrument.

Unlike an attorney-at-law, anyone can be an attorney-in-fact. This person's authority, though, is usually severely limited and always restricted to those things specifically stated in the agreement. A power of attorney conferring the right to sell another's real property must be:

- In writing.
- Signed.
- Witnessed by two competent witnesses.
- Acknowledged before a notary.
- Recorded with the county recorder in the county where the land is situated to become effective.

Listing Agreements. A **listing agreement** of more than one year would have to be in writing under the statute of frauds; however, all listing agreements (regardless of length) should be in writing. As an agreement between the parties, a listing agreement represents an employment contract, which ordinarily would not need to be in writing to be enforced.

 Remember: Ohio's Licensing Law statute requires that listing agreements have expiration dates and that true copies must be left with all parties. Because of these and other precise requirements that need to be stated in listing agreements. Any oral arrangement is extremely difficult to prove, so it is always worth an agent's time to get things in writing.

Type of Writing Required

To satisfy the statute of frauds, the writing does not have to be a formal legal document. A note or memorandum is enough if it indicates there is an agreement between the parties and it is signed by both parties.

Case Example

Mr. McNutt agreed to sell his property to Mr. and Mrs. Sanders. McNutt took out a sheet of paper and wrote down, "Received deposit of $300 on property located at 4228 New Portage Road as binder on sale totaling $12,500; balance to be paid at time of transfer of clear title." He then signed the paper.

Later, however, McNutt refused to go through with the sale. Mr. and Mrs. Sanders sued. The court held that the signed paper was sufficient to make their contract enforceable. *Sanders v. McNutt,* 147 Ohio St. 408, 72 N.E.2d 72 (1947).

A full signature is unnecessary; initials are enough. In fact, anything the signer intends as a signature will do. Just keep in mind that it may be difficult to prove that a wavy line or an "X" was someone's signature if that person later denies it.

Part Performance

The **doctrine of part performance** *allows a court to enforce an oral agreement, which should have been in writing, when the promisee has taken irrevocable steps to perform her side of the bargain, and failure to enforce the contract would result in an unjust benefit for the promisor.* Some cases involving the statute of frauds seem very unfair because one party gets away with breaching an agreement just because the other party did not know the law requires that type of agreement to be in writing. The doctrine of part performance tries to prevent unfairness, in at least a few cases, where one party started to carry out her side of the bargain in reliance on the other party's promises.

In Ohio, the doctrine is applied only when:

- The injured party has taken irrevocable steps, making it impossible to restore the injured party to her original position.

- Failure to enforce the contract would result in fraud and an unjust benefit for the other party.

<hr>

Case Example

A mother was concerned that she might lose her home to foreclosure because she was unable to pay the property taxes. She agreed to deed the property to her adult son if he would pay the taxes and allow her to live in the house for the rest of her life. They did not put this agreement in writing, but the mother executed a deed granting her son title, and he paid the delinquent taxes.

Sometime later, the son decided he wanted to tear down the house and build a new one. He asked his mother to move out, but she refused. The son then filed an eviction suit against his mother.

The court ruled that the mother was entitled to possession of the property for the rest of her life. The mother and son's agreement amounted to an oral lease. Although the statute of frauds requires a lease for more than one year to be in writing, in this case, the court applied the doctrine of part performance. By deeding the property to her son, the mother had taken an irrevocable step in reliance on his oral promise. If the court refused to enforce the lease, the son would receive an unjust benefit, so the court upheld the oral lease. *Egner v. Egner,* 24 Ohio App. 3d 171, 493 N.E.2d 999 (1985).

Interpretation of Written Contracts

In a breach of contract lawsuit, the court has to interpret the parties' agreement and decide if it has been breached. The court tries to decipher and put into effect what the parties intended when they entered the contract. As a general rule, when an agreement is in writing, the court is supposed to determine the parties' intention from the written document alone, if possible.

Parol Evidence Rule. Parol evidence is *evidence concerning negotiations or oral agreements that were not included in a contract, altering or contradicting the terms of the written contract.* The court will generally refuse to admit this kind of evidence.

For Example

A tenant would not be allowed to testify, "Even though the lease says the rent's due on the first, the landlord told me before I signed that I wouldn't have to pay it until the fifteenth."

If, however, the document is unclear or ambiguous, the judge will allow testimony about the contract negotiations in an attempt to clear the ambiguity and show what the parties intended.

Terminating a Contract

A contract can be terminated by:

- Genuine assent.
- Assignment.
- Conditions.
- Mutual agreement.

Genuine Assent

A **genuine assent** means that *consent must be freely given to create a binding contract.* Offer and acceptance as an expression of mutual consent are not freely given when either is the result of:

1. Fraud.
2. Undue influence.
3. Duress.
4. Mistake.

If any of these factors are present, the victimized party may void the contract.

Fraud

As discussed in Chapter 3, **fraud** is *an intentional or negligent misrepresentation of a material fact.* Fraud occurs when a defrauded person had a right to rely on the other person to tell the truth. A fraudulent misrepresentation results in a contract that would not have been entered into had the truth been known. Fraud compromises the assent, allowing the defrauded to escape the contract.

Undue Influence

Undue influence is *exerting excessive pressure on someone so as to overpower the person's free will and prevent him from making a rational or prudent decision.* A contract is voidable if a person persuades another to sign it by taking unfair advantage of the other person's trust, or weakness of mind (due to senility, exhaustion, etc.). Undue influence often involves telling the victim that documents must be signed immediately with no time to consult a lawyer.

Duress

Duress is *threatening violence against, or unlawfully confining, a person (or any member of that person's family) to force him to sign a document.* Duress also includes the threat of injury to reputation (i.e., **blackmail**). **Economic duress** (also called **business compulsion**) *involves threatening to take some action that will be financially disastrous for the victim—* for example, threatening to withhold payment owed to the victim. Any of these actions make a contract voidable.

Mistake

A **mistake** is *when one or more parties to a contract were mistaken about a fact or a law.* Usually, this does not involve any bad faith or sinister intentions. There are two types of mistakes:

1. **Mutual mistake**—Both parties are mistaken about something important to their contract. In this case, either party may disaffirm the contract.

2. **Unilateral mistake**—Only one party is mistaken. The contract is voidable only if the other party knew about the mistake and did nothing to correct it.

Assignment

In **an assignment**, *one party (the **assignor**) transfers her rights or interests under a contract to another (the **assignee**).* In Ohio, all contracts are assignable unless the contract states otherwise. As a general rule, either party can assign the contract without the other's consent unless the contract states that consent is required.

One exception to this general rule concerns contracts for personal services (e.g., a listing agreement). A party to a personal service contract can assign the contract only with the consent of the other party.

For Example

If M hires C to play the organ at M's wedding, she cannot make C play at someone else's wedding instead. Conversely, C cannot send her sister to play at M's wedding instead of showing up herself.

Another exception is that a contract cannot be assigned without consent if the assignment would change the other party's duties or increase her risks.

Liability

When a contract is assigned, the assignor is not relieved of liability under the contract. The assignor remains secondarily liable to the other party and can be sued if the assignee does not perform. This rule applies even when the other party consents to the assignment. Thus, in a loan assumption situation, the owner may assign his mortgage to a new buyer who assumes it. The original owner is still liable, however.

Novation. Novation is *when one party to a contract withdraws and a new party is substituted, relieving the withdrawing party of liability.* This is better than an assignment because the withdrawing party avoids secondary liability. A novation can be arranged only with the other original party's consent.

Novation can also refer to the substitution of a new obligation in place of the original one. If the original parties tear up a two-year lease and execute a five-year lease, that is a novation. Again, both parties must give their consent.

Accord and Satisfaction. Accord and satisfaction is *an agreement to accept something different (and usually less) than what the original contract called for.* To extinguish the original obligation, the promisee must execute a document stating that the promisor's performance has been accepted in satisfaction of the obligation.

Conditions

Conditions are *provisions in a contract or deed that make the parties' rights and obligations depend on the occurrence (or non-occurrence) of particular events.* These are also called **contingency clauses**. Contracts often include one or more conditions. If the event does not occur, the promisor can withdraw without liability for breach of contract.

For Example

Many purchase agreements are contingent on whether the buyers qualify for financing, or on the results of an appraisal, termite inspection, or soil test.

When a contract is conditional, the promisor must make a good faith effort to fulfill the condition. He cannot deliberately prevent its fulfillment in order to get out of the contract.

A condition can be waived by the party it was intended to benefit or protect. But when a condition is included for the benefit of both parties, neither one can waive it without the other's consent.

For Example

B interviewed for a job with a certain company, but it will be another month before he hears whether they have hired him. He explains his situation to L, and she agrees to loan B some money on the condition that B gets the job. This condition protects both B and L. It prevents B from taking out a loan he will not be able repay, and it prevents L from lending to someone who is very likely to default.

Suppose B does not get the job after all, but still wants to borrow the money. He would like to waive the condition, but B cannot waive it unilaterally. L must also agree to waive it, or the contract is void.

Mutual Agreement

There are two ways in which a contract can be terminated by **mutual agreement**:

• Rescission
• Cancellation

Rescission

Rescission is *when a contract is terminated, and each party gives anything acquired under the contract back to the other party.* This occurs when one party to a contract does not want to enforce the other party's promise. Instead, he just wants to undo the contract and go back to square one. In that case, he may ask a court to rescind the contract. When a contract is rescinded, each party returns any consideration given by the other. This is called **restitution.**

 When a contract is rescinded, all contractual obligations are terminated.

Rescission is available under a variety of circumstances:

• When a voidable contract is disaffirmed, a court will rescind it.
• One party can request rescission of the contract if the other party did not provide the promised consideration, or if the consideration turns out to be void.

Cancellation

Cancellation *is the termination of a contract without undoing acts performed under the contract.* In this way, a contract can be rescinded without going to court. Both parties must agree if they prefer to cancel their contract instead of rescinding it. As with rescission, when a contract is canceled, all further obligations are terminated.

Performance and Breach of Contract

If one party to a contract performs his side of the bargain, the other party is required to perform, too. If one party fails to perform and the failure is not excused, he has breached the contract. When one party breaches, the other party is not required to perform: If a person enters a contract to build a house for $250,000 and does not build the house, he is not entitled to be paid the $250,000.

Unfortunately, it is not always so easy to determine whether there has been a breach.

For Example

Suppose A does all the things promised, but the other party (B) feels they were not done well. A does nearly everything promised, but some details are not taken care of; or A does everything promised but takes longer to do it than agreed. In these scenarios, it can be argued whether the contract was breached and whether B is required to perform his side of the bargain.

In the previous example, B's obligation to perform depends on whether there has been **substantial performance** or a **material breach.**

Substantial Performance versus Material Breach

Substantial performance is *when a promisor does not perform all of his contractual obligations but does enough that the promisee is required to fulfill his side of the bargain.* Let's continue with our previous example:

For Example

If A has not fulfilled every detail of the contract but has carried out the main objectives, this may be treated as substantial performance. Although B may be able to sue for damages because of the unfulfilled details, this does not excuse B from performing his side of the bargain.

A **material breach** is *a breach of contract important enough to excuse the non-breaching party from performing his contractual obligations.* Let's take a look at the effect a material breach would have on the previous example:

For Example

If A fails to perform some important part of the contract, or performs very badly, this will be treated as a material breach. If A commits a material breach, B may be able to sue for damages and is excused from fulfilling his promises.

What provisions of a contract are so important that failure to fulfill them amounts to a material breach? That depends on the circumstances of each case. If the promisee emphasized to the promisor that a particular detail of the contract was especially important, failure to comply with that detail may be held to be a material breach.

Time is of the Essence

Many contracts state, "Time is of the essence." The purpose of including this phrase is to emphasize that timely performance is an essential part of the contract and failure to perform on time will be a material breach. When a contract does not provide a "time is of the essence" clause, the general rule is that performance within a reasonable time after the stated deadline is not a material breach.

There is an important exception to that rule—it does not apply to real estate purchase contracts. For those contracts, delay is **always** a material breach, even without a "time is of the essence" clause. However, if a party acts as if the agreed closing date is not particularly important, a court may hold that the party has waived the right to insist on that deadline.

For Example

S agreed to sell B her house with closing set for August 15. That date arrives, but S has not cleared the title or completed the repairs yet. B does not complain.

Finally, three weeks later, S is ready to go. But now B decided he does not want that house, so he refuses to pay S and accept the deed. When S sues, B objects that S breached the contract by missing the deadline.

The court rules that B's actions waived the right to treat S's delay as a material breach. Because of that waiver, B was required to perform his side of the bargain.

Tendering Performance

Tendering performance is *when a party offers to perform his side of a contract.* A **tender offer,** or simply a **tender**, is *an unconditional offer by one of the parties to a contract to perform his part of the agreement.* This is done when the offeror believes the other party is going to breach, because it establishes the offeror's right to sue if the other party does not accept it.

For Example

The time for performance has arrived and B has not taken any steps toward carrying out her side of the bargain. Before A can sue B for breach of contract, she is required to offer to perform her side of the bargain.

Repudiation

Repudiation is when one of the parties to a contract informs the other before the set time of performance that he does not intend to perform as agreed. When a party to a contract clearly and unequivocally states that he does not intend to perform, that party is said to have repudiated the contract. Once one party has repudiated the contract, the other party may immediately file a lawsuit for breach of contract without making any tender offer.

For Example

B tells A that she is not going to go through with the purchase of A's property. A does not have to wait until the scheduled closing date nor tender his performance before suing B for breach of contract.

Remedies for Breach of Contract

When a promisee performs badly or refuses to perform at all (either by repudiation or by rejecting the tender offer), he has breached the contract. The promisor may then turn to the legal system for help. If the court concludes there has been a breach of contract, it must decide on a remedy. The remedies available through the court system include:

- Compensatory damages
- Liquidated damages
- Specific performance

Compensatory Damages

Compensatory damages are *a damage award, usually monetary, intended to compensate the plaintiff for harm caused by the defendant's actions or failure to act.* The most common remedy for a breach of contract is the breaching party is ordered to pay a sum of money to the non-breaching party. The amount rewarded depends on the damage incurred by the non-breaching party. The award amount is supposed to put the non-breaching party in the same position he would have been in if the other party had fulfilled the contract.

For Example

P contracted to clear H's property for $10,000, but he quit the project soon after starting. H then hired L to carry out the job. L charged H $12,000.

H sues P for breach of contract and P is ordered to pay her $2,000. If P had not breached the contract, it would have cost H only $10,000 (rather than $12,000) to have her property cleared. The $2,000 ($12,000 - $10,000) judgment against P represents the difference between what the job actually cost H and what it would have cost her if P had not breached.

In the previous example, if L had charged H only $9,000 to clear the property, H would actually have been better off as a result of P's breach. The job would have cost H $1,000 less than it would have if P had fulfilled their contract. In that case, H would not be entitled to a judgment against P because she was not damaged by his breach. The point of a contract lawsuit is to compensate the promisee for actual damages, not to punish the promisor for breaching. **Punitive damages** are generally awarded only in cases involving a tort or fraud, not for breach of contract (see Chapter 1).

Mitigation of Damages. Mitigation is *when the non-breaching party takes action to minimize the losses resulting from a breach of contract.* The non-breaching party in a contract dispute is required to do whatever he can in order to reduce the losses, or mitigate the damage, resulting from the other party's breach.

For Example

B contracts to buy S's house for $100,000 and then refuses to go through with the purchase. S has to make an effort to find a new buyer—she cannot simply sue B for $100,000.

If S sells the house to her nephew for $60,000, she will not be awarded $40,000 in damages, either. B will only have to pay S the difference between the contract price and the market value. If the court finds the house was worth $92,000 on the closing date set in the original contract, B will probably be ordered to pay S $8,000.

Liquidated Damages

Liquidated damages are *a sum of money that the parties to a contract agree in advance (at the time of entering the contract) will serve as compensation in the event of a breach.* A liquidated damages provision is included in some contracts to lessen the possibility of expensive litigation. Since the parties agreed in advance to set the damages at a specified sum, or to calculate them according to a specified formula, the non-breaching party must accept the liquidated damages instead of suing for actual/compensatory damages.

Of course, sometimes the breaching party will refuse to pay, so the case ends up in court anyway. For a liquidated damages provision to be enforceable, it must have seemed likely (at the time the contract was made) that calculating actual damages in the event of a breach would be difficult. If it was apparent that actual damages would be easy to determine, the court may refuse to enforce the liquidated damages provision of the contract and award actual damages instead.

In addition, the amount of damages agreed to must be reasonable. If the liquidated damages amount specified in the contract is unreasonably large (much more than the actual damages could possibly amount to), the court will regard it as a penalty instead of liquidated damages. If deemed to be a penalty, the court will refuse to enforce the provision since the purpose of damages for breach of contract is compensation, not punishment. In that case, the non-breaching party will be entitled to collect only actual damages.

Specific Performance

Specific performance is *a legal remedy in which a court orders the breaching party of a contract to perform as agreed, rather than simply paying monetary damages.* This occurs most often when the non-breaching party to a contract cannot be compensated for harm that resulted from the other's breach. In such a case, the non-breaching party has the right to compel the other party to do what he promised in the contract.

Courts generally will not grant specific performance when a damages award will be just as effective.

For Example

A car dealer will not be ordered to sell a customer a particular car when that customer could get an identical one from another dealer. If the customer has to pay more at the second dealer, the first dealer will be ordered to pay the difference as a damages award.

When the object of a contract is one-of-a-kind, specific performance is an appropriate remedy. A damages award will not enable a party to buy an identical item if one does not exist. Since real estate is considered unique, specific performance is the remedy generally granted to a buyer when a seller breaches a real estate purchase agreement by refusing to execute the deed.

There are certain circumstances in which a court cannot grant specific performance:

- A court can never grant specific performance as a remedy for breach of a personal service contract since no one can be forced to work for someone or to employ someone.

- A court cannot order a person to perform according to a contract if that person did not receive legally adequate consideration. That person may be forced to pay damages to the other party for his breach, but he will not have to go through with the transaction.

For Example

If X agreed to sell his $200,000 house for $75,000, the contract is enforceable even though the consideration is inadequate. X may be required to pay damages to the buyer, but he cannot be forced to complete the sale.

Real Estate Contracts

A real estate agent is expected to be familiar with several types of contracts. Each type is a particular application of the basic rules of contract law outlined in the first part of this chapter. We'll take a brief look at **listing agreements**, **purchase contracts**, **options**, **leases**, and **land contracts**.

Listing Agreements

A **listing agreement** is *a written agency contract between a seller and a real estate broker, stipulating the broker will be paid a commission for finding (or attempting to find) a buyer for the seller's property.* As such, listing agreements are employment contracts between a seller and a real estate broker. The seller hires the broker to find a buyer and, in exchange for the broker's services, the seller will pay a commission.

The commission rate or amount of commission must be negotiated between the seller and the broker. **It is a violation of federal and state antitrust laws for brokers to set uniform commission rates.** Any discussion of rates among members of competing firms could give rise to a charge of price-fixing.

Payment of Commission

Payment of a broker's commission may be made dependent on any lawful condition. The listing agreement may specify that the commission is due when the seller signs a binding contract with a buyer, or only if the sale actually closes.

But unless otherwise agreed, the broker is entitled to a commission when a **ready, willing, and able** buyer is found:

- A buyer is considered **ready** and **willing** if he makes an offer that meets the terms established by the seller in the listing.

- A buyer is considered **able** if he has the financial ability to complete the purchase.

Under the terms of most listing agreements, once a ready, willing, and able buyer has submitted an offer, the broker has earned a commission—even if the sale never closes.

Case Example

Ms. Cravaack owned a motel. She listed the property with Mr. Scott for $90,000. Scott showed the motel to Mr. Eichenhorst, who later submitted a written offer to purchase it for $80,000. Scott presented the offer to Cravaack. After some discussion, Scott telephoned Eichenhorst and told him Cravaack still wanted $90,000. Eichenhorst agreed to pay that price, and the parties arranged to meet a few days later to sign a formal contract.

Then, Cravaack changed her mind about Eichenhorst's offer and refused to sign the contract. Although the transaction had fallen apart, Scott sued Cravaack for his commission.

In the listing agreement, Cravaack promised Scott a 6% commission for his services, but the listing did not say under what conditions the commission would be paid. The court ruled that Scott earned the commission when he presented Eichenhorst's offer to Cravaack. Eichenhorst was ready, willing, and able to buy on Cravaack's terms, and it was Cravaack's fault that the sale was not consummated. *Scott v. Cravaack*, 53 Ohio App. 2d 248, 372 N.E.2d 1375 (1977).

If a prospective buyer's offer does not precisely match the terms the seller specified in the listing, the seller can refuse to contract without owing the broker a commission. This makes it very important to have the seller's terms spelled out clearly in the listing agreement.

Types of Listing Agreements

A broker's right to a commission also depends on the type of listing agreement used. Four main types of listing agreements are **exclusive right to sell**, **exclusive agency**, **open listing**, and **net listing**.

Exclusive Right to Sell. An **exclusive right to sell** listing agreement *is one that entitles the broker to a commission if anyone, including the seller, finds a buyer during the listing term.*

Exclusive Agency. An **exclusive agency** listing agreement is *one that entitles the broker to a commission if anyone other than the seller finds a buyer for the property during the listing term.*

Open Listing. An **open listing** agreement *is a non-exclusive listing given by a seller to as many brokers as he chooses.* If the property is sold, a broker is entitled to a commission only if she is the *procuring cause* of the sale.

To be the **procuring cause** of a sale, the agent must be primarily responsible for bringing about a sale (e.g., by introducing the buyer to the property, by negotiating the agreement between the buyer and seller). The broker's actions must start a chain of events that results in an agreement. Only the broker who finds a buyer will be paid.

 An open listing is a unilateral contract—the seller promises to pay a commission if the broker is the procuring cause of the sale, but the broker does not actually promise to do anything.

Net Listing. A **net listing** agreement is *one in which the seller sets a net amount he is willing to accept for the property, with the broker being entitled to keep the excess as her commission if the actual selling price exceeds that amount.*

Although not expressly forbidden by Ohio law, net listings are discouraged because they can lead to charges of fraud by a seller who may have not understood the terms of the agreement and feels taken advantage of or misled.

In theory, exclusive listing agreements result in better service for sellers than open listing agreements because the broker's claim to a commission is more secure, so she is likely to work harder to bring about the sale.

Listing Agreement Requirements

Ohio's real estate Licensing Law requires any type of listing agreement to include a **definite expiration date**. Most exclusive listing agreements contain an **extension clause** (also called a **broker protection clause**), which covers a certain period after the listing expires. An extension clause provides that the broker is still entitled to a commission if the property is sold during the extension period and the buyer is someone the broker negotiated with during the listing term. The broker should provide the seller with a list of prospects she introduced to the property. If the seller was not aware that the buyer is someone the broker dealt with, the seller may not have to pay a commission.

Buyer Agency Agreements—Exclusive Purchaser Agency Agreement

An exclusive purchaser agency or a buyer's broker agreement is an agency agreement between a purchaser and broker that meets the requirements of section 4735.55 of the Revised Code and does both of the following:

- Grants the broker the exclusive right to represent the purchaser in the purchase or lease of property; and

- Provides that the broker will be compensated in accordance with the terms specified in the exclusive agency agreement or if a property is purchased or leased by the purchaser during the term of the agency agreement unless the property is specifically exempted in the agency agreement.

 Always give clients copies of all documents they sign! Failure to do so can cause loss of license.

Prohibiting Access to Listed Property by Unlicensed Individuals

In recent years, the Ohio Real Estate Commission and the Division of Real Estate and Professional Licensing have seen an ever-increasing number of enforcement actions involving real estate licensees providing access to listed property to unlicensed and/or unsupervised individuals. It's critical to point out that Ohio real estate law absolutely prohibits providing lockbox codes, keys, keypad codes, or any other means of access to listed property—residential or commercial—to any individual who is not an active real estate licensee. This prohibition applies to unlicensed assistants working at the brokerage as well.

While a licensee may find it convenient to allow a prospective buyer or contractor into a property when the licensee is running late or otherwise unavailable, such action violates the security and sanctity of the owner's property and opens the licensee—as well as his principal broker and any designated management-level licensee in the brokerage—to liability and possible disciplinary action, including license suspension, fines, and required education.

Purchase Contracts

Purchase contracts are *contracts in which a seller promises to convey title to real property to a buyer in exchange for the purchase price*. These are also called:

- Purchase agreements
- Sale contracts
- Sale agreements
- Purchase and sale agreements
- Earnest money agreements

In Ohio, the purchase contract form usually serves three purposes:

1. It is the buyer's offer.
2. It is the receipt for the earnest money deposit.
3. It is the contract between the buyer and seller.

Additionally, in some parts of Ohio where escrow closings are common, the contract may also serve as the escrow agent's instructions.

Purchase Contract Requirements

First, the buyer makes an offer by filling out a purchase contract form—or, more commonly, by having a real estate agent fill it out. At the same time, the buyer gives the agent an earnest money deposit and the agent signs the section of the form acknowledging receipt of the deposit. The agent then submits the offer to the seller. If the seller decides to accept it, he signs the same form, creating a binding contract between buyer and seller.

The purchase contract should at least identify the parties, the property, and the interest to be sold. Ideally, it will state all the terms of the sale as clearly as possible:

- What is and is not included in the sale
- The total price
- The method of payment

Any conditions must be spelled out in the contract. Purchase contracts are often contingent on the buyers being able to obtain financing or sell their current home. Many purchase contracts provide that if the buyer defaults, the earnest money deposit is forfeited to the seller. This is a type of liquidated damages provision—the seller keeps the deposit instead of suing for breach of contract.

Handling Earnest Money

Earnest money is *an inducement to have the buyer's offer accepted and a means of showing the seller that the buyer is serious and able to follow through with the financing necessary to buy the property*. **All purchase contracts must provide written instructions as to the disbursal of earnest money funds**, specifically, whether the funds are "returned to the buyer" or "disbursed to the seller."

Typically, the earnest money is held in the selling broker's trust account. It could, however, be held in the listing broker's trust account if both the buyer and seller agree. In either case, the money will not earn interest. If the buyer wants his earnest money to earn interest, it will have to be held by the seller in an interest-bearing account or the buyer and seller could open an interest-bearing account. Once a contract is entered into and earnest money has been deposited into the broker's trust account, it can be released only if one of the following occurs:

- The transaction closes, and the broker disburses earnest money funds according to the terms in the purchase contract,

- The parties provide the broker with separate written instructions, signed by both parties, that specify how to disburse the earnest money funds,

- The broker receives a copy of a final court order that specifies to whom the earnest money is to be awarded,

- After two years, the broker must report the earnest money deposit as unclaimed funds and remit them to the Ohio Department of Commerce Division of Unclaimed Funds.

Options

Options are *contracts which give one party the right to do something, without obligating him to do it*. Thus, an option is a *unilateral contract*. The most common type of real estate option is an **option to purchase**. An option to purchase *gives one party (the **optionee**) the right to buy the property of another (the **optionor**) at a specified price within a limited time*. Within that period, the optionee may choose to exercise the option (i.e., enter into a contract to buy the property) but the optionee is under no obligation to exercise the option.

An option is supported by consideration. The optionee pays the optionor for the option right.

For Example

If an owner tells a prospective buyer she is willing to sell her house for $100,000, the buyer might pay her $1,000 to keep that offer open for a month. The payment of consideration makes the option irrevocable until it expires. If the optionor dies before the option expires, it is still binding on the optionor's heirs.

An option to purchase real property must be in writing and signed. It must also be exercised in writing if the optionee decides to go through with the purchase of the real property under the option. The option agreement should be as specific as possible, stating all terms of the potential sale. The option document may also serve as the purchase contract if and when the option is exercised.

An option can be recorded (to protect the optionee) only if it states a definite expiration date. The optionee's claim ends automatically on that date, and the recorded option is no longer a cloud on the title.

Right of Preemption

A **right of preemption** *is a right to have the first chance to buy or lease property if the owner decides to sell or lease it*. This is also called a **right of first refusal**. This is not the same thing as an option. An optionee can purchase the property at any time during the option period on the stated terms. Someone who holds a preemption right, however, has the right to purchase the property before anyone else does *only* if the owner decides to sell it. Also, if a third party makes an offer for the property and the owner is willing to accept it, the preemption right holder must match the terms of that offer in order to acquire the property.

Leases

Leases are *contracts in which one party pays the other rent in exchange for possession of real estate*; thus, a lease is the conveyance of a leasehold estate from the fee owner to a tenant. Leases, like all contracts, must:

- Contain all of the elements necessary for a valid contract in order to be legal and enforceable.
- Be in writing if the term will last for more than one year.
- Be attested and acknowledged if the term is for more than three years.

For a more in-depth discussion of the requirements for a valid lease, see Chapter 11.

Types Of Leases

While a residential lease is usually a straightforward exchange of rent for occupancy, commercial leases are usually more complex and varied in their terms. The four main types of commercial leases are **gross lease**, **net lease**, **percentage lease,** and **land lease** (also called **ground lease**).

Gross Lease. A **gross lease** is *a lease for which the owner or landlord pays all property taxes, mortgage payments, insurance, etc., and the tenant pays all utilities.* This is similar to a residential lease except that the commercial version can provide for future rent increases tied to inflation or taxes. A gross lease is usually used for tenants that are professional in nature (e.g., lawyers, doctors, executives).

Net Lease. A **net lease** *is a lease for which the tenant pays all property taxes, mortgage payments, insurance, etc., as well as all utilities, in addition to a monthly rent payment.* This is a variation of the gross lease and is used with similar types of tenants. The main difference is that the owner or landlord has shifted much of the risk for increased costs to the tenants who pay a proportional amount of the property taxes, insurance, and sometimes, maintenance costs.

Percentage Lease. A **percentage lease** is *a lease for which the tenant pays a percentage of gross sales, often in addition to a fixed monthly rental payment.* This type of lease is more commonly used for retail tenants.

Land Lease. A **land lease** (or **ground lease**) is *a lease for which a tenant leases only the land from the landlord, but the tenant actually owns the building.* This, usually, is first done when the land is vacant, but the owner of the building is free to sell the building at will and have the buyer assume the land lease. Likewise, the landlord can sell the land subject to the lease of the building owner. This type of lease usually has a term equal to the life expectancy of the building but can be for up to 99 years.

Land Contracts

Land contracts are *real estate installment agreements for which the buyer (**vendee**) makes payments to the seller (**vendor**) in exchange for the right to occupy and use the property, but no deed or title is transferred until all, or a specified portion of, payments have been made.* Here the seller actually holds title to land as security, not just a mortgage lien. Since actual title will be transferred by deed at a future date, the buyer's present interest in a land contract is called **equitable title**.

In Ohio, a land contract must be executed in duplicate, recorded within 20 days of execution, and must include:

1. Names and address of all parties.

2. Date each party signed in front of a notary public.

3. Legal description of the property.

4. Price of the property.

5. Charges or fees for services separate from the contract price.

6. Down payment amount.

7. Principal amount owed.

8. Amount and due date of each payment.

9. Interest rate and method of computing the interest rate.

10. Encumbrances against the property.

11. Requirement that the vendor deliver a general warranty deed.

12. Requirement that the vendor provide evidence of title.

13. Provision for vendor's default.

14. Requirement that the vendor record the contract.

Because the seller still retains title to the property, there is some risk that the seller could go out and mortgage the property for an amount greater than his interest in the property. Under Ohio law, the seller cannot mortgage the property for more than the balance due under the land contract without the buyer's consent. This protects the buyer's interest in the property. The seller must also give the buyer a statement, at least once a year, or as requested, showing the amount of payments that have been credited to principal and interest, and the balance due under the contract.

Buyer Default

If the contract has been in effect for *less than five years* or the buyer has paid *less than 20%* of the purchase price before default, the seller may initiate **forfeiture proceedings** 30 days after the buyer's default, by giving the buyer written notice of the default and of the seller's intent to declare the contract forfeited, unless the buyer corrects the default. The buyer has ten (10) days to correct the default, thus reinstating contract terms and retaining his rights under the contract. If the buyer fails to remedy the default within the ten-day notice period, he loses all rights to the property, as well as all payments made up to that point.

If the contract has been in effect for *five or more years* or the buyer has paid *20% or more* of the price, upon default, the seller must use **foreclosure proceedings,** the same as under a mortgage, in order to protect the buyer's substantial investment.

Ohio Division of Real Estate and Professional Licensing

The **Ohio Division of Real Estate and Professional Licensing's** position on listing properties sold by land contract is to remind the licensee to exercise extreme caution since a licensee cannot give legal advice on any questions regarding validity of title or other legal issues that may arise from listing or selling property with a land contract. An attorney at law should always be consulted by all parties involved, and a licensee must never draft any documents relating to this, or any other, real estate transaction. Such actions can be grounds for license suspension or revocation.

Summary

1. A **contract** is an agreement to do, or not do, something. Every contract is either **express** or **implied**, **unilateral** or **bilateral**, **executory** or **executed**. Contracts are also **valid**, **void**, **voidable**, or **unenforceable**. The requirements for a valid contract are contractual capacity, offer, acceptance, consideration, and lawful and possible objective.

2. A person lacks **capacity to contract** unless he is mentally competent and at least 18 years old. Failure to meet these requirements results in a voidable contract. A valid contract is based on the parties' mutual consent and achieved through **offer and acceptance**. If the offeree changes the terms of the offer, it is a counteroffer, not an acceptance. If a party obtains another's consent through fraud, undue influence, duress, or mistake, the contract is voidable by the victim. A contract generally is not valid unless there is **consideration**— each party must give something of value to the other. A contract is enforceable even if the consideration given by the parties is unequal. A contract with an unlawful or impossible objective is void.

3. The **statute of frauds** requires certain contracts to be in writing and signed by the party to be charged to be enforceable. This includes contracts concerning interests in real property: Purchase contracts, options, and powers of attorney. A lease also has to be in writing and attested and acknowledged, unless the term is three years or less. The four types of commercial leases are **gross leases**, **net leases**, **percentage leases**, and **land leases**. A **listing agreement** is considered an employment contract and, as such, the statue of frauds does not require it to be in writing.

4. If one party commits a **material breach** of contract, the other is not required to fulfill his side of the bargain. But when there is **substantial performance** by one party, the other is also required to perform. A promisor cannot get out of a conditional contract by preventing the condition from being fulfilled. A condition may be waived by the party it was intended to benefit.

5. The most common remedy for breach of contract is **compensatory damages**. Punitive damages are generally not awarded, except in cases of torts or fraud. The non-breaching party is required to **mitigate the damages**. A **liquidated damages** provision states in advance how much one party will be entitled to collect in the event of a breach. **Specific performance** is available only when a damages award cannot adequately compensate the non-breaching party.

6. Listing agreements, purchase contracts, options, leases, and land contracts must comply with general rules of contract law. Types of listings are **exclusive right to sell**, **exclusive agency**, and **open listings**. **Net listings** are technically not illegal, but are discouraged due to possible charges of fraud. Unless the listing agreement states otherwise, a commission is earned when a **ready, willing, and able** buyer is produced on the seller's terms. It is a violation of federal and state antitrust laws for brokers to set uniform commission rates.

Quiz

1. **Y tells Z, "I'll pay you $15 to mow my lawn on Saturday." Z says, "Sure, I'll do that." What type of contract do they have?**

   a. executed unilateral contract

   b. executory bilateral contract

   c. express unilateral contract

   d. implied bilateral contract

2. **An offer can be revoked at any time before it is accepted UNLESS**

   a. it is an offer to purchase real property.

   b. the offer has a specific termination date.

   c. the offer states that it is irrevocable.

   d. the offeree gives the offeror consideration for keeping the offer open.

3. **On May 15, B offers to buy S's property. On May 18, S mails B a letter accepting the offer. On May 19 (before she receives S's letter), B calls S and tells him the offer is revoked. Do they have a binding contract?**

   a. No, because B had not received the acceptance letter before she revoked her offer.

   b. No, because S should have accepted over the telephone instead of by mail.

   c. Yes, because B waited more than three days to revoke her offer.

   d. Yes, because S's acceptance became effective when he mailed it.

4. **B sends S a letter offering to buy his house. S calls B and rejects the offer, but a few hours later, S changes his mind. He mails B a letter accepting the offer. Do they have a binding contract?**

   a. No, because the offer was terminated when S rejected it.

   b. No, because they have not had a lawyer draw up a formal agreement yet.

   c. Yes, because an offer can be accepted by any reasonable method.

   d. Yes, because an offer cannot be rejected over the telephone.

5. **S offers to sell his house to B for $200,000, if B will pay $45,000 in cash and give S a 15-year mortgage for the balance at 11% interest. B responds, "I accept your offer, provided that I have to pay only $40,000 down." This is a**

   a. counteroffer.

   b. defeasible offer.

   c. partial acceptance.

   d. unilateral acceptance.

6. **B blackmails S into signing a contract to sell him her home for less than half its value. This contract is**

   a. severable due to unlawful purpose.

   b. unenforceable because the consideration is inadequate.

   c. void due to fraud.

   d. voidable due to duress.

7. **Under Ohio's Statute of Frauds, which contract does NOT have to be in writing to be enforceable?**

   a. an option to buy a single-family home

   b. a real estate sales contract

   c. a three-month listing agreement for vacant land

   d. a 24-month residential lease

8. **When a new person takes the place of one of the parties to a contract, and the withdrawing party is relieved of all liability, it is called**

   a. accord and satisfaction.

   b. assignment.

   c. novation.

   d. substantial performance.

9. **X agrees to build Q a house for $250,000, but before construction begins, X breaches the contract in order to take on a more profitable job. Q has to hire another builder, who charges her $285,000. Q sues X for breach of contract and wins. The court will probably award Q**

   a. $35,000 in compensatory damages.

   b. $250,000 in punitive damages.

   c. rescission and $35,000 in punitive damages.

   d. specific performance.

10. *When a contract is terminated and each party returns whatever consideration the other had provided, it is called*

    a. cancellation.
    b. repudiation.
    c. rescission.
    d. a tender offer.

11. *Unless the listing agreement says otherwise, a broker is entitled to a commission only if*

    a. a buyer with a good credit rating makes a reasonable offer.
    b. a ready, willing, and able buyer offers to buy on the seller's terms.
    c. the sale actually closes.
    d. the seller and buyer sign a binding contract.

12. *An option agreement*

    a. can always be revoked, until it has been exercised.
    b. is not a contract.
    c. is supported by consideration.
    d. is terminated by the death of the optionor.

Decedents' Estates

At some point in your real estate career, you will come across property that is part of a deceased person's estate or owned by someone under the care of a guardian. To represent such property, you must know something of the probate process. Knowledge in this area also increases your ability to represent properties in general.

Understand, however, that much of this area falls within the practice of law. Any advice given to a buyer or seller could be construed as legal advice, which is off limits for most agents and brokers. It is always advisable to seek legal advice from your company counsel before discussing such properties with buyers or sellers.

Key Terms

Note: Because terminology is of vital importance on the Ohio Real Estate Examination, these terms should be committed to memory.

Administrator A person appointed by the probate court to manage and distribute the estate of a deceased person when no executor is named in the will or there is no will.

Bequest Personal property transferred by a will.

Devise To transfer real property as a gift by will; also used as a noun to refer to the real property itself, which is transferred by a will.

Escheat When property reverts to the state after a person dies without leaving a valid will and without heirs.

Executor A man appointed in a will to carry out the will's provisions. A woman is called an **Executrix.**

Holographic Will A will written entirely in the testator's (or testatrix's) handwriting, but which was not witnessed. Because it was not witnessed, this type of will is not recognized in Ohio.

Intestate Succession Distribution of property to heirs of a person who died intestate (without a valid will).

Legacy Receiving money by a will.

Probate 1. A judicial proceeding in which the validity of a will is established and the executor is authorized to distribute the property in an estate. 2. When there is no valid will, a judicial proceeding in which an administrator is appointed to distribute the estate to the heirs according to the laws of intestate succession.

Testator A man who makes a will. A woman is called a **Testatrix.**

Probate

Probate is *both the court of jurisdiction over estates and the process of proving the validity of a will.* In order for a will to be valid in Ohio, it must meet strict minimum standards. Should those standards not be met, or the will be challenged on other grounds and thrown out, the estate may become subject to administration as though no will existed. A will transfers property on the death of the maker, never sooner. An expectation of property under a will is not a property right.

Wills

A **will** (also called a **testament**) is *a person's legally binding instructions regarding how his estate should be disposed of after death. A male person making the will* is called a **testator**; a female is referred to as a **testatrix**.

A person who dies with a valid will in place is said to have died **testate**. A valid will appoints an **executor** (male) or **executrix** (female) *who is charged with carrying out the deceased's wishes.* The will sets forth the following items (and to whom they will go):

- **Bequest** (personal property)
- **Legacy** (money)
- **Devise** (real property)

Requirements for a Valid Will

For a will to be valid in Ohio, it must:

- Be in writing (with a minor exception noted later).
- Show **testamentary intent**.
- Be signed by the testator and two disinterested witnesses.

The testator must also have **testamentary capacity**.

Testamentary Capacity

Any person of "sound mind and memory" who is at least 18 years old may make a will in Ohio. This is referred to as **testamentary capacity.** The person's mind must be clear enough that he understands what a will is, understands the nature and extent of his property, and is aware of those who are "the natural objects of his or her bounty" (e.g., spouse, children, close relatives).

Testamentary Intent

A document cannot be a valid will unless the person who executed it had **testamentary intent.** That means *he intended that the document would take effect only after death.* No specific words are required, but the testamentary intent must be apparent from the document itself.

Case Example

A warranty deed that was not delivered before the grantor died was submitted to the probate court as a will. The court rejected it, since there was nothing in the deed itself to indicate that it was supposed to take effect after the grantor's death. *In re Estate of Ike, Deceased*, 7 Ohio App. 3d 87, 454 N.E.2d 577 (1982).

Signed by the Testator

In Ohio, a will ordinarily must be in writing, and the testator's signature must appear at the end of the document. The signature has to be witnessed by at least two competent adults. If the witnesses were not actually present when the testator signed the will, they must hear the testator acknowledge the validity of the signature.

If the witnesses are still alive when the testator dies, they may be asked to testify in probate court as to the validity of the signature if anyone challenges the will. A will may still be upheld even if the witnesses are no longer living.

Disinterested Witnesses

The witnesses should not be beneficiaries under the will. Should a witness be a beneficiary, the will is not invalidated. Instead, the gift to the witness is voided to the extent that it exceeds any share the witness would have received under the **statute of descent and distribution** had the testator died without a will.

Exceptions

There is only one exception to the requirements for a valid will recognized in Ohio: A will must be in writing. The acceptance of an **oral will** requires two disinterested witnesses.

 Real property cannot be devised orally.

Nuncupative Wills. In exceptional circumstances, an oral will is valid in Ohio. *A person on his deathbed may make an oral will bequeathing personal property.* This is called a **nuncupative will**. The will must be put into writing and signed by two disinterested witnesses within ten days after the testator's statement.

Holographic Wills. Ohio does not recognize unwitnessed wills. In some other states, however, *an unwitnessed will is valid if it is written entirely in the testator's own handwriting.* This is known as a **holographic will**.

Family Rights Under a Will

A testator's surviving spouse is entitled to receive $40,000 out of the estate as a support allowance, whether or not the testator bequeathed anything to the spouse. A testator cannot disinherit his spouse. If there is no surviving spouse, the testator's minor children will receive the $40,000 allowance. Aside from that allowance, a testator's children are disinherited if the testator does not leave them anything in the will.

The spouse has the right to elect whether to accept what the testator willed to her or take the share she would have received if the testator had died **intestate** (without a will). The distribution of assets for intestate succession is detailed later in this chapter. Even if the testator attempts to cut the spouse out of the will, the spouse can still get a share of the estate.

A spouse who chooses to take the intestate succession share instead of what is bequeathed in the will (referred to as "taking against the will") can never be awarded more than half the net estate left over after the deceased person's creditors have been paid. If the testator has two or more surviving children or grandchildren, the spouse cannot be awarded more than one-third of the net estate. The remainder of the estate (whatever is left over after the spouse takes his or her share) is distributed according to the terms of the will, as if the spouse had died before the testator.

Mansion House

In some cases, a surviving spouse may elect to take the **mansion house**, which is *considered to be the family home, along with the surrounding land*. The spouse can take the mansion house if the value of the property she is entitled to receive is equal to or greater than the value of the deceased's interest in the mansion house.

For Example

H and W are married with no children. They own their home as tenants in common with each holding an undivided one-half interest in the property. W executes a valid will, leaving everything she owns to a TV game show host.

After W's death, H naturally elects to take against the will. The value of W's net estate is approximately $300,000 and H is entitled to half of that ($150,000). W's one-half interest in their home (the mansion house) is worth about $110,000. H's share in the estate is greater than $110,000, so he may choose to take W's interest in the mansion house as part of his share.

If H did not elect to take the mansion house, he and the game show host would own it as tenants in common. H would have an undivided three-fourths interest—his own, plus half of W's interest—and the game show host would have an undivided one-fourth interest. Since H does not want to share his home with the game show host, he would elect to take the mansion house. (He'll also get $40,000 in cash.)

When the surviving spouse does not have the right to take the mansion house, or chooses not to, she is allowed to go on living there, free of charge, for one year. In some cases, though, the property may have to be sold to pay the deceased person's debts before that year ends. In that case, the estate is required to compensate the surviving spouse in an amount equal to the rental value of the property for the remainder of the year.

Certificate of Transfer

When real property is devised (i.e., given as a gift), the probate court issues a *certificate of transfer*. This **certificate of transfer** *acts as the "deed" to convey a decedent's real property*. This certificate of transfer states the testator's name, the names of the devisees (persons receiving the gift), and a description of the property. A certificate of transfer should be recorded in the county where the property is located.

Intestate Succession

Intestate succession is *when property passes to a person's legal heirs, because he died without a valid will*. The rules of intestate succession determine who is entitled to a share of the property. These rules are set forth in the statute of descent and distribution, Ohio Rev. Code § 2105.06.

Someone who takes property by intestate succession is called an **heir**. The probate court decides who the heirs are, and appoints an **administrator** who is *charged by the court with the responsibility of carrying out the statutory distribution of the property*. If the estate includes real property, the probate court will issue the certificate of transfer for the heirs to record.

Generally, a person's heirs are his spouse and **lineal descendants**, which include the person's children, grandchildren, great-grandchildren, and so on. If no spouse or lineal descendants are living when the intestate person dies, the estate goes to other relatives.

Here is a brief summary of the primary rules of intestate succession in Ohio.

1. When an intestate person is survived by his spouse, but by no lineal descendants, the spouse receives the entire estate.

2. When an intestate person is survived by his spouse and one child:

    a. If the spouse is the natural or adoptive parent of the child, the spouse receives everything.

    b. If the spouse is not the parent of the child, the spouse receives the first $20,000, and divides the remainder of the estate with the child.

3. When an intestate person is survived by his spouse and two or more children:

    a. If the spouse is the natural or adoptive parent of all the children, the spouse receives everything.

    b. If the spouse is the parent of any of the children, the spouse receives the first $60,000, plus one-third of the remainder of the estate, and the children divide the other two-thirds equally.

    c. If the spouse is not the parent of any of the children, the spouse receives the first $20,000, plus one-third of the remainder, and the children divide the other two-thirds equally.

4. If there is no surviving spouse, the entire estate is divided among the intestate person's children.

5. If one of the intestate person's children dies before the intestate person, the share the pre-deceased child would have received (under rule 2, 3, or 4) is divided among that child's lineal descendants.

For Example

E and G had three children together: B, C, and D. Before their marriage, E had another daughter, A.

E dies intestate, leaving a net estate worth $360,000. She is survived by her husband (G), and her children (A, B, C, and D).

G receives the first $60,000 out of the estate, since he was B, C, and D's father. He also receives one-third of the remainder of the estate ($100,000). So, his total share is $160,000.

The other two-thirds of the estate ($200,000) is divided between E's four children.

6. When an intestate person is not survived by a spouse or by any lineal descendants, the estate is distributed in this order:

    a. To the intestate person's parents

    b. To the intestate person's brothers and sisters

    c. To the intestate person's grandparents

    d. To the lineal descendants of the intestate person's grandparents

    e. To the next of kin

    f. To the intestate person's stepchildren or their lineal descendants

If there is no spouse, no lineal heirs, and no step-children, the estate is distributed to the state.

 Members of category (b) get a share only if there are no living persons in category (a) and the members of category (c) get a share only if there are no living persons in either category (a) or (b), and so on down the list.

Mansion House

Just as a person who decides to take against his spouse's will can elect to take the mansion house, so can a person whose spouse dies intestate.

For Example

Continuing with the previous example, G could have chosen E's interest in the family home as part of his intestate share, as long as his share was equal to or greater than the value of her interest in the home.

Designated Heir

In Ohio, it is possible for anyone to be a **designated heir** by filing a declaration with the probate court.

For Example

B made her best friend E her designated heir. Even though E would not ordinarily be entitled to any part of B's estate under the rules of intestate succession, E will inherit part of B's estate as if she were B's child.

Escheat

Escheat is *when property ownership reverts to the state because a person dies intestate without leaving a valid will and no living heirs.* Since the state is the ultimate source of title to property, it's also the ultimate heir when there are no other claimants. In order for a person to die without any heirs, however, there must be no living spouse, children, grandchildren, parents, siblings, nor any other next of kin or step-children.

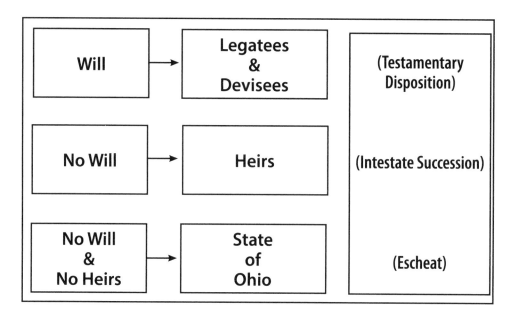

Summary

1. **Probate** is both the court of jurisdiction over estates and the process of proving the validity of a will. A person who dies leaving a will is said to have died **testate**. A person who dies without leaving a will is said to have died **intestate**.

2. A **will** is a person's legally binding instructions regarding how his estate should be disposed of after death. For a will to be **valid** in Ohio, it must be in writing, the testator must have testamentary capacity, the will itself must show testamentary intent, the will must be signed at the bottom by the testator, and it must also be signed by two disinterested witnesses.

3. A surviving spouse cannot be disinherited in Ohio since the spouse can elect to take half of the net estate based on the rules of intestate succession instead of what is **bequeathed** in the will. A spouse can also choose to take the **mansion home** if the spouse's share was equal to or greater than the value of the spouse's interest in the home.

4. **Intestate succession** is when property passes to a person's legal heirs because he died without a valid will. Property passes to the heirs, according to the **statute of descent and distribution**. This statute is non-negotiable, and administration of intestate estates are closely monitored by probate court.

5. A person's **heirs** are his spouse and all lineal descendants. **Lineal descendants** are the person's children, grandchildren, great-grandchildren, and so on. Other relatives, parents, siblings, and next of kin are in line. In Ohio, it is also possible to designate an heir by filing a declaration with the probate court.

6. If a person dies intestate without leaving a valid will and with no living heirs, title to that person's property **escheats** to the state of Ohio since the state is the ultimate source of title to property.

Quiz

1. **H wrote a will leaving everything to his son. When H dies, his wife**
   a. automatically takes title to the mansion house, in spite of the will.
   b. can elect to take against the will, and may be able to take the mansion house.
   c. will receive nothing, unless she can prove the will is invalid.
   d. will receive two-thirds of the estate, in spite of the will.

2. **W died intestate. She is survived by her husband and her daughter from a previous marriage. What share of W's estate is her husband entitled to?**
   a. $20,000, plus half of the remainder of the estate
   b. $60,000, plus one-third of the remainder of the estate
   c. half of the entire estate
   d. one-third of the entire estate

3. **When property escheats, the title**
   a. passes to the heirs.
   b. passes to the next of kin.
   c. reverts to the remainderman.
   d. reverts to the state.

4. **A valid will must be made by a testator who**
   a. has property to dispose of.
   b. is married.
   c. is of sound mind and memory.
   d. is survived by someone.

5. **If one dies intestate, married with two children, what does the spouse (who is the natural parent of the children) receive?**
   a. Nothing, the kids get it all.
   b. the first $60,000
   c. $60,000, plus one-third of the remainder of the estate
   d. the entire estate

6. **The issue in a will contest is**
   a. the issue of holography.
   b. the validity of the will.
   c. whether the testator was married.
   d. whether to appoint an ancillary trustee.

7. **Your role as a real estate salesperson in property held by an estate is**
   a. advisory.
   b. probate avoidance.
   c. to help the heirs to buy cheap.
   d. to list property the executor or administrator has the power to sell.

8. **Real property given in a will is**
   a. always subject to all encumbrances.
   b. called a devise.
   c. subject to adverse possession by the administrator.
   d. usually worthless.

9. **One appointed by the court to distribute the assets of an estate is called a(n)**
   a. administrator.
   b. executor.
   c. intestate.
   d. trustee.

10. **The process of escheat**
    a. allows the next of kin to take title to real property.
    b. allows the surviving spouse to elect against the will.
    c. can exist only when there are no next of kin and the decedent had no will.
    d. determines to whom and in which order the estate will be distributed.

11. **A valid will in Ohio needs two witnesses who**
    a. are not related to each other or to the testator.
    b. can read and write.
    c. have no interest in the will.
    d. sign in the presence of each other and the testator.

Land Use Controls

A prospective buyer considers property with particular plans in mind—for example, remodeling the house, opening a gas station, or planting an orchard. To decide whether the property is suitable, the buyer needs to know if there are any restrictions on its use. This chapter discusses public restrictions on land use imposed by federal, state, and local governments on private owners, and private restrictions imposed by a developer or a previous owner.

Key Terms

Appropriation Taking private property for public use (with just compensation) through the government's power of eminent domain. Also called **Condemnation**.

Brownfield Any real property where redevelopment or re-use may be complicated by the presence or potential presence of a hazardous waste, petrole-um, pollutant, or contaminant.

CC&Rs A declaration of **C**ovenants, **C**onditions, and **R**estrictions; usually recorded by a developer to create a general plan of private restrictions for a subdivision.

Comprehensive Environmental Response, Compensation, and Liability Act (CERCLA) A federal law enacted by Congress whose primary em-phasis is the cleanup of inactive hazardous waste sites and the liability for cleanup costs on arrangers and transporters of hazardous substances and on current and former owners of facilities where hazardous substances were disposed. Also known as **Superfund**.

Comprehensive Plan A long-range plan for development of a city or region.

Conditional Use A land use that does not comply with the general zoning rules for the zone in which it is located but is permitted there because it benefits the public. Also called a **special exception**.

Nonconforming Use A land use that does not conform to current zoning laws but is allowed because the land use was established before the new zoning laws were passed.

Planned Unit Development (PUD) A special subdivision that may combine nonresidential uses with residential uses, or otherwise depart from the ordinary zoning and subdivision regulations. In some PUDs, the lot owners co-own recreational facilities or open spaces as tenants in common.

Police Power The constitutional power of state and local governments to enact and enforce laws that protect the public's health, safety, morals, and general welfare.

(Continued on page 234)

Key Terms (cont.)

Restrictive Covenant A promise to do, or not do, an act relating to real property; usually an owner's promise not to use property in a particular way. It may or may not run with the land.

Rezoning An amendment to a zoning ordinance, usually changing the uses allowed in a particular zone. Also called a **zoning amendment**.

Spot Zoning An illegal rezoning that favors or restricts a landowner (or a small group of owners) without justification.

Variance A permit obtained from the local zoning authority allowing the holder to use property or build a structure in a way that violates, or is a deviation from, the zoning ordinance.

Landownership Restrictions

Land was the first basis for wealth (it had value long before the invention of money); as such, it has always been the subject of scrutiny. In old English common law, under the **feudal system**, the King held title to all land, and those who lived and farmed the land were only tenants. Beginning in the 17th century, land reforms made it possible for tenants (anyone other than the King) to have title to land. This is called the **allodial system**, which we still use today.

Landownership (title) in Ohio can be absolute, but the absolute right to own land is not equal to the absolute right to use and enjoy it. The public sector (government) or the private sector (individuals, companies) may place restrictions on land. In this chapter, we will discuss restrictions on use and enjoyment rights.

Public Restrictions

Public restrictions on the use of privately-owned land have proliferated in the past few decades. They take the form of:

* Zoning ordinances
* Building codes
* Subdivision regulations
* Environmental laws

The government also has the power to take private land for public use, with payment of just compensation to the owner. While this is not a public restriction, per se, **appropriation of private property** is another way in which the government can control the use of private property.

Zoning Ordinances

Zoning ordinances are generally local laws or resolutions that divide the city or county into zones, segregating different types of land use in different zones. The purpose of zoning ordinances is to regulate the types of activity that may be undertaken in different areas to protect the general welfare of the area and its citizens. Early zoning laws usually established four land use categories:

1. Residential
2. Commercial
3. Industrial
4. Agricultural/rural

Modern zoning laws tend to be much more complicated. In addition to the four basic categories, numerous subcategories are used.

For Example

Even a small city might have three types of residential zones:

- R-1—Only detached single-family houses are permitted.
- R-2—Row houses and duplexes (as well as detached houses) are permitted.
- R-3—Multi-family housing is permitted.

Also, there are likely to be separate zones for light industrial and heavy industrial uses.

Each type of zone generally has its own minimum lot size and building height limits. There are usually **setback** and **side yard rules,** requiring buildings to be at least a specified distance from the front and side property lines. There may also be a limit on how much of a lot can be covered by a building, or other similar types of restrictions.

Zoning laws regulate many other aspects of development in addition to type of use, building size, and placement. An ordinance is likely to include requirements for off-street parking, landscaping, outdoor lighting, and other things that a local government may feel are necessary.

For Example

Nowhere City's ordinance provides that office buildings in a C-2 commercial zone may not be higher than ten stories. They must be set back at least 20 feet from the front and rear property lines, and at least 10 feet from the side property lines. In addition, no more than 85% of a lot can be taken up by a building.

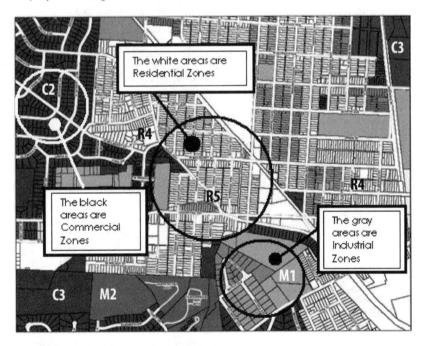

Power to Regulate Land Use

The first zoning laws in the United States were enacted at the beginning of this century. At first, it was argued that zoning was an unconstitutional interference with a landowner's property rights. But in a landmark case concerning a zoning ordinance in the village of Euclid, the U.S. Supreme Court ruled that zoning was a constitutional exercise of the state's police power. (*Village of Euclid v. Ambler Realty Co.*, 272 U.S. 365 (1926).)

Police Power. Police power is *the constitutional power of state (and local) governments to enact and enforce laws that protect the public's health, safety, morals, and general welfare.*

A state may delegate this power to local governments. Because zoning prevents overcrowding and problems with sanitation, fire protection, and law enforcement that overcrowding creates, zoning laws are deemed to protect the public health, safety, and welfare. So, as a general rule, zoning laws are a legitimate use of the government's police power and are not unconstitutional.

Constitutional Challenges to Zoning

The constitutionality of a particular zoning law can be challenged in court. A landowner may argue that the zoning is arbitrary and unreasonable, with no relationship to the public health, safety, or welfare.

However, it is difficult to win this type of case because the court often presumes the zoning ordinance is constitutional. The land owner (plaintiff) has to prove "beyond fair debate" that it is not. If there is room for a reasonable difference of opinion, the court will rule that the zoning ordinance is valid. In this case, the court agrees that the city council (or other local legislative body) is in a better position than a court to determine community needs.

Case Example

A developer bought four lots on Central Avenue in Toledo. The lots were zoned for single-family residential use, but they were on the edge of the residential zone, right beside a commercial zone with gas stations and a shopping center.

The developer wanted to put an office building on the lots. He requested a zoning change, but the city council turned him down. He filed a lawsuit against the city, challenging the constitutionality of the zoning ordinance. He argued it was unreasonable to restrict his lots to residential use when there was commercial development so nearby.

The state supreme court upheld the ordinance. The developer's lots could still be considered part of a residential neighborhood. Putting them to commercial use would probably increase traffic congestion, noise, and air pollution. The developer had failed to clearly show, beyond fair debate, that the city council's decision had no relation to the public health, safety, and welfare. *Leslie v. City of Toledo*, 66 Ohio St. 2d 488, 423 N.E.2d 123 (1981).

Inverse Condemnation. Another type of challenge to a zoning law is based on the just compensation clause in the Constitution. The action is referred to as an *inverse condemnation lawsuit*. An **inverse condemnation** lawsuit is *when a property owner sues the government, asking the court to order the government to either pay compensation or loosen the land use restrictions.* The term "inverse" is used because the landowner is suing the government, instead of the other way around. (The government's right to appropriate private land for public use, called **condemnation** or **appropriation**, is discussed later in this chapter.)

Basically, the owner's lawsuit is based on the fact that the Constitution requires the government to compensate the owner when private property is taken for public use. In an inverse condemnation lawsuit, an owner claims that a zoning law has restricted his property so severely that it amounts to an uncompensated "taking" of the land.

To win an inverse condemnation suit, the owner has to prove the zoning law rendered the property virtually useless by preventing the only kinds of development it was suited for. It is not enough to show that the law:

- Keeps the owner from putting the property to its most profitable use.

- Lowers the value of the property—even if it is lowered substantially.

Case Example

Some developers proved in court that their property would be worth only $11,000 with a single-family home on it but would be worth $165,000 if they were allowed to build an office building on it. Nevertheless, since it was possible to develop the property in compliance with the current zoning (as a single-family home), the court ruled that the zoning law was valid, and the developers were not entitled to compensation. *Mintz v. Village of Pepper Pike,* 57 Ohio App. 2d 185, 386 N.E.2d 849 (1978).

Other Constitutional Challenges. Zoning laws can be challenged on a number of other constitutional grounds. An ordinance cannot be discriminatory—that is, it must be applied in the same manner to all similarly situated property owners. It also cannot be exclusionary—excluding certain groups of people from a community. Some ordinances regulating signs have been struck down because they violated the right to freedom of speech. In a few cases, zoning laws have been invalidated because they violated the right to privacy.

Case Example

To prevent large groups of unrelated people from living together (e.g., commune), East Cleveland enacted a zoning ordinance that limited occupancy of a residential dwelling unit to a single family. The law defined "family" narrowly: Any traditional, nuclear family would fit the definition (no matter how large), but many extended families would not.

Mrs. Moore shared her home with one of her sons and her two grandsons. This use of her residence violated the strict interpretation of the zoning ordinance.

Mrs. Moore sued the city, and the case went all the way to the U.S. Supreme Court. The Court struck down the East Cleveland ordinance. Although it was legitimate to limit occupancy to a single family, the ordinance went too far. With its constricted definition of "family," the court held that the city was unconstitutionally intruding into Mrs. Moore's privacy. *Moore v. City of East Cleveland,* 431 U.S. 494 (1976).

Enacting Zoning Laws

In Ohio, zoning laws can be enacted by any form of local government: Counties, municipal corporations, or townships. If a municipal corporation has more than 5,000 people, it is further categorized as a city; if it has less than 5,000 people, it is categorized as a village. *All laws, including zoning laws, passed by city councils or village councils* are called **ordinances.** *All laws, including zoning laws, passed by county commissioners or township trustees* are called **resolutions.**

The Ohio General Assembly established certain procedures for local governments to follow when they enact zoning laws. State law does not require a local government to zone or regulate land use within its boundaries at all, but if a local government chooses to regulate land use, it must follow the procedures outlined in the state law.

An exception to that rule is *a city or village that has adopted a charter is not required to comply with the state zoning procedures.* This is referred to as the **home rule provision.** The state constitution (Article XVIII, section 7) grants municipal corporations some independence from state law. It empowers a municipal corporation to adopt a charter that can take precedence over certain state laws. If the charter establishes its own zoning procedures, the city or village does not have to follow the state procedures.

The zoning procedures for cities and villages outlined here are the state procedures. These have to be followed by any cities or villages that do not have a charter. They may or may not be followed in a chartered city or village, depending on the terms of the charter

The county and township zoning procedures must to be followed by all counties and townships. The home rule does not apply to them.

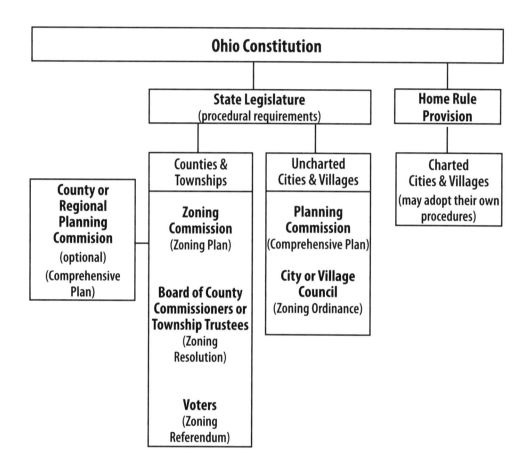

City and Village Zoning. In order for a city or village to enact its own zoning, the city council or village council must first set up a **planning commission**, which is responsible for preparing a *long-term* **comprehensive plan** for development.

The comprehensive plan developed by the city or village may address many issues, including population density, housing, transportation, utility services, parks, historic landmarks, and so on. It will include an overall plan for zoning, dividing the whole community into zones and prescribing general rules for land use and building size and placement.

Once the planning commission prepares a comprehensive plan, it certifies the plan to the city or village council. Now, the council is authorized to adopt zoning ordinances. Because zoning can have far-reaching effects, the council is required to hold at least one public hearing before adopting a new ordinance. The hearing is a chance for citizens, community groups, and developers to voice their opinions about the proposed law.

A zoning ordinance is generally supposed to conform to the guidelines and requirements laid out in the comprehensive plan. An ordinance that is in accordance with the plan can be adopted by a simple majority vote. When a proposed ordinance conflicts with the plan, it can become law only if three-fourths of the council members vote in favor of it.

County and Township Zoning. A county board of commissioners may regulate land use in the unincorporated areas of the county by establishing a **county rural zoning commission**, which prepares a *zoning plan*. A **zoning plan** is more limited in scope than a comprehensive plan, since a zoning plan is exclusively concerned with land use issues.

Before submitting the zoning plan to the board of commissioners, the zoning commission must hold a public hearing in each township in the county. The board of commissioners is also required to hold a public hearing for the entire county before taking any action in regard to the plan.

The board of commissioners then votes on the plan. If the board adopts the plan, it becomes a zoning resolution. However, a zoning resolution does not become law automatically. Instead, the issue gets turned over to the citizens of the county in a **referendum** vote. The citizens vote whether the resolution should be put into effect. It becomes law only in those townships where a majority of voters approve it.

A board of township trustees can pass zoning laws that differ from the county rural zoning laws and apply them only within that township. The procedures are basically the same as the county procedures:

- The trustees set up a **township zoning commission** to prepare a plan.
- Public hearings are conducted.
- The trustees vote to adopt the plan as a zoning resolution.
- The citizens of the township vote on the resolution, and it becomes law if the majority favor it.

County and Regional Planning. A county board of commissioners may establish a county planning commission (not the same as a county rural zoning commission). The **county planning commission** will prepare a comprehensive plan for the entire county, coordinating the development of all municipalities and townships in the county. In addition, local governments in neighboring counties may establish a regional planning commission to prepare a comprehensive plan for the whole region.

When there is a county or regional planning commission in place, a township or county rural zoning commission is required to submit any proposed zoning resolutions to the planning commission for approval. To pass a zoning resolution that differs from the regional or county comprehensive plan, the board of county commissioners must vote for it unanimously.

Zoning by Referendum. Voter approval of a referendum is an essential step in the adoption of a zoning resolution by a county or township. But even though state law does not require city and village councils to refer proposed zoning ordinances to the voters, a city or village charter may require a referendum vote on zoning proposals.

Case Example

Some Ohio developers sued to challenge the constitutionality of zoning by popular vote, but the U.S. Supreme Court ruled that this was a valid application of the referendum process. *City of Eastlake v. Forest City Enterprises, Inc.*, 426 U.S. 668 (1976).

Exceptions to Zoning Laws

Zoning laws are often controversial because they can have a big impact on the use and value of property. A zoning law is constitutional only if it applies in the same manner to all similarly situated property owners. If zoning regulations are rigidly applied, it can lead to unnecessarily harsh results for a few property owners. To prevent this, zoning laws usually provide for limited exceptions to their rules.

These exceptions include:

- Nonconforming uses
- Variances
- Conditional uses

Nonconforming Uses. Nonconforming uses occur *when land use does not conform to current zoning laws but is allowed because the land use was established before the new laws were enacted.* This situation can occur when a new zoning designation is imposed on a neighborhood. Some owners may find the way they are using their property is not permitted under the new law, even though it was perfectly legal before. These landowners are permitted to continue using their land the same way they always have under a nonconforming use.

Case Example

The Grandes bought a large parcel of unzoned property in Highland Heights. The property had been used as a nursery for many years. The Grandes took over the nursery business, maintaining the greenhouses and selling plants on the property.

Then, Highland Heights adopted a zoning ordinance and the Grandes' nursery was in an area zoned for single-family residential use. The nursery became a nonconforming use. *Hunziker v. Grande*, 8 Ohio App. 3d 87, 456 N.E.2d 516 (1982).

In the previous example, Highland Heights could not order the Grandes to stop using the property as a nursery, because it was a nonconforming use, which Ohio law protects. If the use was established and legal when the zoning law went into effect, it must be allowed to continue.

There are strong reasons for this rule. If a local government could terminate a nonconforming use, in constitutional terms, that would be a taking of property without just compensation (which is discussed in Chapter 1 and later in this chapter). Even if the government paid compensation, the power to cut off nonconforming uses would create a lot of uncertainty. Property owners would be much more hesitant about opening a business (or starting any other property use that requires a significant investment) if the government could shut it down at any time.

Although nonconforming uses are allowed to continue, they may be subject to a number of restrictions intended to gradually phase them out.

For Example

A zoning ordinance may provide that nonconforming uses cannot be expanded, and that nonconforming buildings cannot be renovated or rebuilt if they are accidentally destroyed. And under state law, if nonconforming uses are voluntarily discontinued for two years, they are considered abandoned and cannot be resumed later on. A city or village ordinance may make the abandonment period shorter, but not less than six months.

Despite all the restrictions, permission to continue nonconforming uses is not tied to a particular owner. If the property is sold, the new owner can continue the nonconforming use.

Although as a general rule, time limits on nonconforming uses are not permitted in Ohio, some states do set time limits (e.g., five years) on nonconforming uses instead of relying on abandonment, obsolescence, or destruction to phase out nonconforming uses. This is called an **amortization provision.**

However, a local government in Ohio does have the power to terminate nonconforming uses (or any other uses) deemed to be a *public nuisance*. A **public nuisance** is *a land use that threatens the public health, safety, morals, or welfare, or constitutes a substantial annoyance to the public.*

For Example

An unsanitary cattle feed lot next to an expanding business district could be declared a nuisance.

An ordinance terminating a nuisance may include an amortization provision, depending on the nature of the problem.

Variances. **Variances** *grant permission to a property owner by the zoning authority, allowing some deviation from strict compliance with the zoning law.* This occurs because, sometimes, a zoning law creates special problems for a particular owner whose property is unusual in some way. To deal with this, zoning regulations provide for variances that permit a property owner to build a structure or use property in a way that is not otherwise allowed.

Variances fall into two categories:

1. **Area variances**—Bend the rules regarding building size and height limits, setbacks, side yards, etc.

2. **Use variance**—Permit property owners to use the land in a way that is not allowed in that zone (e.g., a commercial use in a residential zone)

To obtain a variance, a property owner applies to the zoning board. In a county or township, this will be the **board of zoning appeals**. A city or village may have a **zoning administrative board** or the functions of a zoning board may be performed by the planning commission. Sometimes a zoning board will hold a public hearing on a variance request, but it may grant minor, routine variances without a public hearing. In any case, board meetings must be open to the public.

Variances are supposed to be granted in special circumstances only. Generally, the property in question must have an unusual size, shape, topography, or location, in comparison to the other properties in the zone. The owner has to show that because of the property's unusual characteristics, he is more restricted by strict application of the zoning law than his neighbors are.

Area Variances. Area variances tend to be easier to get than use variances because area variances usually ask for a less drastic change in zoning policy. To obtain area variances, owners usually need to show only that strict compliance with the zoning laws would cause *practical difficulties*. This standard can be met by showing that the zoning unreasonably prevents the owner from making a permitted use of the property.

Case Example

Montville Township's zoning law allowed swimming pools only in back yards. Pools were prohibited in front or side yards.

The Washington Court Athletic Club bought a piece of vacant land in Montville Township, intending to build a recreation center there. Because of deep ravines on the land, the building could be placed in only one particular position. But with the building in that position, there would be a ravine immediately behind it, preventing installation of a swimming pool there.

The club applied to the township board of zoning appeals for a variance. The board granted a variance allowing the club to install a swimming pool in the side yard. *Peterson v. Washington Court Athletic Club*, 28 Ohio App. 3d 90, 502 N.E.2d 252 (1986).

Use Variances. As previously stated, between use variances and area variances, use variances are usually more difficult to obtain because they tend to have greater impact on the character of a neighborhood. In fact, some local zoning laws do not allow use variances at all. To obtain use variances, property owners must show that strict compliance with the zoning would cause *unnecessary hardship*. To meet this standard, the owner must demonstrate that the permitted uses of the property are not economically feasible and that the property really cannot be used without the variance. It is not enough for a property owner to show that he could make a more profitable use of his property if the use variance were granted. Sometimes, though, use variances are granted for more practical reasons.

Case Example

The First National Bank in the village of Ottawa was located on property zoned for business use. The bank decided it needed more room for employee and customer parking. It obtained an option to purchase a neighboring piece of property, intending to use it as a parking lot. This property was zoned for residential use, however.

The bank applied to the village planning commission for a variance. After a public hearing, the commission granted the bank a variance allowing it to use the residential property as a parking lot. The variance was granted subject to conditions requiring special landscaping, lighting, and fencing. *Schomaeker v. First Nat'l Bank*, 66 Ohio St. 2d 304, 421 N.E.2d 530 (1981).

When a zoning board denies or grants a variance, the applicant or the neighbors can appeal to the court of common pleas. The court is expected to defer to the judgment of the zoning board, unless the board's decision was clearly unreasonable and arbitrary. In the previous case example, the Schomaeker case was appealed up to the Ohio Supreme Court. In upholding the variance, the Supreme Court stated: "A zoning board or planning commission...is vested with a wide discretion with which the courts will not interfere unless that discretion is abused. Whether a hardship or exceptional or extraordinary circumstances exist to justify the issuance of a variance is a question of fact to be determined by the zoning board or commission."

Conditional Uses. Conditional uses are *land usages that do not comply with the general zoning rules for its location but are permitted there because they benefit the public good.* These are also called **special exceptions**. Most zoning laws allow permits to be issued for certain uses that are inconsistent with a neighborhood's zoning designation but are necessary or beneficial to the community. Common examples include:

- Schools
- Hospitals
- Churches
- Cemeteries
- Gas stations

A zoning ordinance or resolution usually has a specific list of conditional uses that may be allowed in a particular zone. The zoning board grants permits for these uses, subject to conditions that limit their adverse effects on neighboring property. In Ohio, the permits are sometimes called **conditional zoning certificates.**

Exceptions to Zoning Regulations

Nonconforming Uses
Variances
Conditional Uses

Rezoning

Rezoning is *a revision in zoning law, usually changing a zone from one type to another*. In many situations, neither a variance nor a conditional use permit is available to the owner of property. Rezoning is one other possibility for a property owner who does not want to accept a zoning law's restrictions on what he can do with a piece of land.

A rezone is actually a change in the zoning law, not just an authorized exception to the law.

For Example

A property owner in an R-1 zone (detached single-family homes only) might ask to have part of that zone designated R-3 (multi-family housing allowed) instead.

Rezoning involves essentially the same steps as the initial adoption of a zoning law:

- Review by the planning and/or zoning commission
- Public hearings
- Approval by the board of county commissioners, the board of township trustees, or the city or village council

An amendment to a township or county rural zoning resolution becomes law 30 days after its adoption by the board, unless local citizens submit a **petition for zoning referendum**, signed by a specified number of voters. In that case, the rezone will go into effect only if a majority of the voters approve it.

A rezone ordinarily must be consistent with the community's comprehensive plan, so drastic changes are rare (e.g., a rezone from residential to industrial use is unlikely). The property owner is often required to show that circumstances have changed since the original law was passed and a new zoning designation would be more appropriate.

For Example

Q owns a lot on the edge of a residential zone. The next street over is zoned for general commercial use. When the zoning ordinance was adopted, there was a row of small, quiet businesses on the commercial street—a book shop, a grocery store, a dry cleaner's, a doctor's office, etc. The street was widened several years later, and the businesses changed. Now there is a car dealership, movie theater, bowling alley, and some fast-food restaurants.

As a result of these changes, property values on Q's street have dropped sharply. People do not want to buy homes right next to the noisy commercial strip. The lots on Q's street would be worth a lot more if apartment buildings could be built there, since renters tend to be less particular than buyers.

So, Q asks for a rezone. There is very little opposition to the proposal at the public hearings; the planning commission approves the change, and the city council votes in favor of Q's request. The boundaries on the zoning map are redrawn to create a multi-family residential zone as a buffer between the single-family zone and the commercial zone.

Spot Zoning. Spot zoning is *an illegal rezoning that favors or restricts one landowner without justification*. In this way, the rezoning process can be abused. Whether a city council's or board of commissioners' actions help or hurt a particular landowner, isolated zoning changes are illegal because the zoning law is not being applied in the same way to all similarly-situated property owners.

For Example

X bought a large piece of commercial property in Nowhere City. The property was in a C-3 zone, where the maximum height limit for buildings was 50 feet. X wanted to build a high-rise office building, so she applied to the city planning commission for a variance. But under the city's zoning ordinance, there was not a legal basis for granting a variance. There was nothing unusual about X's property. It could be developed in compliance with the height limits, even though that would not be as profitable as a high-rise building, so the planning commission rejected X's application.

Then the city council passed an amendment to the zoning ordinance, removing the height limit from X's property. To justify its action, the council claimed the high-rise building would be economically beneficial for the city. Neighboring landowners sued, however, and the court ruled that the rezoning was invalid. The change violated the community's comprehensive plan and gave X special treatment.

Sometimes a legitimate zoning change looks like spot zoning, since it applies to only one or two properties. But as long as there are sound reasons for the rezone and it does not conflict with the comprehensive plan, it probably is not unconstitutional.

Enforcement of Zoning Laws

In order to enforce zoning laws, a board of county commissioners or township trustees may establish a **zoning certificate system**. Under such a system, a property owner cannot construct or alter any building without obtaining a zoning certificate first. The zoning inspector or building inspector will issue a certificate only if the building plans conform to the zoning laws. Cities and villages often have a similar system.

A local government can sue a property owner who violates a zoning law. The court may issue an injunction ordering the owner to tear down an illegal structure or to stop an illegal use. Under certain circumstances, a neighboring property owner also has the right to sue for an injunction, but the neighbor must be able to show that he will be specially damaged by the violation.

In addition to injunctions, fines can be imposed on property owners who violate zoning laws. For violation of township or county rural zoning, an owner can be fined up to $100 for each offense—and each day that a violation continues can be treated as a separate offense.

Building Codes

Building codes *establish standards for construction, requiring builders to use particular methods and materials.* A local government usually has several specialized building codes (e.g., fire code, plumbing code, electrical code). Like zoning laws, they are an exercise of the police power, protecting public health and safety. In Ohio, some minimum building standards are set by state law, but a local government can require more.

Building codes are mainly enforced through the **permit system**:

- A property owner intending to build or remodel a structure must submit plans to the local building department for approval.

- A building permit is issued only if the plans comply with the codes.

- The project may be inspected during construction, and the inspector can issue a stop work order if there are any problems.

- The completed building will be inspected to make sure it actually does comply with the codes.

Every structure must comply with building codes, not just new or remodeled structures. There are routine fire and health inspections for most buildings, other than private homes. And when a new, stricter standard is imposed, a property owner may be required to bring an old building "up to code." Fines and injunctions are used to enforce building codes.

Subdivision Regulations

Subdivision regulations are *state and local laws that must be complied with before land can be subdivided*. In this way, local authorities can also control land use. These regulations may govern the size of the lots in a subdivision and the location of streets, sidewalks, and sewer and water lines. These regulations may also require the developer to provide open spaces and recreational areas within the subdivision.

A local government enforces subdivision regulations by requiring subdividers to submit a *plat* for approval. A **plat** is *a detailed survey map of the subdivision, showing the boundaries of the lots, streets, and so forth*. If the plat is approved, the subdivider files it at the county recorder's office. It is illegal for the subdivider to sell lots in the subdivision before the plat is approved and recorded.

It is not just major developers who have to comply with subdivision regulations. Under state law, a local government can require an owner to submit a plat if the property is being subdivided into two or more lots and any one of the lots is smaller than five acres. If all the lots are five acres or larger, a plat can be required if the subdivision will make it necessary to establish any new streets or access easements, or to widen or extend existing streets.

Planned Unit Developments (PUDs)

A **planned unit development** (**PUD**) is *a special type of subdivision allowed in some communities, which does not necessarily have to comply with all the standard zoning and subdivision regulations*.

For Example

Nonresidential uses may be combined with residential uses in a PUD. And because a PUD developer does not have to follow all of the setback and lot size rules, the buildings may be clustered close together on undersized lots to create larger open spaces than ordinary subdivisions have. In some PUDs, the lot owners co-own these open spaces as tenants in common.

To obtain permission to build a PUD, a developer usually has to submit detailed plans to the planning or zoning commission for approval.

Environmental Laws

Environmental laws are laws enacted by federal and state governments to protect the country's land, air, and water; to keep the land, air and water clean; and to promote conservation of land, air, water, and natural resources. When land use controls were first developed, not much thought was given to protection of the environment. In recent years, however, this has become an area of great concern. Next, we will briefly discuss some of the most important federal and state environmental laws.

Federal Environmental Laws

The **National Environmental Policy Act** (**NEPA**) requires federal agencies to prepare an **environmental impact statement** (**EIS**) for any action that would have a significant effect on the environment. NEPA applies to all kinds of federal development projects, such as dam and highway construction and waste control plans. NEPA also applies to private action when the use or development of land requires a license or permit from a federal agency, or even a federal loan. In those cases, the federal agencies may require submission of an EIS before granting approval.

An EIS should disclose the impact of the development on energy consumption, sewage systems, school population, drainage, water facilities, and other environmental, economic, and social conditions.

Clean Air Act. The **Clean Air Act** requires the federal **Environmental Protection Agency (EPA)** to regulate emission of air pollutants. Each state is required to prepare a **state implementation plan (SIP)** for meeting the national air quality standards issued by the EPA. States are authorized to prevent development that would interfere with attainment or maintenance of clean air objectives.

Clean Water Act. Under the **Clean Water Act**, the EPA sets national water quality standards. Any land use that would discharge an unacceptable amount of pollutants into a lake or waterway is prohibited. The Clean Water Act also addresses wastewater treatment problems. It encourages local governments to investigate new technology and alternatives to traditional sewage treatment plants. The adequacy of available treatment facilities has to be taken into account in deciding whether to permit new construction in a particular area.

Comprehensive Environmental Response, Compensation, and Liability Act (CERCLA). CERCLA, also known as the **Superfund**, created mandatory waste-site requirements and established consequences when hazardous materials were released at the sites. The tax revenue, originally from chemical and petroleum industries, goes into a trust fund used for cleaning up large or abandoned hazardous waste sites where no clearly responsible party can be identified. Over the years, the EPA has examined tens of thousands of sites across the country, placing contaminated properties where hazardous waste is located—called Superfund sites—on a **National Priorities List**. The term **brownfields** refers to *real properties whose expansion, redevelopment, or reuse may be complicated by the presence or potential presence of a hazardous substance, pollutant, or contaminant.* The **Brownfields Revitalization Act** amended CERCLA in 2002 to provide funds for the cleanup of designated brownfield sites. The legislation also provides guidelines and tax incentives for reinvesting in these old industrial properties to protect the environment, reduce blight, and take development pressures off green spaces and working lands.

Ohio's Environmental Protection Laws

In compliance with federal requirements, the Ohio General Assembly passed air and water pollution control legislation and established the **Ohio Environmental Protection Agency (OEPA)** to administer the environmental laws.

A permit from OEPA is required for any significant discharge of pollutants into the water or air. The agency's grant or denial of a permit can be appealed to the state Environmental Board of Review. OEPA does not require submission of environmental impact statements, but it reviews any federal EIS prepared for a project in Ohio.

Appropriation of Private Property

Appropriation is *the taking of private property for public use, with just compensation, through the government's power of eminent domain.* This is also called **condemnation**. This is another way that the government can control the use of private land.

For Example

The government could take someone's home, demolish it, and turn the land into a public park or parking lot.

Both the federal and state constitutions require the government to pay the owner **just compensation** for the property, which is generally the fair market value.

Most government entities (e.g., state director of transportation, city government, board of education) can condemn property. In addition, the government has delegated the power of eminent domain to some private entities (e.g., privately-owned utility companies). Whether the entity is public or private, its intended use of the property must benefit the public.

Before appropriating property, the government agency is first required to simply offer to buy it. If the owner refuses the offer, the agency files an **appropriation lawsuit**. The owner may argue to the court that the agency does not actually need the property, or that the intended use will not benefit the public. Those arguments rarely prevail, however. A jury determines how much compensation must be paid, and the court transfers title from the owner to the agency.

Dedication

Dedication is a *gift of private land to the public*. Unlike appropriation, dedication is more or less a voluntary form of alienation. The government is *not* required to compensate the owner for dedicated land. There are two types of dedication:

1. Statutory
2. Common law

Statutory Dedication. Statutory dedication is *a dedication required by law*. While this may not sound voluntary, it is usually a condition for permission to subdivide.

For Example

When developers subdivide property, they normally dedicate the streets and sidewalks for public use. Usually, they are required by law to do this. The city or county approves the subdivision plat and accepts the dedication. The plat is recorded, and title to the dedicated land passes to the government.

Common Law Dedication. Common law dedication is *dedication resulting from the owner's intention to donate land for public use, along with the government's acceptance of the donation*. This type of dedication does not involve any particular procedure. The owner's intention may be expressly stated (as when a wealthy philanthropist dedicates a portion of his land to the city for use as a public park), or it may be implied. If the public openly uses private property for a long time and the owner does not object, the law presumes an intention to dedicate the land.

The government's acceptance may also be express or implied. There can be a formal declaration, or the government may show its acceptance by taking control and maintaining the property. Without some act by the government, though, public use alone is not acceptance. Just because the public has been using the property for a long time does not mean the government has legal responsibility for maintaining it.

Private Restrictions

In addition to all the laws that restrict use of a particular piece of property, there may be private restrictions. These restrictions are usually imposed by a former owner of the property—often by the original developer. In many cases, private restrictions prohibit a use that the zoning and other land use laws would allow.

For Example

A lot zoned for any type of residential use might be subject to a private restriction that permits only a single-family home to be built there.

Private restrictions take two forms:

1. Conditions
2. Covenants

Conditions

Conditions are *provisions in a deed (or other document) that make the parties' rights and obligations depend on the occurrence (or non-occurrence) of a particular event.* Deed conditions were discussed in Chapter 6, under defeasible fee estates.

When an owner transfers a defeasible fee to someone else, the grantee's title is contingent on compliance with a condition stated in the deed.

For Example

A deed may grant land "To X, on condition that the barn will never be painted orange." If the condition is broken (if the barn is painted orange), a court could rule that the grantee has forfeited title to the property, and ownership would revert to the grantor.

In reality, however, deed conditions are rare.

Covenants

Covenants are *promises or guarantees, either express or implied, in a deed (or other document).* Covenants in deeds are much more common than conditions. "Covenant" is another term for "contract"—a binding promise to do or not do something. A **restrictive covenant** is *a binding promise concerning the use of real property.*

A restrictive covenant in a deed can cover the same issues as a condition.

For Example

A deed may contain a covenant stating, "The grantee covenants never to paint the barn orange." A covenant, though, does not make the grantee's title conditional. If the grantee paints the barn orange, a court may order her to paint it a different color or pay damages to the grantor, but she cannot lose title to the property.

Whether a restriction is a condition or a covenant depends on the language in the deed that created it. Because forfeiture of title is an extremely harsh punishment, though, a court will always try to interpret a deed restriction as a covenant rather than a condition whenever possible. A deed restriction will be enforced as a condition only if the wording makes it absolutely clear that title was contingent on compliance.

 Ohio courts tend to favor free use of land over any form of private restriction. As a result, if there is some ambiguity in the wording of a restrictive covenant, a court will interpret it narrowly rather than broadly, to allow the property owner as much freedom as possible under the terms of the covenant.

Creation of Restrictive Covenants

As just discussed, a restrictive covenant can be imposed on property in a deed. This is especially common when the owner of a large tract of land sells part of it to someone else while retaining the rest. To prevent the new neighbor from using the property in some objectionable way, the grantor imposes restrictions on the grantee's parcel.

But it is not just when property is transferred that restrictive covenants can be imposed. They can also be created by an express agreement between established neighbors.

For Example

A and B have lived next door to each other for several years. A starts worrying that B might put an addition on her house that would block his view of the mountains. He discusses this with B. B says that if A pays her $500, she will not obstruct his view. A puts this agreement in writing, B signs it, and A gives B the $500. This is an enforceable contract between A and B. If B breaks her promise, A can sue her.

However, the following year B sells her property to X, who is interested in astronomy and builds an observation tower that blocks A's view of the mountains. A does not have the right to sue X because he was not a party to the contract between A and B.

By following certain rules, however, A and B could have made their restrictive covenant . in the same way that an easement can (see Chapter 6). In this case, the restriction against blocking the view would apply to X, or anyone else who bought B's property. And if A sold his property to someone else, the new owner would have the right to enforce the restrictive covenant and protect the view, just as A did.

A restrictive covenant can run with the land if the deed or agreement creating the restriction is recorded. The recorded document gives constructive notice of the restriction to anyone buying the burdened property. As a result, the buyer takes title subject to the restriction, and can be required to comply with it. The recorded document should:

- Describe the property that benefits from the restriction as well as the property burdened by the restriction.
- Expressly state that future owners of the burdened property are to be bound by the restriction, for the benefit of the other property.

Many deeds say something to the effect of "subject to restrictions of record." But once a restrictive covenant is in the recorded chain of title for a particular piece of property, subsequent buyers take title subject to the restriction even if it is not mentioned in their deed. However, that rule is limited by the Marketable Title Act, which is discussed later in this chapter.

Related to the Property. Even if a restrictive covenant is stated in a recorded document, it cannot run with the land unless it relates to the use, maintenance, or improvement of the real property. Courts express this requirement by saying that a restrictive covenant has to "touch and concern the land."

For Example

A covenant in a deed stating that the grantee must never smoke cigarettes could not run with the land, but if the covenant prohibited smoking only on the property being transferred, then it might run with the land.

Terminating Restrictive Covenants

Under the **Marketable Title Act** (see Chapter 7), *a restrictive covenant that was created before the current owner's root of title will be extinguished unless it is preserved.* A restrictive covenant can be preserved in a deed or notice recorded at any time after the root of title. The deed or notice must state that the property is subject to the restriction, and specifically mention the deed or other recorded document in which the restriction was created. A general reference, such as "subject to restrictions of record," is not enough to preserve a particular restriction. If a covenant is not preserved, it expires 40 years after the root of title. There are also several other ways to terminate restrictive covenants.

Termination Date. Sometimes, the document creating a restrictive covenant includes a specific time limit. In this case, the covenant becomes unenforceable when the date comes or when time runs out. Most restrictive covenants do not have an expiration date, however.

Release. A restrictive covenant (like an easement) can be terminated by agreement. The owner of the benefited property may agree to release the burdened property from the restriction. In this case, the parties should be sure to record a release.

Merger. A restrictive covenant can also be terminated by merger (again, just like an easement). If the owner of the burdened property acquires title to the benefited property too, the restriction disappears. It will not revive if the two properties are sold again separately in the future.

Abandonment. If a restrictive covenant is not enforced, it may become unenforceable, resulting in termination by abandonment. Even after a developer has taken the right steps to establish a general plan, it will not work unless there is substantially uniform compliance with the restrictions. If several homeowners have already broken a particular rule, it can no longer be enforced against other homeowners.

For Example

The subdivision's declaration of covenants, conditions, and restrictions require each house to be set back at least 20 feet from the front of the lot. The owner of Lot 44 started to build a house that was set back only 16 feet, so the owner of Lot 45 sued to enforce the setback restriction.

The owner of Lot 44 pointed out that the houses on Lots 12, 15, 19, 27, 28, 33, 41, 50, and 56 are all set back less than 20 feet. The court ruled that the 20-foot setback requirement has been abandoned and can no longer be enforced.

Changed Circumstances. Similarly, a restrictive covenant may no longer be enforceable if the character of the restricted neighborhood has changed. This is called "termination due to changed circumstances."

Case Example

In 1913, a developer in Parma subdivided some property on Broadview Road and he restricted all the lots to residential use. By the 1970s, Broadview Road had become a four-lane arterial road with a great deal of traffic and the subdivision was surrounded by businesses.

The Hopkos owned five adjacent lots in the subdivision, all of them with frontage on Broadview Road. They wanted to use the lots for a funeral home and obtained permission from the city to build one there. However, some of their neighbors in the subdivision sued to enforce the covenant restricting the property to residential use.

The Hopkos claimed that the restriction had been extinguished under the Marketable Title Act. The court found that the restriction was extinguished for some of the Hopkos' lots but had been preserved against their other lots. Even so, the court refused to enforce the restriction. The court reasoned that Broadview Road had changed so much since 1913 that the original purpose of the restriction (to protect the residential character of the subdivision) could no longer be realized. *Semachko v. Hopko*, 35 Ohio App. 2d 205, 301 N.E.2d 560 (1973).

Subdivision Restrictions

Today, most private restrictions are imposed by subdivision developers. A developer often places restrictions on all the lots in a new subdivision by recording a **declaration of covenants, conditions, and restrictions**, better known as **CC&Rs**. Note that even though CC&Rs stands for covenants, conditions, and restrictions, they virtually never make a grantee's title subject to forfeiture. The purpose of CC&Rs is to keep the subdivision attractive and protect the market value of the homes.

Through the CC&Rs, the developer can establish a **general plan** of restrictions for the whole subdivision. When there is a general plan, any homeowner in the subdivision can enforce the CC&Rs against any other homeowner there. In other words, it is not just the developer who can enforce the CC&Rs. The lots are mutually burdened and benefited by the restrictions. In many cases, a homeowners association enforces the restrictions on behalf of the whole community.

Case Example

Among many other provisions, the CC&Rs for the Beckett Ridge subdivision stated that residents could not put up clotheslines in their yards without first getting approval from the homeowners association.

Mr. and Mrs. Agne bought a house in Beckett Ridge in 1981. They put up a clothesline in their back yard soon after moving in, without asking for permission from the homeowners association. The line was visible from neighboring yards, the street, and the community golf course. None of the other families in the subdivision used an outdoor clothesline.

Several months after the Agnes put up their clothesline, the homeowners association sent them a notice ordering them to take it down. The Agnes ignored that notice, and also ignored a second notice sent a few months later. Finally, in late 1982, they applied to the homeowners association for permission to use the clothesline. The association denied their request. The Agnes still did not take the clothesline down.

The homeowners association decided to take the clothesline conflict to the court system and filed a lawsuit against the Agnes. The Agnes argued that it was unreasonable for the association to refuse to allow them to use an outdoor clothesline, but the court ruled that the restriction was enforceable. Unless the Agnes could show a compelling need to use the clothesline, the homeowners association could deny them permission to do so. The Agnes had not demonstrated a compelling need, so the court issued an injunction, ordering them to remove the clothesline. *Beckett Ridge Ass'n-I v. Agne,* 26 Ohio App. 3d 74, 498 N.E.2d 223 (1985).

To establish a **general plan**, the CC&Rs should clearly state that the restrictions are mutually binding on all the homeowners. The developer also has to mention the CC&Rs either in the subdivision's recorded plat or in the deed to the first purchaser of each lot. If they are not mentioned in the plat or in a deed in the recorded chain of title for a particular lot, the owner of that lot probably will not be bound by the restrictions. Also, that owner will not be able to enforce the restrictions against other homeowners in the subdivision. Finally, a subdivision's CC&Rs can be terminated in much the same way as other restrictive covenants.

Summary

1. Landownership **restrictions** are either *public* (imposed by government) or *private* (imposed by individuals). Public restrictions may take the form of **zoning ordinances**, **building codes**, **subdivision regulations**, or **environmental laws**. The government may also control the use of private land by using its power of **eminent domain** to take private land for public use. Private restrictions take the form of **conditions** or **covenants**.

2. The government's power to regulate land use is based on the state's **police power** to pass laws to protect the public health, safety, morals, and general welfare. The Supreme Court has upheld the government's right to impose **zoning laws**. Land use laws are unconstitutional if they are discriminatory or exclusionary, or if they are excessive and prevent an owner from using the land.

3. **Zoning laws** divide different types of land use into different areas. They also usually regulate lot size, building height, building setbacks, off-street parking, etc. Zoning laws are local laws, adopted by a county, township, city, or village. A **rezone** is a change in the zoning law. **Spot zoning** is illegal because it benefits or restricts certain owners without justification. Exceptions to zoning laws include **nonconforming uses**, **variances**, and **conditional uses**.

4. **Nonconforming uses** are established uses that violate new zoning laws but must be allowed to continue. They usually cannot be expanded, renovated, rebuilt after destruction, or resumed after abandonment. **Variances** allow an owner to build a structure or use property in a way that violates the strict terms of zoning laws. **Area variances** bend the rules regarding building size, height limits, setbacks, side yards, and so on, and may be granted so the owner can avoid practical difficulties. **Use variances** permit property owners to use land in a way not allowed in that zone and cannot be granted unless the owner would suffer unnecessary hardship. **Conditional uses** allow land to be used in a way that does not comply with the zoning laws, because it benefits the public.

5. **Building codes** set minimum standards for construction and materials. New construction is inspected to ensure it meets the standards. An owner may also have to bring an existing building up to code. **Subdivision regulations** must be complied with before land can be subdivided. These regulations may govern lot size, location of streets and sidewalks, etc., and may also require open spaces or recreational areas. The **National Environmental Policy Act (NEPA)** requires environmental impact statements to be submitted for development projects involving federal funding or federal agency permits. The **Ohio Environmental Protection Agency (OEPA)** regulates pollutant discharges into the air or water.

6. Deed conditions are rare today. Courts try to interpret deed restrictions as covenants. **Restrictive covenants** relate to the use, maintenance, or improvement of property and may *run with the land*. Developers often impose restrictions on an entire subdivision by recording **CC&Rs**. Restrictive covenants can be terminated by termination date (rare), release, merger, abandonment, or because of a change in the character of a neighborhood.

Quiz

1. *The constitutional basis for governmental regulation of the use of private property is*

   a. eminent domain.

   b. the National Environmental Policy Act.

   c. police power.

   d. the zoning clause.

2. *A owns some undeveloped property that is zoned for commercial use. The city later rezones that area to allow only residential use. A's property could be used for residential purposes, but commercial development would be much more profitable. In fact, the property would be worth $500,000 for commercial development, but only $100,000 for residential development. Which statement is TRUE?*

   a. A has a right to develop the property commercially as a nonconforming use.

   b. This zoning law is constitutional, since it does not prevent the only kind of development the property is suited for.

   c. This zoning law is unconstitutional because it prevents A from putting the property to its most profitable use.

   d. Zoning laws that allow only residential use of property are unconstitutional in Ohio.

3. *To enact a zoning ordinance, an unchartered city in Ohio must*

   a. appoint a planning commission to prepare a comprehensive plan for the city.

   b. appoint a zoning commissioner to prepare a zoning plan for the city.

   c. get the approval of a majority of the voters in a local referendum.

   d. get the approval of the state board of zoning appeals.

4. *A section of the neighborhood has recently been rezoned for residential use only. Z's store is located in this section. He will be allowed to continue to use his property as a store. This is known as a*

   a. conditional use.

   b. nonconforming use.

   c. spot zone.

   d. variance.

5. *To be entitled to a use variance, a property owner ordinarily is required to show that*

   a. the character of the neighborhood has changed and the zoning designation is no longer appropriate.

   b. none of the neighbors object to the proposed use.

   c. strict application of the zoning law would cause unnecessary hardship.

   d. strict application of the zoning law would prevent the most profitable use of the property.

6. *A wealthy philanthropist owns some property that is zoned residential. He wants to donate the property for the construction of a charity hospital. Can a hospital be built on this property?*

   a. No, because area variances are illegal in Ohio.

   b. No, because even a non-profit hospital is considered a commercial use, not a residential use.

   c. Yes, because it is a nonconforming use.

   d. Yes, if the zoning board or planning commission issues a conditional use permit for the project.

7. *J owns a tract of property in an area of the city that is zoned for light industrial use. The city council rezones J's tract for commercial use, although the surrounding properties are still zoned industrial. The zoning change enables J to build a very profitable commercial development. This is an example of a(n)*

   a. illegal spot zone.

   b. illegal variance.

   c. legitimate conditional use.

   d. legitimate zoning modification.

8. **The board of township trustees has just rezoned an area of the township to allow multi-family residences to be built there. This zoning change will become law**

   a. as soon as it is published in a newspaper of general circulation within the township.

   b. only if a 2/3 majority of the township voters approve it in the next election.

   c. within 30 days, unless the board of county commissioners unanimously votes to overturn it.

   d. within 30 days, unless a petition for zoning referendum is filed.

9. **The city just adopted a stricter electrical code. T owns a store that was in compliance with the old code but is not up to the new standards. Which statement is TRUE?**

   a. The new code can be applied only to new buildings, so T will not have to change his wiring.

   b. State law requires T to comply with the new code within 120 days.

   c. T can be required to comply with the new code only if he expands or modifies his building.

   d. T may be required to comply with the new code whether or not he modifies his building.

10. **Under Ohio law, a local government can require the property owner to submit a plat for approval whenever a piece of property is subdivided into**

    a. 2 or more lots, if any of the lots is smaller than five acres.

    b. 10 or more lots, if all of the lots are larger than five acres.

    c. 10 or more lots, if any of the lots is larger than five acres.

    d. 25 or more lots, if all of the lots are smaller than two acres.

11. **NEPA requires an environmental impact statement to be prepared for certain development projects. This requirement applies only to**

    a. industrial projects.

    b. projects built on federal land.

    c. projects that would have a significant impact on the environment.

    d. public projects, such as dams and highways.

12. **If the wording of a restriction in a deed is ambiguous, a court usually interprets the restriction as a**

    a. condition rather than a covenant, because a condition can result in forfeiture of title.

    b. condition rather than a covenant, because a covenant can result in forfeiture of title.

    c. covenant rather than a condition, because a condition can result in forfeiture of title.

    d. covenant rather than a condition, because a covenant can result in forfeiture of title.

13. **X and Y are neighbors. Y cannot stand Spanish tile roofs, so he asks X to promise never to put a tile roof on her house. Y pays X $200 and X signs a binding agreement, but Y does not record it. Later, X sells her house to B. B can put a tile roof on the house because**

    a. B did not have notice of the restriction.

    b. private restrictions that control the appearance of buildings are unenforceable.

    c. restrictive covenants do not run with the land.

    d. the tile roof will not lower the value of the neighboring property.

14. **The developer established a general plan of restrictions that applies to every home in the subdivision. This includes a provision prohibiting vegetable gardens. The owners of Lot 60 have planted corn, tomatoes, and rutabagas in their front yard. Who can enforce the restriction against the owners of Lot 60?**

    a. any lot owner who can see the vegetable garden from his property

    b. anyone who owns a lot anywhere in the subdivision

    c. only the developer or the homeowners association

    d. only the next-door neighbors (the owners of Lots 59 and 61)

15. *The CC&Rs for the Lowland Heights subdivision were recorded in 1954. They restrict all lots to single-family residential use. The city has grown, and Lowland Heights is now surrounded by a commercial district. The value of the homes in the subdivision has dropped sharply, but the lots would be quite valuable as commercial property. The residential use restriction*

    a. cannot be enforced, since the zoning allows commercial use of the lots.

    b. has been terminated by abandonment.

    c. is enforceable unless a majority of the homeowners vote to abandon it.

    d. may no longer be enforceable, because the character of the surrounding neighborhood has changed.

Landlord/Tenant

Acommon real estate transaction occurs when an individual desires to rent a place to live or work. Real estate agents need a basic understanding of landlord/tenant law, since they may be asked to act as rental agents or to sell property that is currently being leased. There are also a growing number of agents who specialize in property management, which requires knowledge of landlord/tenant law. This chapter explains the requirements for a valid lease and discusses the rights, duties, and liabilities of landlords and tenants.

Key Terms

Assignment When a tenant transfers his right of possession, or other interest, in leased property to another person for the remainder of the lease term.

Constructive Eviction When a landlord's act (or failure to act) interferes with the tenant's quiet enjoyment of the property, or makes the property unfit for its intended use, to such an extent that the tenant is forced to move out.

Covenant of Quiet Enjoyment A guarantee that a buyer or tenant has the right to exclusive, undisturbed possession of a leasehold estate during the entire term of the lease. It guarantees the tenant will not be disturbed by the previous owner, the lessor, or anyone else claiming an interest in the property.

Forcible Entry and Detainer Action A lawsuit filed by a landlord to evict a defaulting tenant and regain possession of the property. Also called an **Unlawful Detainer Action**.

Implied Warranty of Habitability An implied guarantee that the property is safe and fit for human habitation; treated by law as an implicit provision in every residential lease regardless of the express terms of the lease.

Retaliatory Eviction When a landlord evicts a tenant in retaliation for complaining about the condition of the property, code violations, violations of the Landlords and Tenants Act, or for participating in a tenants' rights group.

Self-Help Eviction When a landlord uses physical force, a lockout, or a utility shut-off to get rid of a tenant, instead of the legal process.

Sublease When a tenant transfers only part of his right of possession or other interest in leased property to another person for part of the lease term.

Leases

Leases are *both a conveyance of a leasehold estate from the fee owner to a tenant and a contract in which one party pays the other rent in exchange for possession of the real estate.* Leases are often called **rental agreements**. As a conveyance, a lease temporarily transfers the right of possession of property from the owner (the **landlord** or **lessor**) to another (the **tenant** or **lessee**). Although the landlord still owns the property in fee simple, the tenant has a leasehold estate. As a contract, a lease states the terms of the parties' relationship.

As with any contract, the landlord and tenant are generally free to negotiate the terms of their lease. However, there are some special limits on freedom of contract with residential leases. Housing shortages often put residential landlords in a much stronger bargaining position than their tenants. Furthermore, residential landlords tend to be more sophisticated than tenants, with a much better understanding of the legal effects of lease provisions. To protect residential tenants against overreaching landlords, the Ohio General Assembly passed the Landlords and Tenants Act in 1974.

Landlords and Tenants Act of 1974

The **Landlords and Tenants Act of 1974** (Ohio Revised Code Chapter 5321) applies only to residential tenancies and:

- Establishes a set of guidelines and imposes duties and responsibilities on each side that cannot be waived.

- Prohibits a landlord from including certain types of provisions in a residential lease, because they are considered unfair (e.g., an exculpatory clause, which is discussed later in this chapter).

The Act also allows a court to refuse to enforce a residential lease provision (even one that is not specifically prohibited by the Act) on the grounds that it is *unconscionable*. An **unconscionable provision** is *one that is so unfair it shocks the conscience of the court, and as such the court will refuse to enforce it.* In addition, the Act imposes a number of duties on residential landlords that apply regardless of the express terms of the lease. Those duties will be discussed later in this chapter.

Requirements of a Valid Lease

Since a lease is a contract, the essential elements of a valid contract are necessary for a valid lease:

- The landlord and tenant must have the legal capacity to contract—they cannot be incompetent or underage.

- There must be an offer and acceptance.

- There must be consideration, which usually is a sum of money paid as rent in exchange for possession of the property.

- The lease must be for a lawful and possible objective.

There are two additional requirements for leases of longer duration. They must be:

1. In writing, witnessed by two witnesses.

2. Acknowledged before a notary public and recorded.

In Writing

To comply with the **statute of frauds**, a lease must be in writing if it will last for more than one year, or if it will expire more than one year after the date on which the parties agreed to it.

For Example

On May 20, 2010, college student T arranges to rent a house for the next school year, from September 1, 2010 through June 30, 2011. The lease is not enforceable unless T and the landlord put it in writing. Even though it is only a ten-month lease, it will expire more than a year after they agreed to it.

Any lease that is required to be in writing must be signed by the landlord. A tenant usually also signs the lease, but the tenant's signature is not essential. A tenant who takes possession and pays rent is considered to have accepted the terms of the lease, even without a signature.

The legal effect of an oral lease for more than one year would be to create a legally enforceable month-to-month periodic tenancy only. In short, the lease is unenforceable as a lease for more than one year but would be enforced as a month-to-month lease.

Acknowledged and Recorded

When the rental term is longer than *three years*, the lease must not only be in writing, but it must also be acknowledged in order to be enforced. Two witnesses have to sign the document and the landlord's signature has to be notarized.

In addition, a lease for more than three years must be recorded to protect the tenant's right to occupy the premises. If it is not recorded, it remains a valid lease between landlord and tenant, but a good faith purchaser without notice of the lease would not be bound by its provisions and could evict the tenant.

For Example

L agreed to rent T his warehouse for five years. L signed a lease, and his signature was properly acknowledged, but the lease was never recorded.

Two years later, L sold the warehouse to X without explaining that it was being leased. X assumed that the equipment currently stored in the warehouse belonged to L and that he would remove it by the closing date.

After closing, X finds out about T. Since X did not have actual or constructive notice of the lease, she is not required to honor it. She can tell T to move his equipment out of the warehouse. T can sue L for damages, because L breached their contract, but T does not have a legal right to continue using the warehouse.

What if the lease between T and L had not been acknowledged, or had not even been put into writing? Then T would probably be completely out of luck, without the right to sue L for breach of contract. A court, though, might be willing to apply the *doctrine of part performance* to allow T to sue L. The **doctrine of part performance** in Ohio is *used to enforce an oral or improperly executed lease if the tenant has taken possession of the property, paid rent, and made some substantial improvements that were authorized by the landlord*. So, if T spent money to modify the warehouse to suit his purposes, a court could allow T to sue L for breach of the lease.

Effect of Option to Renew. Many leases contain an **option to renew**, *giving the tenant the right to extend the lease for an additional period.* When the tenancy would last for more than three years if the option were exercised, the lease must be acknowledged and should be recorded. This is true even if the tenancy would last for only three years or less if the tenant decided not to exercise the option.

For Example

A simple three-year lease does not have to be acknowledged and recorded. But a three-year lease with an option to renew for another two years must be acknowledged and should be recorded. In the same way, a one-year lease with an option to renew for another year must be in writing and signed.

Periodic Tenancies. As we saw earlier, a **periodic tenancy** is *automatically renewed for another period unless one of the parties gives the other notice of termination.* One thing that confuses many people is the length of the lease term in a periodic tenancy (week-to-week, month-to-month, or year-to-year). A month-to-month tenancy is renewed for another month if neither the landlord nor the tenant gives notice. Months can add up to years, though, and a tenant with a month-to-month lease may live in the same apartment for 10 or 20 years. But in the eyes of the law, the length of the tenant's lease term is always just one month. As a result, it is not necessary to put the agreement in writing, or to have it acknowledged or recorded.

 In Ohio, oral leases are considered to be month-to-month periodic tenancies.

> **Lease**
>
> Conveyance: Transfers leasehold estate (temporary possession) to tenant
>
> (Lessor) L ⟶ T (Tenant)
>
> Contract: Capacity, offer, acceptance, consideration, and lawful objective
>
> More than 1 year: In writing and signed
> More than 3 years: Acknowledged and recorded

Basic Lease Provisions

Every written lease should include certain basic information—the parties' names, the amount of the rent, when rent is due, and the duration of the lease. An adequate description of the property is also important. For many leases, the street address is enough, but if the lease is going to be recorded, a full legal description should be used.

The parties do have the option of filing a memorandum of lease instead of the lease itself. The memo states only the parties' names and addresses, property description, length of term, and any renewal rights without giving other details of the tenancy. This is done when the parties want to keep certain provisions (e.g., the rent amount) confidential.

Most leases also contain clauses concerning:

- Acceptable uses of the property.
- The right to assign or sublet.
- The required security deposit.
- The responsibility for repairs and maintenance.
- The landlord's right to access the property during the lease term.
- The tenant's responsibility for alterations or damage to the property.
- Renewal rights.
- The consequences of default.

Ohio law requires a residential lease to state the name and address of the landlord. If the landlord has an agent (e.g., property manager), the name and address of the agent is also required. The tenant must be given this information in writing, even when the lease itself is oral. If the tenant is not given this information, the landlord waives the right to receive certain legal notices from the tenant. Those notices will be explained later in this chapter.

Types of Leases

There are important distinctions between residential and commercial leases, which will be discussed in greater detail later. While residential leases are usually straightforward exchanges of rent for occupancy, commercial leases are usually more complex and can come in many forms. The four main types of commercial leases are:

1. Gross lease
2. Net lease
3. Percentage lease
4. Land lease (also called ground lease)

Gross Lease

A **gross lease** is *a lease for which the owner or landlord pays all property taxes, mortgage payments, insurance, etc., and the tenant pays all utilities.* This is similar to a residential lease except the commercial version can provide for future rent increases tied to inflation or taxes. A gross lease is usually used for tenants that are professional in nature (e.g., lawyers, doctors, executives).

Net Lease

A **net lease** is *a lease for which the tenant pays all property taxes, mortgage payments, insurance, etc., as well as all utilities, in addition to a monthly rent payment.* This is a variation of the gross lease and is used with similar types of tenants. The main difference is that the owner or landlord shifts much of the risk for increased costs to the tenants, who pay a proportional amount of the property taxes, insurance, and, sometimes, maintenance costs.

Percentage Lease

A **percentage lease** is *a lease for which the tenant pays a percentage of gross sales, often in addition to a fixed monthly rental payment.* This type of lease is most commonly used for retail tenants.

Land Lease

A **land lease** (or **ground lease**) is *a lease for which a tenant leases only the land from the landlord but the land tenant actually owns the building.* This usually is first done when the land is vacant, but either party can freely transfer their interests and obligations to subsequent purchasers who agree to abide by the terms of the land lease. This type of lease usually has a term equal to the life expectancy of the building but can be for up to 99 years.

Selling Leased Property

A landlord is free to sell the leased property at any time. The new owner takes the property subject to the existing leases, unless they provide otherwise. Also, in the case of existing leases for more than three years that are not recorded and of which the new owner had no notice, the new owner is *not* required to honor them.

When a new owner takes title subject to an existing lease, all former owner's rights and duties under the lease are transferred to the new owner. If the tenant gave the former owner a security deposit or paid any rent in advance, the former owner should either refund that money to the tenant or turn it over to the new owner (who must agree to hold it as a deposit or apply it to the rent). Unless the new owner is using the same property manager as the former owner, the tenant will have to be told whose name should appear on the rent checks and where to send them. A residential tenant must also be given the names and addresses of the new owner and his property agent.

Assignment versus Subleasing

A tenant can transfer his right of occupancy to another person either by **assignment** or **sublease**. We will examine both and the important distinction between the two.

Assignment

An **assignment** is *when a tenant transfers his entire right of possession or other interest in lease property to another person for the entire remainder of the lease term.* The important point is that an assignment transfers a tenant's entire interest, but this does not transfer a tenant's entire liability under the lease.

With an assignment, the **assignee** (the *second tenant*) and the **assignor** (the *original tenant*) share legal responsibility for paying rent to a landlord. The assignee has primary liability; the assignor has secondary liability. If the assignee does not pay, the landlord has a right to sue both the assignee and the assignor for the rent.

Sublease

A **sublease** is *when a tenant transfers only part of his right of possession or other interest in leased property to another person for part of the lease term.* The important distinction is that a sublease transfers something less than a tenant's entire interest.

Subleases take two forms:

1. A tenant transfers the right to occupy only part of the leased property, while continuing to occupy the rest of it (e.g., a store leasing retail space in a shopping center might sublease a small portion of its space to a salon or a jeweler).

2. A tenant transfers the right to occupy all of the property, but only for part of lease term's remainder.

A sublease does not alter the legal relationship between a landlord and the original tenant. The subtenant usually pays rent directly to the original tenant, who in turn pays the landlord. If the subtenant does not pay as agreed, it is still the original tenant who has full legal responsibility for paying the landlord. If the landlord does not get paid, he will sue only the original tenant.

For Example

T has a two-year lease on an apartment, from January 2010 through December 2011. In July 2011, he has an opportunity to take a three-month trip to South America, so he plans to rent the apartment to X for July, August, and September. Since T has not transferred his entire interest, this arrangement is a sublease. T is the **sublessor**, and X is the **sublessee** or **subtenant**. When T returns from South America at the beginning of October, X will move out and T will resume his tenancy for the rest of the lease term.

Now suppose that T's trip will last six months instead of three, so he will not be back until the beginning of January 2012, after his lease expires. T will rent the apartment to X for July through December 2011. Because T has transferred the entire remainder of his lease to X, their arrangement is an assignment instead of a sublease. T is the **assignor**, and X is the **assignee.**

Why bother to distinguish between an assignment and a sublease? It makes a difference in terms of liability. Neither a sublease nor an assignment lets the original tenant off the hook—the original tenant still owes the rent, whether or not a subtenant or assignee pays as agreed. If the original tenant has to pay the rent, he can sue a subtenant or assignee for reimbursement. But if a subtenant or assignee is judgment-proof, the original tenant—not the landlord—takes the loss.

Novation. A **novation** is *when one party to a contract withdraws and a new party is substituted (this must be done with the landlord's consent)*. By arranging a novation instead of an assignment or sublease, the original tenant is able to escape liability under the lease altogether. A novation replaces the lease between the landlord and the original tenant with a completely new lease between the landlord and the substitute tenant. In this way, the original tenant is released.

Landlord's Consent

Of course, a novation is possible only with the landlord's consent, since it is a new contract between the landlord and the substitute tenant. Landlords are generally unwilling to consent to a novation unless the substitute tenant is just as desirable and financially sound as the original tenant.

By contrast, the landlord's consent is not required for an assignment or sublease unless the original lease expressly states it is required or the original lease expressly forbids it. Many leases do contain a consent requirement, however. Sometimes, a lease forbids assignment without consent but does not require consent for subleasing (or vice versa). This is another reason why the technical distinction between an assignment and a sublease can be important.

Case Example

In 1968, the F.W. Woolworth Company leased space in a Toledo shopping center owned by the Joseph Brothers Company. The initial lease term would expire on January 31, 1990 and Woolworth had the option of renewing it for an additional five years, extending it until January 31, 1995. The lease prevented Woolworth from assigning its interest without Joseph Brothers' consent but permitted subleasing without consent.

Woolworth operated a store in the shopping center space until October 1982, when it decided to close the store. In March 1983, Woolworth executed an agreement transferring possession of the space to SCOA Industries until January 30, 1995. Woolworth then notified Joseph Brothers that it was exercising its option to extend its lease until January 31, 1995.

Case Example (cont.)

SCOA opened a Hills Department Store in the space, paying Woolworth much higher rent for it than Woolworth was paying Joseph Brothers. Joseph Brothers sued Woolworth for breach of the consent requirement in the lease.

Joseph Brothers claimed that the arrangement between Woolworth and SCOA was an assignment, not a sublease. The court, however, ruled in Woolworth's favor. The agreement with SCOA was a sublease, not an assignment, because it did not transfer Woolworth's entire interest. Woolworth would retake possession before its lease expired— although only for a single day (January 31, 1995). That was enough to make it a sublease, and Woolworth did not have to get Joseph Brothers' consent. *Joseph Bros. Co. v. F.W. Woolworth Co.*, 884 F.2d 369 (6th Cir. 1988).

If a lease requires landlord consent for assignment, but does not say anything about subleasing, a tenant can sublease without consent. And if the lease requires consent for subleasing but does not mention assignment, a tenant can assign without consent. In other words, courts will not interpret "assignment" to include "subleasing," or vice versa. This problem occurs because many people assume that assignment and subleasing are the same thing, and carelessly drafted leases often use the terms interchangeably.

 Real estate agents should never draft leases—not even experts in property management. This is an unauthorized practice of law in Ohio.

Withholding Consent. Many leases that require the landlord's consent for an assignment or subleases provide that the lessor cannot unreasonably withhold consent. There must be a good reason for refusing to accept the assignee or sublessee as a tenant.

Case Example

The tenants signed a two-year lease for an apartment. The lease stated they could not assign or sublease without the landlord's written consent, "which shall not be unreasonably withheld."

The tenants lived in the apartment for more than a year and decided to move out. They asked the landlord, Mr. Stern, for permission to sublet the apartment to a friend. Stern refused to consent to the sublease because their friend, Mrs. Hermann, was a widow. He explained that he once had a bad experience with a widow as a tenant. In his former experience, the widow herself was a good tenant but she remarried. Her new husband moved in with her and he turned out to be nothing but trouble for the landlord.

After Stern refused to consent to the sublease, the tenants moved out anyway and stopped paying rent. Stern sued, but the court ruled in favor of the tenants. They did not owe Stern any more rent because his refusal to accept Mrs. Hermann as a subtenant was unreasonable. It was arbitrary and irrational to decide not to rent to any single or widowed women on the basis of his past experience with one widow. *Stern v. Taft*, 49 Ohio App. 2d 405, 361 N.E.2d 279 (1976).

Formal Requirements

The requirements for a valid assignment or sublease are the same as those for a lease. The assignment or sublease must be in writing and signed by the assignor or sublessor if it will end more than a year after it is agreed to. The document must be acknowledged and recorded if the assignment or sublease will last for more than three years.

Occasionally, the terms of an assignment or sublease are just written in the margin of the original lease, which is then recorded a second time. Recording a separate assignment or sublease document is much clearer. This document should state the recording numbers (volume and page numbers) of the original lease for reference purposes.

Rights and Duties of the Landlord and Tenant

In Ohio, there are essentially two bodies of law that govern the rights and duties of landlords and tenants: One covering nonresidential property and the other governing residential property. Generally speaking, the nonresidential and residential markets are governed by different rules:

- **Nonresidential market**—Governed by the common law rules of buyer beware (**caveat emptor**), with severely limited rights on both sides of the lease.

- **Residential market**—The **Landlords and Tenants Act of 1974** creates obligations and remedies for both landlords and tenants which are non-negotiable. These duties and responsibilities imposed by the Act cannot be waived, even if both sides want to waive them or agree to do so.

In a lease, the landlord and tenant each agree to take on certain duties in exchange for certain rights. The law also imposes duties on each party, creating corresponding rights for the other.

Some of these duties and responsibilities imposed by law apply unless otherwise agreed (i.e., unless the lease says that they do not apply). But some of them apply no matter what the lease says—overriding any express lease provisions that conflict with them. In certain cases, the courts refer to a duty imposed by law as an **implied covenant** or **implied warranty**—the law makes it part of the lease, even though the parties did not.

Landlords and Tenants Act of 1974

In Ohio, most of the duties that apply no matter what is stated in the lease are the ones imposed by the Landlords and Tenants Act of 1974. The Act applies to all residential leases except proprietary leases for cooperative apartments, rental space in a mobile home park, and farm rentals with at least two acres of land. The Act also does *not* apply to hotels or motels, or institutional housing (e.g., prisons, hospitals) but it does apply to college dormitories.

The Act provides that the rights it establishes cannot be waived. If the Act imposes a particular duty on a landlord, the lease cannot contain a clause that says the landlord is not required to fulfill that duty—even if the tenant would be perfectly happy to agree to that. In the same way, if the Act gives a landlord a particular right, the lease cannot take that right away. Of course, either party may choose not to enforce his rights when a problem comes up, but neither one can make a binding contract to give up those rights for good.

Any of the rights and duties that are not based on the Landlords and Tenants Act may be waived by the terms of the lease. Thus, in a nonresidential lease, either party may agree to give up virtually any right he would otherwise have. In a residential lease, though, both parties can never give up certain rights. Those rights will be discussed in detail in this chapter. Residential leases may contain a waiver of some rights as agreed by the parties, as long as those rights are not specifically established or protected by the Landlords and Tenants Act of 1974.

Possession

Unless otherwise agreed, there is an implied covenant in every lease that the landlord will deliver possession of the property to the tenant on the date the lease term begins. If the tenant is prevented from taking possession, the landlord has breached this implied covenant.

For Example

The rental agreement says tenancy will begin on August 1st. But when the new tenant shows up on that day ready to move into the house, she discovers that the previous tenant has not moved out yet. It was up to the landlord to make sure the old tenant was out before August 1st and his failure to do so is a breach of the new lease.

When the covenant to deliver possession is breached, the tenant has the option of rescinding the lease. **Rescinding the lease** would involve asking the landlord to return any money already paid and finding another place to live or set up shop. The tenant may also decide not to rescind and wait for the landlord to deliver possession.

If the tenant decides to wait for possession instead of rescinding the lease, she will be entitled to damages because of the delay.

For Example

Continuing with the previous example, suppose the house was not ready for the new tenant until August 6th. If the new tenant chose to wait, she still must pay the August rent, but the landlord may have to reimburse her for the extra costs she incurred. That might include a five-night hotel bill, the cost of storing her furniture for six days, and additional moving expenses.

Rent

The tenant's primary duty is to pay the rent as agreed. Most leases state a specific date when rent is due, usually at the beginning of the rental period. If the lease does not specify when rent is to be paid, it is due at the end of the rental period.

A landlord can terminate a lease and evict the tenant for failure to pay the rent on time. But a landlord who repeatedly accepts late payments (with or without a late charge added) is considered to have waived the right to terminate the tenancy for late payment. To regain that right of eviction, the landlord must notify the tenant before the next rent payment is due that no more late payments will be accepted.

Case Example

Ms. Blackmon had been renting an apartment in Cincinnati from Mr. Spencer for five years. She was supposed to pay $235 at the beginning of each month, but she habitually paid late—sometimes not until the last day of the month. Spencer routinely sent Blackmon a "late notice" requesting her to pay a $10 late charge, and Blackmon routinely added the late charge to her rent when she finally paid.

On January 10, 1985, Spencer sent Blackmon the standard late notice. A few days later, they got into an argument over a matter unrelated to the rent. Spencer then began the eviction process, giving Blackmon a notice terminating the tenancy for nonpayment of rent. Blackmon sent Spencer the January rent check on the eighteenth, but he mailed it back to her.

In the eviction proceedings, the court ruled in favor of Blackmon. By accepting late payments for so long, Spencer had waived his right to terminate the tenancy on that ground. He should have sent Blackmon a notice informing her that the rent for February and all subsequent months would have to be paid on time. Then, if the February check came late, he could have terminated her tenancy. *Spencer v. Blackmon,* 22 Ohio Misc. 2d 52, 490 N.E.2d 943 (1985).

Privacy and Right of Entry

Privacy and the right of entry are part of the implied covenant of quiet enjoyment. The duties and responsibilities of each party vary depending on whether a nonresidential or residential lease is at issue.

Nonresidential

In a nonresidential tenancy, a landlord does not have the right to enter leased property without a tenant's consent, unless the lease specifically gives a landlord that right. The only exception that lets a landlord enter is to stop a tenant from committing **waste**—*abusing or damaging the property*. A nonresidential tenant can withhold consent for any reason, or no reason at all, unless otherwise agreed.

Residential

The **Landlords and Tenants Act** establishes different rules for residential tenancies, giving landlords a right of entry to:

* Inspect the leased apartment or house.

* Make ordinary, necessary, or agreed repairs or improvements.

* Deliver parcels that are too large for the mailbox.

* Supply necessary or agreed services.

* Show the property to prospective buyers, lenders, contractors, or tenants.

The landlord must obtain the tenant's consent to the entry, but the tenant may not unreasonably withhold consent.

To exercise the right of entry, a residential landlord has to follow certain rules. Except in an emergency, the landlord may enter the property only at reasonable times. This is usually interpreted to mean during ordinary business hours. The landlord is also required to give the tenant reasonable notice of his intent to enter, unless it is an emergency. Under state law, 24 hours' notice is presumed to be reasonable, but more or less notice may be reasonable depending on the circumstances.

Spencer v. Blackmon, the case discussed prior in connection with late rent payments, also involved the residential landlord's right of entry.

Case Example

A Cincinnati ordinance requiring landlords to install smoke detectors went into effect January 1, 1985. On January 8, Mr. Spencer went to his apartment building with a carpenter to install smoke detectors in compliance with the new ordinance. He did not notify the tenants in advance.

Spencer went to Ms. Blackmon's apartment and found she was not home. He tried to enter the apartment with a passkey but could not get in because Blackmon had installed an additional lock.

A few days later, Spencer asked Blackmon for a key to the new lock. She refused to give him one but said that she would allow him into the apartment anytime, as long as he notified her in advance. Spencer told her she would have to move if she was not willing to let him have a key and gave her an eviction notice.

In the eviction proceedings, Spencer argued that he was not required to give advance notice of his intent to enter on January 8 because it was an emergency. The court disagreed, ruling that even though Spencer should have complied with the smoke detector ordinance before January 1, his delay did not create an emergency. The court also ruled that Blackmon was not required to give Spencer a key to her lock. Blackmon was allowed to continue her tenancy, and Spencer was ordered to pay Blackmon's attorney's fees. *Spencer v. Blackmon*, 22 Ohio Misc. 2d 52, 490 N.E.2d 943 (1985).

Covenant of Quiet Enjoyment

The original legal basis for a tenant's right to privacy is something the courts call "the implied covenant of quiet enjoyment." The **covenant of quiet enjoyment** is considered part of every lease, unless otherwise agreed and *provides that the tenant has a right to undisturbed possession of the property during the lease term.* The tenant is protected from intrusion by the landlord or by anyone else claiming a right to the property. This covenant is breached if the tenant is wrongfully evicted.

Eviction

Eviction is *dispossessing or expelling someone from real property.* An eviction can be either:

- **Actual eviction**—Physically forcing someone off of property or preventing them from re-entering (e.g., changing the locks), or using the legal process to make someone leave.

- **Constructive eviction**—When a landlord's act (or failure to act) interferes with the tenant's quiet enjoyment of the property, or makes the property unfit for its intended use to such an extent that the tenant is forced to move out (e.g., it has become unsafe or uninhabitable).

For Example

T signed a two-year lease for an apartment in a large building. Sometime after he moved in, the building became infested with cockroaches. T did his best to exterminate them in his apartment, but it was hopeless. The whole building was infested, so the roaches kept coming back. T complained to the landlord, but the landlord did not take any action. T finally felt he needed to move out.

A breach of the covenant of quiet enjoyment (actual or constructive eviction) relieves the tenant of the duty to pay rent. To claim constructive eviction, though, the tenant must actually move off the property. In the previous example, T could not have stopped paying rent because of the roaches if he remained in the apartment.

Not every problem or disturbance can be the basis for a claim of constructive eviction, however. The problem must substantially interfere with the tenant's use of the property and it must be the landlord's responsibility. The following case from California illustrates that rule. An Ohio court would likely reach the same result.

Case Example

Mr. Brown leased an apartment. The lease stated that the landlord was not liable to the tenant for any damage resulting from the acts of other tenants in the building.

It turned out that the family in the apartment beneath Brown liked to sing and quarrel loudly at all hours. Brown could not get a good night's sleep. His complaints to the family and to the landlord had no effect, so he moved out and stopped paying rent. The landlord sued Brown for the rent money.

The court ruled in the landlord's favor. Since the lease expressly stated that the landlord was not responsible for the acts of the other tenants, the neighbors' noise was not constructive eviction. Brown was required to pay his rent. *Conterno v. Brown*, 263 Cal. App. 2d 135, 69 Cal. Rptr. 393 (1968).

```
┌─────────────────────────────────────────────┐
│             Constructive Eviction            │
│                                              │
│   • Substantial interference with use of     │
│     property                                 │
│                                              │
│   • Problem is landlord's responsibility     │
│                                              │
│   • Tenant must actually move out            │
│                                              │
│   • Duty to pay rent ends                    │
└─────────────────────────────────────────────┘
```

Maintenance, Repairs, and Habitability

Both tenants and landlords have some duties for maintenance, repairs, and the habitability of leased property. Again, these obligations vary for nonresidential and residential leases and can be:

- Express.
- Implied.
- Stated in the lease.
- Imposed by law.

Tenant's Duties—Nonresidential

Unless otherwise agreed, a nonresidential tenant is expected to maintain the leased property so that it is in more or less the same condition at the end of the tenancy as it was at the beginning. Of course, in the case of property with more than one rental unit (e.g., an office building), the tenant is not responsible for maintaining the common areas, such as the lobby, hallways, elevators, and parking lot. In some leases, the landlord agrees to maintain or repair the leased unit as well as the common areas.

The tenant must not intentionally or negligently damage any part of the property or permit guests to damage it. The tenant is expected to repair damage caused by:

- Unauthorized alterations.
- Failure to exercise ordinary care.
- Use of the property in a way it was not intended to be used.

If the tenant does not make these repairs, he is liable to the landlord for their cost. A tenant is *not* liable for the ordinary wear and tear that results from normal use of the property, though.

Tenant's Duties—Residential

The **Landlords and Tenants Act** imposes specific maintenance duties on residential tenants. The tenant is required to:

- Keep the rental unit safe and sanitary.
- Dispose of rubbish and garbage.
- Keep the plumbing fixtures clean.
- Use all electrical and plumbing fixtures properly.
- Comply with housing, health, and safety codes.

The tenant may also be responsible for keeping the appliances in working order if the lease specifically gives the tenant that duty. The tenant must not damage the property or remove any fixtures and must also forbid guests from causing damage.

In the lease, a residential landlord may agree to take on any or all of the maintenance duties that the Landlords and Tenants Act would otherwise require the tenant to perform. If the lease is silent, those basic duties are the tenant's responsibility. The lease may give the tenant additional responsibilities only if they are *not* duties the Landlords and Tenants Act specifically imposes on the landlord.

Landlord's Duties—Nonresidential

In Ohio, a nonresidential landlord is:

- Required to warn prospective tenants about known latent defects in the property—just as a seller is required to warn prospective buyers (see Chapter 3).

- Not required to put property into good condition before renting it.

- Not required to make sure that it is fit for the tenant's intended use.

There are no guarantees for a nonresidential tenant, except those expressly stated in the lease.

If the property is in such poor shape that it violates building, health, or fire codes, local authorities can make the landlord bring it into compliance. But disrepair and safety hazards are a breach of the nonresidential landlord's contract with the tenant only if the lease says so (unless the landlord fraudulently concealed the problems). A nonresidential tenant must protect himself or herself by inspecting the property thoroughly before signing the lease.

Furthermore, a nonresidential landlord is not obligated to maintain or repair the leased property once the tenancy begins. Many landlords agree to provide maintenance services (especially in office space leases), but they are not required to by law.

Landlord's Duties—Residential

A landlord's duties are a very different matter with residential property. Under the Landlords and Tenants Act, a residential landlord must:

- Comply with all building, housing, health, and safety code provisions that materially affect health and safety.

- Make all repairs and do whatever is necessary to put and keep the property in a fit and habitable condition.

- Keep the common areas safe and sanitary.

- Provide garbage receptacles and arrange for garbage pickup, if there are four apartments or more.

- Maintain the electrical, plumbing, sanitary, heating, ventilating, and air conditioning equipment in good and safe working order.

- Supply running water, hot water, and heat.

These duties are referred to as the **implied warranty of habitability**. *By offering residential property for rent, the landlord implicitly guarantees to the tenant that it is fit for human habitation.* Disclaimers in the lease cannot change that. If the property is not kept up to minimum standards, the Landlords and Tenants Act provides the tenant with legal remedies to force the landlord to fix the problems.

Residential Tenant's Remedies

When residential property falls below the standards of habitability set by the Landlords and Tenants Act, the tenant is not liable for the full amount of rent he agreed to pay. Instead, the tenant owes the landlord only the reasonable rental value of the property in its substandard condition.

Case Example

In September 1980, Mr. Simon rented an apartment in Shaker Heights from Mr. Howard. The apartment building had an air-conditioning system that was controlled by the landlord. Howard ran the air-conditioning during the summer, but it was his practice to turn the system off on any day when he felt the weather was cool enough.

Simon's apartment had a southern exposure and was directly under the tar roof, which made it much hotter than the outside temperature, and much hotter than the rest of the building. On many occasions when Howard turned off the air conditioning, the temperature in Simon's apartment rose well above 80, and opening the windows did almost nothing to cool it down.

Over the course of two summers, Simon complained to Howard about the air-conditioning 40-50 times. The last time, in July 1982, Simon started shouting and cursing at the landlord. After that incident, Howard decided to terminate Simon's tenancy (which was on a month-to-month basis). Simon refused to move out, so Howard filed suit to have him evicted.

In the eviction proceedings, Simon counterclaimed against the landlord. Simon argued that Howard's practice of turning off the air-conditioning violated the Landlords and Tenants Act's requirement that the system be kept in "good and safe working order." The court agreed. Although Simon was not entitled to stay on in the apartment, he was entitled to damages. The court estimated that the lack of air-conditioning reduced the value of Simon's apartment by $90 per month, for two months out of each of the two summers that he had lived there. Howard was ordered to repay Simon $360. *Howard v. Simon*, 18 Ohio App. 3d 14, 480 N.E.2d 99 (1984).

A landlord's breach of duty is frequently raised as a counterclaim in an eviction suit, as it was in the previous *Howard v. Simon* case. The tenants are often being evicted because they have not been paying the rent, and they claim they were not paying rent because of the property's bad condition. That counterclaim does not prevent the eviction. By not paying the rent, the tenants breached their lease and the landlord has the right to evict them. But the court may rule that the tenants owe the landlord less than the full amount of the agreed rent because of the property's reduced value.

The Landlords and Tenants Act sets up special remedies for tenants so they can force the landlord to fix the property without risking eviction. These remedies can be used if the landlord fails to fulfill any of the maintenance duties imposed by the Act, or any duties he agreed to take on in the lease.

Process for Special Remedies. To take advantage of these special remedies, the tenant's first step is to send the landlord a written notice describing the problem that needs to be fixed. If the lease did not include the names and addresses of the landlord and his agent, the landlord waived the right to receive this notice. The tenant must then give the landlord a reasonable amount of time to take care of the problem. How much time is "reasonable" depends on the severity of the problem and how long it will take to fix. In any case, the landlord must take action within 30 days.

If the landlord does not respond to a tenant's written complaint within a reasonable amount of time, the tenant has three options:

1. Move out and terminate the tenancy.

2. Start depositing the rent with the municipal or county court instead of paying it to the landlord.

3. Apply to the courts for an order directing the landlord to fix the problems.

To use any of these remedies, the tenant must be current in rent payments. When the tenant deposits rent with the court, the judge may allow the tenant to use some of the rent money to pay for the necessary repairs. This is often called the **repair and deduct remedy**.

The landlord may apply for a release of the rent money deposited with the court. The judge will release the money to the landlord after the problems are fixed. The judge will also release some of the deposited rent to the landlord, even before the repairs are made, if the landlord cannot otherwise afford to pay for the property's mortgage, insurance, taxes, or operating expenses, or if the money is needed in order to pay for the required repairs.

The landlord is also entitled to have the rent money released if he proves there was no actual violation of the lease or the Landlords and Tenants Act, or if the landlord proves the violations were caused by the tenant. If the judge determines that the tenant caused the violations or otherwise acted in bad faith, the tenant may be ordered to pay damages to the landlord, along with court costs and the landlord's attorney's fees.

The Landlords and Tenants Act's special remedies apply to all residential tenancies except private college dormitories. A building with three or fewer apartment units can also be exempted. For these properties to be excluded, though, the landlord must include a written provision in the lease explaining those remedies will not be available. Even if it is an oral lease, the landlord must still give this notice to the tenants in writing.

For Example

T rents an apartment in a three-unit building that belongs to L. The lease states that the tenant will not be able to deposit rent with the municipal court or use the other remedies provided in Ohio Revised Code § 5321.07 (if the lease did not include that notice, then T would be able to use the special remedies).

So what can T do if L does not fulfill the duties imposed by the Landlords and Tenants Act or the lease? If the violation is a substantial interference with her use of the apartment, she may be able to move out and claim constructive eviction, terminating the lease. Or T can go on living in the apartment, paying rent, and sue L. Her lawsuit may be based on breach of the lease, breach of a legal duty (a tort), or both.

Any tenant may choose to sue the landlord, whether or not the special remedies are available. The right to sue cannot be waived in a lease. The tenant will have to prove, though, that the landlord was notified of the need for repairs and failed to respond. In this type of situation, the tenant may be entitled to damages that go well beyond a reduction in the amount of rent owed.

Case Example

Mrs. Allen was 58 years old and physically disabled. She signed a one-year lease to rent a single-family home from Mr. Lee for $272 a month. The Cuyahoga County housing authority would pay $226 toward each month's rent, and Allen would pay the additional $46.

The property was in terrible condition when Allen rented it. She claimed that Lee promised to clean the house and perform many repairs before she moved in. Lee, however, did not clean or repair the house. When Allen moved in, there was dirt and grime everywhere; rubbish in the basement; rotting porches; broken windows; holes in interior walls and floors; a corroded, peeling bathtub that would not drain; broken pipes that made it impossible to use the washing machine; and rats and cockroaches—among other problems.

Allen stayed in the house for four months because she could not afford to move again without the housing authority's approval. The housing authority finally terminated the lease and allowed her to move. But while Allen was waiting for the housing authority to respond, she suffered a breakdown and was hospitalized for ten days. She claimed the breakdown was caused by the distress she experienced in her horrible living conditions. She was particularly afraid of the rats that infested the house.

Six weeks after she moved out, Allen sued Lee. The court ordered Lee to pay Allen $4,588 as compensatory and punitive damages, plus $2,820 in attorney's fees. The damages were intended to cover Allen's moving expenses and hospital bills, as well as to compensate her for the emotional distress she suffered as a result of Lee's breach of duty. *Allen v. Lee,* 43 Ohio App. 3d 31, 538 N.E.2d 1073 (1987).

In the previous *Allen vs. Lee* case, the landlord denied promising to clean and repair the property before the tenant moved in. The court held, though, that it did not matter whether or not he made any promises because he had a legal duty to put the house in habitable condition at the beginning of the lease, and to maintain it throughout the tenancy. His failure to do so probably ended up costing him more than the repairs would have.

Security Deposits

Security deposits are required by most landlords as a way of ensuring that tenants comply with all the provisions of a lease. This includes payment of all rents owed. Unfortunately, it is not uncommon for a tenant to move out without paying all the rent due and/or leaving the property in a mess or even badly damaged. To protect themselves, most landlords require a tenant to pay a security deposit before the tenancy begins.

If the tenant pays the rent and keeps the property in good condition, the entire security deposit is to be refunded when the lease ends and possession is returned to the landlord. If the tenant still owes rent, however, the landlord can keep part or all of the deposit to cover the unpaid amount.

Furthermore, if the tenant breaches the terms of the lease or (in a residential tenancy) fails to look after the property to the extent required by the Landlords and Tenants Act, the landlord can keep part or all of the deposit to cover any resulting damages. However, a security deposit is *not* supposed to be used to repair ordinary wear and tear or to put the property into better shape than when the tenant moved in.

Case Example

Ms. Albreqt rented an apartment in Maumee from Dr. Chen. Albreqt gave Chen a $285 security deposit. When Albreqt moved out several months later, Chen returned only part of the deposit. He kept $30 to cover the cost of carpet cleaning, $8 for repairing a towel rack, $65 for repairing water-damaged wallpaper and plaster in the bathroom, and $32 to replace curtain rods that Albreqt had removed.

Albreqt sued Chen to recover the portion of the security deposit he had retained. The court ruled in Chen's favor regarding the curtain rods, reasoning that although Albreqt had put the curtain rods up herself, the lease clearly stated that any fixtures the tenant installed would become the property of the landlord.

The court sided with Albreqt, though, regarding the other items. Albreqt had left the carpet as clean as it was when she moved in (or even cleaner), so she could not be charged for the cleaning costs. She also could not be held responsible for the cost of repairing the towel rack or the bathroom wall, since they were already in bad condition when her tenancy began. *Albreqt v. Chen*, 17 Ohio App. 3d 79, 477 N.E.2d 1150 (1983).

If a tenant (residential or nonresidential) caused severe damage and the repair costs are greater than the amount of the security deposit, the landlord may sue to collect the additional amount. The security deposit does not limit the tenant's liability, because the deposit is not treated as liquidated damages (see Chapter 8 for a discussion of contracts and liquidated damages).

For Example

The tenant gave the landlord a $200 security deposit. When the tenant moved in, the carpet was fairly new and in good condition. When he moved out six months later, the carpet had coffee stains in several places and a rather large number of cigarette burns. Let's suppose that it will cost the landlord $525 to replace the carpet. The landlord could sue the tenant for $325—the amount the security deposit did not cover. The court would consider whether it had been reasonably necessary to replace the carpet. If so, the landlord would be entitled to the full amount of damages.

Residential. Ohio law does not limit the amount a landlord may demand as a security deposit, but the Landlords and Tenants Act requires a residential landlord to pay interest of 5% on any deposit, or portion thereof, which exceeds $50 or exceeds one month's rent, whichever is greater.

For Example

When a tenant rents an apartment for $200 a month with a $275 security deposit, the landlord must pay 5% interest on $75.

The accrued interest must be turned over to the tenant annually. In the event that a tenant stays for less than six months, though, the landlord is not required to pay interest, no matter how much the deposit was.

Within 30 days after a residential tenant moves out, the landlord must return the security deposit, or give the tenant a written itemized statement explaining why all, or part, of the deposit has been retained. If the landlord does not give the tenant an itemized statement or wrongfully withholds part of the deposit, the tenant can sue. The court may order the landlord to pay twice the amount that was wrongfully withheld, plus the tenant's attorney's fees. This is true even if the landlord acted in good faith and was simply mistaken about how much he was entitled to keep.

A tenant who does not leave a forwarding address—so the landlord cannot send the deposit or statement—is not entitled to damages or attorney's fees.

Nonresidential. Remember, these rules do not apply to nonresidential tenancies. A commercial landlord in Ohio is not required to pay interest on a security deposit or to give the tenant an itemized statement at the end of the tenancy. A commercial tenant, however, can sue to recover any part of the deposit he feels was wrongfully withheld.

Liability for Personal Injuries on Leased Property

The legal concept of a **tort** was discussed briefly in Chapter 1. When A injures B, the rules of tort law make A liable to B. A is required to pay damages compensating B for the costs of the injury. Although that simple statement sums up the general idea of tort liability, actual tort lawsuits are not that simple.

Most injuries are accidental, not deliberate, and some accidents are unavoidable. In a tort lawsuit based on accidental injuries, the defendant usually is not liable unless he was negligent. **Negligence** is *any conduct that falls below the standard of care that a reasonable person would exercise under the circumstances.* That means the defendant did not act as carefully as he should have.

How carefully one is required to act depends on the situation: Sometimes, a person has no duty of care towards another person; other times, a person has a great duty of care. Proving that a defendant was negligent involves showing that he had a duty of care toward the plaintiff and breached that duty. To win a tort lawsuit, the plaintiff also must prove that the defendant's negligence caused the injuries.

Torts

There are four basic elements to a tort claim:

1. Duty
2. Breach
3. Injury
4. Causation

The elements must occur in that order from a legal standpoint. First, a person must have a duty to others, which is breached, and a person is injured as a causation of the breach. In reality, of course, the injury occurs first, then someone tries to prove the causation of the injury was the breach of a duty. Proving an injury is usually the easy part, and often showing causation is not difficult either. Where tort claims become complicated is establishing who had a duty to whom (whose fault or responsibility was the injury) and that the breached duty created liability.

Duty and Liability. The law imposes on landowners a duty of care toward other people who enter their property. If the landowner breaches that duty and someone is injured as a result, the landowner can be sued by the injured person.

In Ohio, a landowner's duty of care varies considerably, depending on what the other person is doing on the property.

For Example

If the person is a trespasser, the landowner's duty is very limited—the landowner is merely supposed to avoid "wanton, willful, or reckless misconduct" that is likely to injure the trespasser. (See *Jeffers v. Olexo*, 43 Ohio St. 3d 140, 539 N.E.2d 614 (1989)).

On the other hand, if the person is a business visitor, the landowner is required to exercise reasonable care to protect the visitor from harm. That means inspecting the property for hazards and warning the visitor about hidden dangers. A business visitor is anyone who enters the property at the landowner's invitation, for a purpose that benefits the landowner.

For Example

A mail carrier crossing A's lawn and coming up on the front porch to deliver letters is one example of a business visitor; a customer entering a store is another.

Those rules concerning a landowner's liability apply to leased property, just as they apply to property occupied by the owner. But there is a complication because, in some cases, a landlord can be held liable for injuries that occur on the leased property; in other cases, the tenant can be held liable; and, in still other cases, both can be held liable. With leased property, liability depends on control.

Traditionally, a landlord was held to give up control over the leased property as soon as the tenancy began. The tenant stepped into the role of the landowner.

For Example

If the meter reader broke his leg when the porch railing collapsed, the tenant usually could be held liable, and the landlord could not. In addition, the landlord usually could not be held liable if it was the tenant who got hurt when the porch railing collapsed. The tenant had control of the property and the landlord did not, so the landlord was not responsible for the tenant's injuries, or anyone else's.

There was one main exception: The landlord was liable for injuries caused by a hidden defect if the landlord knew of the defect before the tenancy began and failed to warn the tenant about it.

Nonresidential Leases. For nonresidential property, those are still the general rules. A nonresidential landlord relinquishes control over the leased property when the tenancy begins. Unless otherwise agreed, however, the landlord retains control over the common areas of the property (e.g., office building's elevators, shopping center's parking lot). The landlord can be held liable for injuries that occur in common areas, but not for those that occur in leased areas.

The rules change if the nonresidential landlord takes on the duty of maintaining and repairing the leased property. Then, the landlord can be held liable for injuries caused by a failure to perform that duty.

For Example

A doctor rents a small office building from L. In the lease, L agrees to perform all necessary maintenance and repairs to keep the property safe during the tenancy. One morning when the doctor's receptionist comes to work, she notices the railing on the front stairway is very wobbly. She calls L, who says he will take care of it.

L does not take care of the problem right away, though. A week later, an elderly patient leans on the railing too hard. The railing gives way, and the patient falls off the stairs, cracking his skull. L can be held liable. The doctor (L's tenant) might also be held liable for failing to warn the patient about the wobbly railing. In this situation, the landlord and the tenant share control of the leased property.

Notice is an important factor in determining a landlord's liability. In the previous example, the receptionist gave L **actual notice** that the railing needed to be repaired. If L had not been alerted to the problem, he probably would not have been held liable. In some situations, however, the landlord has **constructive notice** of a problem—he should have known about it even if he did not—and will be held responsible on that basis.

Residential Leases. Just like a nonresidential landlord, a residential landlord can be held liable for injuries that occur in the common areas of the property. In Ohio, a residential landlord's liability extends to the leased unit as well—even if the landlord did not agree to maintain or repair the property in the lease. This is because the Landlords and Tenants Act gives the landlord the duty to "keep the premises in a fit and habitable condition." The landlord can be held liable for injuries caused by conditions that resulted from his failure to keep the property habitable.

For Example

Something is wrong with the wiring in T's apartment and all the electrical outlets on the east wall of the kitchen are dead. To keep the refrigerator running, T plugs an extension cord into an outlet on the other side of the kitchen. Since that outlet is already handling a microwave and some small appliances, it is dangerously overloaded.

T calls the landlord, who lives in one of the other apartments. She comes over to look at T's kitchen and says she will be able to fix the wiring in a day or two. The landlord does not come back as promised, though, so T goes on living with the extension cord. Six weeks later, a fire starts in the overloaded outlet. T and a guest are badly burned and most of T's personal property is destroyed.

If T and his guest sue, the landlord will probably have to compensate both of them for their injuries, as well as for the property loss. The landlord is liable for negligently failing to keep the electrical system in safe working order. She had a duty to T. She breached that duty, and that caused the injuries.

The landlord may argue that T was negligent, too, since he overloaded the electrical outlet.

A plaintiff's negligence may reduce the amount of damages the defendant must pay in certain cases, but it does not eliminate the defendant's liability. In the previous example, the jury might decide to allocate 15% of the responsibility for the fire to T and 85% to the landlord—T's damages award would be reduced by 15%. In addition, T would probably be liable for 15% of the guest's damages. This sharing of responsibility for damages is known as the **comparative negligence rule** in tort law.

Exculpatory Clauses. Sometimes a lease includes an **exculpatory clause**, which states the landlord cannot be held liable if the tenant or someone else is injured on the leased property. In Ohio, an exculpatory clause in a nonresidential lease is enforceable—it lets the landlord off the hook. An exculpatory clause in a residential lease is void. Under the Landlords and Tenants Act, a residential tenant cannot waive the right to sue the landlord for personal injuries.

Termination of a Lease

A lease for a fixed term is an estate for years (see Chapter 6) that terminates on a specific date. Sometimes, when a lease is about to expire, the parties decide to renew it. They may renegotiate the terms of the lease and the rent may be adjusted.

A lease can also be renewed even if a landlord and tenant do not expressly agree to renew. If the tenant retains possession after the lease expires and the landlord continues accepting rent, it is presumed they have renewed the lease on the same terms. With an implied renewal, if rent is paid monthly, the new lease is month-to-month.

For Example

T rented L's house for a one-year term, paying $475 a month in rent. At the end of the year, the lease expires but T does not move out. He continues to pay L $475 a month. This is an implied renewal, and T and L have the same duties as they had under the original lease; though now, instead of an estate for years, T has a month-to-month periodic tenancy.

Nothing seems to have changed. T is paying L $475 each month, just as he always has, but the lease term is now only one month long, not one year. Either T or L can terminate the periodic tenancy by giving notice to the other party.

Nonresidential

Notice of termination for a nonresidential periodic tenancy is controlled by the lease, not by law. The lease may require the notice to be in writing. Thirty days' notice is standard for a month-to-month tenancy, but the lease may set a longer or shorter notice period.

Residential

For residential tenancies in Ohio, the Landlords and Tenants Act governs notice of termination. To terminate a residential month-to-month tenancy, at least 30 days' notice must be given before the end of the period and written notice is not required. If neither party gives notice, the tenancy is automatically renewed for another month. Similarly, a residential week-to-week tenancy requires only seven days' notice and is renewed for another week if no one gives notice. If a lease says more notice is required or less notice is allowed, that provision is unenforceable.

Although a periodic lease can be terminated at any time by giving notice, a lease for a fixed term cannot. Both landlord and tenant are bound by the lease until the term expires, unless otherwise agreed. This is true even if one party dies.

A fixed-term lease can be terminated before it expires in one of four ways:

1. Surrender
2. Destruction of the building
3. Eviction
4. Abandonment

Surrender

Surrender is *giving up an estate before it expires*. In this case, both tenant and landlord would like to terminate the lease before its term expires, so they agree to do so. In this case, the tenant gives up possession and owes no further rent.

Destruction of the Building

Destruction of the building includes fires, floods, tornados, or other disaster. When all or part of a building (e.g., office, apartment) is leased, the lease's purpose is frustrated if the building is destroyed. In Ohio, destruction or severe damage ends the tenancy and releases the tenant from paying rent, unless otherwise agreed.

Eviction

Eviction is *dispossessing or expelling someone from real property*. Eviction is the process by which a landlord regains possession of the property from a tenant who is unwilling to give it up. Here, we will discuss the eviction process and several types of eviction.

In Ohio, a landlord has a right to evict a tenant in one of these circumstances *only*:

- The tenant is holding over after the lease term has expired.
- The tenant has breached an obligation imposed by a written lease.
- A residential tenant has not paid the rent.
- A residential tenant has breached an obligation imposed by the Landlords and Tenants Act that materially affects health and safety.
- For a residential building, compliance with a building, housing, health, or safety code would require demolition or alterations so substantial the tenant could not remain on the property.

Nearly every written lease states that the tenant is required to pay rent; so, failure to pay rent is almost always grounds for eviction. But, if a nonresidential written lease fails to mention the tenant's obligation to pay rent, the landlord cannot evict the tenant for nonpayment. A nonresidential landlord with an oral lease cannot evict the tenant for nonpayment, either. The landlord can sue for payment of the overdue amount but cannot sue to regain possession of the property.

Eviction Process

The eviction process is comprised of three basic steps:

1. Notice to vacate
2. Forcible entry and detainer action
3. Writ of execution

These steps must be followed, in order, as prescribed by law.

Notice to Vacate. A **notice to vacate** (also called a **notice to quit**) is *a notice to a tenant demanding that he vacate the leased property*. For most evictions, this is the landlord's first step. The landlord sends a written notice that tells the tenant to move out and explains that legal action to regain possession will begin if he does not move out. It has to be served on the tenant at least three business days before the landlord files a lawsuit for eviction. If a residential tenancy, the notice must say:

> "You are being asked to leave the premises. If you do not leave, an eviction action may be initiated against you. If you are in doubt regarding your legal rights and obligations as a tenant, it is recommended that you seek legal assistance."

For a residential eviction based on breach of an obligation affecting health and safety, the landlord's first step is to send a notice stating the tenancy will terminate on a particular date unless the tenant takes care of the problem by then. The termination date must be at least 30 days after the notice is delivered to the tenant. If the termination date arrives and the tenant still has not complied with the Landlords and Tenants Act, the landlord may serve a three-day notice to vacate.

Forcible Entry and Detainer. A **forcible entry and detainer action** is *a lawsuit filed by a landlord to evict a defaulting tenant and regain possession of the property*. This is also called an **unlawful detainer action**. The landlord may begin legal proceedings to evict the tenant when a tenant does not move out within three days (or other time specified in the notice) after receiving a notice to vacate. These legal proceedings both use the word "detainer" because the tenant is "detaining" the property without right and against the landlord's wishes.

An unlawful detainer action can be filed in county court, municipal court, or common pleas court, depending on where the property is located and the amount in controversy (see Chapter 1). Because possession of property is at issue (not just money), unlawful detainer suits are supposed to be resolved as quickly as possible and take priority on a court's schedule. Procedures are expedited as well, so a tenant may be given only five days, instead of 28 days, to answer the summons and complaint.

The central issue at trial is whether the landlord has a right to possession of the property. In some cases, other issues are decided at the same time (e.g., whether one party is entitled to damages because the other breached the lease). In other cases, though, those issues will be dealt with later in a separate trial that does not have priority on the court's schedule.

Writ of execution. A **writ of execution** is *a court order directing a public officer (often the sheriff or marshal) to seize and/or sell property to regain possession for the owner and/or satisfy a debt*. If the court finds that the landlord is entitled to possession of the property, a writ of execution is issued to the sheriff. If the tenant does not move out within ten days, the sheriff can forcibly remove the tenant and his belongings from the property. If the tenant files an appeal, the court will issue a stay of execution, directing the sheriff to wait for further orders from the court.

Self-Help Eviction

A **self-help eviction** is *when a landlord uses physical force, a lockout, or a utility shut-off to get rid of a tenant, instead of the legal process*. This occurs despite expedited procedures, because the legal eviction process often seems slow to the landlord. Some leases include a clause giving the landlord the right to retake possession without going through the legal process if the tenant defaults.

Nonresidential. In Ohio, such a "self-help" provision in a nonresidential lease is valid. After following any notice procedures stated in the lease, the landlord can simply demand that the tenant move out immediately. The landlord can send an individual to act as the landlord's agent to oversee the eviction, but the eviction cannot involve a breach of the peace and the landlord's agents cannot use force. If the tenant resists—yells or becomes violent—the landlord's agents must cease and desist. The landlord can avoid that problem by retaking possession in the tenant's absence and changing the locks.

Residential. Under the Landlords and Tenants Act, "self-help" provisions are illegal, and a residential landlord is not allowed to force tenants off the property by any means other than the legal process. It is illegal for the landlord to threaten the tenants, lock them out, or shut off utility services to make them leave. If the landlord takes any of those actions, the tenants can sue, and the court may award the tenants damages and attorney's fees.

Case Example

The Thomases rented an apartment from Mr. Papadelis on November 10, 1982. The lease stated that if tenants caused trouble, Papadelis could give a three-day notice to vacate and lock them out if they did not leave.

After paying their first week's rent on time, the Thomases stopped paying rent altogether. In late November, Papadelis sent them a notice to vacate, but the Thomases did not move. Finally, in January 1983, Papadelis changed the locks while the Thomases were away from the apartment. Two days later, a court ordered Papadelis to allow the Thomases to return to the apartment. He did so, and they stayed until April 1983 without paying any rent.

The Thomases sued Papadelis for wrongful eviction. He countersued for the unpaid rent. The court awarded the Thomases nominal (token) damages of $50, plus $1,500 attorney's fees. It awarded Papadelis $1,127 in unpaid rent.

Papadelis wanted to offset his $1,127 judgment against the Thomases' $1,550 judgment, so he would have to pay them only $423. But the court ordered him to pay the full $1,550, even though the Thomases were probably judgment-proof and might never pay Papadelis the $1,127. However, the court did order that the $1,500 for attorney's fees be paid directly to the Thomases' lawyer, not to the Thomases themselves. *Thomas v. Papadelis*, 16 Ohio App. 3d 359, 476 N.E.2d 726 (1984).

Retaliatory Eviction

A **retaliatory eviction** is *when a landlord evicts a tenant in retaliation for complaining about the condition of the property, code violations, violations of the Landlords and Tenants Act, or for participating in a tenants' rights group.* This is called retaliatory eviction because the landlord is retaliating against the tenant for asserting his rights. The Landlords and Tenants Act makes retaliatory eviction illegal in residential tenancies.

Specifically, the Act prohibits a residential landlord from evicting, or threatening to evict, a tenant if the tenant has:

- Complained to a government agency about violations affecting health and safety.
- Complained to the landlord about violations of Landlords and Tenants Act.
- Joined with other tenants to negotiate terms of the lease with the landlord.

The Act also prohibits a landlord from raising the rent or reducing services in retaliation for the tenant's actions. Of course, the Act does not prevent a landlord from raising the rent for legitimate reasons (e.g., to reflect the cost of property improvements or to cover an increase in operating costs.).

When a landlord takes any type of retaliatory action, the tenant has the right to terminate the tenancy. In addition, or instead, the tenant can sue the landlord for damages. The court may also award the tenant attorney's fees.

In an unlawful detainer action, a tenant who proves that the lawsuit was retaliatory is entitled to stay in possession of the property. But a tenant cannot use the landlord's retaliatory motives as a defense against eviction if the tenant failed to pay rent or is holding over after expiration of the lease.

Abandonment

Abandonment is failure to occupy and use property, which may result in a loss of rights. Sometimes a tenant moves out (or simply disappears) before the lease expires and stops paying the rent. Obviously, an eviction lawsuit is not necessary in these cases, since the tenant has already relinquished possession, but the landlord may still sue the tenant for damages.

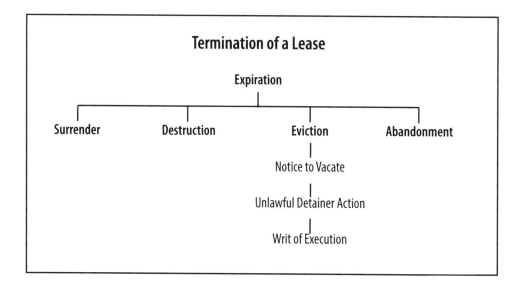

Landlord's Damages

When a landlord sues a tenant for damages, the landlord is entitled to a judgment for any overdue rent and for the cost of necessary repairs, minus the amount of the security deposit. If the tenant abandoned the property before the lease expired, the landlord's damages may also include rent for the time the apartment was vacant while the landlord looked for a new tenant (up to the point when the lease would have expired). In addition, the damages may cover what it cost the landlord to advertise for a new tenant.

For Example

In January 2009, T signed a two-year lease for L's house, giving L a $300 security deposit and agreeing to pay $500 a month for rent. But in June of that same year, T lost her job. She could not pay the rent due on July 1 and a few days later, she moved out and went to stay with her brother.

L cleaned up the house and began advertising it for rent again. She did not find a new tenant until mid-October, however. The new tenancy began November 1.

L sues T for damages. The court orders T to pay L not just the July rent, but the rent due up until November 1—a total of $2,000. T also owes L $135, which was the cost of the classified ads L ran in the newspaper to try and re-rent the apartment. The $300 security deposit that L retained will be deducted from the judgment, and T will be obligated to pay the rest of the damage award to L.

In some cases, the landlord is not able to find another tenant who is willing to pay the same rent as the tenant who abandoned the property.

For Example

Continuing with the previous example, suppose L's new tenant agrees to pay only $450 a month, instead of the $500 T was paying. Then, T could be ordered to pay L an additional $700 in damages: $50 x 14 = $700. That would be the $50 difference for 14 months, from November 2009 through December 2010 (when T's lease term was supposed to end).

Duty to Mitigate Damages

As we saw in Chapter 8, all parties who are wronged by another party in a contract still have an obligation to **mitigate** (lessen) damages. A lease is a contract, so it is no different. If a tenant leaves and still owes the landlord money, the landlord is required to lessen his potential losses.

For Example

A landlord could mitigate his damages by renting the property again after abandonment. By finding a new tenant who will start paying rent, the landlord reduces the amount of damages caused by the former tenant's breach of the lease. As a result, the former tenant cannot be held liable for the full amount of the rent he would have owed under the original lease, since that would overcompensate the landlord and amount to punitive damages against the former tenant.

In most states, it has been ruled by the courts that the landlord has a duty to mitigate damages by finding a new tenant. That is now the rule in Ohio, also. In past Ohio cases, former tenants were ordered to pay the full amount of rent owed for the entire remainder of the lease term, even though the landlord made no effort to rent the property again. Today's courts, though, are inclined to require a reasonable attempt at re-renting. If the former tenant can prove the property could have been rented again sooner than it was, or for more money, the court might reduce the landlord's damage award.

Damages after Eviction

An issue that is not completely settled in Ohio is what damages must be paid by an evicted tenant (as opposed to a tenant who has abandoned the property). At least one Ohio court of appeals has held that a tenant cannot be ordered to pay any rent for the period after the landlord sent a notice to vacate, even though the property was unoccupied while the landlord looked for a new tenant.

In *Cubbon v. Locker*, 5 Ohio App. 3d 200, 450 N.E.2d 697 (1982), the Court of Appeals for Lucas County reasoned that by choosing to evict the tenant, the landlord forfeited the lease and was not entitled to any further rent from the evicted tenant. Of course, the evicted tenant could be held liable for any rent still owed for the period before the notice to vacate was sent.

On the other hand, in *Briggs v. MacSwain*, 31 Ohio App. 3d 85, 508 N.E.2d 1028 (1986), the Court of Appeals for Franklin County specifically disagreed with the Cubbon decision. In Briggs, the tenant had a one-year lease that was due to expire at the end of March 1986. On January 8, 1986, the landlord sent her a notice to vacate because she had not paid the January rent. The tenant moved out on January 31, and the landlord rented the apartment to a new tenant at the same rate beginning on March 1. When the landlord sued the former tenant for damages, the former tenant was ordered to pay the February rent as well as the January rent. The court argued that eviction should not allow a defaulting tenant to escape her obligations under the terms of the lease.

Landlord/Tenant Law in Mobile Home Parks

In a mobile home park (or manufactured home park), residents usually own their homes and rent a small piece of land from the park owners. Tenants in mobile home parks run into a number of problems other residential tenants do not have:

- It is much more difficult for a mobile home owner to move than for an ordinary tenant.

- In many communities, there are very few mobile home parks with very few vacancies.

- It can be expensive to move a mobile home, especially a large one.

To address these problems, the Ohio General Assembly adopted a special landlord/tenant law for mobile home parks, Ohio Revised Code § 3733.09-3733.20. This law gives park owners and park tenants rights and duties that are very similar to the ones established in the Landlords and Tenants Act.

For Example

It requires owners and tenants to keep the park and the mobile homes up to minimum standards of safety and sanitation, and it prohibits retaliatory eviction.

In addition, the law has provisions that give mobile home park tenants more control over the duration of their tenancies than other tenants have. Rather than explaining all of these provisions, let's look at one example:

For Example

Some park owners would prefer to have all tenants on a month-to-month basis so they can get rid of them with 30 days' notice. The law, however, requires a park owner to offer a tenant a lease for a term of one year or more. The terms of that lease must be essentially the same as those offered for a month-to-month tenancy. That prevents park owners from encouraging tenants to take a month-to-month tenancy instead of a year's lease by making the month-to-month rent lower or more attractive in some other way. If the tenant does not want to make a commitment to stay in the park for a year, he can choose the month-to-month lease. There must be the option of a year's lease, however, and there cannot be incentives to try to get tenants to take the month-to-month lease option.

Rent Control

Rent control laws are local ordinances that set maximum limits on the amount of rent a landlord may charge. Many ordinances have a "vacancy decontrol" provision, allowing a landlord to raise the rent at the beginning of a new tenancy. Those ordinances usually restrict the landlord's ability to terminate a tenancy, though. Without such a provision, the landlord would be tempted to trade in old tenants for new ones as often as possible so rent could increase.

The intent of these laws is to make rental property available at reasonable rates when there is a housing shortage. Rent control is very controversial, however. Its opponents argue it actually causes housing shortages by making residential rentals unprofitable for property owners.

Although there are many communities in California and New York that have adopted residential rent control ordinances, rent control has not caught on in Ohio. The Ohio General Assembly considered a state rent control bill at one point, but it did not pass.

Summary

1. A **lease** is both a conveyance and a contract. It creates a **leasehold estate** that temporarily transfers the right of possession of property from landlord to tenant. The requirements for a valid lease are the same as those for a valid contract. Furthermore, a lease must be *in writing* and *signed by the landlord* if it will end more than one year after it was made. A lease for more than three years must also be *acknowledged* and *recorded*.

2. Basic lease provisions include the parties' names, amount of rent, when rent is due, and term of the lease. Four basic types of commercial leases are **gross lease**, **net lease**, **percentage lease**, and **land lease**. A buyer of leased property takes it subject to the existing leases, unless the existing leases provide otherwise or are not recorded. **Assignment** or **subleasing** is allowed unless the lease forbids or conditions it, but the original tenant is still liable for the rent.

3. A **nonresidential landlord** may *not* enter the property without the tenant's permission, unless otherwise agreed. Except in an emergency, a **residential landlord** must obtain the tenant's consent and give reasonable notice before entering. A **residential tenant** may not unreasonably withhold consent. The implied **covenant of quiet enjoyment** gives a tenant the right to undisturbed possession of the property. The covenant is breached by **constructive eviction** when property becomes uninhabitable or unusable. This relieves the tenant of the duty to pay rent. To claim constructive eviction, a tenant must move out.

4. Different standards govern landlord/tenant relationships in nonresidential and residential leases. **Nonresidential leases** are governed by caveat emptor and stated lease terms. **Residential leases** are governed by the **Landlords and Tenants Act**, giving both parties statutory duties that cannot be waived. **Nonresidential landlords** must warn tenants of known latent defects, but do not have to put property into good condition. **Residential landlords** must make buildings fit for human habitation and keep them fit during the tenancy.

5. If a **residential landlord** does not make repairs as agreed, or within a reasonable time as required by law, the tenant can pay rent to the courts. The tenant is liable only for the reasonable rental value of the property in its substandard condition. A landlord can keep a tenant's **security deposit** to cover unpaid rent or damage, but not for ordinary wear and tear. A **residential landlord** must give an itemized explanation if the full deposit is not returned. **Tort** liability for injuries is based on **negligence**. A landlord with a duty to repair may be held liable for injuries that occur because of unrepaired problems.

6. A periodic lease is renewed unless one party gives **notice of termination**. A fixed-term lease expires on a specific date unless the parties agree to renew. It can be terminated early by **surrender**, **destruction of the building**, **eviction**, or **abandonment**. In eviction, the landlord sends a **notice to vacate**. If the tenant does not move out, the landlord files an **unlawful detainer action**. If the court finds the landlord is entitled to possession, a **writ of execution** is issued. **Self-help eviction** and **retaliatory eviction** are illegal for residential landlords.

Quiz

1. **The Landlords and Tenants Act of 1974 applies**

   a. only to cities with a population of 20,000 or more.

   b. only to residential and commercial property.

   c. only to residential property.

   d. to all leased real property in Ohio.

2. **Which lease does NOT have to be in writing?**

   a. a month-to-month lease for a single-family home

   b. a one-year lease that will begin immediately and has an option to renew for one additional year

   c. a one-year lease that will begin in three weeks

   d. a two-year commercial lease with no option to renew

3. **L leases her house to T for a two-year term. Three months after L signs the lease, X makes a very tempting offer to buy the house. Which statement is TRUE?**

   a. L can sell the house, but X will take title subject to the lease.

   b. L cannot sell the house unless T agrees to surrender the lease.

   c. L cannot sell the house until the lease expires, because it is a lease for a fixed term.

   d. L cannot sell the house without T's consent, since this is a residential lease.

4. **T leases an apartment for a one-year term—from November 1 through October 31. But in January, T's brother buys a house and asks T to come live with him. So, T rents his apartment to X from February 15 through October 31. This is called a(n)**

   a. assignment.

   b. novation.

   c. reconveyance.

   d. sublease.

5. **A new tenant signs a two-year lease that begins on March 1, but on March 1, the previous tenant is still living in the apartment. Which statement is TRUE?**

   a. It is up to the new tenant to start eviction proceedings against the old tenant.

   b. The landlord has a duty to get the old tenant out so the new tenant can take possession.

   c. The new tenant is entitled to damages but does not have the right to rescind the lease.

   d. The new tenant will not owe rent for the period that the old tenant remains in the apartment.

6. **T has a five-year lease for an office in a small building. In the lease, the landlord agreed to keep the common areas in good condition and to perform all major repairs. One rainy autumn, the roof starts leaking badly in several places. The leaks threaten T's furniture and papers and make the office impossible to work in. T informs the landlord, but the landlord does not send anyone around to repair the problem, so T moves out. This is an example of**

   a. actual eviction.

   b. constructive eviction.

   c. self-help eviction.

   d. wrongful abandonment.

7. **L rents apartments for $500 a month. What is the most L can require a tenant to give as a security deposit?**

   a. $250, since this is a residential tenancy

   b. $500

   c. $1,500

   d. The law does not set a limit on the amount of the deposit.

8. ***T turns out to be a landlord's nightmare. Before L finally gets T evicted, T has caused at least $1,500 damage to the house. T's security deposit was only $500. Which statement is TRUE?***

   a. L can sue T for additional damages only if the lease states that T is required to repair any damage to the property that occurs during the tenancy.

   b. L can sue T for damages in addition to keeping the security deposit.

   c. Once a landlord has chosen to terminate the lease, the tenant is not liable for property damage.

   d. The security deposit serves as liquidated damages, so T cannot be sued for additional damages.

9. ***When T rented her apartment three years ago, it was in decent condition, but now it is infested with cockroaches, the living room heater does not work, and the stairs are rickety. In spite of T's frequent complaints, the landlord has not taken care of these problems. Which statement is TRUE?***

   a. The landlord is not required to fix these problems unless the lease says the landlord has a duty to keep the property habitable during the tenancy.

   b. These problems are not the landlord's responsibility if the lease expressly states that the landlord has no duty to repair the property.

   c. Until these problems are fixed, T can be held liable only for the reasonable rental value of the property in its substandard condition.

   d. Until these problems are fixed, T cannot be evicted if she stops paying rent.

10. ***T is leasing commercial space from L for an art gallery. The lease states that L cannot be held liable for injuries that occur on the property during the tenancy. One of T's customers trips over a loose board in the gallery floor and breaks a leg. The board was okay when T moved in. Which statement is TRUE?***

    a. Both L and T could be held liable, because an exculpatory clause in a lease is always void.

    b. L could be held liable, but T could not, because a landlord always has a duty.

    c. L could be held liable, but T could not, because T is not the landowner.

    d. T could be held liable, but L could not, because an exculpatory clause in a nonresidential lease is valid.

11. ***A landlord or tenant who wants to terminate a residential month-to-month lease must give the other party notice at least***

    a. one week in advance.

    b. 15 days in advance.

    c. 30 days in advance.

    d. two months in advance.

12. ***A forcible detainer or unlawful detainer action is a lawsuit brought by a***

    a. landlord against a tenant to evict the tenant.

    b. landlord against a tenant who removes fixtures at the end of the lease.

    c. tenant against a landlord who does not refund a security deposit.

    d. tenant against a landlord who wrongfully refuses to perform repairs.

13. ***A notice to vacate must be given to a tenant at least***

    a. 3 business days before an eviction lawsuit is filed.

    b. 30 days before an eviction lawsuit is filed.

    c. 30 days before the lease expires.

    d. 30 days before the writ of execution is issued.

14. ***The tenant in Apartment 6 has a two-year lease. He has so much trash in his apartment that it is a fire hazard and the landlord wants to evict him as quickly as possible. The landlord's first step is to***

   a. file the eviction lawsuit.

   b. send him a notice stating the tenancy will terminate in 30 days if the trash is not removed.

   c. send him a notice to vacate.

   d. file a civil lawsuit to require him to remove the trash since a residential tenant cannot be evicted for this.

15. ***A residential landlord got rid of a bad tenant by shutting off the heat in January. That was legal***

   a. if the tenant was causing a problem that materially affects health and safety.

   b. if the tenant was holding over after the lease expired.

   c. only if the lease expressly stated the landlord had that right.

   d. under no circumstances.

Final Exams

FINAL EXAM #1

1. *P sues D for the breach of a real estate contract, claiming $121,500 in damages. In which court is the case most likely to be tried?*
   a. County Court
   b. Court of Common Pleas
   c. Municipal Court
   d. Ohio Real Estate Court

2. *To start a civil lawsuit, a plaintiff files a complaint. If, in the same lawsuit, the defendant makes claims against the plaintiff, the defendant files a*
   a. counterclaim.
   b. countercomplaint.
   c. deposition.
   d. injunction.

3. *The rule preventing a court from hearing a case if too much time has passed since the facts giving rise to the case have occurred is called the*
   a. rule of equitable remedies.
   b. statute of liability.
   c. statute of limitations.
   d. statute of frauds.

4. *According to Ohio License Law, who does NOT need to be licensed to sell real estate?*
   a. an apartment locator service that charges a fee for its services to the client seeking an apartment
   b. a friend selling a neighbor's property for $100
   c. a property management company that leases to tenants
   d. a salaried employee of ABC Corporation when ABC is selling its own property

5. *When a salesperson or a broker enters the armed services, her real estate license is said to be*
   a. canceled.
   b. in escrow.
   c. inactive.
   d. on deposit.

6. *When a broker returns his own broker's license to the Superintendent of the Division of Real Estate so as to reactivate his salesperson license, the license is said to be*
   a. canceled.
   b. in escrow.
   c. inactive.
   d. on deposit.

7. *Under Ohio Real Estate Law, the Real Estate Commission shall suspend or revoke the license of any salesperson or broker who is found guilty of any of the following EXCEPT*
   a. offering a bottle of wine to anyone who will list a home with his broker (and not disclosing this fact to others).
   b. purchasing a list of names of transferring employees from a nearby major company for $100.
   c. saying to a client, "Buy this listing and I guarantee you will double your money on this property in only one year."
   d. a second violation of a civil rights law.

8. **Suspension of a real estate license is for**

   a. one-half the time of a revocation.

   b. a set period of time, with reactivation by application after the suspension is lifted.

   c. an unspecified period of time.

   d. an unspecified period of time, with reactivation by application.

9. **Which is legal under Ohio Civil Rights Law?**

   a. The landlord/occupant of a four-plex housing unit refuses to rent to an Asian couple.

   b. The owner of vacant land refuses to lease to a woman.

   c. The owner refuses to show his only single-family owner-occupied home (which is up for sale) to a person over 70 years of age.

   d. The owner/occupant of only one single-family home refuses to sell the home to a Roman Catholic couple.

10. **Channeling prospective buyers to a particular neighborhood based on their race is called**

    a. blockbusting.

    b. panic buying.

    c. redlining.

    d. steering.

11. **Under Federal and/or Ohio Civil Rights laws, who is LEAST likely to be held liable for unlawful discrimination?**

    a. multiple listing service

    b. rental agent

    c. resident manager

    d. prospective tenant

12. **For which violation of Ohio Civil Rights law must the Real Estate Commission suspend a real estate license for a minimum of two months, or revoke it?**

    a. first

    b. second

    c. third

    d. fourth

13. **The rule of common law that allows a tenant to re-enter land and harvest crops even after tenancy ends is called the**

    a. doctrine of emblements.

    b. doctrine of trade fixtures.

    c. rule of capture.

    d. rule of fructus industriales.

14. **Under current Ohio law, the most important consideration in the determination of whether a lessee's improvement to real property is a fixture is the**

    a. cost of the fixture.

    b. intention of the court.

    c. intention of the lessee.

    d. size of the fixture.

15. **A trade fixture is**

    a. always constructively annexed.

    b. an item the lessee is allowed to remove.

    c. an item the lessee traded something for to acquire.

    d. a natural attachment.

16. **In Ohio, riparian or littoral property is increased by the process of**

    a. accretion.

    b. alluvium.

    c. erosion.

    d. reliction.

17. **Which is the highest and best real property freehold possessory interest?**

    a. fee simple absolute

    b. fee simple determinable

    c. life estate pur autre vie

    d. conventional life estate

18. **The deed says, "I grant this land to B for life, and then to C." Before the death of B, which future interest does C have?**

    a. dower

    b. life estate pur autre vie

    c. reversion

    d. remainder

19. **Which statement is TRUE of an easement appurtenant that is NOT true of an easement in gross?**

    a. It is for a limited purpose.

    b. There is a dominant tenement.

    c. There is not a dominant tenement.

    d. There is a servient tenement.

20. **X's property has the following liens against it (all in the same year):**

1	A first mortgage that was recorded January 15th
2	A property tax lien that attached May 15th
3	A mechanic's lien recorded on May 20th; however, work began on May 2nd
4	A judgment lien recorded May 1st

When X's property is sold at foreclosure, which is the correct order to pay off the liens?

a. 1, 3, 4, 2
b. 1, 4, 3, 2
c. 2, 1, 4, 3
d. 2, 4, 1, 3

21. **In terms of conveying real estate, which pair of words best matches "deed/will?"**

a. delivery/acceptance
b. grantor/grantee
c. life/death
d. written/oral

22. **Title to real property changes hands when the deed is**

a. delivered.
b. recorded.
c. signed.
d. witnessed or notarized.

23. **A special warranty deed is special because it offers**

a. the lease deed warranties.
b. limited warranties.
c. the most deed warranties.
d. unlimited warranties.

24. **Given no other evidence, the court will presume that co-tenancy is in which form?**

a. joint tenancy
b. survivorship tenancy
c. tenancy by the entireties
d. tenancy in common

25. **With whom can a licensed real estate broker, working for the seller, legally share her commission?**

a. the attorney-at-law who represents the seller
b. the bank that makes the loan on the property in question, if it is HUD property
c. the buyer's broker
d. the seller

26. **In Ohio, for property to escheat to the state, which must be TRUE?**

a. The testator must have tried to cheat the state.
b. There must be no net estate.
c. There must be no will and no living heirs.
d. There must be no will or no living heirs.

27. **Which is NOT an example of an exception to zoning regulations?**

a. area variance
b. conditional use
c. nonconforming use
d. setback

28. **X had a deed with a restrictive covenant—he could paint his house only green. He transferred the property by deed to his son, but the covenant was not recorded in the new deed. Under Ohio's Marketable Title Act, when would the covenant no longer apply to the property?**

a. 21 years from the date of the new deed
b. 40 years from the root of title for the new deed
c. at the death of X
d. A deed with a covenant is not marketable, so the Act does not apply.

29. **Who are the parties to the listing agreement (contract)?**

a. agent and broker
b. agent and seller
c. buyer and seller
d. seller and broker

30. **Who are the parties to the sales contract?**

a. agent and broker
b. agent and seller
c. buyer and seller
d. seller and broker

31. **Which is a broker's favorite type of listing agreement?**
    a. exclusive agency agreement
    b. exclusive right to sell agreement
    c. notarized listing agreement
    d. open listing

32. **X leases a building. The lease states that X must pay, "3% of all monthly gross receipts as rent." This is a**
    a. gross lease.
    b. land lease.
    c. net lease.
    d. percentage lease.

33. **Under Ohio law, a _____ is presumed to be representing the _____, unless there is a specific agreement stating that the _____ is representing the ____.**
    a. broker, buyer, broker, buyer
    b. broker, seller, broker, buyer
    c. sales agent, buyer, sales agent, seller
    d. There is no such presumption.

34. **As an agent working with sellers, a Consumer Guide to Agency Relationships must be given to sellers prior to marketing and showing the property; as an agent working with buyers, a Consumer Guide to Agency Relationships must be given to buyers when the**
    a. closing is held.
    b. first contract is signed.
    c. first substantive contact occurs.
    d. offer is presented.

35. **Sales agent X does not sell client Y's property during a 90-day listing agreement. X immediately thereafter buys the property, makes a few (very obvious) repairs, and sells it for a nice profit. This transaction is probably**
    a. illegal—an agent may never buy a former client's property.
    b. legal—it does not matter why X bought the property as long as X paid the listed price.
    c. legal—the listing agreement had ended so X was not an undisclosed principal.
    d. unethical—it is a breach of loyalty, especially if the repairs were very minor.

36. **X fails to make the home repairs for which he contracted with Y. The contract was for $5,000 and was not paid. Y secures another contractor to perform the work for $6,000. In the subsequent lawsuit of Y against X for breach of contract, Y is most likely to be awarded**
    a. $1,000 in compensatory damages.
    b. $1,000 in punitive damages.
    c. $5,000 in compensatory damages.
    d. $6,000 in compensatory damages.

37. **For which violation would a licensee be LEAST likely to lose his real estate license?**
    a. failure to pay commissions
    b. income tax evasion
    c. a second civil rights law violation
    d. failure to report a change of address

38. **A "due on sale" clause, if present, is normally found in the**
    a. mechanic's lien.
    b. mortgage.
    c. real estate purchase agreement.
    d. resolution.

39. **A one-third (1/3) life estate in a deceased spouse's property transferred without consent is**
    a. dower.
    b. a homestead.
    c. a life estate pur autre vie.
    d. reversion.

40. **A willed gift of money is a**
    a. bequest.
    b. devise.
    c. legacy.
    d. testament.

41. **A probable example of a patent defect is a**
    a. bad well.
    b. deteriorated driveway with visible past repairs.
    c. termite infestation.
    d. worn out septic tank.

42. **Two parcels of land wherein one parcel has the use of another for a specific, limited purpose is called**

    a. easement appurtenant.
    b. easement in gross.
    c. fee simple determinable.
    d. license.

43. **Real estate brokers CANNOT be licensed real estate**

    a. corporations.
    b. partnerships.
    c. salespersons.
    d. trusts.

44. **A prospective buyer signs a contract to buy property Z and makes a generous earnest money deposit with his real estate agent. The contract states that the seller has, "six days from the date of the contract to accept the offer." On day five, the seller has not yet accepted the offer, but the buyer withdraws the contract. The earnest money deposit must be**

    a. divided between the buyer and seller.
    b. divided between the seller and his broker.
    c. given to the seller only.
    d. returned to the prospective buyer only.

45. **Under agency law, a listing broker should NOT**

    a. account for all trust funds.
    b. disclose information about the buyer's financial condition.
    c. disclose the principal's true selling price.
    d. present all offers to the principal, even poor ones.

46. **When a sales agent returns her license to the Superintendent of the Division of Real Estate so as to have it held for a period of time, the license status is**

    a. in escrow.
    b. inactive.
    c. on deposit.
    d. suspended.

47. **The right to reclaim property after a foreclosure due date is**

    a. the homestead right.
    b. reverse condemnation.
    c. the right of redemption.
    d. the right of remainder.

48. **Under Ohio law, it is mandatory that every listing agreement have a(n)**

    a. extension clause.
    b. referral date.
    c. sale date.
    d. termination date.

49. **A is a first-time newly licensed real estate agent. What is the earliest time at which she can practice her profession?**

    a. as soon as her license is issued by the Division of Real Estate
    b. upon accepting a job with a licensed broker
    c. upon notification by the Division of Real Estate of successful completion of the real estate licensing exam
    d. upon registration of her license with the clerk of courts in the county in which her broker maintains a principal place of business

50. **The licensed real estate sales agent is**

    a. always the agent of the broker.
    b. always the agent of the buyer.
    c. always the agent of the seller.
    d. usually the agent of the buyer.

FINAL EXAM #2

1. *A person who has absolute control of a parcel of real estate is said to own a*
   a. fee determinable estate.
   b. fee simple absolute estate.
   c. leasehold estate.
   d. life estate.

2. *The law requiring certain contracts to be in writing in order to be enforceable is called the*
   a. parole evidence rule.
   b. statute of frauds.
   c. statute of limitations.
   d. written instrument law.

3. *A executes a contract for the sale of a property to E. Thirty-one days before the closing, A dies. Which statement is TRUE?*
   a. The deal is canceled.
   b. The deal is in limbo for one year.
   c. The deal is voidable at the option of the deceased's heirs.
   d. E can compel A's executor or heirs to complete the sale.

4. *A unilaterally enforceable contract by which the owner agrees with a buyer that the buyer shall have the right to buy the property at a fixed price (if the buyer so desires) within a certain time period is called*
   a. an escrow agreement.
   b. an exclusive.
   c. an option.
   d. the right of first refusal.

5. *Buildings erected before the enactment of a zoning ordinance and that do not comply with the zoning limitations are called*
   a. nonconforming uses.
   b. outlawed classifications.
   c. rezonings.
   d. variances.

6. *The rate of commission is set by the*
   a. broker and the principal.
   b. multiple listing service.
   c. real estate board.
   d. real estate commission.

7. *When a deed is recorded,*
   a. the deal is completed.
   b. it cannot be unrecorded without a court order.
   c. it may still be changed at any time in the future.
   d. the recording acts as a notice to the world of the buyer's interest in the property.

8. *Mortgages are recorded*
   a. because they are required to be recorded by the county recorder.
   b. to assure that monthly payments are made in a timely fashion.
   c. to give notice of a lien on the property.
   d. to show ownership.

9. *When a new home is not completed by the closing date, what is the buyer's LEAST likely course of action?*
   a. allow the builder to extend the contract
   b. get a promise from the builder that the work will be completed
   c. revoke the contract
   d. demand that the builder gives him a more expensive home

10. *In a real estate transaction, title to the real estate passes from seller to buyer by*
    a. execution of the deed by the seller, and delivery and acceptance of the deed by the buyer.
    b. possession of the property.
    c. recording of the deed.
    d. witnessing of the deed.

11. *A sells a home to B. B takes possession immediately but is slow to record the deed. In the meantime, A sells the same property to C, who immediately records the deed (before B). Who has title?*
    a. A
    b. B
    c. C
    d. B and C

12. *The reversion of real property to the state because of a lack of heirs or other persons legally entitled to hold the property of a deceased person who died intestate is known as*

   a. eminent domain.

   b. escheat.

   c. police power.

   d. right of survivorship.

13. *When a salesperson represents a buyer who needs to sell his present home prior to finishing the purchase of his new home, the agent should*

   a. consult the Ohio Division of Real Estate to make sure the deal is executed according to current regulations.

   b. insist the client buy one of his listed properties.

   c. protect the client by using a contingency clause in the purchase contract relative to the sale of the current home.

   d. protect himself by having the listing agreement notarized.

14. *When a salesperson is the listing agent and is offering a listed property that she feels is overpriced, the correct action is to*

   a. not quote any price.

   b. quote only the listed price.

   c. tell prospective buyers to look at other properties.

   d. tell prospective buyers what she feels the price should be.

15. *Which action would be permitted under the Federal Fair Housing Act?*

   a. advertising property for sale only to a special group

   b. changing the terms of a loan for a member of a minority group

   c. refusing to rent a home to someone because of a poor credit history

   d. telling someone that a place has been rented when it has not

16. *Which item would NOT ordinarily be included in the sale of real estate?*

   a. barn

   b. farm equipment

   c. farm house

   d. fences

17. *Which best describes earnest money?*

   a. advance for closing costs and other expenses the buyer will incur in the transaction

   b. advance on commission to be paid to the broker

   c. consideration for the sale of property to make the contract legal and binding

   d. inducement deposited by the buyer at the time of signing the sales contract

18. *An agent violates the laws against steering by*

   a. referring prospective clients to a broker of their national origin or color.

   b. showing clients homes only in a particular neighborhood based on their race.

   c. both a and b

   d. neither a or b

19. *C received an earnest money check of $1,500. It would be considered commingling of funds if C*

   a. deposited the check in the brokerage commercial account.

   b. deposited the check in a trust account.

   c. gave the check to the seller.

   d. held the check until closing.

20. *In order to be enforceable, the purchase agreement must have*

   a. an attestation by a disinterested third party.

   b. competent parties.

   c. an earnest money deposit.

   d. the signature of a married seller's spouse.

21. *In a foreclosure sale, the*

   a. debtor can be the successful bidder and awarded title.

   b. debtor cannot bid on the property.

   c. debtor is freed of any future responsibility for liens.

   d. lender is always the successful bidder.

22. *Absent a clause in the sales contract, to whom should the sales associate turn over deposit money she receives?*

   a. her broker—for deposit in the brokerage trust account

   b. property owner

   c. seller's attorney

   d. Superintendent of Real Estate

23. **The Real Estate Recovery Account can reimburse a claimant up to a maximum amount of**

    a. $20,000 per licensee.

    b. $20,000 per occurrence.

    c. $40,000 per licensee.

    d. $40,000 per occurrence.

24. **A guarantee by a sales agent that he can get property rezoned**

    a. is against the rules and laws of the Ohio Real Estate Commission.

    b. must be accomplished at the agent's expense.

    c. must be completed within six months after the transaction closes.

    d. must be in writing to be valid because it deals with real property.

25. **Appointments to the Ohio Real Estate Commission are made by the**

    a. Director of Commerce.

    b. Governor.

    c. Secretary of State.

    d. Superintendent of Real Estate.

26. **A sales associate presented a contract for the listing price to a seller from a financially qualified black prospect. Later, the broker presented a lower contract to the same seller from a white prospect. The seller accepts neither of these contracts, but sells the property to a neighbor (through the same sales associate) who has decided to buy the house to prevent the black prospect from purchasing it. Who is NOT liable under the 1968 Federal Fair Housing Act?**

    a. neighbor

    b. sales associate

    c. seller

    d. white prospect

27. **Which is NOT required for a fraud complaint to be actionable in court?**

    a. There must be intentional wrongdoing.

    b. The victim must have relied on what he was told.

    c. The wrongdoing must be material.

    d. The fraudulent information must have been in writing.

28. **A broker's license is suspended for one year. What happens to the sales agents under that broker?**

    a. Their licenses will be revoked.

    b. They may continue to operate the broker's business.

    c. They may make an application to transfer to another broker.

    d. They must remain on inactive status until the broker's license is reinstated.

29. **Which is responsible for the requirement that all listing agreements have a definite expiration date?**

    a. Civil Rights Commission

    b. National Association of REALTORS®

    c. Ohio laws

    d. Ohio Real Estate Commission

30. **All real estate advertising must include the name of the**

    a. agent.

    b. broker or brokerage.

    c. seller.

    d. street.

31. **An owner asks a broker to list a property for sale at $70,000. Upon inspection, the broker believes the property is worth $80,000. The broker should**

    a. buy the property for $70,000.

    b. get a net listing for the property at $70,000.

    c. inform the owner that he believes the property is worth $80,000.

    d. suggest listing the property at $75,000 so there is some bargaining room.

32. **Which is a private restriction on the use of real property?**

    a. health and safety regulations

    b. restrictive covenants

    c. variances

    d. zoning laws

33. Which is the best example of rescission of a contract?

a. lease that is terminated by mutual agreement of the lessor and lessee

b. listing contract that does not result in a commission

c. offer to purchase that is revised by a counteroffer

d. option to purchase that is transferred to a new buyer

34. A broker obtained a 120-day exclusive right to sell listing agreement, but did absolutely nothing to market the property for 60 days. Which statement is FALSE?

a. The broker has breached the listing agreement and his fiduciary duty.

b. The broker has earned a commission even though no work has been done because the listing agreement is valid.

c. The seller can cancel the listing prior to the 120th day for lack of performance.

d. The seller can withdraw the property from the market without consequence.

35. Which statement in regard to an option on real property is TRUE?

a. An option is binding only on the optionee.

b. An option is usually given by the owner of the real property to be optioned.

c. An option is voidable by the optioner.

d. An option must be enforced by a suit filed by the optionor.

36. If the parties to a contract are of legal age and of sound mind, they are said to have

a. consideration.

b. contractual capacity.

c. legality of objective.

d. reality of consent.

37. Who is most likely to be treated as an independent contractor for federal tax purposes?

a. broker in charge

b. personal assistant

c. principal broker

d. sales associate

38. Who does NOT own a future interest in real property?

a. holder of dower rights

b. holder of reversionary interest

c. remainderman

d. a life tenant

39. Which encumbrance would constitute a lien on real property?

a. deed restriction

b. easement

c. encroachment

d. mortgage

40. Which is the most complete freehold estate in real property?

a. estate for years

b. fee simple absolute

c. fee simple determinable

d. tenancy at sufferance

41. P wants to extend the side of the house beyond the setback boundary. P must obtain

a. a nonconforming use.

b. permission from all his neighbors.

c. a rezone.

d. a variance.

42. A riparian owner is one who owns land bounding on

a. a common area.

b. municipal property.

c. a national forest.

d. a waterway.

43. Exclusive ownership of a part of the airspace and co-ownership of the rest of the components of the land characterize

a. a condominium.

b. an easement.

c. eminent domain.

d. a timeshare.

44. Eminent domain is a

a. freehold interest.

b. governmental power.

c. private land use control.

d. type of zoning classification.

45. *Which is NOT an essential element of a valid deed?*
    a. consideration
    b. delivery and acceptance
    c. legal description
    d. recordation

46. *Which is NOT part of the real property?*
    a. emblements
    b. fixtures
    c. improvements
    d. subsurface rights

47. *Tenants' trade fixtures are considered to be personal property because*
    a. it encourages tenants to improve properties while they are still tenants.
    b. it keeps down the cost of fixing up properties after tenants vacate the premises.
    c. it makes it easier to sell rented property.
    d. otherwise the real property owner could charge more for rent.

48. *A deed is the most commonly used legal instrument for the transfer of*
    a. encroachments.
    b. freehold estates.
    c. leasehold estates.
    d. personal property.

49. *Which would be considered the unauthorized practice of law by a real estate agent?*
    a. attesting a deed
    b. drafting a land contract
    c. filling in blanks on a form sales contract
    d. witnessing a will

50. *There are two parcels of land, wherein one parcel has the use of another parcel for a specific purpose. This situation is referred to as a(n)*
    a. appurtenant easement.
    b. easement in gross.
    c. license.
    d. restrictive covenant.

PRACTICE EXAM ANSWER SHEETS

1. ___	1. ___	1. ___	1. ___	1. ___	1. ___
2. ___	2. ___	2. ___	2. ___	2. ___	2. ___
3. ___	3. ___	3. ___	3. ___	3. ___	3. ___
4. ___	4. ___	4. ___	4. ___	4. ___	4. ___
5. ___	5. ___	5. ___	5. ___	5. ___	5. ___
6. ___	6. ___	6. ___	6. ___	6. ___	6. ___
7. ___	7. ___	7. ___	7. ___	7. ___	7. ___
8. ___	8. ___	8. ___	8. ___	8. ___	8. ___
9. ___	9. ___	9. ___	9. ___	9. ___	9. ___
10. ___	10. ___	10. ___	10. ___	10. ___	10. ___
11. ___	11. ___	11. ___	11. ___	11. ___	11. ___
12. ___	12. ___	12. ___	12. ___	12. ___	12. ___
13. ___	13. ___	13. ___	13. ___	13. ___	13. ___
14. ___	14. ___	14. ___	14. ___	14. ___	14. ___
15. ___	15. ___	15. ___	15. ___	15. ___	15. ___
16. ___	16. ___	16. ___	16. ___	16. ___	16. ___
17. ___	17. ___	17. ___	17. ___	17. ___	17. ___
18. ___	18. ___	18. ___	18. ___	18. ___	18. ___
19. ___	19. ___	19. ___	19. ___	19. ___	19. ___
20. ___	20. ___	20. ___	20. ___	20. ___	20. ___
21. ___	21. ___	21. ___	21. ___	21. ___	21. ___
22. ___	22. ___	22. ___	22. ___	22. ___	22. ___
23. ___	23. ___	23. ___	23. ___	23. ___	23. ___
24. ___	24. ___	24. ___	24. ___	24. ___	24. ___
25. ___	25. ___	25. ___	25. ___	25. ___	25. ___
26. ___	26. ___	26. ___	26. ___	26. ___	26. ___
27. ___	27. ___	27. ___	27. ___	27. ___	27. ___
28. ___	28. ___	28. ___	28. ___	28. ___	28. ___
29. ___	29. ___	29. ___	29. ___	29. ___	29. ___
30. ___	30. ___	30. ___	30. ___	30. ___	30. ___
31. ___	31. ___	31. ___	31. ___	31. ___	31. ___
32. ___	32. ___	32. ___	32. ___	32. ___	32. ___
33. ___	33. ___	33. ___	33. ___	33. ___	33. ___
34. ___	34. ___	34. ___	34. ___	34. ___	34. ___
35. ___	35. ___	35. ___	35. ___	35. ___	35. ___
36. ___	36. ___	36. ___	36. ___	36. ___	36. ___
37. ___	37. ___	37. ___	37. ___	37. ___	37. ___
38. ___	38. ___	38. ___	38. ___	38. ___	38. ___
39. ___	39. ___	39. ___	39. ___	39. ___	39. ___
40. ___	40. ___	40. ___	40. ___	40. ___	40. ___
41. ___	41. ___	41. ___	41. ___	41. ___	41. ___
42. ___	42. ___	42. ___	42. ___	42. ___	42. ___
43. ___	43. ___	43. ___	43. ___	43. ___	43. ___
44. ___	44. ___	44. ___	44. ___	44. ___	44. ___
45. ___	45. ___	45. ___	45. ___	45. ___	45. ___
46. ___	46. ___	46. ___	46. ___	46. ___	46. ___
47. ___	47. ___	47. ___	47. ___	47. ___	47. ___
48. ___	48. ___	48. ___	48. ___	48. ___	48. ___
49. ___	49. ___	49. ___	49. ___	49. ___	49. ___
50. ___	50. ___	50. ___	50. ___	50. ___	50. ___

Appendix

CHAPTER QUIZ ANSWER KEY

Chapter 1—Introduction to Law

1. a. compensate a person who has been harmed.
2. a. has violated the standards of reasonable conduct imposed by law.
3. b. exceeds the powers granted to the government.
4. b. the Dayton City Council
5. c. make court decisions more consistent and predictable.
6. d. timeframe of a case being heard
7. c. Court of Common Pleas

Chapter 2—Ohio Statutes

1. b. a salaried employee of ABC Corporation when selling the company's own property
2. d. is part of the Department of Commerce.
3. c. the Real Estate Commission
4. c. offer real estate to the market only on the terms allowed by the seller.
5. b. can personally buy a listing only after disclosure to the seller that the sales associate is a principal.
6. d. must have a place of business to operate as brokers.
7. b. her license has been issued by the Division of Real Estate.
8. b. damaged by a licensee in a real estate transaction.
9. a. 3 hours of core law, 3 hours of civil rights law, and 3 hours of ethics as part of the 30-hour requirement.
10. a. anyone

11. d. protect the public against fraudulent practice.
12. a. he discloses his license.

Chapter 3—Agency Law

1. a. general agent.
2. a. appears to be the agent of another, but does not have actual authority.
3. c. must have an expiration date.
4. b. at any time.
5. a. The listing salesperson dies.
6. d. seller's subagent.
7. a. at the first substantive contact.
8. c. seller.
9. d. the unauthorized practice of law.
10. c. It is legal for X to make an offer only if the seller understands that X himself is the prospective buyer.
11. b. It must be disclosed in writing and consented to by the parties when the agent has an ongoing business relationship with one party and not the other.
12. a. disclose all known latent defects in the property to the buyer, whether or not the buyer asks about them.
13. b. Actual fraud is intentional and constructive fraud is unintentional.
14. b. can be held liable because her statements to the buyer were fraudulent.
15. a. are awarded in addition to compensatory damages in some tort suits.
16. d. A listing licensee may negotiate the sale of the listed property for a buyer client without disclosing to the seller that they represent the buyer.

Chapter 4—Fair Housing

1. d. racial discrimination in the sale or lease of any property.
2. b. Federal Fair Housing Act.
3. d. provide for fair housing throughout the U.S.
4. a. families with children.
5. b. Federal Fair Housing Act.
6. c. the owner of a single-family home in Canton, who owns one other single-family home
7. d. under no circumstances.
8. a. directing customers to different listings based on their race or ancestry and the racial or ethnic composition of the neighborhoods.
9. d. none of these laws, since this is a commercial transaction.
10. b. Ohio Civil Rights Commission.
11. d. 1 year
12. d. Yes, because V's race was a factor in the manager's decision, even though it was not his only reason for rejecting her.
13. d. Yes, because the ordinance has a disparate impact on minority groups.
14. c. The Travelers Club (a private club that admits only men) refuses to let M stay in its lodgings because he is not a club member.
15. c. suspend his license for at least two months, or else revoke his license.

Chapter 5—The Nature of Real Property

1. c. emblements.
2. b. will be considered part of the sale under the doctrine of constructive annexation.
3. a. the intention of the annexer.
4. c. can be removed by the tenant before the lease expires.
5. b. not remove the counter because of the written agreement.
6. a. Colossus can buy the air rights from the railroad.
7. c. legal, if T has an appropriation permit.
8. c. J owns the section of the river bed adjoining her property out to the middle of the river.

9. c. a property owner who drills a well owns all of the oil or gas it produces, even though some migrated under a neighbor's land.
10. b. applies only when the holder of the mineral interest is someone other than the owner of the surface property.

Chapter 6—Interests in Real Property

1. b. fee simple absolute.
2. c. remainderman.
3. a. estate for years.
4. a. encumbrance.
5. a. appurtenant easement.
6. d. merger.
7. c. mechanic's lien.
8. b. a lien for delinquent property taxes always has highest priority.
9. b. can seek a deficiency judgment against the debtor by filing a separate court action.
10. c. 2021

Chapter 7—Deeds

1. d. quitclaim deed.
2. a. against encumbrances.
3. b. fiduciary's deed.
4. c. the signature of a competent grantee.
5. a. delivery and acceptance of the deed.
6. d. not offer advice of this kind because it involves the practice of law.
7. a. one
8. a. buyer's attorney
9. b. automatically confer dower rights.
10. c. present donative intent of the grantor.
11. b. even though the title is in one partner's name alone.
12. a. A blanket mortgage covers the entire condominium property.

Chapter 8—Contracts

1. b. executory bilateral contract
2. d. the offeree gives the offeror consideration for keeping the offer open.
3. d. Yes, because S's acceptance became effective when he mailed it.
4. a. No, because the offer was terminated when S rejected it.
5. a. counteroffer.
6. d. voidable due to duress.
7. c. a three-month listing agreement for vacant land
8. c. novation.
9. a. $35,000 in compensatory damages.
10. c. rescission.
11. b. a ready, willing, and able buyer offers to buy on the seller's terms.
12. c. is supported by consideration.

Chapter 9—Decedents' Estates

1. b. can elect to take against the will, and may be able to take the mansion house.
2. a. $20,000, plus half of the remainder of the estate
3. d. reverts to the state.
4. c. is of sound mind and memory.
5. d. The entire estate
6. b. the validity of the will.
7. d. to list property the executor or administrator has the power to sell.
8. b. called a devise.
9. a. administrator.
10. c. can exist only when there are no next of kin and the decedent had no will.
11. d. sign in the presence of each other and the testator.

Chapter 10—Land Use Controls

1. c. police power.
2. b. This zoning law is constitutional, since it does not prevent the only kind of development the property is suited for.
3. a. appoint a planning commission to prepare a comprehensive plan for the city.
4. b. nonconforming use.
5. c. strict application of the zoning law would cause unnecessary hardship.
6. d. Yes, if the zoning board or planning commission issues a conditional use permit for the project.
7. a. illegal spot zone.
8. d. within 30 days, unless a petition for zoning referendum is filed.
9. d. T may be required to comply with the new code whether or not he modifies his building.
10. a. 2 or more lots, if any of the lots is smaller than five acres.
11. c. projects that would have a significant impact on the environment.
12. c. covenant rather than a condition, because a condition can result in forfeiture of title.
13. a. B did not have notice of the restriction.
14. b. anyone who owns a lot anywhere in the subdivision.
15. d. may no longer be enforceable, because the character of the surrounding neighborhood has changed.

Chapter 11—Landlord/Tenant

1. c. only to residential property.
2. a. a month-to-month lease for a single-family home
3. a. L can sell the house, but X will take title subject to the lease.
4. d. sublease.
5. b. The landlord has a duty to get the old tenant out so the new tenant can take possession.
6. b. constructive eviction.
7. d. The law does not set a limit on the amount of the deposit.
8. b. L can sue T for damages in addition to keeping the security deposit.
9. c. Until these problems are fixed, T can be held liable only for the reasonable rental value of the property in its substandard condition.
10. d. T could be held liable, but L could not, because an exculpatory clause in a nonresidential lease is valid.
11. c. 30 days in advance.
12. a. landlord against a tenant to evict the tenant.
13. a. 3 days before an eviction lawsuit is filed.
14. b. send him a notice stating the tenancy will terminate in 30 days if the trash is not removed.
15. d. under no circumstances.

EXAM 1

1. B. Court of Common Pleas
2. A. counterclaim.
3. C. statute of limitations.
4. D. a salaried employee of ABC Corporation when ABC is selling its own property
5. D. on deposit.
6. D. on deposit.
7. B. purchasing a list of names of transferring employees from a nearby major company for $100.
8. B. a set period of time, with reactivation by application after the suspension is lifted.
9. C. The owner refuses to show his only single-family owner-occupied home (which is up for sale) to a person over 70 years of age.
10. D. steering.
11. D. prospective tenant
12. B. second
13. A. doctrine of emblements.
14. C. intention of the lessee.
15. B. an item the lessee is allowed to remove.
16. A. accretion.
17. A. fee simple absolute
18. D. remainder
19. B. There is a dominant tenement.
20. C. 2, 1, 4, 3
21. C. life/death
22. A. delivered.
23. B. limited warranties.
24. D. tenancy in common
25. C. the buyer's broker
26. C. There must be no will and no living heirs.
27. D. setback
28. B. 40 years from the roof of title for the new deed
29. D. seller and broker
30. C. buyer and seller
31. B. exclusive right to sell agreement
32. D. percentage lease.
33. D. There is no such presumption.
34. C. first substantive contact occurs.
35. D. unethical--it is a breach of loyalty, especially if the repairs were very minor.
36. A. $1,000 in compensatory damages.
37. D. failing to report a change of address
38. B. mortgage.
39. A. dower.
40. C. legacy.
41. B. deteriorated driveway with visible past repairs.
42. A. easement appurtenant.
43. D. trusts.
44. D. returned to the prospective buyer only.
45. C. disclose the principal's true selling price.
46. B. inactive.
47. C. the right of redemption.
48. D. termination date.
49. A. as soon as her license is issued by the Division of Real Estate
50. A. always the agent of the broker.

EXAM 2

1. B. fee simple absolute estate.
2. B. statute of frauds.
3. D. E can compel A's executor or heirs to complete the sale.
4. C. an option.
5. A. nonconforming uses.
6. A. broker and the principal.
7. D. the recording acts as a notice to the world of the buyer's interest in the property.
8. C. to give notice of a lien on the property.
9. D. demand that the builder gives him a more expensive home
10. A. execution of the deed by the seller, and deliver and acceptance of the deed by the buyer.
11. B. B
12. B. escheat.
13. C. protect the client by using a contingency clause in the purchase contract relative to the sale of the current home.
14. B. quote only the listed price.
15. C. refusing to rent a home to someone because of a poor credit history
16. B. farm equipment
17. D. inducement deposited by the buyer at the time of signing the sales contract
18. C. both a and b
19. A. deposited the check in the brokerage commercial account.
20. B. competent parties.
21. A. debtor can be the successful bidder and awarded title.
22. A. her broker--for deposit in the brokerage trust account
23. C. $40,000 per licensee.
24. A. is against the rules and laws of the Ohio Real Estate Commission.
25. B. Governor.
26. D. white prospect
27. D. The fraudulent information must have been in writing.
28. C. They may make an application to transfer to another broker.
29. C. Ohio laws
30. B. broker or brokerage.
31. C. inform the owner that he believes the property is worth $80,000.
32. B. restrictive covenants
33. A. lease that is terminated by mutual agreement of the lessor and lessee
34. B. The broker has earned a commission even though no work has been done because the listing agreement is valid.
35. B. An option is usually given by the owner of the real property to be optioned.
36. B. contractual capacity.
37. D. sales associate
38. D. a life tenant
39. D. mortgage
40. B. fee simple absolute
41. D. a variance.
42. D. a waterway.
43. A. a condominium.
44. B. governmental power.
45. D. recordation
46. A. emblements
47. A. it encourages tenants to improve properties while they are still tenants.
48. B. freehold estates.
49. B. drafting a land contract
50. A. appurtenant easement.

Glossary

The definitions given here explain how the listed terms are used in the real estate field. Some terms have additional meanings, which can be found in a standard dictionary.

Abandonment The failure to occupy and use property, which may result in a loss of rights.

Abstract of Title A brief, chronological summary of the recorded documents affecting title to a particular parcel of real property.

Acceptance 1. Agreeing to the terms of an offer to enter into a contract, thereby creating a binding contract. 2. Taking delivery of a deed.

Accession The acquisition of title to land by its addition to real estate already owned through human actions or natural processes.

Accord and Satisfaction An agreement to accept something different (and usually less) than what the original contract required.

Accretion A gradual addition to dry land by the forces of nature, as when the tide deposits water-borne sediment on shoreline property.

Acknowledgment When a party signing a document formally declares to an authorized official (usually a notary public) that he signed voluntarily. The official certifies that the signature is voluntary and genuine.

Ad Valorem A Latin phrase meaning "according to value;" a tax to be paid based on a value set by authorities—refers to taxes assessed on the value of property (e.g., real property taxes).

Administrative Agency A government agency (federal, state, or local) that administers a complex area of law, adopting and enforcing detailed regulations that carry the force of law.

Administrator A person appointed by the probate court to manage and distribute the estate of a deceased person when no executor is named in the will or there is no will.

Adverse Possession When someone acquires title to real property by openly occupying it without the owner's permission for more than 21 years.

Affiant A person who makes an affidavit.

Affidavit A sworn statement that has been written and acknowledged; may be submitted as evidence in a trial.

Affirm Ruling by an appeals court that the lower court's decision was correct, rejecting the appellant's arguments.

Age of Majority The age at which a person gains legal capacity; in Ohio, 18 years of age.

Agency A relationship of trust created when one person (the principal) gives another person (the agent) the right to represent the principal in dealings with third parties.

Agency, Apparent 1. When someone not authorized to represent another acts as if he or she is that person's agent. 2. When an agent acts beyond the scope of the agent's authority, giving a third party the impression the acts are authorized. Also called **ostensible agency**.

Agency, Dual When a broker or salesperson represents both parties in a transaction, as when a broker represents the buyer and seller.

Agency Coupled with an Interest When the agent has a personal interest in the subject of the agency—as when one co-owner has been authorized by the others to sell their property. This can restrict termination of the agency.

Agent A person licensed to represent another (the principal) in a real estate transaction; a person authorized to represent the principal in dealings with third parties (clients or customers), often referred to as a licensee.

Agent, Dual A licensee who enters into any of the dual agency relationships set forth in Ohio license law; when a licensee represents both the buyer and seller in the same transaction, and all management level licensees at a brokerage. A management level licensee is not a dual agent if there is more than one management level licensee in the brokerage and that licensee either personally represents the buyer or seller or that licensee is the buyer or seller.

Agent, General An agent authorized to handle all of the principal's affairs in one area or in specified areas.

Agent, Special An agent with limited authority to do a specific thing or conduct a specific transaction.

Agent, Split A licensee assigned by a broker to represent a buyer or seller in a transaction, usually in an in-company dual agency situation.

Agent, Universal An agent authorized to do everything that can be lawfully delegated to a representative.

Air Rights The right to undisturbed use and control of the airspace over a parcel of land (within reasonable limits for air travel); may be transferred separately from the land.

Alienation A legal term that encompasses all methods of transfer (voluntary and involuntary) of ownership or interest in property.

Alienation, Involuntary The transfer of an interest in property against the will of the owner, or without action by the owner, occurring through operation of law, natural processes, or adverse possession.

Alienation, Voluntary When an owner voluntarily transfers an interest to someone else.

Allodial System The system of land ownership in which anyone can own land.

Alluvion The solid material deposited along a shore by accretion. Also called **alluvium**.

Amortization Provision In zoning law, a provision that places time limits on nonconforming uses—not permitted in Ohio.

Amount in Controversy The amount of money at issue in a lawsuit; used as a limitation on the jurisdiction of some courts.

Ancillary Trustee A trustee appointed by the Ohio Real Estate Commission to finish the brokerage business of a broker who dies.

Annexation Attaching personal property to land so that the law views it as part of the real property.

Annexation, Actual A physical attachment of personal property to land.

Annexation, Constructive Personal property associated with real property in such a way that the law treats it as a fixture, even though it is not physically attached to the real property.

Answer The document a defendant files with the court in response to a plaintiff's complaint.

Appeal The process in which a higher court reviews the decision of a lower court or an administrative tribunal.

Appellant The party who files an appeal because he is dissatisfied with the trial court's decision. Also called **petitioner**.

Appellee The party in an appeal who did *not* file the appeal. Also called the **respondent**.

Appraisal An estimate or opinion of the value of a piece of property as of a certain date. Also called **valuation**.

Appraiser A person who appraises property; especially an expert qualified to do so by education and experience.

Appropriation Taking private property for public use (with just compensation) through the government's power of eminent domain. Also called **condemnation**.

Appropriative Rights Water rights allocated by government permit, according to an appropriation system. It is not necessary to own property beside the body of water to apply for an appropriation permit.

Appurtenance A right that goes with ownership of real property; usually transferred with the property but may be sold separately.

Appurtenance, Intangible An appurtenant right that does not involve ownership of physical objects— for example, easements (as opposed to mineral rights that involve tangibles).

Arbitration An alternative to going to court, whereby the parties agree to submit facts and evidence to an impartial third party.

Artificial Person An entity created by law, as (distinguished from a natural person, a human being); usually refers to a corporation.

"As Is" Clause A provision in a purchase agreement stating the buyer accepts property in its present condition.

Assessment 1. A government's valuation of property for tax purposes. 2. A special assessment.

Assessor An official who determines the value of property for taxation.

Assignee A person to whom a right or interest has been assigned.

Assignment 1. When a person transfers his interests under a contract to another. 2. When a tenant transfers his right of possession, or other interest, in leased property to another person for the remainder of the lease term.

Assignor A person who assigns a right or interest to another.

Associate Broker A licensed real estate broker with a brokerage who does not function as a principal broker or as a management level licensee.

Attachment Court-ordered seizure of property belonging to a defendant in a lawsuit so it will be available to satisfy a judgment. In the case of real property, attachment creates a lien.

Attachments, Natural Plants growing on land (e.g., trees, shrubs, crops)—considered real property.

Attorney-in-Fact Any person authorized to act for another by a power of—not necessarily a lawyer, who is an attorney-at-law.

Authority, Actual Authority intentionally given to an agent by the principal, either expressly or by implication.

Authority, Express Authority expressly communicated, in words or in writing, by the principal to the agent.

Authority, Implied Authority conveyed by the principal to the agent by the principal's deeds or actions, not words.

Authority, Incidental Authority indirectly given to an agent to do everything reasonably necessary to carry out the principal's express orders.

Bequeath To transfer personal property to another by a will.

Bequest Personal property that is transferred by a will.

Bill A proposed law formally submitted to a legislature for consideration.

Bill of Sale A document used to transfer title to personal property from one person to another.

Blockbusting The illegal practice of inducing owners to sell their homes (often at a deflated price) by suggesting the ethnic or racial composition of the neighborhood is changing, with the implication that property values will decline as a result. Also called **panic selling**.

Bona Fide In good faith; genuine.

Boundary The perimeter or border of a parcel of land; the dividing line between one piece of property and another.

Breach A violation of an obligation, duty, or law.

Breach, Material An unexcused failure to perform according to the terms of a contract, important enough that the non-breaching party is not required to perform his contractual obligations.

Breach of Contract An unexcused failure to perform according to the terms of a contract.

Broker Any person, partnership, association, limited liability partnership, limited liability company, or corporation who, for a fee, sells, lists, leases, exchanges, negotiates, auctions, or otherwise deals in the real estate of others, or represents publicly that he does.

Broker, Associate A person who has qualified as a real estate broker but works for another broker.

Brokerage A broker's business.

Brownfield Any real property where redevelopment or re-use may be complicated by the presence or potential presence of a hazardous waste, petrole-um, pollutant, or contaminant.

Building Code Regulations establishing minimum standards for construction and materials.

Bump Clause A provision in a purchase agreement that allows the seller to keep the property on the market until a condition in the contract is fulfilled.

Bundle of Rights All real property rights conferred with ownership, including right of use, right of enjoyment, and right of disposal.

Buyer Broker An agent representing the interests of the buyer of a property.

Cancellation Termination of a contract without undoing acts that have already been performed under the contract.

Capacity The legal ability to perform some act, such as enter into a contract or execute a deed or will.

Case Law Rules of law developed in court decisions, as opposed to constitutional law, statutory law, or administrative regulations.

Caveat Emptor A Latin phrase meaning "let the buyer beware." The rule that a buyer is expected to examine property carefully, instead of relying on the seller to point out problems.

CC&Rs A declaration of **C**ovenants, **C**onditions, and **R**estrictions; usually recorded by a developer to create a general plan of private restrictions for a subdivision.

Cease and Desist Order A court order requiring the stoppage of certain activities.

Certificate of Judgment A summary of the provisions of a court judgment; when recorded, it creates a lien on all the real property of the debtor in the county where recorded.

Certificate of Transfer A document issued by a probate court showing a transfer of title from a deceased person to his heirs or devisees.

Chattel A piece of personal property.

Chattel Real Personal property that is closely associated with real property (e.g., a lease).

Checker A person working with a fair housing organization who pretends to be interested in buying or renting property from someone suspected of unlawful discrimination. Also called a **tester**.

Civil Law The body of law concerned with the rights and liabilities of one individual in relation to another; includes contract, tort, and property law.

Civil Litigation A lawsuit in which one individual sues another for compensation.

Civil Rights Fundamental rights guaranteed to all persons by the law. The term is primarily used in reference to constitutional and statutory protections against discrimination based on race, religion, sex, or national origin.

Client A person who employs a broker, lawyer, or other professional. A real estate broker's client can be the seller, the buyer, or both, but usually is the seller.

Closing The final stage in a real estate transaction, when the seller receives the purchase money and the buyer receives the deed.

Closing Costs Expenses incurred in the transfer of real estate in addition to the purchase price (e.g., appraisal fee, title insurance premiums, broker's commission, transfer tax).

Cloud on the Title A claim, encumbrance, or defect that makes the title to real property unmarketable.

Codicil An addition to or revision of a will. Must be executed with the same formalities as a will.

Codification The collection and organization of various laws into a comprehensive statutory code.

Collusion An agreement between two or more persons to defraud someone.

Color of Title A title that appears to be good title but which, in fact, is not.

Commercial Property Property zoned and used for business purposes, such as warehouses, restaurants, and office buildings (as distinguished from residential, industrial, or agricultural property).

Commingling Illegally mixing money held in trust on behalf of a client with personal funds.

Commission The compensation paid a broker for services in a real estate transaction; usually a percentage of the sale price, rather than a flat fee.

Common Areas The land and improvements in a condominium, planned unit development, or cooperative that all residents use and own as tenants in common (e.g., parking lot, hallways, recreational facilities); does not include the individual apartment units or homes.

Common Grantor A person who owned two or more neighboring properties and sold them to different buyers.

Common Law 1. Early English law. 2. Long-established rules based on English law, still followed in many states. 3. Case law.

Common Law Marriage When two people of the opposite sex hold themselves out to the world as being married, such as through the use of a joint checking account, even though no formal marriage decree has been issued by a court. No longer available in Ohio.

Community Property In some states, property is owned jointly by a married couple. Only Arizona, California, Idaho, Louisiana, Nevada, New Mexico, Texas, and Washington have community property system laws.

Comparative Negligence Rule When parties share liability based on their partial fault or negligence in causing the injury or tort.

Competent 1. Of sound mind, for the purposes of entering a contract or executing a will; not suffering from mental illness, disability, or senility. 2. Of sound mind and having reached the age of majority.

Complaint The document a plaintiff files with the court to start a lawsuit.

Comprehensive Environmental Response, Compensation, and Liability Act (CERCLA) A federal law enacted by Congress whose primary em-phasis is the cleanup of inactive hazardous waste sites and the liability for cleanup costs on arrangers and transporters of hazardous substances and on current and former owners of facilities where hazardous substances were disposed. Also known as Superfund.

Comprehensive Plan A long-range plan for development of a city or region.

Condemnation 1. Taking private property for public use, through the government's power of eminent domain. Also called **appropriation**. 2. A declaration that a structure is unfit for occupancy and must be closed or demolished.

Condition A provision in a contract or deed that makes the parties' rights and obligations depend on the occurrence (or non-occurrence) of a particular event. Also called a **contingency clause**.

Conditional Use A land use that does not comply with the general zoning rules for the zone in which it is located but is permitted there because it benefits the public (e.g., a hospital in a residential neighborhood). Also called **special exception**.

Condominium A property developed for co-ownership, where each co-owner has a separate interest in an individual unit, combined with an undivided interest in the common areas of the property.

Condominium Declaration The document that must be filed for record when property is developed as or converted to a condominium.

Consideration Anything of value (e.g., money, services, goods, promises) given to induce another person to enter into a contract. Sometimes called **valuable consideration**.

Consideration, Adequate Consideration that is comparable in value to the consideration the other party to the contract is giving. A contract is enforceable even if the consideration is inadequate, but a court cannot order specific performance in that case.

Constitution A fundamental document that establishes a government's structure and sets limits on its power.

Constitutional 1. Pertaining to or based on a constitution. 2. Not in violation of the U.S. Constitution or a state constitution.

Constitutional Law Law derived from the Constitution.

Contemporaneous Offers Offers to purchase or lease on behalf of two or more clients represented by the same licensee for the same property that the licensee knows, has known, or has reason to know will be taken under consideration by the owner or owner's authorized representative during the same period of time.

Contract An agreement between two or more parties to do, or not do, a certain thing. The requirements for an enforceable contract are: **Capacity, mutual consent, lawful objective**, and **consideration**. In addition, certain contracts must be in writing to be enforceable.

Contract, Bilateral A contract in which each party promises to do something.

Contract, Executed A contract in which both parties have fully performed their contractual obligations.

Contract, Executory A contract in which one or more parties have not yet completed performance of their obligations, as they may be in the process of carrying out their duties.

Contract, Express A contract put into words, either spoken or written.

Contract, Implied A contract that has not been put into words but is implied by the actions of the parties.

Contract, Land A real estate installment agreement where buyer makes payment to seller in exchange for right to occupy and use property, but no deed or title is transferred until all, or a specified portion of, payments have been made. Also called **installment land contract, installment sales contract, land sales contract, real estate contract**, and others.

Contract, Oral A spoken agreement, as opposed to a written one.

Contract, Unenforceable A contract that a court would refuse to enforce. For example, a contract may be unenforceable because its contents cannot be proven, it is not in writing, or the statute of limitations has run out.

Contract, Unilateral A contract in which only one party makes a legally binding promise and the other does not. The promise will become legally binding if the other party chooses to accept it (similar to an offer).

Contract, Valid A binding, legally enforceable contract.

Contract, Void A contract that is not an enforceable contract because it lacks one or more of the requirements for contract formation or is defective in some other respect.

Contract, Voidable A contract that one of the parties can disaffirm, without liability, because of a lack of legal capacity or a negative factor (e.g., fraud or duress).

Conversion 1. Misappropriating property or funds belonging to another. 2. Changing an existing rental apartment building into a condominium.

Conveyance The transfer of title to real property from one person to another by means of a written document (e.g., deed).

Cooperative A building owned by a corporation, with residents as shareholders in the corporation; each shareholder gets a proprietary lease on an individual unit and a right to use common areas.

Co-ownership Any form of ownership in which two or more people share title to a piece of property, holding undivided interests. Also called **co-tenancy** or **concurrent ownership**.

Corporation An association organized according to strict regulations, in which individuals purchase ownership shares; regarded by the law as an artificial person, separate from individual shareholders.

Corporation, Domestic A corporation doing business in the state in which it was created (incorporated).

Corporation, Foreign A corporation doing business in one state, but created (incorporated) in another state.

Co-tenant Anyone who shares ownership of a piece of property with another. In Ohio, a co-tenant may be a joint tenant, a statutory survivorship tenant, a tenant in common, a tenant by the entireties, or a tenant in partnership.

Counteroffer A response to an offer to enter into a contract, changing some terms of the original offer. It is a rejection of the original offer (not a form of acceptance) and does not create a binding contract unless the new counteroffer is accepted by the original offeror (the counter-offeree).

Courtesy At common law, a husband's interest in his wife's property; in Ohio, courtesy has been abolished and replaced by dower rights.

Covenant 1. A contract. 2. A promise. 3. A guarantee (express or implied) in a document (e.g., a deed or lease). 4. A restrictive covenant.

Covenant of Quiet Enjoyment A guarantee that a buyer or tenant has the right to exclusive, undisturbed possession of a leasehold estate during the entire term of the lease. It guarantees the tenant will not be disturbed by the previous owner, the lessor, or anyone else claiming an interest in the property.

Creditor A person or other entity (e.g., a bank) who is owed a debt.

Creditor, Secured A creditor with a lien on specific property, enabling him to foreclose and collect the debt from the sale proceeds, if not otherwise paid.

Criminal Law The body of law concerned with crimes—individual's actions against society.

Criminal Litigation A lawsuit in which the government sues an individual to punish the wrongdoer and protect society.

Cure To remedy a default by paying money that is overdue or fulfilling other obligations.

Customer A party in a transaction with whom an agent does not have a fiduciary duty or relationship, but with whom an agent must still be fair and honest.

Damages An amount of money a defendant is ordered to pay to a plaintiff.

Damages, Compensatory Damages awarded, usually of money, intended to compensate the plaintiff for harm caused by the defendant's act or failure to act, including personal injuries (physical and mental), property damage, and financial losses.

Damages, Consequential Damages compensating for losses that were not the direct result of the defendant's wrongful act, but which were a foreseeable consequence of it.

Damages, Liquidated A sum of money agreed to in advance by parties to a contract (at the time of entering into the contract), which will serve as compensation in the event of a contract breach.

Damages, Punitive Damages awarded, added to compensatory damages, to punish a defendant for malicious or outrageous conduct and discourage others from engaging in similar acts.

Debtor A person or other entity (e.g., a company) who owes money to another.

Decedent A person who has died.

Dedication A gift of private property for public use; may transfer ownership or simply create a public easement.

Dedication, Common Law A dedication resulting from owner's intention to donate land for public use and government's acceptance of the donation. Common law dedication may be involuntary (e.g., when owner permits public use of property for a long time, intention to dedicate property may be implied).

Dedication, Statutory A dedication required by law (e.g., dedication of property for streets and sidewalks as a prerequisite of subdivision approval).

Deed An instrument that conveys the grantor's interest, if any, in the real property.

Deed, Bargain and Sale A deed that implies the grantor owns the property and has the right to convey it but does not carry any warranties.

Deed, Correction A deed used to correct minor mistakes in an earlier deed (e.g., misspelled names or errors in the legal description).

Deed, Fiduciary A deed executed by a trustee, executor, or other fiduciary, conveying property that the fiduciary does not own but is authorized to manage.

Deed, General Warranty A deed in which the grantor warrants the title against defects that might have arisen before or during his period of ownership.

Deed, Gift A deed not supported by valuable consideration; often lists "love and affection" as the consideration.

Deed, Limited Warranty A deed in which the grantor warrants title only against defects arising during the time he owned the property and not against defects arising before his time of ownership. Also called **special warranty deed**.

Deed, Quitclaim A deed that conveys any interest in a piece of real property the grantor has at the time the deed is executed. This type of deed is often used to clear up a cloud on title. It contains no warranties of any kind.

Deed, Warranty A deed carrying warranties (guarantees) of clear title and the grantor's right to convey.

Deed, Wild A recorded deed that will not be discovered using the grantor-grantee indexes, because of a break in the chain of title. A mortgage or other document can also be "wild."

Deed in Lieu of Foreclosure A deed given by a borrower to the lender to satisfy debt and avoid foreclosure.

Deed of Trust An instrument rarely used in Ohio. Like a mortgage, it creates a voluntary lien on real property to secure repayment of a debt. The parties to a deed of trust are the grantor or trustor (borrower), beneficiary (lender), and trustee (neutral third party). Unlike a mortgage, a deed of trust includes a power of sale, allowing the trustee to foreclose non-judicially. Also called a **trust deed**.

Default Failure to fulfill an obligation, duty, or promise, as when a borrower fails to make payments, a tenant fails to pay rent, or a party to a contract fails to perform.

Defeasance Clause A mortgage clause used in title theory states, whereby the mortgagee agrees to deed property to the mortgagor after all terms of the contract have been performed satisfactorily. A defeasance clause is used to defeat or cancel a certain right upon the happening of a specific event (e.g., upon final payment, words of grant in a mortgage are void, the mortgage is canceled, and title is re-vested to mortgagor). A defeasance clause can also be used to give borrower the right to redeem property after default on a note by paying full amount due plus fees and court costs.

Defendant 1. A person being sued in a civil lawsuit. 2. An accused person in a criminal lawsuit.

Deferment Permission to delay fulfillment of an obligation (e.g., paying taxes) until a later date.

Delivery The legal transfer of a deed (or other instrument). A valid deed does not convey title until it has been delivered to the grantee.

Deposit 1. Money offered as an indication of good faith regarding future performance of a purchase agreement. Also called **earnest money**. 2. A tenant's security deposit.

Deposition In a lawsuit, the formal, out-of-court testimony of a witness or a party, taken before the trial; used as part of the discovery process to determine the facts of the case or when the witness will not be able to attend the trial. A transcript of a deposition can be introduced as evidence in the trial.

Depreciate To decline in value.

Designated Heir A chosen heir. By filing documents with probate court, a person can choose anyone to be his heir under the law.

Devise 1. (noun) Real property transferred in a will. 2. (verb) To transfer real property by will.

Devisee A recipient of real property under a will.

Disaffirm The act of asking a court to terminate a voidable contract.

Discovery, Pretrial Using depositions and interrogatories to learn more about the disputed facts in a case from opposing parties and reluctant witnesses; when each of the opposing parties in a lawsuit is required to disclose requested information and evidence to the other party, and each is allowed to examine witnesses who will testify for the other side at trial.

Discrimination Treating people unequally because of their race, religion, sex, national origin, age, or some other characteristic of a protected class, in violation of civil rights laws.

Disparate Impact A law that is not discriminatory on face value but has a greater impact on a minority group than on other groups.

Distinguished When the facts of a case differ from a precedent.

Domicile The state where a person has his permanent home.

Donative Intent An intent to transfer title immediately and unconditionally.

Dower In Ohio (and some other states), the interest held by a married person in the real property his or her spouse owns in fee simple during their marriage. (At common law, dower referred only to the wife's interest in her husband's property, while the husband's interest in his wife's property was called **courtesy**—also spelled **curtesy**. Now, dower refers to either spouse's interest in the other's property.)

Dower Rights, Choate Dower rights that have vested in a person, creating a statutory life estate. This occurred because the person's spouse sold the property without a dower release and subsequently died. Also called **vested dower rights**.

Dower Rights, Inchoate Dower rights that have not yet vested, but have the potential to do so; held by a married person in real property currently owned by his or her spouse, or (if the spouse is still alive) in real property the spouse sold without a dower release. Also called **contingent dower rights**.

Due on Sale Clause A mortgage clause that prohibits assignment by making the entire mortgage balance due when property is sold.

Due Process A fair hearing before an impartial judge. Under the U.S. Constitution, no one may be deprived of life, liberty, or property without due process of law.

Duress Threatening violence against or unlawfully confining someone to force him to sign a document; or, threatening or confining the signer's spouse, child, or other close relative.

Duress, Economic Threatening to take action that will be financially harmful to a person to force him to sign a document (e.g., threatening to breach a contract). Also called **business compulsion**.

Easement A right to use some part of another person's real property for a particular purpose. An easement is irrevocable and creates an interest in the property.

Easement, Appurtenant An easement that benefits a particular piece of property (the dominant tenement).

Easement, Negative An easement that prevents the servient tenant from using his own land in a certain way (as opposed to allowing the dominant tenant to use it). Essentially the same as a **restrictive covenant**.

Easement, Positive An easement that allows a dominant tenant to use the servient tenement.

Easement by Express Grant An easement granted to another in a deed or other document.

Easement by Express Reservation An easement created in a deed when a landowner is dividing the property, transferring the servient tenement but retaining the dominant tenement.

Easement by Implication An easement created by operation of law (not express grant or reservation) when land is divided, if there is a long-standing, apparent use that is reasonably necessary for enjoyment of the dominant tenement. Also called an **implied easement**.

Easement by Necessity A special kind of easement by implication that occurs when a dominant tenement would be completely useless without an easement, even if it is not a long-standing, apparent use.

Easement by Prescription An easement acquired by prescription. Also called a **prescriptive easement**.

Easement in Gross An easement that benefits a person instead of land; there is a dominant tenant, but no dominant tenement.

Emblements, Doctrine of The rule that allows an agricultural tenant to re-enter land to harvest crops if the lease ends (through no fault of the tenant) before the crop can be harvested. This rule applies only to the first crop.

Eminent Domain The government's constitutional power to take (appropriate or condemn) private property for public use, as long as the owner is paid just compensation.

Employee Someone who works under the direction and control of another.

Encroachment A physical object intruding onto neighboring property, often due to a mistake regarding the boundary.

Encumbrance A nonpossessory interest in property (such as an easement, lien, or restrictive covenant), which burdens the property owner's title.

Enjoin To prohibit an act, or command performance of an act, by court order; to issue an injunction.

Equal Protection Requirement Under the Fifth and Fourteenth Amendments to the U.S. Constitution, all citizens are entitled to equal protection by the laws; no law may arbitrarily discriminate between different groups or be applied to groups in a discriminatory manner.

Equitable Remedy A judgment granted to a plaintiff that is something other than an award of money (damages); for example, an injunction, quiet title, rescission, and specific performance.

Equitable Right of Redemption The right of a debtor to save or redeem property from foreclosure proceedings prior to the confirmation of sale.

Equity 1. An owner's unencumbered interest in property; the difference between the value of the property and the liens against it. 2. A judge's power to soften or set aside strict legal rules, to bring about a fair and just result in a particular case.

Erosion A gradual loss of soil due to the action of water or wind.

Error, Harmless A mistake by a trial judge that is determined not to have affected the final judgment in a case.

Error, Prejudicial A mistake by a trial judge that may have affected the final judgment in a case. Also called **reversible error** (because it is grounds for reversing the trial court's decision).

Escheat When property reverts to the state after a person dies without leaving a valid will and without heirs.

Escrow The system in which things of value (e.g., money, documents) are held by a disinterested third party (an escrow agent) on behalf of the parties to a transaction until specified conditions have been met.

Escrow Instructions The contract that authorizes an escrow agent to deliver items deposited in escrow, once the parties have complied with specified conditions.

Estate 1. A possessory interest in real property; either a freehold estate or a leasehold estate. 2. The real and personal property left by someone who has died.

Estate for Years A leasehold estate set to last until a definite date, after which it terminates automatically. Also called a **term tenancy**.

Estate of Inheritance An estate that can be willed or descend to heirs (e.g., a fee simple estate).

Estoppel A legal doctrine that prevents a person from asserting rights or facts that are inconsistent with earlier actions or statements, when he failed to object (or attempt to "stop") another person's actions.

Estoppel, Promissory A doctrine applied when someone makes a technically unenforceable promise, but another person acts in reasonable reliance on the promise. If the person who relied on the promise will suffer harm unless it is enforced, a court may enforce it. Also called **doctrine of detrimental reliance**.

Eviction Dispossessing or expelling someone from real property.

Eviction, Actual Physically forcing someone off of property, preventing someone from re-entering property, or using the legal process to make someone leave.

Eviction, Constructive When a landlord's act (or failure to act) interferes with the tenant's quiet enjoyment of the property, or makes the property unfit for its intended use, to such an extent that the tenant is forced to move out.

Eviction, Retaliatory When a landlord evicts a tenant in retaliation for complaining about the condition of the property, code violations, violations of the Landlords and Tenants Act, or for participating in a tenants' rights group.

Eviction, Self-Help When a landlord uses physical force, a lockout, or a utility shut-off to get rid of a tenant, instead of the legal process.

Eviction, Wrongful When a landlord evicts a tenant in violation of the tenant's rights.

Evidence Testimony, documents, and objects submitted in a lawsuit as proof of a fact.

Exculpatory Clause A clause in a contract or lease providing that one of the parties will not be liable in the event the other party (or someone else) is injured. This type of clause is void in residential leases in Ohio.

Execute 1. To sign. 2. To perform or complete.

Execution The legal process in which a court orders an official (such as a sheriff) to seize and sell the property of a judgment debtor to satisfy a judgment lien.

Executive The head of a government, such as a president, governor, or mayor.

Executor/Executrix A person appointed in a will to carry out the provisions of the will. A man is called an **executor**; a woman is called an **executrix**.

Exemption A provision holding that a law or rule does not apply to a particular person, entity, or group. For example, a company with a property tax exemption does not have to pay property taxes.

Exhibit 1. Documentary or physical evidence submitted in a trial. 2. An attachment to a legal document.

Express Stated in words (spoken or written).

Extender Clause A listing agreement clause stating that for a specified period after the listing expires, the broker will still be entitled to a commission if the property is sold to someone the broker dealt with during the listing term. Also called **carryover clause** or **safety clause**.

Failure of Purpose When the intended purpose of an agreement or arrangement can no longer be achieved; in most cases, this releases the parties from their obligations.

Familial Status A protected class under the Federal Fair Housing Act and the Ohio Civil Rights Act, which makes it illegal to discriminate against persons who are the parent or guardian of a child under 18 years of age.

Federal Question A legal issue involving the U.S. Constitution, a treaty, or a federal statute. Federal courts have jurisdiction to hear federal question cases, but they may also be decided in state court.

Fee An estate of inheritance; title to real property that can be willed or descend to heirs.

Fee, Conditional A type of defeasible fee; title that may be terminated by a former owner if conditions stated in the deed are not met. The former owner has a power of termination. Also called **fee simple subject to a condition subsequent**.

Fee Simple An inheritable, transferable, perpetual ownership interest.

Fee Simple Absolute The greatest estate one can have in real property; freely transferable and inheritable, and of indefinite duration, with no conditions on the title. Often called **fee simple** or **fee title**.

Fee Simple Defeasible A type of real property ownership that may be defeated or undone if certain events occur or certain conditions are not met. Also called **defeasible fee**.

Fee Simple Determinable A defeasible fee that is terminated automatically if certain conditions occur. The grantor (or his heirs) has a possibility of reverter. Also called a **determinable fee**.

Feudal System The system of land ownership where a king or queen owns all of the land and all others are merely tenants.

FHA The Federal Housing Administration; a government agency that insures mortgage loans.

Fiduciary Someone in a position of trust and confidence, held by law to high standards of good faith and loyalty.

Fiduciary Relationship A relationship of trust and confidence in which one party owes the other (or both parties owe each other) loyalty and a higher standard of good faith than they owe to third parties. For example, an agent is a fiduciary in relation to the principal; husband and wife are fiduciaries in relation to each other.

Financing Statement A brief document that, when recorded, gives constructive notice of a creditor's security interest in an item of personal property.

Finder's Fee A referral fee paid to someone for directing a buyer/seller to a real estate agent.

First Lien Position The spot held by the lien with highest priority when there is more than one mortgage or other debt or obligation secured by the property.

Fixed Term A period of time with a defined ending date.

Fixture An item of personal property that may or may not be attached to real property but is closely associated with real property in such a way that it has legally, and is intended to, become part of real property.

Foreclosure When a lien holder causes property to be sold so unpaid debt secured by the lien can be satisfied from the sale proceeds.

Foreclosure, Judicial A lawsuit filed by a lender or other creditor to foreclose on a mortgage or other lien.

Foreclosure, Nonjudicial Foreclosure by a trustee under the power of sale clause in a deed of trust, without the involvement of a court. Not used in Ohio.

Foreclosure, Strict Foreclosure with a strict deadline, past which a mortgagor can no longer reclaim his interest in the real property out of the foreclosure proceedings by bringing the mortgage current.

Foreign Real Estate Any real estate situated outside the state of Ohio.

Forfeiture Loss of a right or something else of value as a result of failure to perform an obligation or condition.

Fraud An intentional or negligent misrepresentation or concealment of a material fact; making statements that a person knows, or should realize, are false or misleading.

Fraud, Actionable Fraud that meets certain criteria, so that a victim can successfully sue. The victim/plaintiff must prove the defendant concealed a material fact or made a false statement (intentionally or negligently) with intent to induce the victim to enter a transaction, and that the victim was harmed because he relied on the misrepresentation.

Fraud, Actual An intentional misrepresentation or concealment of a material fact; when a person actively conceals material information or makes statements known to be false or misleading.

Fraud, Constructive A negligent misrepresentation or concealment of a material fact; when a person carelessly fails to disclose material information or makes statements that he should realize are false or misleading.

Freehold Estate An ownership estate in real property; either a fee simple or a life estate. The holder of a freehold estate has title.

Fructus Industriales Plants sowed and cultivated by people ("fruits of industry").

Fructus Naturales Naturally occurring plants ("fruits of nature").

Future Interest An interest in real property that may, or will, become a possessory interest at some point in the future.

Garnishment The legal process by which a creditor gains access to a debtor's personal property or funds in the hands of a third party. If a debtor's wages are garnished, the employer pays part of the paycheck direct to a creditor.

Government Survey System A legal description for land referencing principal meridians and baselines designated throughout the country.

Grant To transfer or convey an interest in real property by means of a written instrument.

Grantee A person receiving a grant of real property.

Granting Clause A deed clause stating a grantor's intent to transfer an interest in real property.

Grantor A person who grants an interest in real property to another.

Gross Lease A lease for which the landlord pays all property taxes, insurance, etc.

Guardian A person appointed by a court to administer the affairs of a minor or an incompetent person.

Habendum Clause A clause included after the granting clause in many deeds; begins "to have and to hold," describing the type of estate granted.

Heir Someone entitled to inherit another person's real or personal property under the laws of intestate succession.

Home Rule A rule that says a city or village that has adopted a charter is not required to comply with state zoning procedures.

Homeowners Association A nonprofit association comprised of homeowners in a subdivision, responsible for enforcing the subdivision's CC&Rs and managing other community affairs.

Homestead Protection Limited protection for a debtor against claims of judgment creditors; applies to property of the debtor's residence.

Hostile and Adverse When possession or use of land is without the owner's permission and against the owner's interests; one condition necessary for an easement by prescription.

HUD The Department of Housing and Urban Development; a government agency that deals with housing issues.

Hung Jury A jury that cannot agree on a verdict after deliberating for a long time, resulting in a retrial of the case with a new jury.

Hypothecate To make property security for a loan without giving up possession of it (as with a mortgage).

Implied Not communicated in words, but is understood from actions or circumstances.

Implied by Law Required by law to be part of an agreement and treated by a court as part of an agreement even if it contradicts the express terms to which the parties agreed.

Implied Warranty of Habitability An implied guarantee that the property is safe and fit for human habitation; treated by law as an implicit provision in every residential lease, regardless of the express terms of the lease.

Improvements Man-made additions to real property; substantial fixtures (e.g., buildings).

Incidental Secondary or minor, but happening as a result of or in association with something else.

Incompetent Not legally competent; not of sound mind; mentally ill, senile, or feebleminded.

Independent Contractor A person who contracts to do a job for another but maintains control over how the task will be carried out, rather than following detailed instructions.

Index, Direct An index kept by the county recorder, with each recorded document listed in alphabetical order according to the last name of the grantor. Also called a **grantor/grantee index**.

Index, Reverse An index kept by the county recorder, with each recorded document listed in alphabetical order according to the last name of the grantee. Also called a **grantee/grantor index**.

Index, Sectional An index that lists recorded documents under the tax parcel number of the property they apply to, grouping together all recorded documents affecting a particular piece of property. Also called a **tract index**.

Ingress and Egress Entering and exiting; usually refers to a road or other means of access to a piece of property. An easement for ingress and egress is one that gives the dominant tenant access to the dominant tenement.

Inherit In strict legal usage, to acquire property by intestate succession, but commonly used to mean acquiring property either by intestate succession or by will.

Injunction A court order prohibiting an act or compelling an act to be done.

Instrument Any document that transfers title (e.g., deed), creates a lien (e.g., mortgage), or gives a right to payment (e.g., contract).

Integration Clause A provision in a contract document stating the document contains the entire agreement between the parties.

Intent, Donative A grantor's intent to transfer title immediately and unconditionally.

Intent, Objective A person's manifested intention; what someone appears to intend, whether that is actually what is intended.

Intent, Subjective What a person actually intends, whether that is apparent to others.

Interest 1. A right or share in something (e.g., real estate). 2. A charge a borrower pays to a lender for the use of the lender's money.

Interest, Undivided A co-tenant's interest, giving him the right to possession of the whole property, rather than a fraction of it.

Interpleader A court action filed by someone holding funds that two or more people are claiming. The holder turns the funds over to court; the court resolves the dispute and delivers the money to whoever is entitled to it.

Interrogatories Written questions submitted to the opposing party in a lawsuit during discovery, which the opposing party is required to answer in writing and under oath.

Intestate Dying without leaving a will.

Intestate Succession The distribution of property to heirs of a person who died intestate (without a valid will).

Invalid Not legally binding or legally effective; not valid.

Inverse Condemnation Action A court action by a private landowner against the government, seeking compensation for damage to property that resulted from government action.

Inverted Pyramid A way of visualizing ownership of real property; theoretically, a property owner owns all the earth, water, and air enclosed by a pyramid that has its tip at the center of the earth and extends up through the property boundaries out into the sky.

Issue A person's lineal descendants: Children, grandchildren, great-grandchildren, and so on.

Joint Venture Two or more individuals or companies joining together for one project or a related series of projects, but not as an ongoing business.

Judgment 1. A court's binding determination of the rights and duties of the parties in a lawsuit. 2. A court order requiring one party to pay the other damages.

Judgment Creditor A person who is owed money as a result of being awarded a judgment in a lawsuit.

Judgment Debtor A person who owes money as a result of a judgment in a lawsuit.

Judicial Review When a court considers whether a statute or regulation is constitutional.

Jurisdiction The extent of a particular court's authority; a court cannot hear a case that is outside its jurisdiction.

Jurisdiction, Appellate The authority to hear an appeal (as opposed to conducting a trial).

Jurisdiction, Concurrent When there is more than one court with jurisdiction over a particular case, thus the plaintiff may choose in which court to file suit.

Jurisdiction, Diversity The power of federal courts to hear cases in which a citizen of one state sues a citizen of another state (or country) in a dispute concerning more than $50,000.

Jurisdiction, Exclusive When there is only one court in which a particular type of case can be filed.

Jurisdiction, General When a court's subject matter jurisdiction is not limited to specific types of cases.

Jurisdiction, Original The authority to conduct a trial (as opposed to hearing an appeal).

Jurisdiction, Personal A court's authority over a particular individual; usually obtained by service of process.

Jurisdiction, Subject Matter The types of cases a particular court has authority to hear.

Jurisdiction, Territorial The geographical area that a particular court has authority over.

Just Compensation The appropriate or fair value for private land taken by the government for public use.

Land Lease A lease in which the tenant leases only the land from owner, but the tenant owns the building.

Landlocked Property 1. Land without access to a road or highway. 2. Land not beside water.

Landlord A landowner who has leased his property to another. Also called a **lessor**.

Latent Defect A defect that is not visible or apparent; a hidden defect that would not be discovered in a reasonably thorough inspection of property.

Lawful Objective A legal purpose.

Lease Conveyance of a leasehold estate from the fee owner to a tenant; a contract where one party pays the other rent in exchange for possession of real estate.

Leasehold Estate An estate that gives the holder (tenant) a temporary right to exclusive possession of the estate, but without having title. Also called **less-than-freehold estate**.

Legacy Receiving money by a will.

Legal Description A precise description of property.

Legal Remedy Money awarded to the plaintiff in a civil lawsuit; damages. Also called a **remedy at law** or **common law remedy**.

Legatee A person who receives money (a legacy) under a will.

Legislature The arm of government that has primary responsibility for passing laws.

Lessee A person who leases property from another; a tenant.

Lessor A person who leases property to another; a landlord.

Levy 1. To impose a tax (verb); 2. A tax (noun).

Liable Legally responsible.

License 1. Official permission to do a particular thing the law does not allow everyone to do. 2. Revocable, non-assignable permission to enter another person's land for a particular purpose.

License, Inactive The license status of any salesperson who returns his or her license to the Division of Real Estate, or whose broker does not want to maintain sponsorship of the licensee. A license may remain inactive indefinitely, as long as it is timely renewed and continuing education requirements are met.

License On Deposit 1. A special license status that is available only to brokers who wish to return their broker's license to the Division of Real Estate in order to reactivate their license as a salesperson. A broker's license may remain on deposit indefinitely if timely renewed and continuing education requirements are met. 2. A special license status available to any licensee who enters the military or whose reserve military status is activated. The license remains inactive until the next renewal date following honorable discharge from the military.

Lien A nonpossessory interest in property, giving a lienholder the right to foreclose if the owner does not pay a debt owed the lienholder; a financial encumbrance on the owner's title.

Lien, Attachment A lien intended to prevent transfer of property pending the outcome of litigation.

Lien, Equitable A lien arising as a matter of fairness, rather than by agreement or by operation of law.

Lien, General A lien against all the property of a debtor, rather than a particular piece of property.

Lien, Involuntary A lien that arises by operation of law, without the consent of the property owner. Also called a **statutory lien**.

Lien, Judgment A general lien against a judgment debtor's property, which the judgment creditor creates by recording a certificate of judgment in the county where the property is located.

Lien, Materialman's Similar to a mechanic's lien, but based on a debt owed to someone who supplied materials, equipment, or fuel for a project (as opposed to labor).

Lien, Mechanic's A specific lien claimed by someone who performed work on the property (construction, repairs, or improvements) and has not been paid. This term is often used in a general sense, referring to materialmen's liens as well as actual mechanics' liens.

Lien, Specific A lien that attaches only to a particular piece of property (as opposed to a general lien, which attaches to all of the debtor's property).

Lien, Tax A lien on real property to secure payment of taxes.

Lien, Vendor's A lien to secure payment of the balance of the purchase price, held by a real estate seller if the buyer does not pay the seller in full at closing (unless the buyer gives the seller a mortgage for the balance).

Lien, Voluntary A lien placed against property with the consent of the owner; a mortgage (or, in other states, a deed of trust).

Lien Priority The order in which liens are paid off out of the proceeds of a foreclosure sale. Tax liens always have the highest priority.

Lien Theory States States in which a mortgagee only holds a lien against property (not actual title) until a loan is repaid, and mortgagor has actual title.

Lienholder, Junior A secured creditor whose lien is lower in priority than another lien against the same property.

Life Estate A freehold estate that lasts only as long as a specified person (the **measuring life**) lives.

Life Estate, Statutory A life estate held by a person whose dower rights have vested (because the person's spouse sold the property without a dower release and subsequently died).

Life Estate Pur Autre Vie A life estate "for the life of another," where the measuring life is someone other than the life tenant.

Life Tenant Someone who owns a life estate; the person entitled to possession of the property during the measuring life.

Limited Liability Companies A new form of association in Ohio that may own land. Structure is similar to a corporation, but has tax benefits of a partnership (e.g., no double taxation).

Limited Real Estate Broker/Salesperson A person licensed exclusively to sell cemetery interment rights for a fee.

Lineal Descendants A person's children, grandchildren, great-grandchildren, and so on.

Lis Pendens A recorded notice stating there is a lawsuit pending that may affect title to the defendant's real estate.

Listing A written agency contract between a seller and a real estate broker, stating that the broker will be paid a commission for finding (or attempting to find) a buyer for the seller's real property.

Listing, Exclusive Agency A listing agreement that entitles the broker to a commission if anyone other than the seller finds a buyer for the property during the listing term.

Listing, Exclusive Right to Sell A listing agreement that entitles the broker to a commission if anyone, including the seller, finds a buyer for the property during the listing term.

Listing, Net A listing agreement in which the seller sets a net amount he is willing to accept for the property; if the actual selling price exceeds that amount, the broker is entitled to keep the excess as commission. Net listings are discouraged in Ohio.

Listing, Open A non-exclusive listing, given by a seller to as many brokers as he chooses. If the property is sold, a broker is entitled to a commission only if he is the procuring cause of the sale.

Litigant A party to a lawsuit; a plaintiff or defendant.

Litigation A lawsuit(s).

Littoral Rights The water rights of a landowner whose property is adjacent to a lake or contains a lake; often called riparian rights (although that term originally referred only to the water rights of a landowner on a river).

Lot A parcel of land; especially, a parcel in a subdivision.

Lot and Block Description The type of legal description used for platted property. The description states only the property's lot number and block number in a particular subdivision. To find the exact location of the property's boundaries, the plat map for that subdivision must be consulted at the county recorder's office.

Mailbox Rule The acceptance of a contract offer is effective as of the moment it is mailed, even though the other party has not yet received it.

Management Level Licensee A licensed broker or salesperson who is affiliated with a real estate brokerage and who has supervisory responsibility over other licensed brokers or salespersons affiliated with that brokerage.

Mansion House The family home and the land on which it is located; referred to in this way when part of a deceased person's estate.

Marketable Record Title Under the Marketable Title Act, an unbroken chain of recorded title going back at least 40 years.

Marketable Title A title free and clear of objectionable encumbrances or defects; so, a reasonably prudent person with full knowledge of the facts would not hesitate to buy the land.

Marketable Title Act An Ohio law that extinguishes certain old, dormant claims against a title, to simplify the title search process.

Material Fact An important fact; one that is likely to influence a decision.

Materialman A person who supplies materials, equipment, or fuel for a construction project.

Measuring Life A person whose life determines the length of a life estate.

Mechanic A person who performs work (construction, remodeling, repairs, or demolition) on real property.

Mediation The process whereby cases already filed with the court are accelerated by referring certain matters to a court referee.

Merger Uniting two or more separate properties by transferring all ownership to one person.

Metes and Bounds Description A legal description that starts at an easily identifiable point of beginning (POB), then describes the property's boundaries in terms of courses (compass directions) and distances, ultimately returning to the point of beginning.

Mineral Rights The rights to the minerals located beneath the surface of property.

Minor A person who has not yet reached the age of majority; in Ohio, a person under 18 years of age.

Misrepresentation A false or misleading statement.

Mistake, Mutual When both parties to a contract were mistaken about a fact or a law.

Mistake, Unilateral When only one of the parties to a contract was mistaken about a fact or a law.

Mitigation When the non-breaching party takes action to minimize the losses resulting from a breach of contract.

Mortgage An instrument that creates a voluntary lien on real property to secure repayment of a debt. The parties to a mortgage are the mortgagor (borrower) and mortgagee (lender).

Mortgage, Blanket 1. A mortgage that covers more than one parcel of real estate. 2. A mortgage that covers an entire building or development, rather than an individual unit or lot.

Mortgage, Satisfaction of The document a mortgagee gives a mortgagor when the mortgage debt has been paid in full, acknowledging the debt has been paid and the mortgage is no longer a lien against the property.

Mortgagee A lender who accepts a mortgage as security for repayment of the loan.

Mortgagor A person who borrows money and gives a mortgage to the lender as security.

Mrs. Murphy Exemption An exemption to the Federal Fair Housing Act for an owner-occupied dwelling of four units or less provided the owner occupies one unit, does not use discriminatory advertising, and does not use a real estate agent. Ohio does not recognize this exemption.

Multiple Listing Service (MLS) A listing service whereby local member brokers agree to share listings and commissions on properties sold jointly.

Mutual Consent When all parties freely agree to the terms of a contract, without fraud, undue influence, duress, or mistake. Mutual consent is achieved through offer and acceptance.

NAR The National Association of REALTORS®.

Natural Person A real human being (as opposed to an artificial person, such as a corporation).

Negligence Conduct that falls below the standard of care a reasonable person would exercise under the circumstances; an unintentional breach of a legal duty resulting from carelessness, recklessness, or incompetence. Negligence that causes harm is a tort.

Net Lease A lease for which tenants pay all taxes, insurance, etc., plus utilities and rent.

Nonconforming Use A land use that does not conform to current zoning laws but is allowed because the land use was established before the new zoning laws were passed.

Nonpossessory Interest An interest in property that does not include the right to possess and occupy the property; an encumbrance (e.g., lien, easement).

Notary Public An official whose primary function is to witness and certify the acknowledgment made by someone signing a legal document.

Notice, Actual Having actual knowledge of a fact, as opposed to knowledge imputed or inferred by law.

Notice, Constructive Knowledge of a fact imputed to a person by law. A person is held to have constructive notice of a fact because it was a matter of public record, even if the person was not actually aware of it. For example, everyone is held to have constructive notice of the contents of recorded documents, since everyone is expected to protect their interests by searching the public record.

Notice, Inquiry Having notice of a problem because circumstances should have alerted a person to a problem that needed to be investigated further, even if actual knowledge of a particular fact does not exist.

Notice to Quit A notice to a tenant, demanding that the tenant vacate the leased property. Also called a **notice to vacate**.

Novation 1. When one party to a contract withdraws and a new party is substituted, with the consent of all parties, relieving the withdrawing party of liability. 2. The substitution of a new obligation for an old one.

Nuisance Interference with the right of quiet enjoyment of property.

Occupying Claimant One who makes improvements to real property in a good faith but mistaken belief that he or she has title. Also called **good faith improver**, **innocent improver**.

Offer When one person proposes a contract to another; if the other person accepts the offer, a binding contract is formed.

Offeree A person who receives an offer or to whom an offer is made.

Offeror A person who makes an offer.

Open and Notorious When possession or use of land is obvious and unconcealed; a condition necessary for easement by prescription.

Opinion, Judicial A judge's written statement of a decision in a court case, outlining the facts of the case and explaining the legal basis for the decision.

Option A contract giving one party the right to do something within a designated time period, without obligation to do it.

Option to Purchase A contract giving the optionee the right, but not the obligation, to buy property owned by the optionor at an agreed price during a specified period.

Optionee A person to whom an option is given.

Optionor A person who gives an option.

Ordinance A law passed by a local legislative body; in Ohio, more specifically, a law passed by a city council or village council.

Ownership The title to property, dominion over property; the rights of possession and control of real or personal property.

Ownership, Concurrent Ownership by more than one person; co-ownership.

Ownership in Severalty Ownership by a single individual, as opposed to co-ownership.

Parcel A lot or piece of real estate, particularly a specified part of a larger tract.

Parol Evidence Evidence concerning negotiations or oral agreements that were not included in a written contract, altering or contradicting the terms of the written contract.

Part Performance A legal doctrine that allows a court to enforce an oral agreement that should have been in writing, when the promisee has taken irrevocable steps to perform his or her side of the bargain and failure to enforce the contract would result in an unjust benefit for the promisor.

Partition, Judicial A court action to divide real property among its co-owners, so each owns part of it in severalty or (if it is not practical to divide the property physically) each gets a share of the sale proceeds.

Partition, Voluntary When co-owners agree to terminate co-ownership and divide a property so that each owns a piece of it in severalty.

Partner, General A partner who has the authority to manage and contract for a general or limited partnership and who is personally liable for the partnership's debts.

Partner, Limited A partner in a limited partnership who primarily is an investor and does not participate in the management of the business and who is not personally liable for the partnership's debts.

Partnership The association of two or more people to carry on a business for profit. The law generally regards a partnership as a group of individuals, not as an entity separate from its owners.

Partnership, General A partnership in which each member has an equal right to manage the business and share in the profits, as well as an equal responsibility for the partnership's debts. All of the partners are general partners.

Partnership, Limited A partnership comprised of one or more general partners and one or more limited partners.

Partnership Property All property that partners bring into their business at the outset or later acquire for their business; property owned as tenants in partnership.

Patent The instrument used to convey government land to a private individual.

Patent Defect A visible, apparent defect that can be seen during a reasonably thorough inspection of property.

Percentage Lease A lease for which a tenant pays a percentage of gross sales instead of or, usually, in addition to rent.

Permit System A system used by state and local governments to monitor compliance with and enforce building codes and other regulations.

Personal Property Any property that is not real property; movable property not affixed to land. Also called **chattels** or **personalty**.

Personalty Personal property.

Petitioner 1. An **appellant**. 2. A **plaintiff** (in some actions, such as a dissolution of marriage).

Plaintiff The party who brings or starts a civil lawsuit; the one who sues.

Planned Unit Development (PUD) A special type of subdivision that may combine nonresidential uses with residential uses, or otherwise depart from the ordinary zoning and subdivision regulations; in some PUDs, the lot owners co-own recreational facilities or open spaces as tenants in common.

Planning Commission A local government agency responsible for preparing the community's comprehensive plan for development.

Plat A detailed survey map of a subdivision, recorded in the county in which the land is located. Subdivided property is often called platted property.

Plat Book A book containing subdivision plats and kept at the county recorder's office.

Pledge When a debtor transfers possession of property to the creditor as security for repayment of the debt.

Police Power The constitutional power of state and local governments to enact and enforce laws that protect the public's health, safety, morals, and general welfare.

Possession 1. The holding and enjoyment of property. 2. Actual physical occupation of real property.

Possessory Interest An interest in property that includes the right to possess and occupy the property either now or in the future; an estate. May be either a freehold or leasehold.

Possibility of Reverter The interest held by a grantor (or grantor's heirs) who has transferred a fee simple determinable.

Power of Attorney An instrument authorizing one person (called an attorney-in-fact) to act as another's agent to the extent stated in the instrument.

Power of Termination The right to terminate a conditional fee estate if the estate holder fails to meet the required conditions. Also called a **right of re-entry**.

Practical Difficulties The reason for a zoning variance, because the zoning prevents the owner from making a permitted use of a property.

Precedent A previously decided case concerning the same facts as a later case; a published judicial opinion that serves as authority for determining a similar issue in a later case.

Precedent, Binding A precedent that a particular court is required to follow because it was decided by a higher court in the same jurisdiction.

Prescription Acquiring an interest in property (usually an easement) by using it openly and without the owner's permission for at least 21 years. In contrast to adverse possession, a prescriptive use does not have to be exclusive (the owner may be using the property, too), and the user does not acquire title to the property.

Principal 1. A person who grants another person (an agent) authority to represent him in dealings with third parties. Also referred to as the **client. 2.** One of the parties to a transaction (e.g., buyer or seller), as opposed to those involved as agents or employees (e.g., broker or escrow agent). 3. With regard to a loan, the amount originally borrowed, as opposed to the interest.

Principal Broker A licensed real estate broker who oversees and directs the daily operations of the brokerage.

Probate 1. A judicial proceeding in which the validity of a will is established and the executor is authorized to distribute the property in an estate. 2. When there is no valid will, a judicial proceeding in which an administrator is appointed to distribute the estate to the heirs according to the laws of intestate succession.

Probate Court A court that oversees the distribution of property under a will or intestate succession.

Procedural Law A law that establishes a legal procedure for enforcing a right.

Procuring Cause The real estate agent who is primarily responsible for bringing about a sale, such as by introducing the buyer to the property or by negotiating the agreement between the buyer and seller (sometimes more than one agent contributes to a sale).

Promisee A person who has been promised something; a person who is supposed to receive the benefit of a legally binding contractual promise.

Promisor A person who has made a contractual promise to another.

Promissory Note A written, legally binding promise to repay a debt.

Proof, Burden of The responsibility for proving or disproving a particular issue in a lawsuit. Usually, plaintiffs have the burden of proof.

Proof, Standard of The extent to which the plaintiff or prosecutor must have convinced the jury or judge in order to win the case. In most civil suits, a preponderance of the evidence must support the plaintiff's case. In a criminal action, the prosecutor's case must be proven beyond a reasonable doubt.

Property 1. The rights of ownership in a thing, such as the right to use, possess, transfer, or encumber the thing. 2. Something that is owned, real or personal, tangible or intangible.

Property Manager A person hired by a real property owner to administer, market, merchandise, and maintain property, especially rental property.

Proprietary Lease An exclusive, longer term lease given to a person who lives in a cooperative and owns stock in the cooperative.

Public Nuisance A land use that threatens public health, safety, morals, or welfare, or constitutes a substantial annoyance to the public.

Public Record The official collection of legal documents that individuals have filed with the county recorder in order to make the information contained in them public.

Puffing Superlative statements about the quality of a property that should not be considered assertions of fact (e.g., "The best buy in town").

Purchase Agreement A contract in which a seller promises to convey title to real property to a buyer in exchange for the purchase price. Also called **purchase and sale agreement**, **purchase contract** or **earnest money agreement**.

Question of Fact In a lawsuit, a question about what actually occurred, as opposed to a question about the legal consequences of what occurred (question of law).

Question of Law In a lawsuit, a question about what the law is on a particular point; what the legal rights and duties of the parties were.

Quiet Enjoyment The use and possession of real property without interference from the previous owner, the lessor, or anyone else claiming title.

Quiet Title Action A lawsuit to determine who has title to property or to remove a cloud from the title.

Race/Notice Rule When the same property has been sold to two different buyers, the buyer to record his deed first has good title to the property, as long as he did not have notice of the other buyer's interest.

Ratification The later confirmation or approval of an act that was not authorized when it was performed.

Reactivate The process to remove a license from inactive, suspension, or deposit status (broker's license only).

Ready, Willing, and Able Making an offer to purchase on terms acceptable to the seller and having the financial ability to complete the purchase.

Real Estate Contract 1. A purchase agreement. 2. A land contract. 3. Any contract having to do with real property.

Real Estate Investment Trust (REIT) A real estate investment business with at least 100 investors, organized as a trust.

Real Property Land and everything attached to it or appurtenant to it.

REALTOR® A broker or salesperson who is an active member of a state or local real estate board that is affiliated with the National Association of REALTORS®.

Realty Real property.

Receiver A person appointed by a court to manage and look after property or funds involved in litigation.

Reconveyance An instrument that releases the security property from the lien created by a deed of trust; the equivalent of a satisfaction of mortgage.

Recording Filing a document at the county recorder's office so it is placed in the public record.

Recording Numbers The numbers stamped on documents when they are recorded; used to identify and locate public record documents.

Redlining Refusing to make loans secured by property located in certain neighborhoods for discriminatory reasons.

Referendum When citizens vote on an issue.

Reformation A legal action to correct a mistake (e.g., typographical error) in a deed or other document. The court will order the execution of a correction deed.

Regulation 1. A rule adopted by an administrative agency. 2. Any government order having the force of law.

Release 1. To give up a legal right. 2. A document in which a legal right is given up.

Reliction When a body of water gradually recedes, exposing land that was previously under water. Also called **dereliction**.

Remainder A future interest that becomes possessory when a life estate terminates and that is held by someone other than the grantor of the life estate; as opposed to a reversion, which is a future interest held by the grantor.

Remainderman The person who has an estate in remainder.

Remand An appellate court ordering further trial proceedings in a case, sending the case back to the court that originally tried it or to a different trial court.

Rent Consideration paid by a tenant to a landlord in exchange for possession and use of property.

Rent Control Governmental restrictions on how much rent a landlord can charge.

Renunciation A person who has been granted something, or has accepted something, later giving it up or rejecting it (as when an agent withdraws from an agency relationship).

Repair and Deduct Remedy When a tenant is paying rent to the court, the judge may allow the tenant to use some of the rent money to pay for necessary repairs.

Repudiation When one party to a contract informs the other before the time set for performance that he does not intend to perform as agreed.

Res Judicata A legal doctrine holding that once a lawsuit between parties has been tried and a final judgment issued, neither party can sue the other over the same dispute again.

Rescission When a contract is terminated and each party gives anything acquired under the contract back to the other party (the verb form is **rescind**).

Reservation A right retained by a grantor when conveying property (e.g., mineral rights, an easement, or a life estate can be reserved in the deed).

Resigned The license status in which a license has been voluntarily and permanently surrendered to or is otherwise in the possession of the Division of Real Estate and Professional Licensing, is not renewed, and is not associated with a real estate broker.

Resolution In Ohio, a law passed by a county board of commissioners or a board of township trustees.

Respondent 1. An **appellee**. 2. In a dissolution of marriage, the party who did not file the action.

Restitution Restoring something to a person of which he was unjustly deprived.

Restriction A limitation on the use of real property.

Restriction, Deed A restrictive covenant in a deed.

Restriction, Private A restriction imposed on property by a previous owner or the subdivision developer; a restrictive covenant or a condition in a deed.

Restriction, Public A law or regulation limiting or regulating the use of real property.

Restrictive Covenant A promise to do or not do an act relating to real property; usually an owner's promise not to use property in a particular way. It may or may not run with the land.

Reverse To overturn a lower court's decision on appeal, ruling in favor of the appellant.

Reversion A future interest that becomes possessory when a temporary estate (such as a life estate) terminates and that is held by the grantor (or his successors in interest).

Reversionary Interest Holder The person who has a future estate interest in reversion.

Revocation 1. When someone who granted or offered something withdraws it; as when a principal withdraws the authority granted to the agent, an offeror withdraws the offer. 2. When the Real Estate Commission permanently withdraws a real estate agent's license.

Rezoning An amendment to a zoning ordinance, usually changing the uses allowed in a particular zone. Also called a **zoning amendment**.

Right of Disposal A right to transfer all or some of a person's ownership interest in real property.

Right of Enjoyment A right to enjoy the benefits of land ownership without outside interference.

Right of Preemption A right to have the first chance to buy or lease property if the owner decides to sell or lease it. Also called a **right of first refusal**.

Right of Survivorship A characteristic of statutory survivorship tenancy, joint tenancy, and tenancy by the entireties; surviving co-tenants automatically acquire a deceased co-tenant's interest in the property.

Right of Use A right of land ownership to make the property productive.

Right of Way An easement that gives the holder the right to cross another person's land.

Riparian Rights The water rights of a landowner whose property is adjacent to or crossed by a river (or, more generally, any body of water).

Rule of Capture A legal principle that grants a landowner the right to all oil and gas produced from wells on her land, even if it migrated from land belonging to someone else.

Running with the Land Binding or benefiting the successive owners of a piece of property, rather than terminating when a particular owner transfers his interest. Usually refers to an easement or restrictive covenant, but it must touch and concern the land.

Salesperson Any licensed agent who is associated with a broker and, as such, may perform most of the acts of a broker, on behalf of the broker. A salesperson has the same fiduciary duty to a broker's client that a broker does.

Secret Profit A financial benefit that an agent takes from a transaction without authority from the principal or without informing the principal of the benefit retained; usually the result of self-dealing.

Security Agreement An instrument that creates a voluntary lien on property to secure repayment of a loan. For debts secured by real property, a security agreement is either a mortgage or a deed of trust.

Security Deposit The money a tenant gives a landlord at the beginning of the tenancy to ensure the tenant will comply with lease terms. The landlord may retain all or part of the deposit at the end of the tenancy to cover unpaid rent, repair costs, or other damages.

Security Interest The interest a creditor may acquire in a debtor's property to ensure the debt will be paid.

Seisin The possession of a freehold estate; ownership. Also spelled **seizen** or **seizin**.

Self-Dealing When a real estate agent buys the principal's property (or sells it to a relative, friend, or associate, or to a business he has an interest in), without disclosing that fact to the principal, and then sells it again for a profit.

Seller Financing When a seller extends credit to a buyer to finance the purchase of the property, as opposed to having the buyer obtain a loan from a third party (e.g., an institutional lender).

Separate Property In states with a community property system, any property owned by a married person that is not held jointly with the spouse as community property.

Service of Process The delivery of a legal document (especially a summons) to a person in accordance with the rules prescribed by statute, so he is held to have legally received the document (whether he actually did).

Setback Requirements The provisions in a zoning ordinance that do not allow structures to be built within a certain distance of the property line.

Settlement 1. An agreement between the parties to a civil lawsuit, in which the plaintiff agrees to drop the suit in exchange for a sum of money or the defendant's promise to do or refrain from doing something. 2. Another term for **closing**.

Settlement Statement A document that presents a final, detailed accounting for a real estate transaction, listing each party's debits and credits and the amount each will receive or be required to pay at closing. Also called a **closing statement**.

Severable When one part or provision in a law or a contract can be held unenforceable without making the entire law or contract unenforceable.

Shareholders The stockholders in a corporation.

Sheriff's Sale A foreclosure sale held after a judicial foreclosure. Sometimes called an **execution** or an **execution sale**.

Side Yard The area between a building and one side boundary of the lot it is located on.

Special Assessment A tax levied only against the properties that have benefited from a public improvement (e.g., sewer, street light), to cover the cost of the improvement; creates a **special assessment lien**, which is an involuntary lien.

Specific Performance A legal remedy in which a court orders the breaching party of a contract to perform as agreed, rather than simply paying monetary damages.

Standing to Sue Generally meaning that a lawsuit can be filed only by someone who was personally harmed by the potential defendant's action. The Supreme Court has interpreted this very broadly with regard to housing discrimination lawsuits.

Stare Decisis The legal doctrine that requires a judge to follow a precedent (decided in the same jurisdiction) to make the law consistent and predictable.

State Action In constitutional law, action by a government (federal, state, or local) rather than by a private party.

Statute A law enacted by a state legislature or the U.S. Congress.

Statute of Frauds A law that requires certain types of contracts to be in writing and signed in order to be enforceable.

Statute of Limitations A law requiring a lawsuit to be filed within a specified time after the event giving rise to the suit occurred.

Statutory Construction When, in the course of resolving a lawsuit, a judge interprets and applies a statute.

Statutory Law The laws adopted by a legislative body (Congress, state legislature, or a county or city council), as opposed to constitutional law, case law, or administrative regulations.

Statutory Redemption This lets a mortgagor redeem property for a set period of time after a foreclosure sale, regardless of the timing of other events. Time frames for **statutory right of redemption** vary by state.

Steering Channeling prospective buyers or tenants to particular neighborhoods based upon their race, religion, national origin, or ancestry.

Strict Liability When someone is held legally responsible for an injury to another, even though he did not act negligently.

Subagent An agent of an agent; a person an agent has delegated authority to so that the subagent can assist in carrying out the principal's orders.

Subdivision 1. Land divided into two or more parcels. 2. A residential development.

Subdivision Regulations State and local laws that must be complied with before land can be subdivided.

Sublease When a tenant transfers only part of his right of possession or other interest in leased property to another person for part of the lease term.

Subpoena A document ordering a person to appear at a deposition or court proceeding to testify or produce documentary or physical evidence.

Substantial Performance When a promisor does not perform all contractual obligations but performs enough so the promisee is required to fulfill his side of the bargain.

Substantive Law A law that establishes a right or duty.

Successor in Interest A person (such as a buyer or an heir) who has acquired property previously held by someone else.

Summons A document informing a defendant that a lawsuit has been filed against him and directing the defendant to file an answer to the plaintiff's complaint with the court.

Support, Lateral The support that land receives from land adjacent to it.

Support, Subjacent The support that the surface of land receives from land beneath it.

Support Rights The right to have one's land supported by the land adjacent to and beneath it.

Surrender Giving up an estate (e.g., life estate, leasehold) before it has expired.

Survey The process of precisely measuring the boundaries and determining the area of a parcel of land.

Suspension The temporary withdrawal of a real estate agent's license for a certain and specified period of time. Usually reactivation is automatic the day after the suspension is lifted and is often conditioned on the fulfillment of certain requirements by the person whose license has been suspended.

Syndicate An association formed to operate an investment business. A syndicate is not a recognized legal entity; it can be organized as a corporation, partnership, or trust.

Tacking When successive periods of use or possession by more than one person are added together to make up the 21 years required for prescription or adverse possession.

Taking When the government acquires private property for public use by appropriation it is called "a taking." The term is also used in inverse condemnation lawsuits, when a government action has made private property useless.

Tax, Property An annual tax levied on the value of real property.

Tax, Real Estate Transfer A tax levied on the transfer of a piece of real property.

Tax Sale The sale of property after foreclosure of a tax lien.

Tenancy The lawful possession of real property; an estate.

Tenancy, Joint A form of co-ownership in which the co-owners have equal undivided interests and the right of survivorship. In Ohio, joint tenancy has been replaced by the statutory survivorship tenancy; joint tenancies established before 1985 still exist, but no new ones may be created.

Tenancy, Periodic A leasehold estate that continues for successive periods of equal length (e.g., week-to-week or month-to-month), until terminated by proper notice from either party. Also called **month-to-month tenancy**.

Tenancy, Statutory Survivorship A form of co-ownership created by the Ohio General Assembly to replace joint tenancy and tenancy by the entireties in Ohio; each co-tenant has an equal undivided interest in real property and the right of survivorship.

Tenancy at Sufferance The possession of property by a holdover tenant.

Tenancy at Will When a tenant is in possession with the owner's permission, but with no definite lease term and no rent paid (or rent paid on an irregular basis); as when a landlord allows a holdover tenant to remain on the premises without paying rent until another tenant is found, or an apartment manager exchanging maintenance duties for occupancy.

Tenancy by the Entireties A form of property co-ownership by husband and wife, in which each spouse has an undivided one-half interest and right of survivorship, with neither spouse able to convey or encumber his or her interest without the other spouse's consent. In Ohio, tenancy by the entireties has been replaced by statutory survivorship tenancy; tenancies by entireties from before 1985 still exist, but new ones may not be created.

Tenancy in Common A form of co-ownership in which two or more persons each have an undivided interest in the entire property (unity of possession), but no right of survivorship.

Tenancy in Partnership The form of co-ownership in which general partners own partnership property, whether or not title to the property is in the partnership's name. Each partner has an equal undivided interest, but no right to transfer the interest to someone outside the partnership.

Tenant Someone in lawful possession of real property; especially, someone who has leased property from the owner, but can also refer to sublessees.

Tenant, Dominant A person who has easement rights on another's property; either the owner of a dominant tenement or someone who has an easement in gross.

Tenant, Holdover A lessee who remains in possession of property after the lease term has expired; a tenant who refuses to give up possession of property when tenancy ends.

Tenant, Servient The owner of a servient tenement; that is, someone whose property is burdened by an easement.

Tender An unconditional offer by one of the parties to a contract to perform his part of the agreement; made when the offeror believes the other party is going to breach, it establishes the offeror's right to sue if the other party does not accept it. Also called a **tender offer**.

Tenement, Dominant Property that receives the benefit of an appurtenant easement.

Tenement, Servient Property burdened by an easement. In other words, the owner of the servient tenement (the servient tenant) is required to allow someone who has an easement (the dominant tenant) to use his property.

Tenements Everything of a permanent nature associated with land and ordinarily transferred with the land. Tenements are both tangible (e.g., buildings) and intangible (e.g., air rights).

Term A prescribed period of time; especially, the length of time a borrower has to repay a loan or the duration of a lease.

Testamentary Capacity A person making a will who is of sound mind and memory and at least 18 years of age.

Testamentary Intent A person making a will who intends to do so and can understand the consequences of his actions.

Testate Refers to someone who has died and left a will.

Testator A man who makes a will.

Testatrix A woman who makes a will.

Time is of the Essence A contract clause that means performance on the exact dates specified is an essential element of the contract; failure to perform on time is a material breach.

Timeshare An ownership interest giving the owner a right to possession of the property only for specific, limited periods each year.

Title 1. Lawful ownership of real property. 2. The deed or other document that is evidence of that ownership (informal usage).

Title VIII Another name for the Federal Fair Housing Act, which is Title VIII of the Civil Rights Act of 1968.

Title, After-Acquired A title acquired by a grantor after he attempted to convey property he did not own.

Title, Chain of The chain of deeds (and other documents) transferring title to a property from one owner to the next, as disclosed in the public record.

Title, Clear A title that is free of encumbrances or defects; marketable title.

Title, Equitable The vendee's (seller's) interest in property under a land contract. Also called **equitable interest**.

Title, Legal 1. Having good title to property. 2. The vendor's (buyer's) interest in property under a land contract.

Title, Root of Under Marketable Title Act, the deed (or other document of conveyance) that, 40 years earlier, was most recently recorded.

Title Company A title insurance company, usually where closings take place (documents signed and funds dispersed).

Title Insurance Insurance that indemnifies against losses resulting from undiscovered title defects and encumbrances.

Title Plant A duplicate (usually microfilmed) of a county's public record, maintained by a title company at its offices for use in title searches.

Title Report A report issued by a title company, disclosing the condition of the title to a specific property.

Title Search An inspection of the public record to determine all rights and encumbrances affecting title to property.

Title Theory States States in which a mortgagee holds actual title to property until the loan is repaid.

Torrens System A title registration system administered by the state; adopted in Ohio and other states, but is costly and rarely used.

Tort A breach of the standards of reasonable conduct imposed by law (as opposed to a duty voluntarily taken on in a contract) that causes harm to another person, giving the injured person the right to sue the one who breached the duty. Also called a **civil wrong** (in contrast to a criminal wrong, a crime).

Trade Fixtures Articles of personal property annexed to real property by a tenant for use in her trade or business.

Transactional Brokerage An arrangement allowed in some states (not Ohio) in which a licensee serves as a facilitator to assist in the timely and accurate conclusion of a sales transaction but does not act as an agent for either party. Also called **Nonagency**.

Trespass An unlawful physical invasion of property owned by another.

Trial The fundamental court proceeding in a lawsuit, in which a judge (and, in some cases, a jury) hears evidence presented by the plaintiff and defendant and issues a judgment.

Trial Record All documents and transcripts from a trial.

Trier of Fact A person who decides questions of fact in a lawsuit. In a jury trial, it is the jury; in a non-jury trial, it is the judge. Questions of law are always decided by the judge, regardless of the presence of a jury.

Trust A legal arrangement in which title to property (or funds) is vested in one or more trustees who manage the property (or invest the funds) on behalf of the trust's beneficiaries and in accordance with instructions set forth in the document establishing the trust.

Trust Account A bank account, separate from a real estate broker's personal and business accounts, used to segregate trust funds from the broker's own funds.

Trust Funds Money or things of value received by an agent, not belonging to the agent but being held for the benefit of others.

Trustee A person appointed to manage a trust on behalf of the beneficiaries.

Trustee's Sale A nonjudicial foreclosure sale under a deed of trust.

Unconscionable Provision A contractual provision so unfair it shocks the conscience of the court; thus, a court will not enforce it.

Unconstitutional Violating a provision of the U.S. Constitution or a state constitution.

Undue Influence Exerting excessive pressure on someone so as to overpower the person's free will and prevent him from making a rational or prudent decision; often involves abusing a relationship of trust.

Unit Owners Association The organization that manages the operation of condominiums, imposing assessments, and arranging maintenance of common areas. Association members are unit owners and elect a board of directors. Also called a **condominium association**.

Unities, Four The unities of time, title, interest, and possession, required for a joint tenancy.

Unity of Interest When each co-owner has an equal interest (equal share of ownership) in a property.

Unity of Possession When each co-owner is equally entitled to possession of the entire property because the ownership interests are undivided.

Unity of Time When each co-owner acquired title at the same time.

Unity of Title When each co-owner acquired title through the same instrument (e.g., deed, will, or court order).

Unjust Enrichment An unfairly obtained benefit.

Unlawful Detainer Action A summary legal action to regain possession of real property; especially, a lawsuit filed by a landlord to evict a defaulting tenant and regain possession of the property. Also called a **forcible detainer action**.

Unnecessary Hardship A reason for a zoning use variance because permitted uses of the property are not economically feasible and the property cannot be used without a variance.

Untenantable Not fit for occupancy.

Usury Charging an interest rate that exceeds legal limits.

Valid The legal classification of a contract that is binding and enforceable in a court of law.

Value The amount of goods or services offered in the marketplace in exchange for some thing.

Value, Assessed The value placed on property by the taxing authority (e.g., county assessor) for the purposes of taxation.

Value, Fair Market The amount of money that property would bring if placed on the open market for a reasonable period of time, with a buyer willing (but not forced) to buy, and a seller willing (but not forced) to sell, if both buyer and seller were fully informed as to the possible use of the property. Also called **market value**.

Variance A permit obtained from the local zoning authority allowing the holder to use property or build a structure in a way that violates, or is a deviation from, the zoning ordinance.

Variance, Area A variance that permits an owner to build a structure that does not strictly comply with the zoning law's setback requirements, height limits, or other rules affecting the size or placement of buildings.

Variance, Use A variance that permits an owner to use property in a way not ordinarily allowed in that zone (e.g., commercial use in a residential zone).

Vendee A buyer or purchaser; particularly, one buying property under a land contract.

Vendor A seller; particularly, someone selling property by means of a land contract.

Vested When a person has a present, fixed right or interest in property, even though she may not have the right to possession until sometime in the future. For example, a remainderman's interest in property vests when it is granted, not when the life estate ends.

Veto When the president or governor formally rejects a bill that Congress or legislature passed. The bill will not become law unless the legislature votes to override the veto.

Void Having no legal force or effect.

Waiver The voluntary relinquishment or surrender of a right.

Warranty, Implied A guarantee created by operation of law, whether or not the seller intended to offer it.

Waste The destruction, damage, or material alteration of property by someone in possession who holds less than a fee estate (e.g., life tenant, lessee).

Water Rights The right to use water in or from a river, stream, or lake.

Will A person's legally binding instructions regarding how her estate should be disposed of after death. Also called a **testament**.

Will, Formal A written, witnessed will.

Will, Holographic A will that is written entirely in the testator's/testatrix's handwriting but which was not witnessed. This type of will is not recognized in Ohio because the will was not witnessed.

Will, Nuncupative An oral will made on a person's deathbed; can transfer only personal property, not real property.

Witness, Expert A person who has expert knowledge of a subject, either through education or experience, who testifies in a court case.

Witness, Fact A person who witnessed actual events connected to a dispute.

Writ of Execution A court order directing a public officer (often the sheriff or marshal) to seize and/or sell property to regain possession for the owner and/or satisfy a debt.

Writ of Possession A court order issued after an unlawful detainer action, informing a tenant that he must vacate the landlord's property within a specified period or be forcibly removed by the sheriff.

Zoning Government regulation of the uses of property within specified areas.

Zoning, Exclusionary A zoning law that effectively prevents certain groups (e.g., minorities or low-income individuals) from living in a community.

Zoning, Spot An illegal rezoning that favors or restricts a landowner (or a small group of owners) without justification.

Index

Attorney
  -in-fact 54
  -in-Fact 205
  Power of 54, 205
Authority 54
  Actual 54
  Express 54
  Implied 55
  Incidental 55
Avulsion 139

B

Bargain and Sale Deed 180
Beckett Ridge Ass'n-I v. Agne 251
Bequest 225, 226
Bilateral Contract 198
Bill of
  Rights 6
  Sale 134
Bishop v. Pecsok 115
Blanket Mortgage 184
Blockbusting 103, 108
Board of Zoning Appeals 241
Breach of Contract 212
Broker 25, 26
  Lien Law 44
  Protection Clause 216
Brownfields 246
  Revitalization Act 246
Building
  Code 244
  Destruction of the 279
Bundle of Rights 128
Burden of Proof 20
Business Name Certificate 182
Buyer
  Broker 57
    Contract 55
  Default 220
  Ready, Willing, and Able 215
Bylaw 184

C

Campbell v. Storer 192
Cancellation 210
Canon of Ethics 96
Care 74
Case Law 1
Caveat Emptor 85
CC&Rs 233, 251
Cease and Desist Order 113

Certificate
  Business Name 182
  Fictitious Name 182
  of Judgment 163
  of Limited Partnership 182
  of Transfer 228
Chain of Title 191
Chattel 128
Checkers 110
Cincinnati M & M Realty, Inc. v. Uckotter 186
City and Village Zoning 238
City of Eastlake v. Forest City Enterprises, Inc. 239
Civil
  Law 2
  Lawsuit 17
  Litigation 1, 3
  Rights Act of 1866 104
  Rights Act of 1968 105
Clause
  "As Is" 95
  Broker Protection 216
  Contingency 209
  Defeasance 159
  Due-on-Sale 161
  Exculpatory 277
  Extension 216
  Granting 174
  Habendum 174
  Transfer of interest 161
Clean
  Air Act 246
  Water Act 246
Client 57
Clouds on the Title 179
Code
  Building 244
  Ohio Revised 7
Commingle 74
Commingling 42
Commission
  Splitting 41
Common
  Area 183
    Limited 183
  Law 8
    Dedication 247
    Marriage 150
Comparative Negligence Rule 277

Compensation
  Just 6, 247
Compensatory Damages 3, 96, 105, 212
Competent Grantor 172
Complainant 111
Complaint 17
  Procedure 34
Comprehensive Environmental Response, Compensation, and Liability Act (CERCLA) 246
Comprehensive Plan 233
Concurrent
  Jurisdiction 14
  Ownership 185
Condemnation 246
  Inverse 236
Condition 209
Conditional
  Use 233, 242
  Zoning Certificate 242
Conditions 248
Condominium 183
  Declaration 183
  Encumbrance and Transfer 184
  Timesharing 184
Confidentiality 74
Confirmation
  of Sale 160
Consent
  Withholding 264
Consideration 171, 174, 197, 203
  Adequacy of 204
  Good 175
  Valuable 203
Constitution 5
Constitutional Law 5
Constructive
  Annexation 127, 132
    The Doctrine of 132
  Eviction 257, 268
  Fraud 93
  Notice 171, 190, 277
Consumer Guide to Agency Relationships 59
Conterno v. Brown 268
Contingency Clause 209
Continuing Education 38
Contract 4
  Bilateral 198
  Breach of 212

W

Warranty
  Deed 176
    General 176, 179
    Limited 176, 179
    Special 179
    Standard 179
  Implied 265
  of Habitability
    Implied 270
Waste 149, 267
Water Right 136
Waters v. Monroe Coal Co. 148
Will 226
  Family Rights Under a 227
  Holographic 225, 227
  Nuncupative 227
  Requirements for 226
  Taking Against the 227
Withholding Consent 264
Witness
  Expert 19
  Fact 19
Words of Conveyance 174
Writ of Execution 280

Z

Zoning
  Administrative Board 241
  Appeals, Board of 241
  by Referendum 239
  Certificate, Conditional 242
  Certificate System 244
  City and Village 238
  Commission
    County Rural 239
  Constitutional Challenges 236
  County and Township 239
  Exclusionary 103, 119
  Laws
    Enacting 237
    Enforcement of 244
    Exceptions to 239
  Ordinance 234
  Plan 239
  Referendum, Petition for 243
  Spot 234, 243